Health, Economic Development and Household Poverty

In recent years, there has been increased interest in how ill health affects household productivity, the local economy, and national and global economic development. Emerging evidence on the strength of these links has led to a call for greater investment in the health sector of developing countries. However, in order to alleviate poverty and enhance countries' chances of equitable economic development, health sector investment needs to ensure that the poor gain access to priority health services. Mounting evidence that health systems in the developing world typically favour the better off has stimulated innovative approaches to health financing and service delivery that can better reach the poor. This book provides an accessible summary of a burgeoning field of research.

The book is split into three parts: the first part concentrates on the evidence regarding the links between health, economic development and household poverty; the second part focuses on evidence on the extent to which health systems address the needs of the poor and the near poor; and the final part considers innovative measures to make health interventions widely available to the poor. Bennett, Gilson and Mills have gathered essays written by academics and experts in the fields of health policy and economic development, each underscoring the need for political commitment to meet the needs of the poor and for developing strategies to build this commitment.

This book will be of great current interest to policy makers and practitioners in the field of international health and development and to researchers engaged with global health and poverty. It would also make an interesting supplementary text for students of international health and development.

Sara Bennett is the Manager of the Alliance for Health Policy and Systems Research, based at the World Health Organization. **Lucy Gilson** is Professor of Health Policy and Systems at the London School of Hygiene and Tropical Medicine and Associate Professor at the Centre for Health Policy at the University of Witwatersrand, South Africa. **Anne Mills** is Professor of Health Economics and Policy at the London School of Hygiene and Tropical Medicine.

Routledge international studies in health economics
Edited by Charles Normand
London School of Hygiene and Tropical Medicine, UK

and

Richard M. Scheffler
School of Public Health, University of California, Berkeley, USA

Health, Economic Development and Household Poverty

From understanding to action

Edited by Sara Bennett, Lucy Gilson and Anne Mills

Routledge
Taylor & Francis Group

LONDON AND NEW YORK

First published 2008
by Routledge
2 Park Square, Milton Park, Abingdon, Oxon OX14 4RN

Simultaneously published in the USA and Canada
by Routledge
270 Madison Ave, New York, NY 10016

Routledge is an imprint of the Taylor & Francis Group, an informa business

© 2008 Selection and editorial matter, Sara Bennett, Lucy Gilson and
Anne Mills; individual chapters, the contributors

Typeset in Times by Wearset Ltd, Boldon, Tyne and Wear
Printed and bound in Great Britain by TJI Digital, Padstow, Cornwall

British Library Cataloguing in Publication Data
A catalogue record for this book is available from the British Library

Library of Congress Cataloging in Publication Data
A catalog record for this book has been requested

ISBN10: 0-415-34428-X (hbk)
ISBN10: 0-203-02357-9 (ebk)

ISBN13: 978-0-415-34428-9 (hbk)
ISBN13: 978-0-203-02357-0 (ebk)

Contents

Figures

Tables

Boxes

Contributors

Marcella Alsan is a physician in the Howard Hiatt Global Health Equity Residency, led by Paul Farmer and Jim Kim at Brigham and Women's Hospital Boston, MA, USA. At the same time, she is completing the Ph.D. program in Economics at Harvard University as well as a fellowship in infectious diseases. After graduating magna cum laude from Harvard College in 1999, she earned a medical doctorate from Loyola University in 2005 and a Masters in Public Health from Harvard in 2006.

Sara Bennett is the Manager of the Alliance for Health Policy and Systems Research, an international collaboration based in the World Health Organization, Geneva, which aims to promote the generation and use of health policy and systems research as a means to improve the health systems of developing countries. Sara has a Ph.D. in health economics from the London School of Economics and Political Science, and has conducted research, and provided policy advice, on a variety of issues including health financing, the role of the private sector, health worker motivation and the impact of global health initiatives on health systems.

David E. Bloom is the Clarence James Gamble Professor of Economics and Demography and Chair of the Department of Population and International Health at the Harvard School of Public Health. He received a Ph.D. in Economics and Demography from Princeton University in 1981, taught at Carnegie-Mellon University and chaired the Department of Economics at Columbia University. A fellow of the American Academy of Arts and Sciences and a faculty research associate of the National Bureau of Economic Research, his recent work has focused on the links between health status, population dynamics, and economic growth, and on education in developing countries.

David Canning is Professor of Economics and International Health in the Department of Population and International Health at the Harvard School of Public Health. His research focuses on the role of demographic change and health improvements in economic development. He received a Ph.D. in Economics from Cambridge University in 1984. Before taking up his position at Harvard, Professor Canning held faculty positions at the London School of Economics, Cambridge University, Columbia University and Queen's University, Belfast. He has served as a consultant to the World Health Organization, the World Bank, and the Asian Development Bank.

Mirai Chatterjee is the Coordinator of Social Security at SEWA. She is responsible for SEWA's Health Care, Child Care and Insurance programmes. She is currently Chairperson of the SEWA-promoted health cooperative – Lok Swasthya. Mirai has a BA from Harvard University and a Masters from Johns Hopkins University's School of Hygiene and Public Health. She is on the Board of several organizations in India including the Friends of Women's World Banking (FWWB), Public Affairs Centre (PAC), Health Watch and the Public Health Foundation of India (PHFI), and is currently advisor to the National Commission for the Unorganised Sector and the National Rural Health Mission.

Matthew Fox is a lecturer in the Center for International Health and Development at Boston University and has recently completed his D.Sc. in the Department of Epidemiology at Boston University (BU). He teaches at BU in the Department of International Health and the Department of Epidemiology. Matthew's research interests include HIV, respiratory infections and epidemiological methods. He is currently involved in a study of the impact of HIV/AIDS and HAART therapy on labour productivity in Kenya, and does data analysis and study design for various projects in the Center. He also does research on quantitative sensitivity analysis.

Lucy Gilson is Professor of Health Policy and Systems at the London School of Hygiene and Tropical Medicine, UK and holds a joint appointment with the University of Witwatersrand, South Africa. She has a background in health and development economics and over twenty years of experience in health policy and systems research, primarily in southern and eastern Africa. She has a particular interest in health and health care equity, and her research work has focused on issues of health care financing, organization, management and policy change. She has also led and supported a range of capacity development activities and provided consultancy and advisory support to governments and international agencies.

Kara Hanson is a Senior Lecturer in Health Economics at the London School of Hygiene and Tropical Medicine. She holds a Doctor of Science degree from Harvard University. Her research has focused on the financing and organization of health services in low- and middle-income countries, on the economics of delivering malaria interventions, and on the role of the private sector in health.

Dean T. Jamison is the Visiting Angelopoulos Professor in Public Health and International Development at Harvard University's John F. Kennedy School of Government and Harvard School of Public Health. An economist and

Professor in the Department of Education at UCLA, his research focuses on education, public health policy and global health. He is a Fellow at the Fogarty International Center at the National Institute of Health, an economic advisor to the World Bank, an Adjunct Professor at Peking University and the University of Queensland and an honorary member of the Institute of Medicine of the National Academy of Sciences.

Rene Loewenson is a Zimbabwean epidemiologist with the Training and Research Support Centre (www.tarsc.org). She has research and training experience in work on participation and health, equity in health and health and employment, particularly through participatory and community based methodologies. She is the programme manager of the Regional network for Equity in Health in east and southern Africa (www.equinetafrica.org) and has carried out technical work with WHO, UNICEF, ILO and UNRISD.

Di McIntyre, Ph.D., is an Associate Professor at the University of Cape Town, South Africa. She founded the Health Economics Unit in 1990 and was Director of this Unit for 13 years. She has served on numerous policy committees and has extensive research, technical support and capacity development experience, both within South Africa and other parts of the African region. Her particular research and technical support experience relates to health care financing (especially user fees and social health insurance), health equity issues, resource allocation (including needs-based formulae and fiscal federalism issues), public–private mix issues and pharmaceutical regulation.

Anne Mills is Professor of Health Economics and Policy at the London School of Hygiene and Tropical Medicine, and Head of both the Department of Public Health and Policy and the Health Economics and Financing Programme. She has over 30 years' experience in health economics-related research in low- and middle-income countries, and has published very widely in the fields of health economics and health systems. She has had extensive involvement in supporting capacity development in health economics in low- and middle-income countries. She has advised a number of multilateral and bilateral agencies, notably the UK Department for International Development and the World Health Organization.

Natasha Palmer is a lecturer in Health Economics and Health Policy at the London School of Hygiene and Tropical Medicine. She holds a Ph.D. from London University. Her research interests include health financing, involvement of non-state providers in service delivery and the motivations of different (state and non-state) health providers. She has a particular interest in understanding the role of non-financial incentives and motivations in the way that health systems run in low-income countries.

Supasit Pannarunothai obtained his medical degree from Ramathibodi Hospital, Mahidol University. He worked in Bhuddhachinaraj Hospital, a regional hospital, for more than ten years and in the Provincial Hospital Division, Ministry of Public Health, for some time. After completing his Ph.D. at the London School of Hygiene and Tropical Medicine, he returned to Bhuddachinaraj Hospital to work as a full-time researcher. In 1998, he joined the Faculty of Medicine, Naresuan University, engaging in teaching and research at the Centre for Health Equity Monitoring, and is currently the Dean of the Faculty of Medicine.

M. Kent Ranson is Research Director, Regional Trauma Services, Calgary Health Region and an Honorary Lecturer in health economics at the London School of Hygiene and Tropical Medicine. He has an MD (McMaster University), MPH (Harvard) and Ph.D. (London). His research interests include community-based health insurance, the equity impact of health and health financing interventions, community randomized trials and cost-effectiveness analysis.

Sydney Rosen is an Assistant Professor of International Health at the Center for International Health and Development at Boston University and the Director of the Health Economics Research Office at the University of the Witwatersrand in Johannesburg, South Africa. She holds a BA and a master's degree in public administration from Harvard University. Her research focuses on the impact of HIV/AIDS on households, private sector companies and public sector agencies in sub-Saharan Africa, on the benefits and costs of prevention and treatment interventions and on sectoral and societal responses to the epidemic.

Steven Russell is a lecturer at the School of Development Studies, University of East Anglia, United Kingdom. His Ph.D. was based on research in Sri Lanka on the economic burden of illness for households. His current research interests cover a variety of health policy questions and are currently focused on the demand-side issues of treatment behaviour, vulnerability and the economic burden of illness for households, social protection, and the social and economic implications of antiretroviral therapy for people living with HIV in resource-poor settings.

Jonathon Simon, MPH, D.Sc., is the Chair of the Department of International Health, Director of the Center for International Health and an Associate Professor of International Health in the School of Public Health, all at Boston University. He received his Doctorate of Science from the Harvard University School of Public Health. Before joining Boston University, he was a Fellow of the Harvard Institute for International Development. Dr Simon has had extensive experience, working in more than 20 developing countries and especially in Africa, particularly on issues including child survival, infectious diseases and capacity strengthening. He has recently been involved in evaluating the economic impact of the HIV/AIDS epidemic on sectors of the African economy.

Tara Sinha is Research Coordinator at Vimo SEWA, Self-Employed Women's Association, India. She has an M.Phil. in Sociology from Jawaharlal Nehru University, India, and a Masters in Public Policy from the University of California, Berkeley. She has worked both as programme manager and researcher. Her recent research has been in the areas of microfinance and microinsurance. She has carried out consultancy work for non-government organizations in India, working in the areas of community development, livelihood promotion and local self-government.

Michael Thiede is Associate Professor in health economics and the Director of the Health Economics Unit, University of Cape Town. His research focuses on health care inequities, pro-poor strategies in health reform and the economics of pharmaceutical markets. He has worked as a consultant for public and private sector clients, including projects in pharmaceutical pricing strategies, hospital management and related issues of public-private mix. Michael received his Ph.D. in economics from the University of Kiel, Germany.

Virginia Wiseman is a Senior Lecturer at the London School of Hygiene and Tropical Medicine. She has a Ph.D. from Curtin University in Australia and has published widely on the economics of malaria. Her current research focuses on the evaluation of different mechanisms for delivering malaria treatment and prevention in sub-Saharan Africa.

Eve Worrall is the Health Economics and Policy Adviser at Liverpool Associates in Tropical Health (LATH), the consultancy company of the Liverpool School of Tropical Medicine. After obtaining her Ph.D. from the Liverpool School, she spent a number of years working at the London School of Hygiene and Tropical Medicine where her research interests included malaria, equity, and the role of the private sector in delivering health interventions. Her work at LATH has a broad focus, including consultancy work in the field of health policy and planning at the international, country and community level.

Preface

In recent years there has been increased interest and understanding amongst development economists about how ill health affects household productivity, the local economy and in turn national and global economic development. Emerging evidence on the strength of these links has led to calls for far greater investment in the health sector of developing countries, such as those issued by the Commission on Macroeconomics and Health. However, in order to alleviate poverty and enhance countries' chances of economic development, health sector investment needs to ensure that the poor gain access to priority health services. There is now substantial evidence that health systems in the developing world tend to favour the better-off. This evidence has stimulated many decision makers to seek new approaches to the organization of health systems and service delivery, that are more successful at reaching the poor, and in turn have stimulated a greater research effort to evaluate such innovations.

This book reviews and summarizes the evidence regarding links between three key concerns – health, economic development and household poverty – with a particular focus on how investment in the health sector can help alleviate poverty, promote health and accordingly assist broader economic development efforts. The book focuses largely on the evidence from and experience of developing countries.

The book is divided into three parts that address:

- evidence regarding the links between health, economic development and household poverty;
- evidence on the extent to which health systems address the needs of the poor, including (i) equity in access to, and utilization of, health services, and (ii) the extent to which health systems provide financial protection against the costs of ill health and thus prevent households that are experiencing ill health from falling into poverty; and
- innovative measures to make health interventions widely available to the poor, to ensure that the poor are adequately protected against health care expenditure, and to give the poor a voice in shaping health services.

Each of these parts includes both chapters that review and summarize the evidence available in the field, and in-depth case studies that vividly illustrate the issues, or new approaches. The case studies are drawn from throughout the developing world.

The topic of the book represents a burgeoning research field, and the book summarizes the most important research findings. As such, the book is intended to be of great practical use to both students and practitioners.

The editors would particularly like to thank Tamsin Kelk for her sterling efforts at editing the final version of the text.

Sara Bennett, Lucy Gilson, Anne Mills

1 Health, economic development, and household poverty:

The role of the health sector

Anne Mills, Sara Bennett, and Lucy Gilson

Introduction

In recent years there has been a significant shift in the attention being paid to health within development policies. Once seen as a 'non-productive' sector, to be given resources only to the extent permitted by economic growth, it is now viewed as an important driver of economic growth. However, there remains considerable scepticism on whether the key players (national governments, international and bilateral agencies, non-governmental organizations (NGOs), and private agencies) are capable of acting on this knowledge and ensuring that increased resources to the health sector are translated into improved health, especially for the poorer sections of country populations.

The purpose of this book is to lay out the arguments and evidence on the relationships between health and economic development, and between health and poverty, and then to examine what we know about how to ensure that the poor benefit from increased resources flowing into the health sector. The book's intended readership comprises those who make, or seek to influence, health sector policy, especially in low-income countries. In keeping with this health policy orientation, the material on health, economic development, and poverty, taking up roughly half of the book, is intended to acquaint readers with the most recent evidence of the importance of health in economic development and of the impact of ill health on poverty. The other half of the book is devoted to discussing how the health of the poorest can best be improved, and to presenting particularly relevant and useful country experiences. This first chapter sets the international scene, and then provides an overview of the key issues raised in the subsequent chapters.

Changing global paradigms

Over the last few years, health has received significantly greater attention in discussions of development policies, and there appears to be acceptance that health merits a special place, along with other social sectors such as education, in international development policies. Historically, this has been the case before. For example, the 'basic needs' approach of the 1970s included health as a priority along with other important social services, and redistribution with growth was a valued and legitimate development strategy that formed the foundation for the Alma Ata Declaration on primary care of 1978. What is new, however, is the much greater degree of international consensus on the importance of improved health in contributing to economic development, i.e. health as a driver of economic performance rather than its beneficiary.

While it is difficult to explain how shifts in beliefs have come about, a number of key international processes have contributed to this new vision of the importance of health. In 2000, the then new Director-General of the World Health Organization (WHO), Gro Harlem Brundtland, set up the Commission on Macroeconomics and Health, chaired by Jeffrey Sachs. The purpose of the Commission was to assess the place of health in global economic development. In addition to re-examining the evidence on the impact of health on economic development, it also addressed how best to improve health through health sector action, including what interventions should be prioritized and how they should be financed. While the latter remain areas of controversy, especially with regard to delivery mechanisms, there has been little challenge to the Commission's basic argument on the fundamental role of health, which was published in its report in 2001 (Commission on Macroeconomics and Health 2001).

Second, and parallel to the Commission, was the process of developing and agreeing the UN Millennium Development Goals (MDGs) (Figure 1.1), which represent a compact between rich and poor nations to improve human development and to eliminate poverty. Of the eight goals, three directly concern health, and health is an important element of Goal 1 on eradicating poverty and hunger and Goal 3 on gender equality. A number of development agencies, such as the UK Department for International Development (DFID), are using the MDGs to guide their own funding plans. Hence the prioritization inherent in the goals is being translated into bilateral funding commitments. In addition, during the UK Presidency of the G8 in 2005, a comprehensive plan to fight poverty was agreed, which included major commitments of funding to tackle communicable diseases.

This emphasis on health is also being encouraged by a new international funding environment where greater resources are flowing into research and development of new drugs and vaccines, and then into support for introducing these at country level. The creation of the Bill and Melinda Gates Foundation

Goal 1: Eradicate extreme poverty and hunger
Goal 2: Achieve universal primary education
Goal 3: Promote gender equality and empower women
Goal 4: Reduce child mortality
Goal 5: Improve maternal health
Goal 6: Combat HIV/AIDS, malaria and other diseases
Goal 7: Ensure environmental sustainability
Goal 8: Develop a global partnership for development

Figure 1.1 The Millennium Development Goals.

has revolutionized funding for research on tropical diseases, with the Foundation now being the largest single supporter of such research, spending $843 million on global health in 2005 (Bill and Melinda Gates Foundation 2006). The Foundation gives substantial support to some specific global initiatives which support country programmes, notably the Global Alliance on Vaccines and Immunization (GAVI) and the Global Fund for AIDS, TB and Malaria (the Global Fund).

Indeed, the creation of the Global Fund in 2001 has opened up a new window through which increased support to the health sector can flow. Between 2001 and 2006, its portfolio grew to $5.5 billion, invested in 131 countries (Feachem and Sabot 2006). Actual disbursement of funds grew from $1 million in the first year, during which systems and structures were being established, to more than $1 billion in 2005 and to a total of $2.4 billion by mid-2006.

GAVI and the Global Fund represent only two of what has become a proliferation of disease-specific initiatives, many of them taking the form of public–private partnerships. They include product-based partnerships, which donate specific drugs; product development-based partnerships, which seek to develop (and sometimes introduce as well) new drugs, diagnostics, and vaccines; and issues/systems-based partnerships such as GAVI and the filariasis elimination programme (Buse and Walt 2000). A key characteristic of such initiatives has been that they focus on a specific product, disease or delivery approach such as community-directed treatment. This greatly increased emphasis on disease control has resurrected the historical debate about vertical and horizontal approaches to disease control – whether health improvement is best gained by focused, self-contained efforts or by broader systems development (Mills 2005). Moreover, those global initiatives that engage at the country level have rapidly learnt that weak health systems provide perhaps the greatest barrier to their success. This is especially so for malaria, tuberculosis (TB), and acquired immunodeficiency syndrome (AIDS) treatment, which need to draw for support on the broader health service infrastructure. Key weaknesses include shortage of staff and, more particularly, of well-trained staff, a poorly motivated workforce due to low pay and poor working conditions, weak drug supply systems, lack of information for management, and weak supervisory and accountability structures at all levels, from the local clinic to the Ministry of Health (Hanson *et al.* 2003).

In response, in the last few years, an emphasis on strengthening health systems has been added to international policy themes and initiatives. Recognition that strong health systems are needed to achieve disease-specific objectives has driven the Global Fund to expand its mandate to support strengthening of health systems in addition to funding programmes specific to malaria, TB, and human immunodeficiency virus (HIV) infection/AIDS. Appreciation for the importance of strong health systems has motivated GAVI to launch a new grants window dedicated to strengthening health systems. The Millennium Project's review of the MDGs, and specifically the report of the task force on child and maternal health (UN Millennium Project 2005), located the importance of strengthening health systems in human rights debates. The Global Health Watch report (People's Health Movement, Medact and GEGA 2005), led by prominent civil society activists, also emphasized the importance of health systems.

As yet another indicator of the greatly increased acknowledgement of the importance of health systems, the second edition of the book *Disease Control Priorities in Developing Countries* (Jamison *et al.* 2006) included substantial material on implementation constraints and on how best to strengthen the various functions of the health system. The first edition, published in 1993, focused exclusively on analysing the burden of disease and the cost-effectiveness of interventions (Jamison *et al.* 1993). The new edition, however, includes chapters on, for example, levels of care (e.g. primary care and community-based programmes) as well as human resources and management.

The greatly increased volume of discussion of health systems is coming up against a lack of research evidence on which decision makers can draw and hence has stimulated an interest in health systems research. The Ministerial Summit on health research, held in Mexico in November 2004, addressed the role of research in the improvement and sustainable development of population health, with specific emphasis on how to translate knowledge into action. Health systems research was a key theme at the Summit, whose declaration stated that research has a crucial but under-recognized part to play in strengthening health systems, improving the equitable distribution of high quality health services, and advancing human development (WHO 2004a). The declaration called for funders of health research to support a substantive and sustained programme of research on health systems.

Thus in the space of only six years or so, the profile of health on the international agenda has greatly increased; mechanisms have been put in place for improving disease prevention and treatment technologies and for channelling much greater support to disease control efforts and country health systems; and there is much greater attention focused on the vital role played by health systems and the need for better evidence. An emphasis on the need to improve the functioning of health systems and better meet the health care needs of the poor is coming not just from donors and global public–private initiatives, but also from academics, practitioners, and civil society groups. Indeed, many of the latter groups have consistently advocated over several decades the strengthening of health systems, but they now see an international environment that is much more receptive to these issues.

But increasingly there is concern that the window of opportunity is limited – many funding agencies want quick results, and if these are not forthcoming, then their attention may switch to other sectors. There is also concern that international attention is still at the level of rhetoric and that there is little awareness that a 'magic bullet' approach is not available nor indeed appropriate to tackle the complex web of constraints that currently hamper health system functioning in low-income countries. Hence the challenge to countries, funding agencies, academics, and practitioners seeking to strengthen health systems is not only to ensure effective use of increased funds but also to change the terms of the debate so that there is recognition of the complex needs, and associated investment requirements, of sustained improvements in health systems.

The following two sections summarize the arguments relating to health and economic development, and health and poverty, before returning to the theme of health sector action and then providing an overview of the book's content.

Health and economic development

We illustrate the role of health in economic development, drawing on the framework from the report of the Commission on Macroeconomics and Health (Figure 1.2). Economic development – as indicated by a high level of gross national product (GNP), growth of GNP per capita, and poverty reduction – is shown to be influenced by economic policies and institutions, governance structures, and supply of public goods; and factor inputs comprising human capital, technology, and enterprise capital. As shown in Figure 1.2, the most important influence of health is on human capital and enterprise capital.

There are numerous pathways through which health (or illness) influences these factor inputs. The key ones are shown in Figure 1.3. Effects are felt both

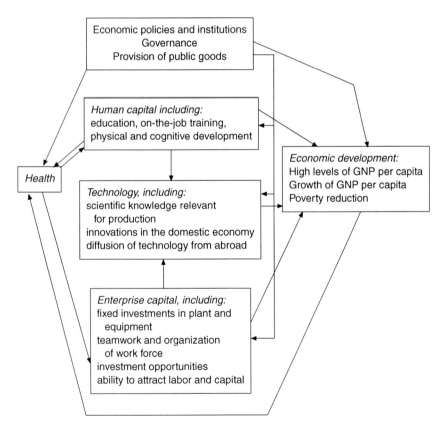

Figure 1.2 Health as an input to economic development (source: Commission on Macroeconomics and Health 2001).

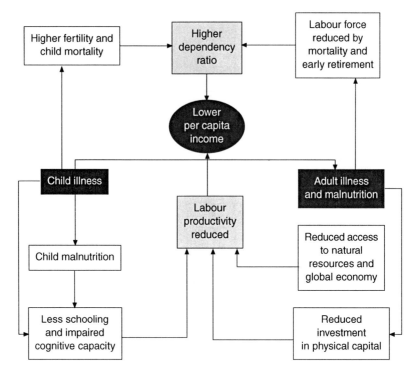

Figure 1.3 Channels through which illness reduces income.

directly, through the immediate impact of ill health on productive activities such as farming, and indirectly, through the effects of illness on fertility, morbidity, mortality, and intellectual capacity and hence on the size, composition, and quality of the labour force, and on the capacity of a country to engage in the global economy. While not all these relationships are yet well documented, there is at least some evidence on all of them, as Chapter 2 makes clear.

Health and poverty

Health and poverty are associated in a number of ways. In general, the poorer someone is, the worse is their health. Thus studies of the socio-economic distribution of ill health generally find that the poor suffer a much higher burden of ill health than richer groups. Mortality statistics in particular show a very clear socio-economic gradient: for example, Figure 1.4 shows the considerable differential in under-five mortality between the richest and the poorest quintiles of the population for each developing region of the world (Gwatkin *et al.* 2005a). Not only are child mortality gaps wide, they are also growing (Victora *et al.* 2003).

The poor face both a higher burden of disease and worse access to preventive

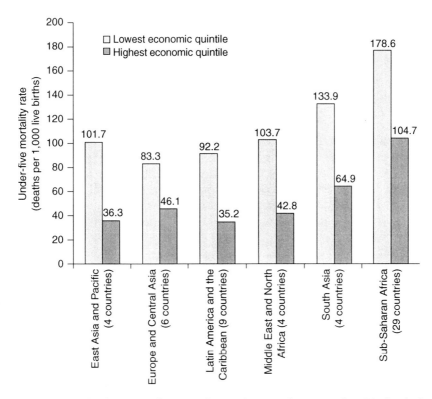

Figure 1.4 Under-five mortality rate by socioeconomic status for 56 developing
    countries.

and curative care. For example, antenatal care coverage (the proportion of
women who make at least one antenatal care visit to a medically trained person)
is 92 per cent in the richest quintile but as low as 60 per cent for the poorest fifth
of the population in developing countries. Similarly, only 35 per cent of children
in the poorest quintile of the population are medically treated for acute respiratory illnesses, while coverage is 59 per cent amongst the richest (Gwatkin *et al.*
2005a). Lower use can stem from a number of barriers, including physical inaccessibility to services, financial inaccessibility where charges are made, and lack
of responsiveness of health providers to the needs of poorer groups.

The relationship flows not just from poverty to ill health, but also from ill
health to poverty. As reviewed later in this book, ill health is a major cause of
households becoming, and staying, poor. This is because of both the direct costs
of ill health – the need to pay for advice, medicines, special food – and the indirect costs which include inability to earn a living or work on the land. Evidence
is now abundant that ill health is an important cause of chronic poverty (Hulme
and Shepherd 2003).

Health sector action

The case for increased support to improve the health of the poor is clear. However, there is considerable lack of agreement on the mechanisms through which an increased volume of resources might best be applied in order to improve health. The following are the key issues.

First, how can health systems be developed to respond better to the needs of the poor? Should governments aim to develop universal services – services available to everyone – or should they seek to target services specifically at the poor? While universal services may be attractive theoretically, poor countries lack the resources to provide truly universal access, and richer groups may be more able to benefit from the limited services available than poorer groups. However, policies that target services at the poor are often not well implemented (Mkandawire 2006) and so may also fail to provide benefits, not least because a programme which benefits only the poor may attract insufficient political support.

Second, what are the best ways of ensuring the accountability of services to poorer groups? Frequently the poor feel marginalized and excluded from services ostensibly provided for their benefit. What governance and involvement mechanisms might help address this problem?

Third, what should be the main sources of funding for health services, and how can the poor be best protected from the costs of health care? What might be ideal in theory must be set against country realities, namely a context of very limited funding, and often limited political commitment to ensuring removal of financial barriers for the poor. The current user fee debate best exemplifies these dilemmas – while there is a strong, evidence-based case for protecting the poor from user charges, simply removing a source of income from under-funded health services is unlikely to improve the services available and accessible to the poor. Replacing user fee income with other funding, as well as broader action to strengthen quality and responsiveness of services, is likely to be required (Gilson and McIntyre 2005).

This debate also exemplifies many of the issues relating to the availability of evidence to inform policy – while we know a lot about the problems of current arrangements, we know much less about the relative merits of specific changes to the status quo. The contents of this book, summarized below, seek both to lay out what is known and to indicate areas where more and better evidence is needed.

Overview of the book

The book is divided into three parts that address:

- evidence regarding the links between health, economic development and household poverty;
- evidence on the extent to which health systems address the needs of the

poor, including (i) equity in access to and utilization of health services, and (ii) the extent to which health systems provide financial protection against the costs of ill health and therefore prevent households experiencing ill health from falling into poverty;
- innovative measures to make health interventions widely available to the poor, to ensure that the poor are adequately protected against health care expenditure, and to give the poor a voice in shaping health services.

Each of these parts includes chapters that review and summarize the evidence available in the field, and in-depth case studies that vividly illustrate the issues or new approaches. The case studies are drawn from throughout the developing world.

While the book frequently refers to 'the poor', poverty is a broad concept, and different chapters of the book focus on different dimensions of poverty. Poverty has often been seen as a lack of financial resources, particularly in terms of having insufficient resources to cover basic needs. This is commonly referred to as absolute poverty (Bourgignon 1999). By contrast, relative poverty looks more at issues of inequity and the nature of deprivation faced by households that have fewer resources at their disposal than others in their society. Increasingly poverty is viewed as a multidimensional concept – linked to gender, age, access to services and social exclusion. Broadening the concept of poverty and distinguishing different forms of poverty has allowed for a finer consideration of how households fall into poverty and strategies that enable households to escape poverty. In many low-income countries, a substantial proportion of the population is in absolute poverty, and so discussion also focuses on the poorest or the 'ultra poor'. Particularly with respect to debates about financial protection in the health sector, consideration is also given to the 'near poor', who may be thrown into poverty through ill health.

Part I: Health, development and poverty

Chapter 2, by Alsan, Bloom, Canning, and Jamison, reviews the evidence on the relationship between health and wealth. Traditional economic thinking has asserted that income growth is a key factor underpinning improved population health. The chapter goes beyond this traditional economic thinking by presenting evidence that population health is an important factor in strengthening economies and reducing poverty. It argues that better health does not have to wait for an improved economy; measures to reduce the burden of disease, to give children healthy childhoods, and to increase life expectancy will in themselves contribute to creating healthier economies.

The chapter presents data on the links between health and income, discussing the two-way relationship which makes interpretation and determination of causality difficult. Inter-country comparisons of health outcomes and gross domestic product (GDP) levels weaken the case for a strict wealth-to-health causal linkage. Cross-sectional data demonstrate that some countries at low levels of income have excellent health status, and some wealthy countries have poor health status. Recent attention has focused on the relationship between population health and rates of economic growth. For example, a WHO analysis found that over the period 1952–92, income growth was less important for improving health outcomes than other factors 'exogenous to wealth', namely technological progress and knowledge diffusion through, for example, health systems. Econometric studies, using data from many countries, have found compelling evidence of a strong causal relationship from health to wealth.

Chapter 2 provides detailed discussion on the mechanisms through which health may contribute to economic growth and poverty reduction. Healthier populations usually have higher labour productivity since workers are physically and mentally more robust. Health improvements change the age-structure of society, giving a substantial, though time-limited, boost to productive capacity. People who live longer tend to save more, so increasing investment in physical and human capacity, and a healthy labour force encourages foreign investment. Finally, improved health in children enables them to make better use of education and become more productive as adults. The chapter concludes that improving the health of nations is a powerful instrument for promoting the wealth of nations.

Chapter 3, by Rosen, Simon, and Fox, provides a case study of the impact of illness on rural labour productivity, drawing evidence from rural Kenya. There is a long history of studies of the impact of tropical disease on labour productivity, but surprisingly little strong evidence. Key reasons, as the authors state, are that neither health nor productivity of individual workers can readily be observed, and that labour substitution – especially within households – can reduce the impact of illness on productivity. The chapter focuses on HIV/AIDS, which might be expected to have a serious impact on productivity since it is a chronic disease largely affecting adults (in contrast to diseases such as malaria, which in Africa mainly affects children). The study took advantage of worker records of a Kenyan tea estate, which, since it provided medical care, had records of morbidity.

The study found a clear impact of AIDS on the productivity and wages of affected workers. Of particular note is the relative magnitude of losses for worker and employer. The tea company paid for the leaf plucked (not for daily or weekly hours worked) and had a very flexible labour supply, so sick workers were readily replaced. Costs to the employer were thus largely confined to paid sick leave and medical care. For the household of the sick worker, however, illness caused a substantial loss of income, and loss of house and related employment benefits following the worker's death.

The existence of a pool of unemployed workers has frequently been noted as likely to mitigate the consequences of illness for productivity in low-income countries. This study is one of the first to show this so clearly, but also to demonstrate the severe impact of illness on affected households.

Part II: The effectiveness of health care systems in addressing the needs of the poor

Chapters 4–6 address the effectiveness of the health care system in meeting the needs of the poor. Two review chapters examine evidence on patterns of access to health care in resource-constrained settings, and the costs that access to health care impose on households. A study from Sri Lanka explores how poor households cope with these costs of illness, and the factors that affect whether households are resilient or vulnerable.

Chapter 4, by Palmer, starts by exploring what is meant by equity and access, focusing on whether all population groups 'have' access (have the potential to use services when needed) and 'gain' access (can actually use services), or whether being poor decreases the likelihood of being able to have and gain access to services of reasonable quality. Evidence of access by socio-economic status is still somewhat limited, so the review also examines proxy evidence such as disparities between rural and urban residence.

The chapter documents a substantial body of evidence that poor people often neither have access nor gain access. For example, as against 68 per cent of urban pregnant women, only 39 per cent of rural pregnant women have access to an adequate range of maternal health services, and seeking no recourse to medical attention even in the case of quite severe illness is often very common. Benefit incidence analyses (BIA), which combine the cost of providing public services with information on their use to show how the benefits of government spending are distributed across different population groups, tend to show that, on balance, government spending on health benefits wealthier groups more in African countries, while Asian countries show a more mixed picture.

Studies of health-seeking behaviour often document quite frequent use of private sector services even by poorer socio-economic groups, despite their lack of resources, and find that this is often a response to the greater availability and responsiveness, and sometimes lower cost, of private services. However, there is some evidence that poorer groups may receive poorer quality of care, even from the practitioners also used by richer groups. The chapter concludes that the evidence paints a bleak picture of failure to reach the ideal of a publicly funded, professionally staffed health system that many countries subscribe to and argues that a wide-ranging package of interventions will be needed to revitalize health systems. Responses need to include both increased funding and a renewed focus on designing policies that will lessen social exclusion and encourage access for disadvantaged groups.

Chapter 5, by McIntyre and Thiede, examines the evidence on the consequences of illness for households, and especially the costs associated with health service use and strategies adopted to cope with them. 'Coping strategies' is the term commonly used to describe how households respond to and manage the demands and stresses placed on them by ill health, but does not necessarily imply successful coping. McIntyre and Thiede find that the combination of both the direct and the indirect costs of illness often well exceeds 10 per cent of household income. Studies which quantify this proportion by socio-economic group find a very clear inverse relationship, with the poorest group facing very much higher burdens than richer groups.

The chapter reviews evidence on the strategies used by households to cope with such costs, and considers whether the strategies are sustainable or serve to drive households deeper into poverty. Which is the case depends not just on the characteristics of a particular strategy but also on a household's inter-household relations and social networks, access to community organizations, and sources of credit. These can play a vital role in supporting households' capacity to cope successfully.

Chapter 5 draws a number of policy implications from its review of evidence. One lesson is the importance of improving the information available to households on how to deal with illness and from where help can be sought. Another is the importance of providing financial protection at the time of illness through prepayment or insurance mechanisms. A third is encouraging community-based mechanisms to support struggling households. And finally, the evidence suggests that the importance of direct non-medical costs – such as transport – has been underestimated and requires greater attention. Cash transfers may be one approach to providing assistance with such costs.

Chapter 6, by Russell, provides a case study of how poor households in urban Sri Lanka coped with illness costs and the consequences of the costs and responses for household livelihoods and poverty. Of especial interest were the factors that contributed to household resilience or vulnerability to illness shocks.

Household asset portfolios (human, physical, financial, and social), and the social and financial resources available to people in the wider community, influenced capacity to cope. Of particular importance were household social networks, financial capital (savings and jewellery that could be pawned), and access to financial institutions offering credit. Coping strategies differed by level of household vulnerability, with consequences for household livelihoods. Highly vulnerable households had weak asset portfolios, weak social networks, and low and irregular incomes and relied heavily on borrowing. Over time these households were struggling and increasingly impoverished. Less vulnerable households had stronger asset portfolios, stronger social networks with resources to offer, and borrowed less. They were on steady livelihood paths and were coping to different degrees. Resilient households had the strongest asset portfolios and faced few or no financial stresses.

Across all households, it was clear that public health services free at the point of delivery protected the majority of households from high direct cost burdens, especially those stemming from costs of hospitalization and chronic illness. However, there was extensive use of private primary care because of problems with public primary care: long waiting times, poor interpersonal quality, and lack of a family doctor system. Improvements in public primary care would greatly benefit poor households.

For vulnerable households, little protection was available against the damaging income losses caused by serious or frequent illness. The study highlights the vital role that social protection measures, such as pensions and targeted social grants, could play in mitigating household impoverishment caused by illness.

Part III: Restructuring health care systems to reach the poor

Chapters up to this point have documented the importance of health and the health system, but also the failings of the system to ensure access of the poor to health care, or to protect the poor from the cost implications of ill health. Several chapters did marshal their evidence to point to important policy implications, such as that of free hospital care in Sri Lanka. But on the whole the chapters paint a depressing picture of the failure of health systems to meet the needs of the poor.

This final section of the book turns directly to ask what can be done. Again it includes both review chapters and specific case studies. In general, there is as yet only limited evidence on how health systems can be improved, so in some cases the chapters offer conceptual clarity and likely strengths and weaknesses of alternative strategies rather than firm evidence.

Chapter 7, by Bennett, reviews alternative approaches to reaching the poor. Building on the barriers to service utilization identified in Chapter 4, it classifies strategies as universal or targeted, and addressing demand-side or supply-side problems. It then selects three universal approaches for in-depth examination: strengthening private sector service provision, introducing essential packages of interventions, and decentralization of health care management.

Constant themes in the chapter are the difficulty of identifying clearly effective approaches, and the absolute lack of evidence, especially with respect to whether the poor benefit or not. For example, mechanisms through which governments can seek to promote improved quality of care, or greater coverage of priority services, by private providers include training private providers (including traditional practitioners such as birth attendants), franchising, regulation, accreditation, and providing additional inputs such as equipment and pre-packaged drugs. Review of evidence of success suggests that there are currently few clearly effective strategies to improve quality of care in the private sector, and very little evidence of positive impact on poor populations. Franchising appears to hold promise, but no studies were found on whether it improves access of the poor. With respect to decentralization, the evidence on its impact is mixed and discouraging overall. A key element appears to be the extent of central government commitment to decentralization and poverty reduction: where this is weak, results may be more negative than positive and may in fact strengthen local elites rather than improve the position of the poor.

Chapter 7 concludes that while universal strategies may have advantages, they are frequently not as effective as hoped. Evidence suggests that multiple complementary approaches are likely to be needed to address health system deficiencies, encompassing strengthening not just of planning and management, but also of regulation and quality assurance procedures, and governance and accountability structures.

Chapter 8, by Hanson, Worrall, and Wiseman, complements Chapter 7 by reviewing targeting mechanisms and their effectiveness. Targeting is the identification and selection of certain groups, households, or individuals, and the distribution of benefits to them. It is a phrase very commonly used to imply the concentration of resources on the most needy. The chapter provides a unifying terminology and conceptual framework for describing the different elements and key choices involved in a targeted transfer programme, and reviews how six different targeting mechanisms have been applied in the health sector (resource allocation formulae, contracting NGOs, user fee exemptions, cash transfer programmes, voucher schemes, and market segmentation).

Available evidence focuses more on documenting coverage, under-coverage, and leakage, with few studies explaining these outcomes or providing insights into how problems might be addressed. Three general lessons are drawn from the evidence. First, the design, implementation, and evaluation of programmes is critically dependent on good information. This is especially the case where targeting requires individual beneficiaries to be identified.

Second, the incentive effects that targeting mechanisms create for providers and users are crucial. For example, exemption mechanisms are unlikely to be successfully implemented if the facility that must apply them thereby loses revenue, or if the poor do not believe that they will be offered an exemption when they visit a facility and also face other costs of accessing services.

Third, limited evidence suggests that individual targeting can be costly to administer. It cannot be assumed that targeting is always a more cost-effective way of reaching the poor, especially where a large proportion of the population is poor.

Chapter 9, by Bennett and Gilson, focuses on alternative approaches for raising and pooling revenue for the heath sector and their implications for the poor. It reviews strategies to improve the fairness of health financing and financial protection for the poor, emphasizing that the degree to which a financing system is pro-poor depends crucially on how different financing mechanisms interact.

The chapter examines three main options for improving the protection of the poor: repealing user fees, expanding tax-based financing, and expanding insurance coverage. The evidence on user fees – both of the impact of fees on the poor and of the impact of removing fees – suggests that their repeal is likely to increase financial accessibility, particularly for the poor. However, this action needs to be accompanied by complementary policies, including additional funding to compensate for the loss of user fee revenue. Tax-based financing is usually less pro-rich than other sources of health financing, but key in producing an equitable outcome is whether use of publicly funded services is pro-poor. This will depend, in considerable part, on whether services are equitably distributed geographically. Neither social health insurance nor community-based health insurance have a record of being especially pro-poor and their potential to protect a substantial proportion of the poor is limited, but interesting insurance developments such as those in Ghana and Rwanda merit further study as the schemes develop and expand.

The chapter ends by discussing the implementation process of health financing reform. Health financing reforms frequently encounter opposition amongst stakeholders, including providers, and are poorly communicated to users. The chapter emphasizes that how health financing reforms are developed, planned, and implemented significantly affects their impact on the poor, and that implementation must be seen as a task of political management rather than an unproblematic technical process.

Chapter 10, by Loewenson, builds on the concluding arguments of Chapter 9 and develops the theme of how people as citizens can play a role in defining, guiding and monitoring the policies that shape health systems. The chapter examines the concept of 'participation' and considers the evidence on its impact, finding that participation does have a positive impact on health systems and health outcomes, though this depends on the nature of services provided and the features of communities. For example, weak participation from the poorest groups, limited access to resources, information and training, resistance from health professionals, and weak formal authority have represented barriers to effective participation in health centre committees.

Social networks, faith-based organizations, trade unions, and other community organizations have provided important means for poor households to respond to a range of health challenges. The chapter provides examples of informal, civil society-based approaches, including ones which seek to obtain sustained representation from the poorest groups. It also examines the very mixed experiences of formal mechanisms to build accountability and responsiveness into health systems, such as district and national boards, hospital boards, and national coordinating committees, finding that poorly defined legal frameworks and inadequate resources are particular barriers to arrangements working effectively. At the global level, the chapter notes that civil society engagement has come largely from Northern pressure groups, and calls for further investigation of the role that Southern community groups can and might play in initiating, supporting, and responding to global campaigns.

The chapter emphasizes that the positive examples indicate that meaningful participation is underpinned by shared values of equity and solidarity, and by health systems which provide specific resources, technical and service support to the primary health care interface between services and society. It warns against 'token' participation, which uses up the time of poor people and communities but does not offer real engagement or ability to influence service provision.

In searching for country case studies on how health systems might be restructured to reach the poor, the editors found a number of examples of health financing reforms, with remarkably little good evidence on reforms to health care provision operating at scale or on wider system changes. What evidence is available on health provision reforms, such as extending services through contractual arrangements, improving private sector provision, and increasing accountability and responsiveness, has been summarized in the review chapters. The two final case studies of the book examine financing issues: reforming the national structure of health financing in Thailand and the experience of one of the largest community-based health insurance schemes in India.

Chapter 11, by Pannarunothai, provides an overview of one of the most significant financing reforms of recent decades: the introduction of universal coverage in Thailand, to provide financial protection for all except civil servants and those employed in the formal sector, who have their own schemes. Responding to the emphasis of Chapter 9 on the vital role in financing reform played by political interests and political management, the chapter examines the historical, economic, and social context of the universal coverage policy, stressing how long it was before political developments were conducive to a focus on equity. It identifies increased democracy, academic pressure groups, and the middle class as the driving forces behind political, bureaucratic, and health reforms. Research and evidence played an important part in bringing the universal coverage policy to fruition, and the chapter summarizes the types of data that are useful in monitoring health equity and how they can be obtained.

Universal coverage has had some notable successes. Although not everyone has chosen to use their entitlement (preferring instead to use other services, especially the private sector), the uptake of subsidized care has been highest for more expensive care (hospitalization), and amongst rural inhabitants, poorer population groups, and the elderly. The proportion of households incurring catastrophic expenditure as a result of health care has clearly fallen. In considerable part because of the design of the new system, including an emphasis on primary care and a new payment system, there has been a marked shift of utilization towards health centres and community hospitals, and away from provincial and regional hospitals.

The chapter identifies some continuing issues and problems. Maintaining the social solidarity needed to ensure political support for the universal coverage policy is a continuing issue, especially impeding any moves towards greater harmonization of this scheme with the other, better-funded schemes for civil servants and the formally employed. Also, maintaining the public sector workforce needed to staff the public services, especially in rural areas where private sector options are not available, is an increasing problem with the liberalization of international trade laws and an increase in medical tourism in Thailand.

Universal coverage in Thailand was accompanied by a very significant increase in tax funding which, for a rapidly growing middle-income country, can be argued to be readily affordable. Low-income countries have less scope to exploit increased tax financing, and hence there has been considerable interest in other approaches to domestic resource mobilization, especially community-based health insurance.

Chapter 12, by Ranson, Sinha, and Chatterjee, reviews the experience of Vimo SEWA, the insurance arm of the Self Employed Women's Association based in Gujarat, India, which has been providing a voluntary insurance policy covering life, assets, and hospitalization to informal sector workers since 1992. The chapter assesses Vimo SEWA in terms of whether it has made health care interventions more widely available to the poor; provided protection against health care costs; and given the poor a voice in shaping health care services.

Vimo SEWA has been remarkably successful with respect to size – its over

100,000 members is unusually large for a voluntary insurance scheme – and enrolment of the poorer segments of the population. However, the degree of financial protection has been limited by two features of scheme design: the need to claim retrospectively for hospitalization costs, and a cap of Rs.2,000 on reimbursements. With respect to 'voice', all elements of SEWA, including Vimo SEWA, are managed by elected member representatives, and members play an active role in shaping the scheme, with popular participation in managerial functions and scheme governance, and a culture of responsiveness.

The chapter concludes with some useful points for other countries with respect to using community-based insurance to protect the poor. It points out how tricky it is to use such schemes to target services to the poorest, and indeed to monitor the extent to which such a scheme is pro-poor. It also points out the limitations of a scheme which focuses on financial barriers, when there are many other barriers to the poor accessing care, especially lack of service provision in remote areas and transport difficulties. On the positive side, the experience demonstrates how different agencies can work together – Vimo SEWA uses public insurance companies as reinsurers and thus helps them deliver their mandate to deliver insurance services to the poor, while SEWA itself benefits from their experience and technical skills. Moreover, Vimo SEWA seeks to encourage its members to use public hospitals because of their lower charges and greater technical skills, and also works with such hospitals to improve their responsiveness.

The final chapter of the book seeks to consider the implications of the arguments and evidence presented in the book for health care policies in developing countries and for international development assistance. It summarizes how policies can be made more pro-poor, and identifies areas where evidence is still lacking. It especially focuses on:

- the need for political commitment and a stronger focus upon strategies to build political commitment;
- the importance of recognition of the inter-linkages between health and other sectors, and the imperative of inter-sectoral action;
- the importance of an effective, well-functioning public health care system which is free at the point of use and has broad geographic coverage;
- the need for an increased focus on the specific details of policy design and process of implementation, as they may significantly affect the extent to which a policy or strategy serves the interests of the poor; and
- the importance of developing a stronger evidence base to guide decisions on how best to make health systems better serve the needs of the poor.

Conclusions

This book provides evidence on the vital role that improved health can play in economic development and in reducing poverty. It also demonstrates that much is known about the extent to which the health systems of low-income countries fail to meet the health needs of the poor.

However, the book highlights the lack of strong evidence on what approaches might improve this situation. It reflects the grossly inadequate attention that has been given by research funders, and by policy makers requiring evidence to inform their actions, to the need for large-scale health systems research. The great majority of current health systems research is very small scale, and countries have very limited health systems research capacity (Alliance for Health Policy and Systems Research 2004). There is a vicious circle, with limited funding limiting capacity, and limited capacity limiting the extent to which larger-scale studies can be set up.

It is true that conclusions drawn from health systems research are to a considerable degree country or setting-specific. Actions to improve health systems, as many chapters emphasize, require complex approaches, tackling a number of facets of the problem at once. Differing circumstances will demand different elements. However, the introduction of similar approaches to a problem in differing contexts, as well as the introduction of different approaches in similar contexts, provides the opportunity for disentangling the relationship between policy design and country context. Yet the literature is notably thin on cross-country comparative studies, which might begin to explore the influence of context on policy success (Palmer *et al.* 2004). Country case studies of specific policies do abound in the literature, but often without exploration of how and why the results occur.

The health policy field also appears prone to fashions – policies are picked up and prescribed, with little accompanying evaluation on whether the desired results are obtained. Many of the policies reviewed in this book – such as community-based health insurance, making greater use of private providers, franchising, cash transfers and vouchers as targeting mechanisms, decentralization – have been widely advocated. But for none of these is the evidence such that they can be confidently predicted to be desirable approaches. Changing health policy fashions in low-income countries appear largely driven by external agencies, who pay little attention to the evidence base justifying them in the first place, give too little time and funding to allow them to 'work', and do little to develop the learning capacities of country health systems so that countries can test out the new ideas and adapt them, as well as develop their own approaches to making things work better. The focus of international debates tends to be on the development of new policy interventions to be added to, or implemented in parallel with, existing systems, rather than enabling and supporting improvements within systems that take account of their existing strengths and weaknesses.

What, then, can readers get out of this book? We hope that they will find the evidence they need to help them make the case for the importance of health in their own particular contexts. We also hope that they will gain from the analytical frameworks presented, to help them think through what might be useful approaches to improving the access of poorer groups to health services. And finally, we hope the book will encourage readers to advocate, support, and even initiate attempts to improve the evidence base on what works in improving health systems.

Part I

Health, development and poverty

2 The consequences of population health for economic performance

Marcella Alsan, David Bloom, David Canning and Dean Jamison

Introduction

Among the most important recent advances in thinking on international development is the idea that population health has a significant effect on economic
performance. Although the effects of individuals' health status on their productivity and earnings are readily observable and widely acknowledged, the consequences of population health for economic performance at the macro level,
and for the well-being of individuals, families and firms, are more difficult to
discern and have been, until recently, rather neglected.

This chapter goes beyond the traditional economic thinking about the relationship between health and income – simply stated, wealth is needed to achieve
health – by presenting evidence that population health is an important factor in
strengthening economies and reducing poverty. The world's overarching framework for reducing poverty is expressed in the United Nation's eight Millennium
Development Goals. Three of these eight goals pertain to health: reducing child
mortality, improving maternal health and combating human immunodeficiency
virus (HIV)/acquired immunodeficiency syndrome (AIDS), malaria and other
diseases. These potentially huge improvements in health are extremely important goals in themselves, and they serve as beacons towards which numerous
development efforts are oriented. But these potential improvements in health are
not only end points that we seek through a variety of means. The improvements
are actually *instruments* for achieving economic growth and poverty reduction.
That is to say, better health does not have to wait for an improved economy;
measures to reduce the burden of disease, to give children healthy childhoods
and to increase life expectancy will in themselves contribute to creating healthier economies.

This insight is relatively new and has significant political implications.
Finance ministers whose concerns have been tightly tied to national budgets and
staving off crises have a new tool to work with, since devoting resources to
health improvements can be a powerful means of stimulating economic growth
and mitigating poverty.

This chapter first looks at some straightforward data about the links between
health and income, and notes the traditional thinking that explains this

connection. It then describes how views are changing and, in particular, focuses on new evidence that good health can promote economic growth and well-being. After focusing on the specific connections between health and poverty, the chapter explores the mechanisms by which improved health can lead to better economic outcomes. The final sections discuss HIV/AIDS as a window into the issues addressed throughout the chapter and the policy directions that flow from the research and views presented here.

Some basic facts and the traditional view of their implications

Table 2.1, which groups countries by their infant mortality rate (IMR) (the number of infants who die before reaching one year of age per 1,000 live births) and income level in 1960, illustrates the general pattern connecting health and economic well-being. It shows that, within a given income classification, countries with higher IMRs in 1960 generally experienced lower rates of economic growth between 1960 and 2000, though de la Croix and Licandro (1999) offer a cautionary note on a related point, finding that 'the effect of life expectancy on growth is positive for economies with a relatively low life expectancy, but could be negative in more advanced economies [where life expectancy is higher on average]'. For example, on average, countries that had a gross domestic product (GDP) per capita between $3,500 and $7,000 in 1960, and IMR less than 50 per 1,000, experienced an average annual growth rate of 3.5 per cent over the subsequent 40 years. By contrast, a country with a GDP per capita less than $1,000 in 1960 and IMR greater than 150 per 1,000 experienced an average of 0.8 per cent per capita GDP growth over the subsequent 40 years.

Indeed, the positive correlation between income per capita and good health (the latter often assessed by life expectancy; see Figure 2.1) is one of the best-

Table 2.1 Annual growth rate of per capita income, 1960–2000 (by income per capita and infant mortality rate, 1960)

Initial income, 1960 (Constant 2000 US$, PPP)	Initial infant mortality rate, 1960			
	IMR ≤ 50	50 < IMR ≤ 100	100 < IMR ≤ 150	IMR > 150
GDP ≤ $1,000	–	3.9 (1)	2.0 (11)	0.8 (9)
$1,000 < GDP ≤ $2,000	–	4.8 (3)	1.5 (7)	0.5 (7)
$2,000 < GDP ≤ $3,500	–	1.6 (6)	1.7 (6)	1.0 (4)
$3,500 < GDP ≤ $7,000	3.5 (6)	2.1 (9)	0.7 (2)	1.0 (1)
GDP > $7,000	2.5 (17)	0.9 (1)	–	–

Source: Heston *et al.* (2006) for income and growth rate data. World Bank (2006) for IMR data.

Notes
PPP = Purchasing Power Parity.
The reported growth rate is the simple average of the GDP growth rates of all countries in the specific cell. The number of observations in each cell is displayed in parentheses next to the average growth rate.

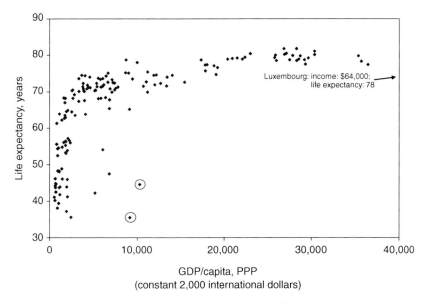

Figure 2.1 Life expectancy vs. income, 2004 (source: World Bank 2006, data are for 2004).

Note
The circled outliers, from lower to higher income, are Botswana and South Africa.

established facts in the field of international development. However, determining causality in the relationship between high incomes and good health remains a vexing issue. Good health could lead to high incomes; the reverse could be true; both could be true; or some other variables could be driving both health and income thereby creating the appearance of a health–wealth link.

To explain the apparent health–wealth relationship, traditional economic thinking (e.g. World Bank 1993a) has asserted that income growth is a key factor underpinning improved population health. The title of a journal article, 'Wealthier is healthier' (Pritchett and Summers 1996), succinctly captures this view. The assertion has a strong theoretical and intuitive basis. Higher incomes lead to greater command over many of the goods and services that promote health, such as better nutrition, safe water and access to quality health services. Higher incomes also promote technical progress and dissemination of new health technologies, which have been the major force behind health improvements (Easterlin 1999; Cutler *et al.* 2006). Consistent with this perspective, policies prescribed by international financial institutions for developing countries have focused on growth in GDP to the neglect and even the detriment of population health (Navarro 2004: 1322).

Evolving views of health, wealth and development

An early and influential analysis suggesting that rising income is not the only driver of health improvements comes from Samuel Preston (1975), who plotted the relationship between life expectancy and national income per capita during the 1900s, 1930s and 1960s (Figure 2.2). Preston's curves reveal two important insights. First, a rise in per capita GDP is associated with greater gains in life expectancy in poor countries than in wealthy ones. Second, the curve shifts up over time. For a given level of income per capita, life expectancy rose substantially over the study period. For example, an individual from a country with per capita GDP of $500 could expect to live around 59 years in the 1930s and 68 years in the 1960s. Preston calculated that if income was the sole determinant of mortality, then gains in life expectancy would have been small (2.5 years between 1938 and 1963). Yet, when he accounted for the upward shift of the curve during the same period, significantly larger health gains were predicted (12.2 years). Preston concludes that factors exogenous to a country's level of income accounted for 75–90 per cent of the rise in life expectancy, worldwide, over this period. These exogenous factors include medical and scientific breakthroughs – such as the development of vaccines and antibiotics – as well as advancements in sanitation and hygiene. Income growth per se accounted for only 10–25 per cent of the gain in life expectancy.

Preston summarizes his findings: 'There is no reason to expect a direct influence of national income per head on mortality . . . its influence is indirect; a higher income implies and facilitates, though it does not necessarily entail, larger real consumption of items affecting health such as food, housing, medical and public health services, education, leisure and health-related research, and, on the negative side, automobiles, cigarettes, animal fats and physical inertia' (Preston 1975: 232).

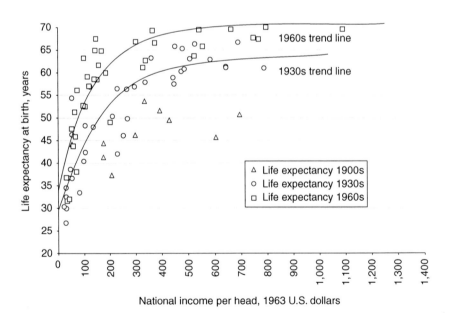

Figure 2.2 Relationship between life expectancy at birth and national income per capita, for countries in the 1900s, 1930s, 1960s (source: Preston 1975).

Preston's investigations drew the attention of economists and others to the links between income and population health. Bloom and Canning (forthcoming) provide a contemporary take on Preston's seminal work and its continuing importance. They note the importance of technological progress (i.e. not just income growth) in spurring health gains and point out why income per capita is an imperfect proxy of well-being. They also delve into the causality questions raised by the simultaneous improvement of health and income.

Specific inter-country comparisons of health outcomes and GDP levels, such as those given in Table 2.2, also weaken the case for a strict wealth-to-health causal linkage. Despite having an average per capita income that is four times higher than Costa Rica's, the United States has a lower life expectancy. Similarly, South Africa has double the per capita income of Cuba, but life expectancy in South Africa is 32 years lower.

Juxtaposing Cuba and the United States further illustrates this point. The two countries have similar life expectancies and equivalent IMRs (seven per 1,000). Yet these countries differ significantly in terms of income per capita. *World Development Report 2003* characterized Cuba as a 'puzzle' of 'good health without growth'. Cuba's impressive health outcomes are thought to be attributable to the priority assigned by the government to health care, as evidenced by the establishment of well-staffed community clinics, immunization campaigns, vector control and a commitment to minimizing inequality in access to health care.

So higher incomes *can* lead to improvements in population health, but sometimes they do not. Presumably, the distribution of income among members of society, a country's economic and social policies, and the strength of its institutions are also important.

In recent years, economists have focused increasingly on the links between population health and levels of income. Such research has been spurred by recognition of the global transformation in human health in the last 150 years, during which people have lived longer and led healthier, more productive lives. Between the sixteenth and the mid-nineteenth centuries, life expectancy around the world fluctuated but averaged less than 40 years, with no upward trend. Lifespan slowly but steadily increased in the second half of the nineteenth century and then jumped markedly in the twentieth century, initially in Europe and then

Table 2.2 Cross-country comparison of life expectancy and GDP per capita

Country	Life expectancy (2004)	GDP per capita (2004 PPP)
United States	77.4	36,465
Costa Rica	78.7	8,714
South Africa	44.6	10,286
Cuba	77.0	5,259

Source: World Bank (2006). Data for GDP per capita for Cuba are from UNDP (2003).

Note
PPP = Purchasing Power Parity.

in the rest of the world. Although there is still debate about the cause of these changes, demographers and economists increasingly attribute the modest declines in nineteenth century mortality rates to rising incomes. Then during the latter half of the twentieth century, global life expectancy increased by almost 20 years, from 46.6 years in 1950–5 to 65.4 years in 2000–5 (United Nations 2005). This represents a global average increase in life expectancy of more than four months per year. Technical advancements appear to be the catalyst for this more recent, more dramatic decline. For example, the World Health Organization (WHO), analysing data from 1952–92, found that income growth is less important to improving health outcomes than are other factors. In the period studied, average per capita income increased from $1,530 to $2,560 (in 1985 international dollars). If the relationship between income and IMR had remained as it was in 1952, IMR would have dropped from 144 per 1,000 to 116 per 1,000 by 1992. In reality, however, it dropped much more sharply to 55 per 1,000. This discrepancy is attributed to factors 'exogenous to wealth', namely technological progress and knowledge diffusion (WHO 1999: 5).

How have these improvements in population health affected economies? Fogel (1990) states, 'Improvement in nutrition and health may account for as much as 30 per cent of the growth in conventionally measured per capita income between 1790 and 1980 in Western Europe.' Arora (2001) investigates the influence of health on the growth paths of ten industrialized countries between the 1870s and the 1990s. Arora finds that changes in health increased the pace of income growth by 30 to 40 per cent, altering permanently the slope of these countries' income trajectories. The reported results hold for five different measures of long-term health and are largely unchanged when controlling for investment in physical capital. Fogel (1994) presents evidence of the historical impact of poor health on labour productivity. Using data from France circa 1790, he estimates that the bottom 10 per cent of the French labour force lacked the energy for regular work, and the next 10 per cent only had enough energy for three hours per day of light work.

Econometric studies that build on data from a large set of countries provide strong evidence that health is a significant predictor of income growth. Economists have expended a great deal of effort determining why growth in some countries is faster than it is in others. Studies have identified many determinants of economic growth, e.g. initial level of income per capita, geographic location, institutional environment, economic policy and investments in education. To this list, health has recently been added. A substantial body of evidence demonstrates that health, as measured by life expectancy or adult survival rates, has a significant effect on the pace of subsequent economic growth (e.g. Barro and Sala-i-Martin 1995; Barro 1996, 1997; Hamoudi and Sachs 1999; Bhargava *et al.* 2001; Bloom *et al.* 2004a). The work of Knowles and Owen (1997) is also consistent with the positive effect of health status on productivity. Taken together, these studies provide compelling evidence of a strong causal relationship from health to wealth. The effect is in addition to other influences on economic growth, emerges consistently across studies and is strikingly large.

Suppose we compare two countries that are identical save for a five-year difference in life expectancy. Several studies have shown that real income per capita in the healthier country will grow 0.3 to 0.5 percentage points per year faster than in its less healthy counterpart. This represents a sizeable boost to growth, given that global per capita income grew by roughly 2 per cent per year from 1965 to 1990. Bloom *et al.* (2004a) show that one extra year of life expectancy raises steady-state income by about 4 per cent.

To be complete, we must note that the case for the effect of health on economic well-being is still a matter of dispute. For example, Acemoglu *et al.* (2003) argue that health differences are not large enough to account for much of the cross-country differences in incomes, and that the variation in political, economic and social institutions is a more central factor. Acemoglu and Johnson (2006) go further, finding that 'there is no evidence that the large exogenous increase in life expectancy led to a significant increase in per capita economic growth'. For a detailed critique of their paper, see Bleakley (2006). In an effort to arrive at policy recommendations, Webber (2002) argues that life expectancy does not necessarily reflect investments in health. He uses nutrition, instead, as a proxy for health and finds that 'reducing undernutrition would only make a modest contribution to economic growth'.

Practical experience provides some relevant evidence about the links between health and economic performance. During the 1980s and 1990s, health sector budgets in developing countries were reduced as part of a package of austerity measures designed to promote economic growth (Périn and Attaran 2003: 1216). These austerity measures took the form of Structural Adjustment Programmes and were adopted by many developing countries during the 1980s and 1990s. Périn and Attaran (2003: 1216) describe the evolution and content of such programmes as follows:

> With the 1982 Mexico debt crisis, development became dominated by an obsession with macroeconomic fundamentals (tellingly, since the same donor countries were also the creditors whose unpaid loans were at risk) . . . The World Bank became the leading purveyor of structural adjustment . . . economic stability and development were best achieved through disciplined privatisation, deregulation, and trade liberalisation, often at the expense of social spending.

The belief that income growth is necessary for health improvements underlay the formulation and enactment of many of these policies. However, in practice these measures have often proved unsuccessful. In Africa, for example, where many countries adopted austerity measures, life expectancy reversals occurred while the economy stagnated (McMichael *et al.* 2004: 1155). By contrast, in Southeast Asia, prioritization of investment in the health of populations contributed to the economic prosperity this region enjoyed (Bloom *et al.* 2000: 257). The work of Easterly (1999) also weakens the argument for a focus on increasing incomes as a strategy for improving health. In an examination of outcomes over a reasonable period of time, Easterly finds only a weak effect of changes in income on population health.

Views that acknowledge the economic value of health improvements have gained greater currency in recent years. In 2000, the then Director-General of WHO, Gro Harlem Brundtland, established the Commission on Macro-economics and Health (CMH). The Commission's mandate was to 'assess the place of health in global economic development'. The CMH report, released in 2001, underscores the importance of health as an instrument for economic development and poverty reduction. The Commission notes that modest investments in health could save 8 million lives per year, resulting in an estimated 330 million disability-adjusted life years (DALYs) saved and about $200 billion in direct economic benefits *per year* by 2010 (Commission on Macroeconomics and Health 2001: 12). The CMH report suggests that good health is not just a consequence but also a cause of economic development.

Of course, the conventional view that wealthier implies healthier (i.e. the causal relationship opposite to that discussed above) is also true. These two views – that health promotes wealth and vice versa – are compatible. Causality running in each direction can give rise to cumulative causality, a so-called virtuous circle in which health improvements promote economic growth, which in turn promotes health.

The mutual reinforcement between health and income can also operate in reverse: sick people are more likely to become poor, and those who are poor are more vulnerable to disease. Often, the poor suffer from ill health because they lack access to clean water and sanitation, live in the most environmentally fragile areas and have difficulty getting medical care and information. Because many of the poor earn their livelihood by engaging in manual labour, health setbacks experienced by the breadwinner of a poor family may prove economically devastating. The household not only loses income, but may also be forced to sell off assets to pay for medical costs. Health problems can also plunge non-poor families into poverty; in countries that provide some level of safety net for the poor, downturns in health will increase the burden on the state while reducing state revenue. Increasingly, economists are recognizing that disease itself may thwart the economic growth that is presumed to prevent it. The vicious circle of poverty and disease is readily observable. Bloom and Canning (2001) describe the process of cumulative causality that can lead to the scenarios described here. An estimated 8 million children under the age of five die each year from easily preventable and treatable conditions, almost exclusively within the developing world (WHO 2003). Lorentzen *et al.* (2005) focus on adult mortality and find that it is such a large factor in reducing economic growth that it 'explains almost all of Africa's growth tragedy'.

The intrinsic value of health merits increased attention in economic analyses (see Marks and Mahal 2006). Health is enshrined as a fundamental human right and a component of individual freedom in numerous national and international legal frameworks. For example, Article 25 of the Universal Declaration of Human Rights states:

Everyone has the right to a standard of living adequate for the health and well-being of himself and of his family, including food, clothing, housing and medical care and necessary social services, and the right to security in times of unemployment, sickness, disability, widowhood, old age or other lack of livelihood in circumstances beyond his control.

Article 12 of the International Covenant on Economic, Social and Cultural Rights (ICESCR) states: 'The State Parties to the present Covenant recognize the right of everyone to the enjoyment of the highest attainable standard of physical and mental health' (Center for the Study of Human Rights 2001). Kinney (2001) documents that 110 national constitutions refer to the right to health care. Amartya Sen characterizes unnecessary morbidity and premature mortality as 'unfreedoms' that constrain human capability (Sen 1999: 24). Both equity- and rights-based approaches to development strongly support devoting additional resources to health.

To these perspectives we now add the macroeconomic argument: investing in population health can spur economic growth. We can therefore view health, along with education, as a form of human capital and an essential investment in a productive society. Chakraborty (2004) expresses this point quite succinctly: 'When human capital drives economic growth, countries differing in health capital do not converge to similar living standards.'

Health and poverty

A simple scatter plot shows the relationship between life expectancy and the poverty rate. Using the widely cited criterion of a $2/day (Purchasing Power Parity (PPP)-adjusted) poverty level, Figure 2.3 shows that countries with higher life expectancy have lower poverty rates. The correlation is not exceptionally strong, but the overall pattern is clear and unsurprising. This chart does not in itself imply causality.

Bloom *et al.* (2006) report on the relationship between health and poverty, finding that the effect of improved health on economic growth extends to the positive effect of health improvements on reducing poverty. They review and detail some of the mechanisms by which this effect can occur and offer evidence about the possible scale of the effect. Poverty reduction is a function of two separate phenomena: the overall growth of income, and changes in the dispersion of that income (which is a reflection of the extent to which the poor benefit from economic growth). Overall growth itself, in the absence of any change in the dispersion of income, will lower the number of people in poverty. Independently of this fact, a changing dispersion of income will change the number of people in poverty. If this distribution is in the direction of greater equality, the poverty rate will fall as those below the poverty line see their incomes rise.

The authors examine three different health scenarios to investigate the possible effect of improved health (as proxied by improved life expectancy) on poverty reduction. (One scenario is life expectancy as estimated and predicted

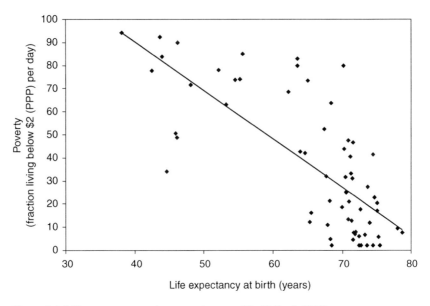

Figure 2.3 Life expectancy and poverty (source: World Bank 2006).

Notes
Life expectancy data are for 2004. Poverty data are for most recent year since 2000.
PPP = Purchasing Power Parity.

by the United Nations, and the other two are life expectancies higher than observed and predicted.) The simulations cover 31 countries with a combined population of 3.1 billion in 1990. With a dollar-a-day poverty rate of 30 per cent at that time, roughly 900 million people in those countries were living in poverty. The simulation results show that if life expectancy in 1990 had been 10 per cent higher and had followed a path leading to its being 10 per cent higher in 2015, then 30 million more people would have risen above poverty than in the scenario that follows actual life expectancy data and current projections. This change is not as sizable as the effect of health on economic growth rates, but it is definitely not negligible. The authors point out that because the poor rely disproportionately on manual labour, it makes sense that they should benefit disproportionately from improvements in health.

Broader arguments support the importance of the link between health and poverty. Since the poor rely on their good health in order to work, any diminution of their health can make them fall even further into poverty; health shocks to a family or community can quickly reverse years of improved health and income gains. Large and unanticipated health care costs can quickly appropriate a significant portion of a family's income and make it impossible for the family to maintain even the often low standard of living it formerly experienced. By contrast, health improvements can offer the poor a chance to work more productively and to be able to pay for schooling, both of which offer a path out of poverty.

Bloom and Canning (2003) point out that health improvements reduce poverty at the national level and also help families emerge from poverty. With better health having the potential to reduce poverty, there is a new rationale for greater spending on health. A new emphasis in this direction will require significant institutional changes at the international, national and local levels.

Healthier to wealthier: mechanisms

There are several channels through which health may contribute to economic growth and poverty reduction. Healthier populations tend to have higher labour productivity because their workers are physically and mentally more robust than those suffering from disease or disability. As detailed below, health improvements in a population change the age structure of society, offering a potentially substantial, albeit time-limited, boost to the productive capacity of an economy (on a per capita basis). Investment in physical and human capital, as well as research and development, is augmented as longer-lived individuals tend to increase their savings for retirement and foreign investment inflows tend to gravitate towards a healthy labour force. Improved health encourages stability in society and can increase the return to other forms of human capital, such as education and job experience. These mechanisms are explored in greater detail below.

Health to family welfare and labour and firm productivity

Health has a direct effect on the productivity of the labour force. Case studies compiled by the World Bank that involved interviews with over 60,000 people living in poverty revealed that their single greatest concern was the health of the household breadwinner. If he or she dies or requires expensive medical care, a family can be financially or economically crippled (World Bank and World Health Organization 2002), possibly entering a vicious circle of poverty and disease, from which it cannot escape.

Studying the effects of health on households and individuals is the purview of microeconomics. Such analyses employ anthropometric measures and indexes of morbidity as measures of health and human capital. The results consistently indicate that health affects worker earnings and productivity. Many studies use adult stature as a proxy for long-term health. Although there is clearly a genetic component to height determination, bouts of infirmity throughout childhood arrest growth, leaving height as an indicator of the frequency and duration of childhood illness. Microeconomic analyses attempt to isolate the wage effects of height variations due to environmental health differences (see Schultz 1999). Using this method, Schultz and Tansel (1997) and Ribero and Nunez (2000) demonstrate that one centimetre of additional height due to health inputs when young adds about 6 per cent to wages. Health interventions to overcome specific health problems can also boost labour productivity. Thomas *et al.* (2005) find improvements in the health and economic productivity of men who received treatment for iron deficiency; after treatment, they 'are more likely to be working, sleep less, lose less work time to illness, are more energetic, more able to conduct physically arduous activities, and their psycho-social health is better'.

In addition to the costs to individuals and households, disease has spillover effects that can impose a high cost on the larger economy. For firms, disease can have dire consequences for both productivity and profitability and thereby decrease competitiveness. The labour force in a society with a high burden of disease experiences higher rates of turnover and absenteeism. Strategic management of the firm can be compromised if its managerial staff become ill. Although it has been argued that surplus labour makes sick workers easily replaceable, this case may be overstated. A study of the effect of HIV on nearly 1,000 firms in sub-Saharan Africa found that replacing the skilled staff presented a serious problem (Biggs and Shah 1997). The death of a worker represents lost human capital investment in job training and worker experience. Worker morale may plummet as friends and co-workers fall sick and die, further diminishing firm productivity.

Firm profitability generally suffers as health costs rise. When workers get sick, they claim more health benefits. Expenditures may shift from productive inputs towards health services or funeral costs. As a precautionary measure, some businesses in sub-Saharan Africa have reportedly started training each skilled labourer in numerous jobs so that the company can operate more easily when skilled workers fall ill. Other firms are hiring multiple workers for each skilled position, to ensure trained replacements when incumbents die (*Economist* 2001). Disease may also affect the demand for a firm's product. A declining consumer base translates into a diminishing market for the firm's products. In the aggregate and over time, these firm and household level effects could contribute to a slowdown in the national economy.

Health to demography

Health improvements also affect demography, in ways that can possibly offer a boost to developing economies. There is a strong association between infant and child mortality and fertility (defined as the number of children a woman bears, rather than how likely or how easy it is for her to become pregnant and bear children). Families in unhealthy societies tend to compensate for expected and actual child deaths by having more children. Although many other factors contribute to fertility, such as mother's level of education, access to reproductive health services and entrenched gender inequalities, the relationship between fertility and IMR is compelling. Countries with an IMR of less than 20 have a 1.7 average total fertility rate (TFR) ('the average number of children women would bear if they follow the age-specific childbearing patterns that characterize a country at a particular time', Menken and Rahman, 2001: 83). By contrast, the TFR is 6.3 for countries with an IMR over 100 (Commission on Macroeconomics and Health 2001: 36). In many instances, high fertility rates reflect purposeful attempts by parents to achieve desired family size: having many children increases the likelihood that at least one or two will survive into adulthood. Bearing a large number of children taxes a mother's health. Large family size also taxes household

resources, which must be spread more thinly with less investment in the education of each child. High fertility (in a context of overall diminished mortality and,
hence, rising population) increases the dependency ratio, i.e. the ratio of the
dependent population (those aged 0–14 and 65 plus) to the working-age population (aged 15–64). A high dependency ratio resulting from high fertility means
that a larger proportion of earnings are channelled into supporting children.

When childhood survival rates rise, families tend to have fewer children.
Low-cost interventions such as vaccinations, vitamin A supplementation, oral
rehydration therapy (ORT) and breastfeeding have ushered in dramatic reductions in infant and child mortality over the past four decades. Globally, child
mortality has declined from 192 per 1,000 live births in 1960 to 79 per 1,000
live births in 2004 (World Bank 2006). The reduction in child mortality has been
particularly dramatic in Southeast Asia, the Eastern Mediterranean and Latin
American regions (WHO 2003: 9). As noted above, when infant and child mortality falls and survival to adulthood becomes more likely, parents can feel more
confident having fewer children. The combination of an initial drop in the IMR
(resulting in there being more children) and the subsequent fall in fertility
(leading eventually to smaller age cohorts) creates a 'bulge' generation that
moves through the age structure of the population. This bulge is the inevitable
result of the 'demographic transition' (i.e. the move towards lower mortality,
followed by a move towards lower fertility). When the bulge generation represents a large number of working-age people, their contribution to the economy
can cause income per capita to rise dramatically. This effect is called the demographic dividend, and its realization is heavily reliant on policies that allow extra
workers to be absorbed into the workforce (Bloom and Canning 2001: 187;
Bloom *et al.* 2004a; Lee and Mason 2006).

East Asia provides a compelling example of how improvements in public
health contribute to economic growth via demographic change. A growing body
of evidence suggests that the East Asian countries that sustained high rates of
economic growth in the second half of the twentieth century did so thanks to
high rates of growth of labour and capital. Growth in labour supply largely
resulted from changes in the age structure of the population that followed from
improved sanitation, safer water, the development of antibiotics and application
of the anti-malarial insecticide dichlorodiphenyltrichloroethane (DDT). Life
expectancy increased from 39 years in 1960 to 67 years in 1990. Infant mortality
declined, from 175 per 1,000 in 1950 to 52 per 1,000 in 1995 (Asian Development Bank 1997), followed by a precipitous drop in fertility. A greater number
of surviving children, followed by smaller birth cohorts, created relatively large
'baby boom' cohorts in a number of countries. When these cohorts reached
working age, the dependency ratio was dramatically lower than in the past. The
working-age population rose from about 55 per cent of East Asia's total population in 1965 to 70 per cent in 2001. A beneficial policy environment, which
focused on education and selective openness to trade, allowed this 'boom' generation to be integrated into the economy. East Asia reaped the productivity
benefits of the swollen workforce. Between 1965 and 1990 per capita income

rose by over 6 per cent per year. This phenomenal growth was given the name the East Asian 'miracle' (World Bank 1993b). However, Bloom and Williamson (1998) and Bloom *et al.* (2000) demonstrate that no less than a third of the 'miracle' could be explained by the demographic dividend.

Health to savings and investment

Another key element in East Asia's economic success was the region's high rate of capital accumulation, driven by an extraordinarily high savings rate of around 30 per cent of income. There are two channels, one accounting and the other behavioural, through which the health of East Asia's population contributed to this high level of savings. Common to both channels is the well-established life-cycle theory of how consumption and savings decisions are made at the house-hold level (see Modigliani and Brumberg 1954). According to this model, households earn an income stream over their lifetime and must choose a con-sumption path consistent with these earnings. It is assumed that, in general, people save when they are young to finance their retirement. Peak savings typ-ically occur between the ages of 40 and 65. Dissaving of the old, assuming no motive to bequeath, should offset the savings of the young in a stationary popu-lation (i.e. a population with a stable age distribution and no population growth). In this situation, there are no aggregate savings.

If the age structure of the population is unstable, aggregate savings or dissav-ings may occur according to the rise or fall of the share of the population at the high-savings ages – this is the effect considered by the accounting channel. In the case of East Asia, the demographic dividend resulted in a large fraction of its population being in the peak savings range of 40–65 years of age. Furthermore, this was the first cohort in the region to be living in a low-mortality environment and to be saving for retirement on a large scale (Bloom *et al.* 2004b: 12). Age-structure effects appear to account for perhaps one-quarter of East Asia's savings boom (Bloom *et al.* 2003).

The behavioural channel highlights the fact that improvements in health and longevity likely affect life-cycle behaviour as individuals look forward to longer, healthier lives (see Bloom *et al.* forthcoming). Increases in longevity tend to increase the relative length of retirement, thereby raising the need for retirement income and generating higher savings rates among the young. Bloom *et al.* (2003) model and empirically investigate the effect of increasing longevity on the national savings rate. They report that a ten-year rise in life expectancy is associated with about a 4-percentage-point rise in the savings rate. Lee *et al.* (2000) argue that rising life expectancy can account for the boom in savings in Taiwan since the 1960s. Rising longevity in developing countries could there-fore magnify the current generation's incentive to save – a development that may have sizable effects on domestic investment. Although this saving and investment boom may only last for one generation and is offset by the needs of the elderly once the population ages, it can substantially boost economic growth rates while it lasts.

Health also affects foreign direct investment (FDI). A high burden of disease enervates the labour force. Perhaps also for fear of endangering their own health, foreign investors and executives tend to shun areas where disease is rampant and where access to health care is limited. By contrast, a healthy, productive workforce will tend to attract FDI inflows. Research has demonstrated that life expectancy exerts an independent influence on FDI: every additional year of life expectancy contributes to about a 9 per cent increase in gross FDI inflows in low- and middle-income countries (Alsan *et al.* 2004: 11). These empirical results are supported by historical evidence. The textbook instance of disease interference in investment is that of the building of the Panama Canal. Yellow fever and communicable diseases claimed the lives of 10,000 to 20,000 workers between 1882 and 1888, forcing Ferdinand de Lesseps and the French to abandon the construction project (Jones 1990).

Health to education

Another mechanism by which health affects income is through its relationship to education. There is an extensive and longstanding literature demonstrating that education increases productivity and wages. A typical estimate is that a year of education increases wages by about 10 per cent (Psacharopoulos and Patrinos 2004). Healthier households generally have more income for many of the reasons discussed above. Their enhanced productivity allows them to earn higher wages, they have fewer health-related expenses and they are able to attain desired family size at lower fertility rates. Healthy families can therefore afford to spend more on their children's education. Given the importance of education to income, it is significant that health can serve as a complementary input to education. In this regard, Finlay (2006) makes a significant finding: that the effect of health on economic growth is stronger in countries where education is weak, because a population that relies more on unskilled labour is more dependent on good health.

Healthier children have enhanced cognitive function and higher school attendance, enabling them to become better-educated, higher-earning adults. Bleakley (2003) finds that deworming of children in the American South had an effect on their educational achievements while in school. Miguel and Kremer (2004) find that deworming of children in Kenya increased school attendance (though it did not enhance academic performance). In a study in India, Bobonis *et al.* (forthcoming) find that deworming and treating anaemia promoted school attendance.

Increased longevity can make investing in education more attractive because it affords a longer time horizon over which to reap the benefits of more schooling (Kalemli-Ozcan *et al.* 2000). Bils and Klenow (2000) find an effect of life expectancy on investments in education at the national level. In addition, lower infant mortality may encourage parents to invest more resources in fewer children, leading to low fertility but high levels of human capital investment (including in education) in each child (Kalemli-Ozcan 2002).

There are numerous paths from impaired health to the inadequate education of children. Leslie and Jamison (1990) review the links between health conditions and what they see as the three main educational problems in developing countries: children who are unprepared to attend school, the failure of many students to learn in school and the unequal participation of girls in schooling.

Children's readiness for school may be hindered by cognitive and physical impairments. These problems may begin *in utero* due to inadequate nutrition and poor health of the mother. An estimated 30 million infants are born each year in developing countries with impaired growth due to poor nutrition during foetal life (United Nations 2000). For example, cretinism, which can be avoided if iodized salt is provided to the mother, is the most common preventable cause of mental retardation worldwide (Cao *et al.* 1994: 1739). Moreover, malnourished children are less likely to enrol in school; those who do enrol do so at a later age (United Nations 2004).

The failure of children in developing countries to learn in school is often attributable to illness. The most important causes of morbidity among school-age children include helminthic infections, micronutrient deficiencies and chronic protein malnutrition. When not fatal, these conditions impair children's ability to learn by directly contributing to disease, absenteeism and inattention among children. Micronutrient deficiencies have a variety of adverse health effects. Vitamin A deficiency contributes to measles mortality and diarrhoeal illness (WHO 2004b), and is the leading cause of preventable paediatric blindness in low-income countries (Sommer and West 1996: 649ff.). Impaired vision is a huge barrier to receiving an education, particularly in resource-poor settings. Globally, 4.4 million children and 6.2 million women of childbearing age manifest varying degrees of vision impairment from vitamin A deficiency (United Nations 2004). Iron deficiency is a well-documented cause of impaired cognitive development and lowered school achievement and has a high economic cost (Grantham-McGregor and Ani 2001). It is also one of the most prevalent nutrient deficiencies in the world, affecting an estimated two billion people (WHO 2004b). Horton and Ross (2003) estimate that income forgone due to iron deficiency ranges from 2 per cent of GDP in Honduras to 7.9 per cent in Bangladesh. The higher estimates are associated with severe iron deficiency and higher returns to educational attainment in the labour market for a given country.

Biological and cultural forces affect the health of girls and can impede their educational attainment. Attending to remediable medical problems could help keep girls in school. Menstruation exacerbates iron-deficiency anaemia, and at around the same developmental stage, iodine-deficiency disorders also begin to affect more girls. Pregnancy increases nutrient demands and the risk of morbidity and mortality from a multitude of associated causes. An estimated 15 per cent of women develop potentially life-threatening complications associated with pregnancy, such as haemorrhage, infection, unsafe abortion, eclampsia and obstructed labour (WHO 2004c). Early marriage and childbearing may account for the drop-off in number of girls enrolled in secondary and tertiary school. A ubiquitous and disturbing pattern is that when illness strikes a family, girls often discontinue studies to assume responsibilities for household chores. Overviews of the interaction between health and education appear in Bloom (2005) and Bloom (2006).

The AIDS epidemic demonstrates particularly starkly the interplay between disease and education. Educational opportunities erode as families are forced to pay more for medical and burial costs. A study in rural districts in Uganda found that one in five children living in HIV/AIDS-affected households was removed from school because school fees could not be paid or the child was required to work (Topouzis 1994). The generation of orphans HIV is creating (14 million, mostly in Africa) strains household resources and affects educational attainment (WHO 2004d). Orphans have lower school enrolment rates and live in more impoverished households. Families who receive orphans often cannot afford to send all children in the household to school and must decide which children to enrol. Boys are usually chosen over girls, and biological children are selected over orphans (Ableidinger *et al.* 2002). Indeed this study finds that school enrolment rates reflect the degree of kinship between the child and the head of the household. HIV/AIDS also affects the supply of education, damaging both its quantity and quality. A sharp increase in mortality rates among teachers and administrators accounts for this setback. Twelve per cent of teachers in South Africa, 19 per cent of teachers in Zambia, and more than 30 per cent of teachers in Botswana are infected with HIV (BBC 2002). In Zambia, the number of teachers killed by AIDS in 1998 was equivalent to two-thirds of the number of teachers trained in the same year (WHO 2004d). Even where teachers are present, they may be sick and ineffective.

HIV/AIDS as a window into the relationship between health and economic outcomes

Economists have studied not only the role that HIV/AIDS can play in economic outcomes via its detrimental effect on educational attainment; much more broadly, the epidemic provides an interesting perspective on the standard economic view of the relationship between health and wealth.

The argument that population health is an important determinant of income growth implies that countries with waning health due to high rates of HIV/AIDS have poor economic prospects. For example, Haacker (2004) argues that HIV/AIDS 'is the most serious impediment to economic growth and development' in countries with severe epidemics. However, a number of other analyses conclude that HIV/AIDS has had no measurable effect on income per capita (Bloom and Mahal 1997a; Mahal 2004; Werker *et al.* 2006). Still others, such as Young (2005), suggest that, despite the obvious human cost, HIV/AIDS might actually promote growth of income per capita. According to this last argument, the reduction in the labour force resulting from AIDS may increase worker productivity because surviving workers have more land and capital at their disposal, and because the capital/labour balance is pushed in a direction that benefits workers. Thus, the heightened mortality from disease may boost living standards. (The origins of this view can be traced to Thomas Malthus (1798), who believed epidemics and famines were 'natural checks' on unfettered population growth. This bleak outlook led economics to be labelled 'the dismal science'.)

The description of events provided by Young may accurately describe the mortality 'shocks' that characterized epidemics throughout history (see Bloom and Mahal 1997b for detail on AIDS, influenza and the Black Death). Yet the short-lived epidemics of the past, such as epidemic cholera or the 1918 Spanish flu, bear little resemblance to the current epidemic of HIV/AIDS. The AIDS virus kills but does so slowly. Because it is most frequently transmitted via sexual activity, it preferentially infects young and middle-age adults. As a result, HIV/AIDS affects societies in different ways than other epidemics and leads to higher burdens of youth (orphan) and elderly dependency. Because the possibility of contracting HIV reduces the incentives and opportunities for education and savings, it likely magnifies the intergenerational transmission of poverty.

It is estimated that approximately 39 million people are infected with HIV (UNAIDS 2006) and that AIDS is now the world's leading killer of adults aged 15–59 (WHO 2003). Co-infections of HIV and malaria or tuberculosis can exacerbate an already dire health situation. A high prevalence of some diseases negatively impacts economies and is associated with lower economic growth rates. Gallup and Sachs (2001) demonstrate that countries heavily burdened with malaria experienced an average growth rate in per capita GDP of about 0.4 per cent per year between 1965 and 1990, in comparison with an average growth rate of 2.3 per cent in other countries. Moreover, a consideration of GDP per capita alone does not fully express the economic losses; it refers to the effects of disease on the income of survivors but does not reflect the monetary value of the loss of life.

Because GDP per capita is not a complete measure of well-being, a 'full income' indicator can be used to convey a more accurate picture of the economic effect of AIDS. Full income consists of two components: GDP per capita for survivors and the estimated value of life for decedents. The latter is derived from the 'value of a statistical life' (VSL) literature. This literature places a dollar value on human life using information from individuals' choices to take life-threatening risks, no matter how small. This method has drawbacks, but it enables governments to compare public health and other development interventions that reduce mortality risks.

Estimates of the monetary value of life are often very large (Viscusi and Aldy 2003). A typical range for a country's VSL is around 100–200 times GDP per capita, with richer countries located at the higher end of the range. Using full income, a conservative estimate of the cost of Africa's mortality change due to AIDS is 1.7 per cent of Africa's income per year from 1990–2000, which is a far higher number than earlier estimates for the effect of AIDS on GDP over the same period (Bloom *et al.* 2004b: 14). More broadly, using techniques that do not rely solely on GDP per capita as the outcome of interest, studies of many countries have shown the intrinsic value of health gains to have been comparable to or higher than the value of income gains due to health improvements (Nordhaus 2003; Becker *et al.* 2005).

The way forward

This chapter has summarized the evidence on the contribution of population health to economic growth and poverty reduction, and the mechanisms through which this takes place.

The next logical step is to determine what fraction of societal resources should be allocated to the health sector. We do not attempt to provide an answer to that question, but the CMH report makes explicit recommendations regarding domestic and international financial contributions towards health. The report estimates that total health outlays for improving population health among low- and middle-income countries would approach $57 billion by 2007 and $94 billion by 2015. The low- and middle-income countries could commit an additional $35 billion per year by 2007 and $63 billion by 2015. In addition, the report calls for concessionary grants totalling $22 billion by 2007 and $31 billion by 2015 from wealthy countries and international development banks. The recommended rise in donor funding for health represents 0.1 per cent of donor country GDP.

It is clear that where disease is most rampant, among poor populations within and across countries, the resources necessary to improve health are most scarce. Wealthy countries could contribute more financial resources towards reducing the burden of disease in the developing world. Low- and middle-income countries could also do much more to improve the transparency, accountability and equity of national health systems. Health is proving to be a worthwhile investment. Improved health will allow developing countries to enjoy higher rates of economic growth and faster poverty reduction; wealthy nations will benefit from reduced expenditures on global public health threats, expanding markets and enhanced global security.

If history serves as a harbinger of things to come, the financial rewards of global health investments are reaped many times over. Smallpox eradication obviates the need for preventive measures and treatment facilities. The cost to the United States for the successful 13-year campaign was about $30 million; since smallpox was eradicated in 1977, the total investment has been returned to the United States every 26 days (CISET 2006).

In sum, investments in population health can be considered integral to economic development and to promoting the wealth of nations. Improving the health of nations is a powerful instrument to this end.

Acknowledgements

The authors are grateful to Larry Rosenberg, and to Helen Curry, Guenther Fink and Jocelyn Finlay, for their assistance in the preparation of this chapter.

3 Illness and labour productivity:
A case study from rural Kenya

Sydney Rosen, Jonathon Simon and Matthew Fox

Kenya I 12 J24
O15 J22
O18 I30

Introduction

As the previous chapter in this book has demonstrated, there are multiple pathways by which ill health can contribute to household poverty. In this chapter, we take a closer look at one of those pathways, labour productivity. Using a detailed case study of human immunodeficiency virus (HIV)/acquired immunodeficiency syndrome (AIDS) among agricultural workers in western Kenya, we explore the relationship between adult morbidity and labour output and discuss how changes in individual-level labour productivity might affect household incomes as well as firm profits, which are important to households because firms provide employment and thus contribute to household economic welfare, even in rural areas.

Background: what do we know about illness and labour productivity?

It is reasonable to suppose that when a worker falls ill, the quantity and quality of that worker's labour deteriorates. For workers who have formal jobs, this loss of productivity might manifest itself in greater absenteeism, poorer performance when at work, or changes in the types of work assigned. For workers who have informal jobs, are self-employed or do unpaid work at home, the impacts of illness are likely to be more direct: fewer goods or services sold, less land planted or harvested, fewer meals cooked.

Earlier research on infectious diseases and productivity

Although these impacts seem obvious, there is in fact surprisingly little quantitative evidence of the consequences of ill health for individual labour productivity. Among the common causes of adult morbidity in the developing world, malaria and schistosomiasis may be the most frequently investigated for labour productivity effects. Most studies have found that an episode of malaria results in at least several days of lost working time or absenteeism: 9.9 days of full disability and 2.7 days of partial disability in Nepal (Picard and Mills 1992); 14 days in rural Ethiopia (Cropper *et al.* 1999); and an average of 5–20 days in multiple studies reviewed in earlier years (Najera *et al.* 1993). In none of these cases was there a direct measure of productivity available, so lost work time, rather than output, was the outcome variable estimated. That was not the case for five studies that examined the impact of schistosomiasis on the productivity of sugar cane cutters, cotton pickers and rice growers in sub-Saharan Africa. Three found no difference in daily output between infected and uninfected workers (Foster 1967; Collins *et al.* 1976; Parker 1992), though absenteeism increased by 2.7 per cent in one. One found an output loss of 3 per cent among infected workers (Fenwick and Figenschou 1972), while the last estimated a 4.9 per cent loss in output per 10 per cent increase in disease prevalence (Audibert 1986).

A handful of studies have examined the productivity effects of other infectious diseases. Two studies analysed the effect of onchocercal skin disease on coffee plantation workers in Ethiopia; one found that severely infected workers worked two fewer days per month than healthy workers and were 16 per cent less productive while on the job (Kim *et al.* 1997), while the other found that infected workers worked 9.1 fewer days per month and earned 25.2 per cent less (Workneh *et al.* 1993). Chronic lymphatic filariasis was found to reduce the daily output of Indian weavers by 27.4 per cent, though it did not affect the number of hours they worked (Ramu *et al.* 1996).

The relationship between labour productivity and HIV/AIDS is even less understood, particularly in developing countries. While the illnesses associated with HIV infection are known to diminish physical and cognitive functioning (O'Keefe and Wood 1996; Gill *et al.* 2002; Robertson *et al.* 2004), we do not know to what extent these symptoms translate into lower labour productivity. The research that has been done has been limited to lost work time. Several studies have documented increases in absenteeism among formally employed workers in sub-Saharan Africa, particularly in the mining and manufacturing sectors. A recent study in South Africa and Botswana, for example, reported that employees who died of AIDS-related causes took an average of 35.4 more days of sick leave in their last year of service than the annual average for the workforces as a whole, which was 6.3 days of sick leave per year. Once again, no direct measures of individual labour productivity were available at the companies studied (Rosen *et al.* 2004).

Why is a direct relationship between health and labour productivity so hard to quantify? One important reason is that, in most settings, neither the health nor the productivity of an individual worker can be observed directly. Employees have an incentive to conceal their health status, as obvious illness could result in demotion, dismissal or denial of health benefits (Pauly 1997). In most workplaces, tasks are performed by teams of people, making the contribution of any one individual difficult to ascertain (Pauly *et al.* 2002). As a result, most estimates of the economic impact of adult disease have relied on self-reported health status, which is known to be an unreliable indicator of clinical status (Behrman and Deolalikar 1988; Strauss and Thomas 1994), or have calculated productivity costs by applying an arbitrary value of worker time, such as the wage rate for unskilled labour, to an extrapolated number of days of labour lost per disease event (Ettling and Shepard 1991; Sauerborn *et al.* 1991; Najera *et al.* 1993; Cropper *et al.* 1999). This approach, while easy to apply, fails to capture the true opportunity cost of a worker's time, which might not be well reflected by the wage rate, and rarely incorporates the loss of productivity on days when a worker is present at work but performs poorly due to illness.

A second important constraint to measuring the impact of health on productivity is the role of labour substitution. Labour substitution can reduce the productivity costs of disease to both households and firms by shifting tasks to other members of a household or to temporary workers hired by the company. Research on malaria has found household labour substitution to be very common, particularly in agricultural settings. One study (Nur 1993) showed that malaria-related productivity losses among Sudanese farmers were entirely offset by household labour substitution. Another study (Cropper *et al.* 1999), in Ethiopia, found that because of labour substitution, the net loss of labour to a household per case of malaria was just 36 per cent of the patient's own labour loss (the additional time required to care for the patient, however, brought the total household labour loss to 107 per cent of the patient's own loss). Workers also frequently 'cover' for sick colleagues, making the true loss of productivity nearly impossible to discern.

The importance of HIV/AIDS

HIV/AIDS is arguably the most devastating epidemic to strike sub-Saharan Africa in recorded history. By the end of 2003, adult prevalence exceeded 10 per cent of adults (aged 15–49) in ten countries (UNAIDS 2004). In a few countries in southern Africa, nearly a third of pregnant women tested positive for HIV. As a result, by 2010 life expectancy at birth was projected to fall to less than 40 years, levels not seen for many decades (Stanecki 2004).

Unlike malaria, diarrhoeal diseases and most other common infectious diseases, which afflict and kill primarily children and old people, HIV/AIDS takes its greatest toll on young working-aged adults. HIV incidence in countries like Kenya begins to rise in the late teenage years and is believed to peak in the early twenties (for women) to mid-thirties (for men). In the absence of effective treatment, most people with HIV will become symptomatic six to eight years after infection (Jaffar *et al.* 2004). The median survival time – the interval between infection and death – is approximately nine to ten years (UNAIDS Reference Group on Estimates, Modelling and Projections 2002). Morbidity and mortality from the disease thus hit hardest when most adults are in their most productive years as workers, parents and citizens.

Because of the concentration of AIDS mortality among working-aged adults, the consequences of the epidemic for labour productivity in sub-Saharan Africa are of serious concern. But how much does HIV/AIDS diminish productivity, and to what extent will labour substitution offset these losses? The case study that follows attempts to answer these questions in a setting in which both the health and productivity of individual workers can be observed directly, that of plantation agriculture.

Case study: tea pluckers in western Kenya

Commercial agriculture plays an important role in many developing countries, employing large numbers of unskilled workers and generating substantial shares of export earnings. Large agricultural estates tend to pay the workers who harvest the crop on a piece-work basis, by the kilogram or ton of spices, fruits, flowers, leaves or vegetables harvested. Because they are located away from large towns and cities, agricultural estates often provide onsite medical care to workers and their households. They thus collect data on both the daily output and the health of each worker. For this reason, most of the studies on morbidity and productivity cited earlier in this chapter used agricultural estates as their research sites.

In 2000, we began a study on a set of commercial tea estates in Kericho District in the highlands of western Kenya. Tea is Kenya's most important export crop, accounting for 18 per cent of the country's export earnings in 2003. Because global tea markets are extremely competitive and the margins earned on most of Kenya's tea are very low, any factor that could cause the production costs of tea to rise was treated with concern. For companies dependent on large numbers of manual labourers, HIV/AIDS was such a factor. For this reason, one of the largest of the multinational tea companies in Kenya invited us to conduct research on the impact of HIV/AIDS on labour productivity on its estates.

Methods

Study site and population

The tea company involved in the study employs nearly 15,000 workers, of whom 10,000 harvest tea as their primary job. These tea pluckers are paid a fixed amount (KSh.4.09, or $0.055) per kilogram of tea they pluck each day. For payroll purposes, the company must therefore keep records of every worker's output every working day of the year. Tea pluckers work six days a week. The average amount harvested per worker is 42.8 kg of tea per day.

The company provides housing, medical care and schooling free of charge to workers and their dependents. Including dependants, the population on the company's estates was estimated at 67,000 in 2000. The medical system includes a central hospital and a network of referral dispensaries and clinics, and is used by almost everyone on the estates, with the exception of senior managers who can afford private health care outside the company system.

In 1999, just before our study began, a survey had been conducted to determine the prevalence of HIV infection among workers and adult dependants on the estates. There were a number of biases in the sample tested, making it not representative of all adults, but the survey provided the only evidence available of the extent of the epidemic among the workers. Adult HIV prevalence was estimated to be 11 per cent. At the time of the study, the company's medical facilities provided treatment of AIDS-related opportunistic infections but did not have a disease management programme for HIV/AIDS or offer antiretroviral therapy.

Data

Our analysis required data about two groups of tea pluckers: (1) pluckers who were known to have died or taken medical retirement as a result of AIDS-related illnesses between 1997 and 2002 (hereafter called 'index subjects'); and (2) pluckers who were working in the same fields on the same days as the index subjects but known not to have died of AIDS (hereafter called 'reference subjects'). Index subjects were identified from medical records at the company hospital. Reference subjects were included in the analysis to represent the normal productivity of 'healthy' workers. Because 'normal' tea output is determined in part by environmental factors such as day-to-day plant growth, the age and variety of the plants, season and weather conditions, we matched each index subject with four reference subjects who had been in the same fields on the same days. The matching allowed us to control for environmental factors about which data were not available.

For each worker in each group, we needed two types of data: basic demographic information and daily records of job assignment and tea output (productivity). We knew from previous research in South Africa that HIV/AIDS-related morbidity could cause additional absenteeism at least two years before death, but we did not know if productivity would be affected even before that. We decided to look backward in time for four years from each index subject's date of death (called the index date). For each matched 'index/reference set' (one index subject with four matched reference subjects), we therefore collected up to four years of daily observations. The time period of interest was defined in relation to each index/reference set's index date, so time does not refer to calendar time, but instead to time before the index subject left the workforce. Because many of the index subjects had been employed for less than four years, and because some older records were missing, we ultimately analysed only the three-year period prior to the index date.

The demographic data, which were extracted from company personnel records, were used to adjust for differences between index and reference subjects on expected predictors of productivity (i.e. years of experience, sex, age, etc.). If, for example, pluckers who died of AIDS were younger, on average, than those who did not, any differences observed in the productivity of the two groups might be attributable to age, rather than health. The demographic data allowed us to control for these differences in the multivariate analysis by including the demographic indicators as independent variables in our equations.

Productivity records were extracted from hand-written payroll registers kept at each estate office and entered into a computerized database by study staff. For each working day, the registers recorded one of three possible assignments for each worker.

1   *Tea plucking.* On days when the worker was engaged in plucking tea, the payroll register contained the number of kilograms of tea leaf harvested.
2   *Other unskilled tasks such as weeding, pruning, packing tea into bags, standing guard.* Even workers whose primary task is tea plucking are occasionally assigned to other tasks, for which they earn a flat daily wage, not an amount based on productivity. These other tasks are usually less strenuous than tea plucking, and we refer to them as 'light duty'. The flat daily wage paid for light duty is the equivalent of plucking 33.2 kg of tea; since the average plucker produces 42.8 kg per day, light duty represents a loss of income.
3   *Absent.* If the worker is not present, the register indicates the type of leave taken, such as sick leave, annual leave, absent without pay, etc. The tea company allowed workers to take several types of paid leave, including sick leave; for a day of paid leave, the wage is the same as that for light duty (the equivalent of plucking 33.2 kg of tea). Many workers also take unauthorized (and thus unpaid) leave.

We hypothesized that HIV/AIDS-related morbidity would affect productivity in three ways. First, HIV-positive workers might produce less on days spent plucking tea. Second, they might be assigned more often to light duty because they are not well enough to spend the whole day plucking tea. And third, they might be absent from work more often. Our analysis was designed to test each of these hypotheses.

Analysis – daily output (tea produced)

To estimate the impact of HIV/AIDS-related morbidity on each measure of productivity, we used a regression analysis aimed at determining how much of the observed variation between index and reference subjects could be explained by HIV/AIDS. For the first measure – differences in quantities of tea plucked per day – the challenge in constructing the regression equation was that each subject had hundreds of daily observations (up to 320 per year for up to three years). Simple linear regression was therefore not appropriate because the correlation among each of the observations on a single subject would provide biased standard errors. To account for the correlations, we modelled each subject's mean weekly output (in kilograms) over time using a random intercept, random slopes linear regression model. The model allowed each subject to have an individual specific intercept, representing that subject's output level at time 0, and an individual slope, representing the subject's output trajectory over time. The intercepts and slopes could then be averaged to get a population mean intercept and slope for both the index and the reference subjects.

To find the model that best fits the shape of the population mean curves of

output over time, we specified models with time as linear (each group represented by a straight line over time), as quadratic (each group represented by a curve
over time), and as higher order specifications. We also included an interaction
term (time multiplied by group). This interaction term represented the added
effect of being in the index group over time and allowed the mean slope of the
two lines (or curves) to deviate from parallel. From the model we could then cal-
culate the differences in output at any time. A more detailed description of the
model we used is presented in Annex 1.

Analysis – light duty and absenteeism

The other two measures of productivity – light duty and absenteeism – were somewhat easier to analyse, as each one involved a number of entire days (rather than
kilograms/day) and there were fewer observations per subject. Because we had
data on entire days, we had no need to use more complicated regression methods
that account for the fact that we had many observations per person, and therefore
each observation was correlated with other observations for the same plucker. For
each of the three years before the index date, we first counted the number of days
of sick leave, annual leave, absence without pay, and light duty for each subject.
We then estimated the differences between index and reference subjects using
Tobit regression. (Tobit regression is similar to linear regression but is appropriate
to use when the data are left censored, or truncated, at some value. In our case,
because the number of days of absenteeism and light duty were not likely to be
zero for any individuals, Tobit regression was more appropriate to use than linear
regression.) We adjusted our estimates for age, sex and years of experience.

Results

Mortality

At the tea company with which we worked, there were 778 deaths of employees
and dependants due to natural causes (disease rather than accidents or violence)
between January 1997 and December 2003. The data showed that the number of
deaths had roughly quadrupled over that period, though the population on the
estates had remained the same (Figure 3.1). The data also showed a distinctive
age-specific pattern of deaths, as illustrated in Figure 3.2.

While a large number of under-five child deaths would have been expected in
any rural community in a developing country, the fact that nearly half (44 per
cent) of those who died were between the ages of 15 and 49 – normally a period of
very low mortality, particularly from natural causes – was a clear indication of the
impact of AIDS. Figure 3.3 indicates what a large share of mortality among adult
workers was attributable to AIDS. (All deaths attributed to AIDS in Figure 3.3 –
and throughout this chapter – are of individuals who had tested HIV positive at the
company's hospital prior to death. Some deaths that are attributed to other causes
may in fact have been HIV-related, but no HIV-positive test result was on record.)

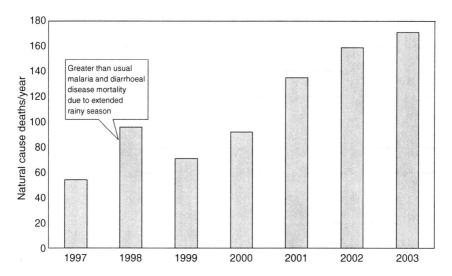

Figure 3.1 Number of natural cause deaths, 1997–2003.

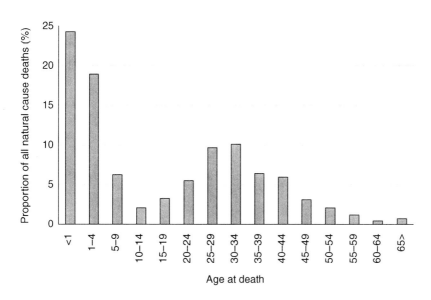

Figure 3.2 Age distribution of natural cause deaths, 1997–2003.

Note

Age at death was not recorded for 14 per cent of those who died during this period. These subjects are not included in this figure.

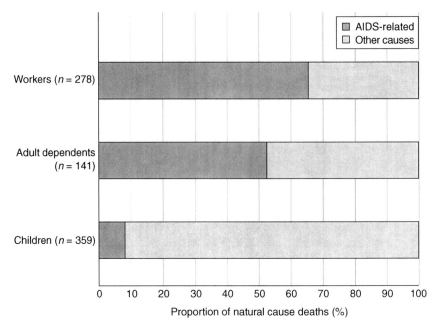

Figure 3.3 Proportion of deaths attributable to AIDS, 1997–2003.

Daily output

From the records of deaths due to natural causes available at the company's hospital and the retirement records at the company, we identified 54 tea pluckers who died or were medically retired due to HIV/AIDS-related causes. The rest of the workers who had died of AIDS-related causes were not tea pluckers. We did, however, include 11 tea pluckers who were medically retired, rather than dying in service, because the medical staff and supervisors reported that, by the time a medical retirement is requested and processed, the employee is usually extremely ill and expected to die within a very short time. As explained above, we also identified an average of four reference subjects for each of these index subjects. The reference subjects and index subjects were similar to one another in terms of age, sex and years of experience, as shown in Table 3.1, suggesting that workers with HIV/AIDS did not differ systematically from other workers along these dimensions.

The mean amount of tea plucked per day by the reference subjects, who represented 'healthy' workers in our analysis, was 42.8 kg, with an interquartile range of 29.0–49.5 kg. The corresponding figure for index subjects was 38.9 kg, with an interquartile range of 23.5–47.5 kg. The unadjusted changes in daily output in the three years prior to the death or retirement of the index subjects are shown in Figure 3.4.

The lower curve in Figure 3.4 can be thought of as the history of productivity decline caused by HIV/AIDS.

Table 3.1 Comparison of index and reference subjects

Parameter	Index subjects		Reference subjects		
	Value	Std Dev	Value	Std Dev	p-value
N	54		217		
Age (mean)*	35.74	7.26	37.33	8.17	0.21
Years of service (mean)*	5.15	3.37	6.20	2.42	0.06
Sex (proportion male)	61%		71%		0.16

Note
* At date on last day of observation.

The adjusted results of the productivity regression analysis are presented in Table 3.2. The final model included only age, a dummy variable for matched group, the variables for time and a dummy variable for AIDS death. Sex and years of service were left out of the model, as they were not found to be predictive of amounts of tea plucked. (We also found no significant statistical interactions between age or sex and being an index subject.) We computed the expected differences at half-year intervals between cases and comparison pluckers after controlling for age and matched group using the modelled coefficients and changing values of time. Because time was included in the model as a

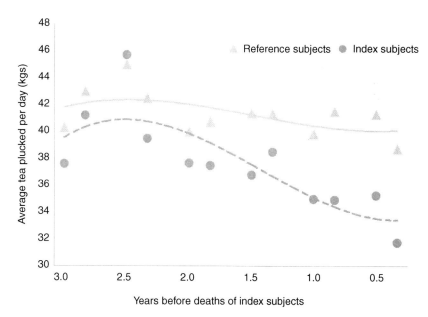

Figure 3.4 Unadjusted daily output on days spent plucking tea.
Note
Curves shown are trend lines using polynomial regression.

Table 3.2 Differences between index and reference subjects on days spent plucking tea at six-month intervals prior to death or retirement of index subjects

Years before death	Difference (kg)	% difference[a]	SE	p-value
3.0	−1.689	−4	2.732	0.536
2.5	0.466	1	2.224	0.834
2.0	2.400	6	1.956	0.220
1.5	4.113	10	1.871	0.028
1.0	5.605	13	1.940	0.004
0.5	6.876	16	2.191	0.002
Last working day	7.927	19	2.684	0.003

Note
a Expressed as a percentage of the average kilograms plucked by reference subjects, 42.8.

continuous variable, each expected difference calculated represents the expected difference between index pluckers and reference pluckers *on the day for which we computed the difference*, not for the entire six-month period. The time periods chosen were used to illustrate the changes over time. Although there is between a −1.7 to 2.4 kilogram difference (−4.1 to 5.8 per cent) between cases and comparison pluckers in the period from two to three years before death, this difference does not reach conventional statistical significance. Starting around 1.5 years before death, differences become statistically significant and much larger in magnitude.

Light duty and absenteeism

In addition to the fall-off in productivity on days spent plucking tea that is shown in Figure 3.4 and Table 3.2, we hypothesized that tea pluckers with HIV/AIDS were more frequently assigned to 'light duty' than other tea pluckers and were absent from work more often. Table 3.3 shows the values and differences in these outcome indicators for index and reference subjects.

During their last three years of life, tea pluckers who ultimately died or retired due to AIDS spent 41 more working days on 'light duty' than did other tea pluckers and were absent from work almost twice as often. A majority (58 per cent) of the additional absenteeism was comprised of unpaid (and unauthorized) leave, most of which occurred earlier in the time period; the rest was divided between additional sick leave (24 per cent) and additional annual leave (18 per cent). The use of unpaid leave declined markedly in the last year of life, from 41 days per year to 33. We speculate that as HIV-positive employees become sicker, they are physically less able to travel away from the estate and need to remain close to the estate medical facilities. They are thus more likely to be present at work.

Table 3.3 Light duty and absenteeism among index and reference subjects

Indicator	Unit	Reference subjects	Index subjects (period before death or retirement)		
			2–3 years	1–2 years	0–1 years
Light duty	No. days per year	32.8	32.8	52.0	54.6
	% difference from reference subjects		0	58.5	66.4
	p-value		N.A.	0.016	0.041
Sick leave	No. days per year	5.4	8.8	14.6	16.4
	% difference from reference subjects		63	171	204
	p-value		0.034	<0.0001	<0.0001
Annual leave	No. days per year	8.8	12.0	15.2	17.1
	% difference from reference subjects		37	73	95
	p-value		0.237	0.016	0.019
Unpaid leave	No. days per year	21.4	46.6	41.3	33.2
	% difference from reference subjects		117	93	55%
	p-value		<0.0001	<0.0001	0.032
Total leave	No. days per year	35.6	67.3	71.1	66.6
	% difference from reference subjects		89	100	87

Note
p-values are from Tobit regression model comparing use of leave by case pluckers to comparison pluckers controlling for age, sex and years of experience.
N.A. = not available.

Overall effect on tea produced and income earned per worker

Since the primary job of the tea pluckers is to harvest tea leaf, it made sense to combine the various effects on productivity presented above into a single measure of the quantity of tea leaf harvested per year by index and reference subjects. Relative to reference subjects, index subjects harvested less tea on days spent plucking and spent more days not harvesting any tea at all, either because they were absent from work or they had been shifted to light duty. The aggregate shortfall in tea output was 30.5 per cent in the index subjects' second-to-last year of service and 35.1 per cent in the last year.

The effect on the index subjects' income was much smaller than the actual shortfall in tea harvested. Although the index subjects did not pluck any tea during their extra days on light duty or on sick leave, they did get paid for those days. The rate for light duty days and sick days is the equivalent of plucking 33.2 kg of tea. The average 'healthy' worker would have plucked more than that – the mean for the reference group alone was 42.8 kg/day – so a day spent on light duty or paid leave still represented a loss of income for the index subjects. On average, the index subjects in our study suffered an income loss of 16 per cent in their second-to-last year of service and 17.7 per cent in the last. These differences are considerably smaller than the differences in annual tea leaf output, reflecting the important role of paid leave and light duty in smoothing workers' incomes.

Summary of results

The results of the case study presented above can be summarized as follows. Relative to other tea pluckers, in the last 365 days on the job a tea plucker who eventually dies or is medically retired due to an AIDS-related condition:

- is absent from work 31 days more often (an increase of 87 per cent);
- spends 22 more days on light duty (an increase of 66 per cent);
- harvests an average of 7.1 kg less tea leaf per day (a decrease of 17 per cent);
- harvests an average of 3,555 kg less tea over the course of the year (a decrease of 35 per cent); and
- earns $117 less in wages (a decrease of 17.7 per cent).

There are smaller but still significant changes in all of these indicators in the second-to-last year before death or retirement.

Limitations of the case study

The study reported above was a retrospective cohort study. The data used in the study were not collected for research purposes, but rather as part of the routine operations of the tea company and its medical system. The data were remarkably well suited to our research needs, but despite this there were a number of limitations to what we could do. Some limitations were overcome through study design and analytical approach. Others could not be overcome. Stating the limitations of what we learned is an essential aspect of presenting the study.

What were the main limitations? First, we did not have disease status data on our reference subjects. Overall HIV prevalence in the workforce of the Kericho tea estates was estimated at 11 per cent, implying that a substantial number of our reference subjects were also HIV positive. If HIV-related illness had already begun to affect their work performance, then we would probably have underestimated the true difference between HIV-positive and HIV-negative subjects.

Second, on days when the yield of tea in the fields is high, tea pluckers are permitted (and even encouraged) to bring family members to pluck alongside them. These 'helpers' contribute their output to the daily totals of the regular employees they are helping. The amount a helper contributes cannot be distinguished from the regular tea plucker's total in our data set, nor can we determine which pluckers are accompanied by helpers on any given day. In aggregate, the presence of helpers mainly reflects field conditions, but estate managers also reported that sick tea pluckers often deliberately bring helpers to the fields to ensure their daily income and hide the worker's illness from management. This practice would be consistent with the literature on labour substitution, which suggests that other household members are frequently pressed into service to make up for the labour of a worker who is sick. If there is systematically greater use of helpers by sick tea pluckers – and we believe that there is – then the true effect of HIV/AIDS on individual labour productivity will be masked.

Finally, our estimates included only tea pluckers who died at a company medical facility or were retired on medical grounds. There is anecdotal evidence that many workers who are severely ill simply walk away from their jobs to return to their home villages, which are typically in other districts or villages of Kenya. These employees did not enter into our analysis, as they had no diagnosis of HIV/AIDS. We do not know the direction of the bias that this practice might have created. If only those HIV-positive pluckers who died in service were those employees who were well enough to work occasionally, our results will underestimate the impact of the disease on productivity. If, on the other hand, the HIV-positive pluckers who died in service were those who were too sick to travel home, then the bias would probably be in the opposite direction.

Interpreting the results: HIV/AIDS, labour productivity and household poverty

Despite the limitations discussed above, the case study helps us to decipher some of the relationships among health, labour productivity and poverty. We know from the case study that HIV/AIDS-related morbidity affects both the job performance and job attendance of an HIV-positive tea plucker and that these changes have consequences for both the tea company (less tea plucked) and the individual plucker (less income earned). While neither of these results is surprising, the relative magnitude of the impacts for the employer and the employee is important to consider.

For the employer, a very large tea company with some 10,000 workers engaged solely or primarily in plucking tea, the reduction of productivity that occurs when one worker (or even many workers) fall ill is of little concern. This is because the company pays *only for the quantity of tea leaves plucked*. If one tea plucker fails to produce the amount expected or cannot adequately harvest his or her assigned field, then another plucker – who could be another employee, a casual worker hired only for a day or a helper from the plucker's own family – will make up the difference and will earn the same amount per kilogram of tea leaf as the sick worker would have. From the tea company's perspective, the same amount of tea will be produced, at essentially the same cost, as if the original worker were not sick at all. The existence of a pool of experienced helpers and casual workers, moreover, ensures that a permanent tea plucker who dies of AIDS can be replaced immediately with another competent and fully productive worker, at little or no cost to the company. Very few industries have as flexible a labour supply as does commercial agriculture in countries with high unemployment, like Kenya. Other companies, in mining, manufacturing, service or other sectors, would probably face at least some costs to replace a worker lost to AIDS, e.g. to recruit and train the new worker.

There are, of course, some additional costs to the employer even when a piece-rate worker falls ill. Paid sick leave, in which HIV/AIDS causes a significant increase, is a clear cost to the tea company. Transfers to light duty, which are also much more frequent for those with HIV/AIDS, may also impose costs on the company if there are more tea pluckers in need of such re-assignment than there are 'light' tasks available. The company also pays in full for medical care for sick workers, including expensive, if ineffective, antibiotics for those with late-stage opportunistic infections. These costs are not negligible, and management has expressed concern about rising absenteeism and the upward trend in its budget for medical care. Because of its very flexible labour management system, however, the tea company avoids most of the costs incurred by other kinds of employers (Rosen *et al.* 2004).

While the company may face little financial fallout from the high rate of HIV/AIDS among tea pluckers, the same cannot be said of the workers themselves. For the employee, the illness caused by HIV/AIDS leads to a substantial loss of income. The average daily wage of healthy workers on the tea estates is $2.37. The reduction of 18 per cent found by the study cuts the average wage to just $1.95 per day. This loss of wage income, moreover, probably reflects only a fraction of the total cost of illness to the household. The income decline we measured includes the contribution of helpers, who are almost always members of the same households as the sick workers. The opportunity cost of the helper's time is not taken into account. If the helper is the worker's wife, for example, her time spent in the tea fields, substituting her labour for that of her sick husband, may be time taken away from working in the family's own garden or engaging in other income-generating activities, such as petty trading. The helper may, alternatively, have to abandon tasks that are essential to the family's welfare even though they do not generate income, such as childcare and food preparation. The same types of opportunity costs apply to family members who must stay home to care for the sick worker and assist him or her to seek medical care if needed.

These opportunity costs, combined with the loss of income, ensure that the worker's illness impoverishes the household and diminishes the welfare of all household members. The damage becomes worse, however, after the worker dies, because the family's house, which is a benefit of employment on the tea estates, must ultimately be vacated. The family thus loses its wage income, house, access to company medical care and access to subsidized schooling – and also suffers the emotional trauma of the death itself.

The morbidity and mortality caused by HIV/AIDS thus have very different consequences for the tea company and for its employees, a divergence that is probably repeated in similar agricultural settings throughout sub-Saharan Africa. The impact of the AIDS epidemic on the company, and on tea production in Kenya in general, is moderate. Production costs may rise slightly, and replacing managers, supervisors and skilled workers who fall ill is difficult. Replacement of a handful of particularly skilled employees (like the tea 'tasters' who oversee the quality of the finished product) may require a substantial investment in recruitment and training. But the quantity and quality of tea produced suffer little, if at all. The impact on individual workers and their households, in contrast, is severe. Tea pluckers with AIDS cannot sustain their incomes, and when they die, their families are forced to return to their home villages or seek jobs in the city, where unemployment is already rampant.

Although the conditions of employment on the tea estates heighten the divergence between the firm-level and individual-level impacts of AIDS, the general pattern described above – modest firm-level costs, high household-level costs – probably prevails in many industries and for many diseases, not only HIV/AIDS. This is in part because high unemployment in many developing countries ensures a plentiful supply of replacement workers. There are many strategies, moreover, that businesses can pursue to protect themselves from the effects of worker illness, while households have few options but to bear the costs (Rosen and Simon 2003). By illustrating this divergence, the case study can help policy makers, company managers, health care professionals and others to understand the dynamics of health, labour productivity and household poverty.

This case study would not be complete without a note about the tea company's response to the AIDS epidemic. Despite the relatively small financial impact that AIDS is having on production costs, the company in the case study is a leader in developing and implementing HIV/AIDS programmes for its employees and their households. In partnership with a large clinical research project funded by an international donor, the company has implemented an active programme of education and awareness training, distribution of condoms, voluntary counselling and testing, prevention of mother-to-child transmission, and prophylaxis for opportunistic infections. When workers die in service, the company frequently offers their jobs to other members of their families, allowing households to remain on the estates and mitigating some of the most serious social and financial consequences of AIDS. While the company undoubtedly has many reasons for taking these actions, its motives appear to be as much ethical and personal as they are financial, reflecting the company's long involvement in Kericho and the managers' own ties to the tea pluckers' community.

Annex 1

The regression model we used to predict the quantity of tea plucked per day was a random intercept, random slopes model, which is a generalization of the simple linear model. We modelled the number of kilograms individual i plucked in week t as:

$$y_{it} = \alpha_i + \beta_{time}t + \beta_{time^2}t^2 + \beta_x x + \beta_{x*time}xt + \beta_{x*time^2}xt^2 + \beta_{age}age + \beta_m M' + \varepsilon_{it}$$

(1)

where t is time in years before the death of the index subject (-3 to 0), x is a dummy variable for indicating membership in the index group ($1 =$ index, $0 =$ reference), M' is a vector of dummy variables indicating the matched group and $\hat{a}_m$ is a vector of $\hat{a}$ coefficients for the matched groups. In this model, $\hat{a}_i$ and the $\hat{a}$ coefficients for time were modelled with random components by including additional error terms. Inclusion of the error terms prevents bias in the standard errors of the $\hat{a}$ coefficients that results from including numerous observations of weekly kilograms of tea plucked from a single individual.

At each time point, the mean number of kilograms of tea plucked can be calculated by writing out the regression equations. For space considerations we have left out the dummy variables for the matched group, but this will not affect our comparisons since the indicator will cancel out in the comparison. Mean quantity plucked at time t can be calculated as:

$$[\alpha_i + \beta_{time}t + \beta_{time^2}t^2 + \beta_{index}x + \beta_{index*time}xt + \beta_{x*time^2}xt^2 + \beta_{age}age]$$

(2)

where x is 1 for subjects in the index group and 0 for subjects in the reference group, and t is the time specified from -3 to 0. For a subject in the index group, the mean quantity plucked would be:

$$[\alpha_i + \beta_{time}t + \beta_{time^2}t^2 + \beta_{index} + \beta_{index*time}t + \beta_{x*time^2}t^2 + \beta_{age}age]$$

(3)

and for subjects in the reference group it would be:

$$[\alpha_i + \beta_{time}t + \beta_{time^2}t^2 + \beta_{age}age]$$

(4)

The difference in the mean quantity of tea plucked by the index group compared with the reference group, controlling for matched group and age, can be calculated at any time t as the difference between equations (2) and (3):

$$[\beta_{index} + \beta_{index*time}t + \beta_{x*time^2}t^2] \tag{5}$$

Part II

The effectiveness of health systems in addressing the needs of the poor

4   Access and equity

Evidence on the extent to which health services address the needs of the poor

Natasha Palmer

> ... effective health interventions exist. They are well known and well accepted.
> They are generally simple and low-tech. They are even cost-effective.
>   Yet, vast swathes of the world's population do not benefit from them. For hundreds of millions of people, a huge proportion of whom live in sub-Saharan Africa and South Asia, the health systems that could and should make effective interventions available, accessible, and utilized are in crisis – a crisis ranging from serious dysfunction to total collapse.
>
> (UN Millennium Project 2005)

Introduction

Good-quality health services, accessible to those with greatest need, is a common policy goal. However, in many parts of the world, health systems fall far short of delivering this. Gaining access to any service may be a struggle and is likely to be harder for the poor. The *World Health Report 2005* (WHO 2005a) identified exclusion from appropriate care as one of the key causes of inequity in the health of mothers and children. Analysis of immunization rates in 20 sub-Saharan African countries shows that, on average, rich children are twice as likely to be immunized as poor (Gwatkin 2002a). Whilst this problem is clear, exploring the meaning of concepts such as equity and access is more complex. This chapter will first highlight some key conceptual elements of these notions and then present evidence on the extent to which the poor are gaining access to adequate health services. Finally, some causal factors that underlie these patterns are briefly discussed.

Equity

Whilst equality is an empirical concept, equity is a normative one, meaning that it is a value judgement (Gwatkin 2002a). It introduces the notion of fairness or social justice (Gulliford *et al.* 2002). Whilst equality can be objectively measured (e.g. whether two people have made the same number of antenatal care visits), equity is a value judgement (*should* they have made the same number of antenatal care visits?). Therefore, definitions of what is equitable can vary greatly between individuals and societies (Donaldson *et al.* 2004). Trying to achieve equity may mean treating people equally or differently.

The concept of equity can be applied to a number of dimensions of health care services. For instance:

- Is health status fairly distributed amongst the population?
- Are health facilities evenly distributed around the country?
- Do people incur costs fairly when they seek health services?
- Does government spend its health budget fairly between different parts of the population?

Access

Access is also a complex notion. It encompasses a number of dimensions which mean that it is not synonymous with use. Mooney (1983) points out that 'equality of access is about equal opportunity: the question of whether or not the opportunity is exercised is not relevant to equity defined in terms of access'. Therefore, looking at health service utilization alone does not explain what form of access people have, or whether their or others' health care needs are being met. What people do when they are ill, or need preventive health care, is determined by a range of factors including knowledge, beliefs, availability of health facilities, drugs and money (Hausmann-Muela *et al.* 2003).

For instance, if people do not attend a health facility, does it mean:

- that they do not need to attend it?
- that they do not realize that they need to attend it?
- that they do not know it is there?
- that they cannot afford to get to it?
- that they do not like it and would prefer to go elsewhere?

Aday and Anderson (cited in Gulliford *et al.* 2002) first made the distinction between 'having access' (potential to utilize a service if required) and 'gaining access' (initiation into the process of utilizing a service). Building on this, Gulliford *et al.* proposed a number of components to equity of access:

1 *Health service availability* – is there an adequate supply of health services available?
2 *Health service utilization* – which may include overcoming personal barriers, financial barriers, or organizational barriers.
3 *Health service outcomes* – what is the relevance and effectiveness of the services? Are they of decent quality?
4 *Equity of access* – do different groups of people get access to services in equal proportion according to their need?

An initial prerequisite of access is the availability of services, but whether these services can be used by their intended beneficiaries is of equal importance. Factors that will determine this second type of access (utilization) include geographical availability and financial and cultural accessibility. Determinants of the acceptability of services include the attitude of health workers to patients, the condition of premises, waiting times and the duration of consultations. Even strong performance in these features does not, however, equate to access to good health service outcomes, the third aspect of access. Even if services are accessible for the poor, there is still the question of whether they meet their health needs. Consumers are often poorly equipped to judge the technical merits of alternative services. Therefore, they may access services that provide poor quality of care. They may do so because there are no alternatives or because such services meet other qualitative criteria that they value (e.g. short waiting times, low cost). Equally, they may not attend a service that is of good technical quality because they perceive it to be of poor quality (for instance, because it is a public sector clinic) or because they fear that they will be treated badly. The final aspect of access, central to this chapter, is the consideration of whether the forms of access described above are available equally to different groups of the population, or whether being poor may further decrease the likelihood of gaining access to good services.

Measuring 'equity' and 'access'

Due to the complexities of defining the concepts of equity and access, measuring *equity* of *access* is often forsaken for measuring simpler, more objective indicators such as *equality* of *expenditure* (does everyone get the same amount of money spent on them?) or *equality* of *utilization* (does everyone go to a health facility equally often?) (Donaldson *et al.* 2004). Other outcomes or indicators that are taken to reflect on access to health services include health status, mortality, health care use, out-of-pocket payments or funding allocations from government (Brockerhoff and Hewett 2000; Castro-Leal *et al.* 2000; Makinen *et al.* 2000; Wagstaff 2000). Such indicators are commonly measured across different population subgroups, such as the richest 20 per cent versus the least rich 20 per cent. Individuals are characterized into subgroups on the basis of factors that reflect broader economic, social and political variation. The use of subgroups allows the study of differences between these groups that are caused by factors outside each individual's choice, such as the lack of opportunity, which lies outside the control of an individual. This allows analysis of differences which can ultimately be judged to be unfair and avoidable. Therefore, subgroups can be defined by economic status (for instance, Castro-Leal *et al.* 2000; Makinen *et al.* 2000; Wagstaff 2000), gender and ethnicity (for instance, Brockerhoff and Hewett 2000), health condition (Gakidou *et al.* 2000), geographical location, age, education or occupation (Gwatkin 2000a).

In the case of socio-economic standing, there are a variety of approaches for creating these categories. For instance, household asset ownership, income,

expenditure or consumption could all be used. Levels of consumption are generally considered the best measure of a household's socio-economic welfare.
However, consumption data are difficult and time consuming to collect and
often cannot be combined with surveys that seek to collect health indicators,
because they are also quite time consuming. Measures of income are frequently
used, but also criticized, since an estimate of income reflects neither longer-term
income nor permanent wealth. Income measures can also be seasonally variable
and there may be a tendency to under-declare income (Makinen *et al.* 2000). In
many low-income settings, especially rural subsistence farming areas, the
concept of a formal, monetized income may also be inappropriate. In such settings, education and occupation are often used as proxies for social standing, and
there is also a recent trend to use data sets such as the Demographic and Health
Surveys (DHS). Here wealth of households is ranked by converting records of
household asset ownership to an asset index, using the method of principal components analysis (Filmer and Pritchett 2001).

Access: what patterns do we see?

Below, the findings of some recent studies are highlighted to demonstrate the
dominant patterns of access in resource-constrained settings. Studies were identified by a search of PubMed and manual searching of recent volumes of the
Bulletin of the World Health Organization, Social Science and Medicine and
Health Policy and Planning. References from relevant papers were also followed up. The search focused on papers from Africa, Asia and Latin America
within the last five years. Following up key references also led to some older
papers being included. Search criteria aimed to locate papers that presented data
on utilization by socio-economic status (SES) or other equity-related subgroups
and papers that provided explanation of observed patterns of access by using
qualitative and case study methods.

A large number of papers were located, mainly from Africa but also with a
significant number covering Asia. Some countries feature more heavily in the
results reported, e.g. Tanzania, South Africa and Bangladesh. This only reflects
that they appear to have more active researchers working in those areas.

The nature of the evidence falls into two groups. Larger, more comprehensive
sources of information include a number of multi-country studies that examine
the role of the private sector (Makinen *et al.* 2000; Prata *et al.* 2005) and the
extent to which the poor are benefiting from health services (Gwatkin 2001).
The latter is an extensive body of work produced by analysis of the DHS using
the asset index approach to establish household wealth. Data are also available
per country on the World Health Organization's website (http://www.who.
int/countries) for indicators related to health outcomes such as child and adult
mortality and immunization rates. The second set of evidence is available from
smaller case studies, which give greater detail but about a smaller subset of
cases.

A number of studies now disaggregate their results by SES. Others study the behaviour of the general population, but tend to be conducted in areas where most residents are poor.

Do poor people 'have access' and 'gain access'?

For access to maternal and obstetric care, a survey of 49 developing countries assessed that 68 per cent of urban pregnant women and 39 per cent of rural pregnant women have access to an adequate range of maternal health services (Bulatao and Ross 2002). Utilization of assisted deliveries was also low. In the Matlab subdistrict of Bangladesh between 1997 and 2001, over 74 per cent of 12,080 births monitored were delivered at home without a skilled attendant (Anwar *et al.* 2004). Full immunization coverage is also alarmingly low in many countries. In Cameroon, it has been estimated at between 34 and 37 per cent (Waters *et al.* 2004). In Nigeria, 39 per cent of children under one year of age have been routinely immunized with at least three doses of oral polio vaccine (OPV). Full immunization rates among poor and rich in developing countries are shown in Figure 4.1.

As for curative care, studies suggest that a large number of those who report having been ill did not access any form of formal care. For instance, in Bangladesh 55 per cent of people who had had fever, bodily pain or gastrointestinal illness reported that they self-treated (Ahmed *et al.* 2003). In Kenya, of 138 episodes of febrile illness, 60 per cent were treated at home with herbal remedies or with medicines purchased from a local shop (Ruebush *et al.* 1995).

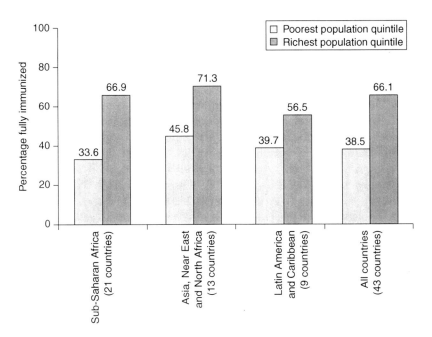

Figure 4.1 Full immunization rates among poor and rich in developing countries.

In Ghana, Hill *et al.* (2003) asked respondents to rank the severity of the illness and found that 50 per cent of children considered by their caregivers to have an illness that was 'severe/could have killed' were not taken to a health facility. Finally, Prata *et al.* (2005) analysed DHS data from 22 countries and found that only 34.3 per cent of children from the poorest quintile who were sick with diarrhoea consulted a medical practitioner (see Table 4.1).

Do the poor benefit equally from public spending?

Benefit incidence analysis (BIA) combines the cost of providing public services with information on their use to show how the benefits of government spending are distributed across different groups within the population (Castro-Leal *et al.* 2000; Demery 2000). In health, it measures the extent to which government financing for health is spent fairly across all groups, usually classified by SES. It combines issues of where spending is focused with the question of who is accessing services. Results from Africa emphasize the extent to which wealthy groups benefit more from government spending (Castro-Leal *et al.* 2000), with a more mixed picture from recent work in Asia and Latin America (Gwatkin 2002a; Suarez-Berenguela 2002; O'Donnell *et al.* 2005).

Using data from the Living Standards Measurement Survey (LSMS), Castro-Leal *et al.* (2000) did a comparative BIA of spending on curative health care across seven African countries. Findings are summarized in Table 4.2. They found that the wealthier groups accessed publicly funded care considerably more than the poor, estimating that the richest 20 per cent of the population receive well over twice as much financial benefit than the poorest 20 per cent from all government expenditure. The difference was strongest at hospital level but also clear for primary care. Results from studies in Asia and Latin America present a more mixed picture – in Indonesia, Mongolia and Vietnam the rich gained far more than the poor; in Malaysia and the Philippines government health spending was found to be pro-poor (Gwatkin 2002a). A recent study examining the shares of public health utilization consumed by the richest and the poorest fifths of the population in ten countries in Asia found that public spending on health care in Malaysia, Thailand and Hong Kong was pro-poor. In the remainder of countries, non-hospital care tended to be marginally pro-poor while hospital-based care was clearly pro-rich (O'Donnell *et al.* 2005). Ensor *et al.* (2002) did a BIA for subdistrict services in two divisions of Bangladesh and found that the poor were accessing primary care services more than the rich, but that at higher levels of care public expenditure favoured the rich relative to the poor. For Latin America and the Caribbean, a Pan American Health Organization (PAHO)/World Bank study (EquiLAC) also found a more mixed picture, with government spending in Jamaica pro-poor, in Peru neutral and pro-rich in Ecuador and Guatemala (Suarez-Berenguela 2002). Finally, in Peru it was found that among adults who had been sick in the last four weeks of the study, utilization of services had a clear trend in favour of the wealthier – 48 per cent of the richest quintile sought care when sick, compared with 25 per cent of the poorest (Valdivia 2002).

Table 4.1 Mean percentages of ill children and reported use of health services for treatment of diarrhoeal disease and acute respiratory infections by socio-economic group from selected African countries* (population 0–5 years old ill two weeks preceding the survey)

	% ill					% of those ill who were seen by a medical practitioner					% of those seen by a medical practitioner who were seen in public facilities				
	Poorest	2nd quintile	Mid	4th quintile	Richest	Poorest	2nd quintile	Mid	4th quintile	Richest	Poorest	2nd quintile	Mid	4th quintile	Richest
Diarrhoeal disease	24.5	23.3	22.5	22.6	18.2	34.3	36.2	37.5	40.8	47.3	22.7	23.7	25.2	28.5	30.4
Acute respiratory infections	17.9	17.8	16.0	15.5	14.3	33.2	38.9	43.9	46.7	59.1	26.2	30.3	34.8	37.5	42.5

Source: Prata et al. (2005).

Note
* Benin, Burkina Faso, Cameroon, Central African Republic, Chad, Comorros, Côte d'Ivoire, Ghana, Kenya, Madagascar, Malawi, Mali, Mozambique, Namibia, Niger, Nigeria, Senegal, United Republic of Tanzania, Togo, Uganda, Zambia, Zimbabwe.

Table 4.2 Benefit incidence of public spending on health in selected countries

Country	Quintile shares of								Total subsidy as % of per capita expenditure	
	Primary facilities		Hospital outpatient		Hospital inpatient		All health			
	Poorest	Richest	Poorest	Richest	Poorest	Richest	Poorest	Richest	Poorest	Richest
Africa										
Côte d'Ivoire (1995)[a]	14	22	8	39			11	32	2.0	1.3
Ghana (1992)	10	31	13	35	11	32	12	33	3.5	2.3
Guinea (1994)[a]	10	36	1	55			4	48		
Kenya (1992)[a,b]	22	14	13	26			14	24	6.0	1.1
Madagascar (1993)[a]	10	29	14	30			12	30	4.5	0.5
United Republic of Tanzania (1992–93)	18	21	11	37	20	36	17	29	N.A.	N.A.
South Africa (1994)[a]	18	10	15	17			16	17	28.2	1.5
Others										
Indonesia (1990)	18	16	7	41	5	41	12	29	1.0	0.5
Vietnam (1993)	20	10	9	39	13	24	12	29	2.1	0.9

Source: Castro-Leal et al. (2000).

Note
a Hospital subsidies combine inpatient and outpatient spending.
b Rural only.
N.A. = not available.

Such analysis by population subgroup yields important, if somewhat crude, results. Due to the expense of large-scale surveys, studies rarely give a comprehensive picture of what is happening at all levels of care or encompass both public and private sectors in a country and are rarely comparable across countries. In addition, simple measures of utilization cannot indicate differences in quality, need or the benefit derived from using a service. For instance, on the rare occasion where use is high amongst poorer groups, this may actually reflect the fact that the quality of service is considered to be of such a low standard that only those who have little choice would consider accessing the service. Better-off groups may go straight to the private sector, and this is encouraged by the health systems of some countries. This appeared to be the case with Voluntary Counselling and Testing for HIV in South African public sector clinics (Thiede *et al.* 2005), where quantitative evidence indicated relatively high use by lower SES quintiles, but qualitative evidence explained that this was due to poor perceptions of confidentiality. Distinctions between 'poor' and 'rich' using measures such as quintiles of SES can also be rather illusory. SES is not distributed evenly in a linear fashion. The 'rich' in many countries are probably only a subsection of the top quintile, with the rest of the SES groupings having very narrow and possibly arbitrary differences between them.

Use of the private sector

There is growing evidence that the poor use a wide range of private sector providers. There is a vast choice of private sector practitioners available to them, both philanthropic and commercial, including doctors, nurses, midwives and those with less formal qualifications, as well as shopkeepers (Mills *et al.* 2002). An eight-country study of health service utilization found that the private sector played an important role in service delivery (Makinen *et al.* 2000). It was estimated to deliver between 50 and 60 per cent of services in Guatemala, South Africa and Paraguay. Prata *et al.* (2005) showed that, in 22 African countries, of those children with diarrhoea who were brought to see a medical practitioner, almost 80 per cent saw a private sector practitioner. Of 801 people interviewed at a public tuberculosis (TB) unit in Vietnam, 39 per cent had attended a private pharmacy or private provider as their first attempt to seek care (Lönnroth *et al.* 2001). Goodman *et al.* (2004) cite a series of studies showing that over 50 per cent of febrile illness episodes in many African settings are treated through retailers (pharmacists, drug shop staff with minimum qualifications, shopkeepers and street vendors). Finally, a study in Egypt found that a preference for private sector providers was so strong that a majority of those with insurance still paid out of pocket to use the services of private providers (PHR*plus* 2004).

An increasing number of studies have examined private sector use by SES. Poorer groups may use lower cadre providers in the private sector. For instance, in Nigeria, Onwujekwe (2005) found a statistically significant likelihood that poorest households were more likely to patronize patent medicine dealers, community-based health workers and traditional healers. Wealthier households used a higher cadre of providers such as primary health care centres, pharmacy shops and hospitals. However, other studies find little difference in care-seeking behaviour by socio-economic quintile in the private sector, suggesting that the poor are likely to be spending a higher proportion of their income than richer groups, if they are being charged the same fees. A recent household survey in Tanzania found that of those having fever in the previous two weeks, 57 per cent went to drug stores or general shops, with no statistically significant difference across socio-economic groups (Njau *et al.* 2006). In Vietnam, it was estimated that the private sector provided 60 per cent of all outpatient contacts and the difference in use of private sector between low and high socio-economic quintiles was not significant (Ha *et al.* 2002).

Quality of care provided to different income groups in the private sector has received some scrutiny in Tanzania. A number of studies suggest that the richer receive a higher quality of care. Schellenberg *et al.* (2003) studied children under five in rural Tanzania who had had an illness episode in the previous two weeks. It was less likely that the poorer children would access appropriate care and the rate of hospital admissions in the lowest socio-economic quintile was almost half that of the highest. The wealthier children were more likely to get antimalarials and antibiotics for pneumonia and were more frequently admitted to hospital. Njau *et al.* (2006) found individuals in the better-off third were more likely to receive antimalarials and this differential was even more pronounced when effective antimalarials were considered. Also in Tanzania, Goodman *et al.* (2004) found that general retailers were much less likely to stock antimalarials, but that when they did, it nearly always included chloroquine, a drug no longer on the treatment regimen in Tanzania. If poorer groups were more likely to use lower levels of private provision, such as that sold by general shops compared with drug shops (the evidence is currently ambiguous), then this would also imply that they were receiving a poorer quality of care. A study in South Africa has also found that receiving appropriate drug treatment for a sexually transmitted infection from a private general practitioner (GP) was significantly correlated with having health insurance, itself a proxy for wealth.

What underlies uneven patterns of access?

What prevents the poor from accessing public sector services more? What is driving high private sector use? As well as traditionally important issues such as geographical accessibility and cost, there is growing evidence that the perceived quality of care of health services has a strong impact on utilization patterns (Gilson *et al.* 1994a; Baltussen *et al.* 2002; Acharya and Cleland 2000; Mills *et al.* 2004) and, in particular, that interpersonal quality of care is very relevant in determining people's willingness to access services. Some important system and patient-related factors are highlighted below.

Lack of 'having access'

Geographical accessibility is the starting point for any discussion of access. Where it is low, it increases costs dramatically. Hjortsberg and Mwikisa (2002) observe that in Zambia 'large distances make it very costly for rural dwellers to seek medical care, especially during the high season for farming'. The decision to seek care at a local drug shop or general store may reflect an assessment of the greater travel time and costs associated with travelling to a more distant public sector provider or private medical practitioner. It may also reflect the longer business hours of retailers in comparison with public sector facilities. Njau *et al.* (2006) found that care seekers spent significantly longer period waiting at government and non-governmental organization (NGO) facilities than at shops and also spent more time travelling to them.

A study from Peru (Valdivia 2002) shows that expansion of facilities is a necessary but not sufficient criterion to increase equity in utilization. An expansion programme between 1992 and 1996 saw an 82 per cent increase in the number of public sector facilities for districts in the poorest quintile of Peru, but the equity-enhancing effect of this massive increase in infrastructure was limited. The author identified other cost barriers for the poor, such as the costs of consultations and drugs. This demonstrates that even where the problem of geographical access or travelling time and cost has been solved, financial factors can prevent access to some health systems in which the poor incur charges for care.

Lack of 'gaining access'

Where services are available, they may still not be utilized. People in need may be near to services, yet encounter difficulties in utilizing them, or else consider them too poor in quality. Some of these barriers are outlined below.

Financial barriers

Despite consistent debate over their value in the last decades, user fees remain widespread in Africa and Asia. A series of reviews of studies show that they have significant effects on utilization (Gertler and Hammer 1997; Gilson 1997; Palmer *et al.* 2004) and act as a barrier to access for poorer and more vulnerable groups. Another consistent feature appears to be the failure of exemptions for poor and vulnerable groups (Gilson and Mills 1995; Russell and Gilson 1997; Kivumbi and Kintu 2002). It is clear that policies of charging for services may deter use and present a barrier to access. Again, however, even the removal of official user fees may not end the problem. Widespread underfunding of health systems means that unofficial charges and quality of care problems may continue or even be exacerbated if user fees are abolished. Gilson and McIntyre (2005) stress the importance of supply-side improvements alongside fee removal to impact on adequate access for the poor.

In many countries, there is evidence both of informal charging in systems that are meant to be free at the point of use or informal charging in addition to existing user fees, such as is described below for Vietnam and is also widely recognized in neighbouring Cambodia (Soeters and Griffiths 2003).

> ... when you go to the hospital, just buy the coupon as usual, and then put 5000 Dong into your medical book, you will be attended quickly. If you don't put some money in, you will have to wait longer and the staff's attitude is not pleasant.
>
> (Anh in Sepehri *et al.* 2005)

Whilst costs in the private sector may be higher, private physicians may give more flexible pricing and accept credit and payment in kind (Lönnroth *et al.* 2001). This may contribute to high private sector use. Equally, once time and travel costs for attendance at a distant public sector facility have been taken into account, use of a drug shop or general store to buy medicines may be more financially affordable.

Personal and system barriers to access

Patient-related factors are also involved in the failure of people to access health services adequately. In a meta-analysis of evidence on maternal mortality, Sundari (1992) found that up to 48 per cent of maternal mortality was blamed on patient factors, with non-arrival or delayed arrival featuring prominently. Some of the reasons underlying this are eloquently described in a paper by Kyomuhendo (2003), which studies the attitudes of some women to maternity services in Uganda:

> Here there is still a preference for traditional birthing practices and pregnancy is seen as a test of endurance. The maternal deaths that ensue are considered a sad but normal event and the use of primary health units and referral hospitals even when complications occur are considered a last resort ... Most mothers expressed cynicism about the efficacy and nature of maternity services at local health facilities ... Midwives ignored the value and meaning that they attached to their birthing experiences ... Health workers were seen as rude, poorly trained and unwilling to dispense drugs, deliberately avoiding maternity patients, abandoning them in a critical situation and expecting to be bribed and lacking in ethics.
>
> (Kyomuhendo 2003)

Failure to recognize symptoms or the severity of a condition is another aspect of people's failure to seek care on time (Sundari 1992; Hill *et al.* 2003). In many countries, socio-cultural differences, in addition to physical and financial problems of access, separate certain groups, often women, from the health system (Mumtaz and Salway 2005). A recent study in Bangladesh found that even when financial barriers were removed, poor women were still less likely to use trained birth attendants at home or in a facility (Chowdhury *et al.* 2006). The authors conclude that 'poor women face barriers other than financial or education-based when seeking maternal health services' (p. 330).

Hartigan (2001) has also suggested that there are differences in providers' attitudes to male and female patients, providing further links between gender and barriers to adequate quality of care.

Availability of drugs and the attitudes and behaviour of health workers have been highlighted as further important system-related barriers to access by many studies. In a survey of user satisfaction in northeast Brazil, Atkinson and Haran (2005) found that lack of availability of prescribed drugs at the pharmacy was the issue most often complained about. A number of earlier studies have also emphasized this point (Litvack and Bodart 1993; Haddad and Fournier 1995; Baltussen *et al.* 2002).

Absent, harassed, rude, overworked, dismissive or plain unhappy health workers, as exemplified in the earlier quotation, are increasingly recognized as one of the key problems in health service delivery (Jewkes *et al.* 1998; Andersen 2004). Schuler *et al.* (2002) observe that in Bangladesh:

> people are prepared to travel further and pay more for higher quality services ... NGOs are effectively addressing key aspects of quality that clients value. Paramount among these is the interpersonal dimensions of quality – treating clients kindly, tactfully and with respect, whether poor or comparatively better off.

Other studies describe how the attitude and behaviour of health workers is supportive towards patients of a higher status in the community (Bulatao and Ross 2002), or how health workers can act as a block to appropriate referral due to their own status anxiety or professional insecurity (Bossyns and van Lerberghe 2004). In contrast to these frequent realities, the importance of relationships of trust and understanding between providers and those needing and seeking care has been stressed by recent literature (Russell 2005; Tibandebage and Mackintosh 2005). The inability of many health workers to act in a caring way may itself be a reflection of their own negative experiences within failing health systems (Jewkes *et al.* 1998; Gilson *et al.* 2005).

Conclusion

As the quote at the beginning of this chapter suggested, many health systems are still failing to meet the needs of the poor. The evidence presented above paints a bleak picture of a failure to reach the ideal of a publicly funded, professionally staffed health system that many countries have subscribed to. The response of many potential clients to the poor quality treatment available is to avoid attending public health facilities or to pay for private sector treatment. To worsen matters, the extent to which private sector treatment is better quality is highly variable, with some evidence that the poorest will also receive the poorest quality of care within the private sector. Recent initiatives to address these widespread failings of the health system include the recognition of the need for increased funding for the health system itself, and a renewed focus on designing policies that will lessen social exclusion and encourage access for disadvantaged groups (Gwatkin *et al.* 2005). Increasing attention to the support needs of health workers is also called for. The complexity of health systems, as well as the demand and supply factors that underlie inequitable access for the poor, suggest that a wide-ranging package of interventions will be needed to revitalize this crucial tool for social justice.

5 Illness, health service costs and their consequences for households

Di McIntyre and Michael Thiede

LDCP I12 I11
O15
I30 I18

Introduction

There is growing interest in the impact on households of the costs of illness and of health service use, and an increasing recognition that these costs can lead to household impoverishment. This interest has partly arisen from the reconsideration of various health sector reforms implemented in recent decades.

In particular, there are concerns about the effect on households of the policy of charging user fees for public sector services. Even the main proponent of user fee policies in the 1980s and 1990s, the World Bank, has more recently urged caution, noting that 'out-of-pocket payments for health services . . . can make the difference between a household being poor or not' (Claeson *et al.* 2001). These payments are related to fees not only at public facilities. As noted in Chapter 4, there is extensive use of private providers in developing countries (by up to 60 per cent of those seeking health care in some countries), even amongst the poorest groups (Makinen *et al.* 2000). Factors contributing to this trend of utilization include ease of access and perceived higher quality of care than in the public sector, the latter being partly due to declining funding of public sector services in the context of macroeconomic crises and structural adjustment programmes. The extent of private health care services, whose growth has been promoted by health sector reforms, and the high levels of use of these services, in the light of user fees at public facilities, have contributed to growing concern about the economic consequences of illness and health care use.

This chapter focuses on a key theme of the book, namely household poverty and its inter-relationship with ill health. It particularly highlights the impact on households of the costs associated with health service use.

These considerations need to be viewed from a broader context of factors relevant to the inter-relationship of ill health, cost burden and poverty. First, illness perceptions and treatment-seeking behaviour are influenced by, and in turn influence, the extent and nature of the cost burden on households. Second, there is not only a range of direct financial costs arising from the treatment-seeking process, but indirect costs, in the form of productive time lost, can also be incurred whether one seeks care or not. As the indirect costs of ill health are covered in some detail in the Kenyan case study presented in Chapter 3, relatively limited attention is paid to this issue here. Finally, various strategies can be adopted to cope with both direct and indirect costs of illness, either drawing on resources and strategies internal to the household or available via social resource networks. The success or failure of households to cope with the economic consequences of illness determines whether they are able to protect their asset base and incomes or whether the household falls into (or more deeply into) poverty.

This chapter briefly considers each of these issues in turn, with particular consideration of the direct costs and related coping strategies. It places particular importance on the unequal burden of these costs across households of different socio-economic status. It concludes with a reflection on the policy options for financial protection suggested by this analysis.

The chapter content is based on an extensive review of the literature, using a search of electronic databases (Medline, Social Science Citation Index, Science Citation Index, Cinahl, Science Direct and Social Sciences Abstracts) as well as relevant websites (id21, WHO, World Bank, Equinet, PHR*plus*, etc.). Inclusion criteria were broadly specified as studies considering the economic consequences of illness and health service use and social resources and strategies for coping with these consequences. The key exclusion criterion was studies that did not focus on the individual or household level. Abstracts were screened by both the authors using these criteria, and a total of 62 were included in the review. Information was initially abstracted in the form of an annotated bibliography and then analysed to identify key issues and trends.

Costs, illness perception and treatment-seeking behaviour

Two broad categories of costs are of concern in this chapter. Direct costs refer to all financial payments made in the process of seeking and obtaining care. Indirect costs refer to the costs of time lost because of inability to undertake normal productive activities due to illness and health care-seeking activities; and the costs of time so lost include not only those of the ill person but also those of other household members.

The potential economic burden of illness and health care use, particularly in the context of differences in household socio-economic status and vulnerability, can have a considerable influence even in the initial stages of the illness cycle, especially in relation to perceptions of ill health. Many household surveys, using self-reported illness as the health status measure, have found that low-income groups report illness less frequently than higher-income groups (Baker and van der Gaag 1993; Falkingham 2004). For example, a study in South Africa found that households in the richest income quintile were 2.3 times more likely to report illness than those in the lowest-income quintile, using a two-week illness recall period (McIntyre and Gilson 1998). These findings are somewhat counter-intuitive, given the overwhelming empirical evidence of higher levels of medically confirmed ill health in the lowest socio-economic groups.

Sauerborn *et al.* (1996a) noted that one of the key ways in which the economic costs of illness can be avoided is 'by modifying illness perception (the phenomenon of ignoring disease)'. This phenomenon was explored through a comparison of illness perceptions between the dry and rainy seasons in Burkina Faso, the latter being the time of major agricultural activity but also the time when the frequency and severity of biomedically verified disease, such as malaria, are at their highest. Fewer people perceived an illness in the month recall period during the rainy season (13.7 per cent) than in the dry season (18 per cent). The illness episodes that were reported were also perceived as less severe in the rainy or harvest season: 8 per cent viewed as severe compared with 36 per cent viewed as severe in the dry season (Sauerborn *et al.* 1996b).

For those who do perceive an illness, they then confront the choice of whether or not to seek care. As highlighted in the preceding chapter, a range of health care access constraints impact on treatment seeking. Empirical evidence indicates that many people do not seek care (even in the form of self-treatment) when ill, as a result of these access constraints. For example, one comparative analysis of household survey data found levels of non-use of health services ranging from over 50 per cent in Thailand and about 40 per cent in Paraguay to about 20 per cent in South Africa (Makinen *et al.* 2000). There were significant differences between socio-economic groups with, for example, 27 per cent of South Africans in the lowest-income quintile not seeking care, compared with 15 per cent of those in the highest-income quintile (McIntyre and Gilson 1998).

The relationship between the absence of mechanisms for protection against the financial consequences of health care use, on the one hand, and illness perception and treatment-seeking behaviour, on the other, has been highlighted by some authors. For example, McIntyre and Gilson (1998) noted that the poor 'cannot "afford" to be ill', while higher-income groups with jobs in the formal sector are likely to have better financial protection against health care costs as well as access to sick leave benefits.

In the context of poor or non-existent cost protection mechanisms, efforts to avoid these costs by 'ignoring' illness and not seeking professional health care may ultimately lead to even higher costs. This occurs when the illness becomes even more serious and results in greater loss of time for normal activities and requires even more expensive health care services. Falkingham (2004) confirms that '[t]he poorest may be deferring health care (and the recognition of illness) until their illness is severe'.

The costs of illness and health care use

Most studies present information on direct (and indirect) costs in relation to household income. Some commentators regard 10 per cent of annual household income being consumed by health care expenditure as the cut-off point for catastrophic expenditure levels (Prescott 1999; Ranson 2002). However, this is a somewhat arbitrary cut-off point, and much lower expenditure levels may be catastrophic for some households. This may apply to households who, for example, devote their entire current income to meeting basic needs such as food purchases (generally the poorest households) and who have limited ability to cope (see next section) with unexpected health care costs. With these caveats in mind, it is informative to review evidence from the literature.

Extent of costs and influence of type of illness

Direct cost estimates vary widely across countries depending upon the methodology of the study (e.g. many studies focus only on the direct costs of health care goods and services and ignore transport and other costs). However, the majority of studies suggest that direct costs tend to be less than 10 per cent of household income on average (Sauerborn *et al.* 1996a; Lucas and Nuwagaba 1999; Makinen *et al.* 2000; Russell 2001).

Indirect costs are less frequently quantified than direct costs in studies on the costs of illness, partly due to the methodological challenges of obtaining accurate indirect cost estimates. The majority of studies that have quantified both cost categories suggest that indirect costs of illness are often greater than the direct costs (Koopmanschap and Rutten 1994). The ratios of indirect costs to direct costs from recent studies range from indirect costs being 3.6 times greater than direct costs in the case of malaria in Rwanda (Ettling and Shepard 1991) to indirect costs being lower than direct costs in Nigeria for malaria (ratio of 0.7) as well as for non-malarial illnesses (ratio of 0.4) (Onwujekwe *et al.* 2000).

When one combines the direct and indirect costs of illness, the total economic effect of illness on households is frequently above 10 per cent of household income. For example, the total household costs of malaria per year were as much as 18 per cent of annual income in Kenya, 13 per cent in Nigeria (Leighton and Foster 1993) and nearly 19 per cent in a new settlement in the Amazon region in Brazil (Sawyer 1993). The costs for all forms of illness totalled 11.5 per cent of monthly household income in Sri Lanka (Russell 2001) and about 11 per cent of average monthly income in Nigeria (Onwujekwe *et al.* 2000). It should be noted that the disease-specific studies include data only on households that have experienced that disease, whereas the studies on costs of the full range of illness present an average for all households whether or not they have experienced illness. While the latter studies present a more accurate picture of the impact on households overall, the disease-specific studies highlight the very high costs for individual households who experience illness, particularly endemic infectious diseases such as malaria.

As suggested by the data presented above, the percentage of household income devoted to direct health care costs varies according to the type of illness or health care event. Hospitalization is recognized as potentially imposing catastrophic costs on individual households. Maternity care can also impose considerable costs on households. A study in Bangladesh – where there is only a nominal registration fee for maternity care but high direct costs for medicines, transport, food, etc. – found that while the majority of households (52 per cent) spent less than 50 per cent of their monthly household income on the direct costs of delivery, 21 per cent spent 50–100 per cent of their income and a further 27 per cent spent one to eight times their monthly income (Nahar and Costello 1998). In countries where substantial hospital fees are charged for maternity care or other related costs are high, the birth of a baby can result in significant financial consequences for households.

The direct costs of long-term fatal illness, particularly acquired immunodeficiency syndrome (AIDS), have the most devastating effects on households. A study in Tanzania has estimated that the direct costs of treatment, during a six-month period, for a person living with AIDS is about 64 per cent of per capita household income for the same period (Tibaijuka 1997).

Similarly, indirect costs differ considerably, both in absolute terms and relative to direct costs, between different types of illness. Certain chronic illnesses can impose a considerable burden on households. A study in India found that patients with chronic lymphatic filariasis lose up to 19 per cent of productive workdays per year (Babu *et al.* 2002). A number of researchers have noted that the time costs of healthy household members are often as large as the time costs of those who are ill (Sauerborn *et al.* 1996a). The care-taking burden on other household members can be particularly severe in long-term terminal illness such as AIDS (Hansen *et al.* 1998).

Distribution between different types of direct costs

The distribution of direct costs between different components is highly variable according to the health system of each country. It is therefore difficult to generalize the results of such context-specific findings, but certain broad trends can be identified.

The empirical evidence suggests that the cost of drugs often contributes a sizeable share of direct costs. For example, drugs accounted for 62 per cent of direct costs for mild malaria and 70 per cent for severe malaria in Ghana (Asenso-Okyere and Dzator 1997). Similarly, drugs contributed 63 per cent of the costs of treating lymphatic filariasis in India (Babu *et al.* 2002). In the case of a normal delivery in Bangladesh, drugs accounted for 39 per cent of direct costs and 55 per cent for caesarean section deliveries (Nahar and Costello 1998). As an average of all direct costs of health care, irrespective of type of illness, drugs accounted for 33 per cent in Sri Lanka (Russell 2001).

It has also been found that transport costs, either for the patient or for both the patient and an accompanying person, are not insignificant. Transport costs accounted for 14 per cent of the direct costs of malaria in Ghana (Asenso-Okyere and Dzator 1997), 22 per cent of that of malaria in Sri Lanka (Attanayake *et al.* 2000), 20 per cent of that of maternity care in Bangladesh (Nahar and Costello 1998) and 14 per cent of that of overall health care in Sri Lanka (Russell 2001).

Costs that are often not taken into account, such as costs of nutritious food for a sick family member and the costs of accommodation and food for an accompanying household member, can also be considerable. For example, these 'other' direct costs were found to be as high as 18 per cent in India for chronic lymphatic filariasis (Babu *et al.* 2002), 27 per cent and 24 per cent, respectively, for normal and caesarean section deliveries in Bangladesh (Nahar and Costello 1998) and 46 per cent for malaria treatment in Sri Lanka (Attanayake *et al.* 2000).

Another direct cost that can impose a substantial burden on households is that of unofficial, informal or 'under-the-counter' fees. While Russell (2001) found that informal fees were virtually non-existent in Sri Lanka, a recent study in Bulgaria specifically focused on this issue and found that they can be substantial. Nearly one-quarter of interviewees had made informal payments, the majority in the form of gifts (equivalent to 7 per cent of the minimum monthly salary) but some in the form of cash (21 per cent of minimum monthly salary) (Balabanova and McKee 2002). Another study found that, on average per patient, unofficial payments at public health facilities in Bangladesh were 12 times more than official fee payments. Although high-income patients pay the highest level of unofficial fees in absolute terms, for the lowest-income group unofficial fees amounted to nearly 72 per cent of average monthly income, while these payments were only 43 per cent and 32 per cent of average monthly income for the middle- and high-income groups, respectively (Killingsworth *et al.* 1999). In many countries, the household burden of paying informal fees reflects the decline in public funding of health services and the fall in the real salaries of health workers.

Cost burden across different socio-economic groups

There is considerable and consistent evidence that the direct costs of health care impose a far greater burden on poor families than on higher-income households. For example, a study in Thailand found that annual household direct costs were equivalent to 21.2 per cent of annual household income in the lowest-income quintile, but only 2.1 per cent for the highest-income quintile (Pannarunothai and Mills 1997). In this study, the greater relative burden on poor households is attributable not only to the lower income levels, but also to the lower insurance coverage (33 per cent) for households in the lowest-income quintile, compared with 62 per cent for those in the highest-income quintile.

A study of hospitalization costs in China found even greater differentials, with the costs per hospital admission accounting for 59 per cent of net annual household income for the poorest, 18 per cent for the middle-income group and 8 per cent for the highest-income group (Wilkes *et al.* 1997).

As in the case of direct costs, similar unequal cost burdens are found in relation to total economic costs too. While the average total costs of malaria were 7.2 per cent of the overall annual household income in Malawi, they were as high as 32 per cent of household income in the lowest-income households, even though the absolute value of these costs for the poorest households, at \$25 per annum, was lower than the average, which was \$40 (Ettling *et al.* 1994). A more recent study considered the distribution of costs for all forms of illness among households of different socio-economic status. While total illness costs were

11.5 per cent of monthly income on average, 65 per cent of households faced a total cost burden of 5 per cent of income or less, while 5 per cent of households had an illness cost burden exceeding 40 per cent of income (Russell 2001).

Key issues on economic consequences of illness

The preceding sub-sections have highlighted that it is not only the cost of health care services themselves that imposes economic burdens on households. Other direct costs associated with the use of health services, such as transport costs, as well as indirect costs, may be of even greater importance. There is consistent empirical evidence that illness costs consume a greater share of household income in poorer households than in higher-income households. It is these vulnerable households that require particular attention in evaluating strategies for coping with these costs and in assessing the likelihood of their falling into poverty, and also for policy interventions to protect their livelihoods.

The vicious cycle of ill health and poverty

The costs of ill health can drive vulnerable households into poverty and can deepen the poverty gap for households that could have been categorized as poor even before the accrual of illness-related costs (Russell 2001; Wagstaff and van Doorslaer 2003). For example, if the head of a household with very young children, which relies on subsistence agriculture, has an episode of severe malaria during harvest time, the household may have to incur debts to pay for health care and may also lose most of their harvest (as the wife attempts to reap the harvest by herself while also caring for a sick husband and infants). Some refer to this link between costs of ill health and persistent poverty as the 'medical poverty trap' (Whitehead *et al.* 2001). Others refer to it as a 'poverty ratchet effect' to describe the plight of households that fall into poverty as a result of an accumulation of illness-related direct and indirect costs and do not manage to move out of poverty again (Chambers 1989).

Whilst the mutual relationships between poverty and ill health in general are recognized and a plethora of studies on this issue have been published over the last decade, the specific effects of costs associated with ill health at the household level have received far less attention. However, in recent years, concerns surrounding the impact of specific diseases, especially the 'ATM' or 'big three' diseases affecting the developing world – human immunodeficiency virus (HIV)/AIDS, tuberculosis (TB) and malaria – have produced important insights into disease-specific economic and social effects (Jayawardene 1993; Topouzis and Hemrich 1994; Asenso-Okyere and Dzator 1997; Tibaijuka 1997; Munthali 1998; Rugalema 1998; Attanayake *et al.* 2000; Wyss *et al.* 2001; Russell 2004). The studies reveal that economic consequences of households' exposure to costs of ill health are not only disease specific, but also depend heavily on the particular socio-economic, cultural and geographic environment. Thus, the poverty dynamics associated with illness vary across households and contexts.

It is appropriate to investigate more closely these determinants in order to identify policy measures that may prevent households from falling into poverty and the deepening of the poverty gap as a result of illness. Among the determinants of the poverty effects of illness costs, the following two categories of variables play the key roles. The first category of variables comprises the factors defining a household's vulnerability, where increasing vulnerability is synonymous with a decreasing ability to protect the household against livelihood risks and shocks. These include factors internal to the household, such as number of household members, dependency ratio, asset base, sanitary conditions and other factors impacting on the household's economic stability and its susceptibility to diseases, as well as external or contextual factors. Contextual factors include the nature and type of 'policy resources' available to households (e.g. food grants), access to other social resources (e.g. non-governmental organizations (NGOs), community-based organisations (CBOs)), features of the social context including social capital and cultural norms, as well as environmental characteristics such as geography and climate. The second category of variables concerns the type of disease underlying the economic hardship the household is facing. In particular, it is necessary to classify diseases by their patterns of occurrence and duration. If a disease is a one-off occurrence, even if the associated costs are relatively high, a household may be better prepared to cope with the costs than if a disease represents a permanent burden. The situation is different when a household is confronted with the effects of a permanent disease or disability (Chale *et al.* 1992; Elwan 1999). A common disease with a high probability of seasonal recurrence again poses a different risk to households' economic and social welfare (Sauerborn *et al.* 1996b). Thus, not only is the absolute and relative dimension of associated costs important, but also their time profile in terms of the duration and frequency of their recurrence.

The analysis of poverty dynamics can be facilitated dramatically by moving from a static view on the determinants of poverty effects to a dynamic view taking into account the strategy options available to a household in distress. This means analysing households' choice sets with respect to viable ways of moving households out of a poverty situation resulting from health-related costs as well as preventing households from falling into poverty as a consequence of ill health in the first place. Even if there is not a one-size-fits-all policy solution to break the vicious cycle of ill health and poverty – an implicit assumption that has guided many policy makers in the past – there are certainly common lessons to be learned from the study of the ways in which households currently deal with economic distress resulting from illness and health service costs.

Coping or struggling with the economic and social consequences of ill health

The impact of the direct and indirect costs of illness on households and their livelihoods can be severe. Households use a range of strategies to cope with these serious economic impacts. Before investigating household responses that have been observed in different settings, it is appropriate to outline the premise underlying the literature around so-called household coping strategies. The concept stems from the literature on household responses to food shortages that developed in the 1980s (Corbett 1988; de Waal 1989). The use of the term coping strategy assumes that there is a particular set of possible activities members of the household can undertake that help the household to deal successfully with the economic impact of the crisis, i.e. to succeed in sustaining a livelihood. Obviously, households' responses to crises depend on their very specific situation – geographically, culturally, socially and economically. In the context of famines, Amartya Sen described meticulously how responses to crises depend on households' entitlement sets, which, besides the possibility of food production, include resource endowments and money or commodities of exchange value (Sen 1981).

The idea of coping strategies lends itself to studies of the economic and social consequences of ill health. One of the first systematic studies of strategies to cope with costs of illness was described for rural households in Burkina Faso by Sauerborn and colleagues (Sauerborn *et al.* 1996a). Their report distinguishes the type of coping behaviour, the level at which support occurs and the success of coping behaviour, which allows the authors to present a type of algorithm describing the sequence of strategies to cope with financial costs of illness. As indicated previously, a key coping strategy that they identify is that of ignoring illness and hence attempting to avoid incurring illness-related costs altogether. When costs are incurred, they report that, in most cases, households chose more than one strategy and the sequence of coping strategies started with households using savings if available, then selling animals, taking loans, accepting gifts and diversifying income in favour of wage labour.

The literature published since Sauerborn and colleagues' study illustrates that there is a similar set of possible responses to costs of ill health across country settings and illness scenarios (McIntyre and Thiede 2003). Yet the actual choice of strategies adopted is dependent on factors deeply rooted in the households' immediate economic, social and cultural environments.

Once health service costs have been incurred, the use of available cash and savings is a logical first step of coping with direct costs of illness. Yet in most low- and middle-income country settings, this option is limited for many people (Sauerborn *et al.* 1996a; Wilkes *et al.* 1997; Kabir *et al.* 2000). A study from Sri Lanka shows that, for chronic, acute and inpatient care, the majority of households had sufficient available cash to at least pay for the immediate direct costs of illness, especially given free hospital services (Russell 2001), but this is not always the case.

The sale of household assets is logically next in line. Different household assets exhibit different characteristics with regard to their saleability and their importance to the socio-economic stability of the household. The characteristics of the set of household assets available to an urban household differ fundamentally from those to a rural household. Assets differ not only in their degrees of 'liquidity'; they also differ in their significance for a household's livelihood. In a rural context, for example, the sale of livestock may mean the loss of food security. A parallel step to the sale of assets in many settings is a change in consumption patterns and the reduction of food intake (Foster 1994; Tibaijuka 1997).

The uptake of loans might be a choice that is preferred by the household to the sale of assets. Across all geographic and cultural settings, borrowing is the most common response in order to cope with medical costs (Abel-Smith and Rawal 1992; McPake *et al.* 1993; Nahar and Costello 1998; Falkingham 2004). The likely effect of loans on household livelihoods can be distinguished by the characteristics of the loan-giver and the business terms of the loan. There is a high risk that the repayment of the initial loan plus (possibly ruinous) interest can plunge a household into further distress.

In a number of contexts – health allowing – people try to diversify their activities to generate quick cash income. This may include activities such as collecting and selling firewood or fruit growing on communal land. In some cases, people usually involved in subsistence agricultural production undertake wage labour to meet pressing financial needs (Sauerborn *et al.* 1996a). There are serious implications for the structure of community livelihoods from changes in local labour market structures motivated by short-term economic imperatives.

A different set of strategies is employed in order to counterbalance illness-related production losses or indirect costs. Often, tasks are reallocated among household members, and in some cases, external labour is hired or advantage is taken of free community labour, if available. Intra-household labour substitution may have drastic social consequences, particularly when children take on the economic activities of a sick parent. In some cases, children are taken out of school. It has been reported that, in sub-Saharan Africa, girls are more likely to be taken out of school than boys, creating yet another disadvantage for young women in securing an adequate education (Mutangadura *et al.* 1999). Another way to counterbalance illness-related shortfalls in household labour in rural areas is a shift to less labour-intensive crops or a change of the capital-labour mix of production. Again, the choices are subject to availability in the specific context.

It is in some ways somewhat 'academic' to distinguish coping strategies for direct and indirect costs, as the household's objective is always to secure a particular level of consumption, whatever the characteristics of the economic shock. Should this level of consumption be jeopardized by the requirement to pay medical bills or by the temporary loss of income due to the ill health of a breadwinner, the economic challenge the household is confronted with is similar.

Even if the general sequence of response categories is quite stable across countries and regions, there are differences in the sequencing of strategies across individual households, partly due to the wide variation in the choices available to them and the relative importance that is assigned to a particular coping strategy within the household's set of choices. In some instances the term coping strategy does not adequately indicate the extent of a household's plight. Household responses to the economic and social consequences of illness often reflect mere 'struggling' (Rugalema 2000), namely when households' access to real strategies, which hold a chance of taking them out of economic distress, is limited.

A clear definition of the key characteristics of a coping strategy is required to explore whether and when a coping strategy is feasible and sustainable. First, the term strategy implies that there is some freedom to plan. Any set of activities that emerges as a forced and inadvertent reaction to a crisis cannot be labelled a strategy. Second, coping with a crisis means that the set of activities undertaken by the household in reaction to the crisis actually helps overcome or promises to overcome the crisis. Only by identifying the circumstances under which coping strategies are chosen by households, because they promise to be successful and sustainable, will mechanisms be revealed for protecting households from sliding into a medical poverty trap.

A key issue in sustainable coping is the access that households have to feasible strategies, where such access is again determined by household characteristics and the socio-economic environment. Different dimensions of access to coping strategies can be described, namely the availability, affordability and acceptability of strategies. The idea of availability is straightforward. If, for example, potential money lenders consider a household too poor or possess too little information on the characteristics of the needy household, they may not want to enter into negotiations (Kabir *et al.* 2000). The option of borrowing money from a money lender is consequently not available to the household. If, however, borrowing money would constitute an available option but the household cannot meet the expense of the trip to the money lender, then the option is not affordable. Lastly, an option may not be acceptable. This may be the case if a strategy is in conflict with cultural rules or religious beliefs.

Having characterized access and its dimensions, there remains the concern around the household's awareness of an option. Coping strategies may not be accessed because they are not within the scope of awareness of the distressed household. For that reason, an important approach to making coping strategies accessible is by means of awareness creation and the improvement of health communication in a broad sense. Initiating and supporting communication within communities around ways of coping with the economic and social burden of illness broadens the perceived or subjective set of strategy choices. It creates awareness of all existing strategy choices and can stimulate community action towards improving and extending the set of accessible strategies. Relational networks and social proximity foster communication and the diffusion of health information (Rutenberg and Watkins 1997; Goldman *et al.* 2001).

Social resources and networks play other important roles in access to several of the coping strategies mentioned. For example, a social network facilitates access to sources of credit, just as it makes the temporary substitution of labour easier. The acceptance of a particular coping strategy is determined by an interplay of the degree of stress under which the household has to act and the tolerability of the conditions of access. The higher a household's stress level, the higher is its acceptance of detrimental conditions. For instance, a desperate household is more likely to accept loans at ruinous interest rates (Kabir *et al.* 2000). A social network can moderate household stress levels, while at the same time these social resources act as an automatic regulator of the conditions under which certain strategies can be accessed. In general, a household's ability to cope with the costs of illness is facilitated by inter-household relations and social networks, community organizations and sources of credit (Russell 2001).

Family ties often form the nucleus of a social network. In many societies, these family ties reach beyond the common core of economic activity to include extended families, for instance, in supporting each other at times of economic distress imposed by illness. Strong family ties are often reflected in direct financial support, intra-family loans and temporary labour supply. In some cases 'family' may encompass the community which gives economic support, for instance, in the form of low-interest cash loans (Mock *et al.* 2001; Ayé *et al.* 2002).

The key mechanism on which many social networks are based is reciprocity. Reciprocity may reach well beyond bilateral relationships. This means that expectations of returns extend to third parties and well into the future. Interestingly, the case in which free care has been provided to the extremely poor is rarely found (Wilkes *et al.* 1997). Yet health care provided free of charge to the 'wealthy' seems to be less uncommon (Sauerborn *et al.* 1996a), which may indicate expectations of some future return. The principle of reciprocity is central to a range of community organizations that can play an important role in enabling households to cope with illness-related costs. Such organizations include rural co-operatives, savings clubs and collective community funds that may require regular contributions and adequate security (Lucas and Nuwagaba 1999; Schneider *et al.* 2001a; Ranson 2002).

Policy implications

One of the policy lessons that can be derived from observations on how poor households deal with the economic consequences of disease is the need to improve information and communication on health and health services, particularly among the poor. This may range from promoting earlier care seeking for certain conditions to advocating specific services and (economic) protection. Communication may also include the creation of forums to learn jointly from local experiences around successful coping. This may lead to the design of community programmes to address various forms of social protection beyond the financial dimension. These programmes could, for example, include an organizational framework for the substitution of labour across the community, taking into account individuals' possible limitations resulting from ill health. This also has implications for the responsibility of employers, who could assist workers in coping with the consequences of illness by assigning tasks compatible with an affected employee's reduced capabilities.

Clearly, a key policy focus of relevance to minimizing the impact of illness-related costs is health care financing. In the context of stagnant or declining tax funding for health services in many low- and middle-income countries, the evidence on the economic consequences of ill health strongly suggests that health care financing mechanisms that offer financial protection at the time of illness (i.e. de-link health care payment from health service use) are preferable. Thus, out-of-pocket payments in the form of user fees to public sector facilities or direct, immediate payments to private providers are the least desirable financing mechanisms as they will have the greatest adverse economic consequences for households. In contrast, prepayment or insurance mechanisms may offer considerable financial protection to vulnerable households.

In particular, community-based strategies that incorporate the principle of reciprocity on a broad basis are important risk-pooling and coping strategies. The economic risk rests on many shoulders and is spread over time. Risk-pooling strategies can provide sustainable protection against the economic consequences of illness as they are characterized by a continuum of flows into and out of the financial pool. There are other advantages of community-based coping approaches. For one, they strengthen the social fabric of communities (Soriano *et al.* 2002), which again has positive effects at several levels. Not only will uptake of services increase when illness occurs, the organization of a community network will also automatically imply an increased level of communication. This itself has affirmative effects on households' knowledge around managing social and economic consequences of illness. As a whole, a community-based scheme means that access to a sustainable strategy will be improved via all three channels identified as key to household coping – availability, affordability and acceptability.

In practice, the establishment of a community-based safety net usually takes the form of a health insurance scheme that focuses on people outside formal sector employment. While there are some successful examples of such community-based health insurance schemes (Musau 1999; Ranson 2002), there is still only a relatively weak empirical basis to advocate for the implementation of these schemes on a widespread basis (Ekman 2004). A particular advantage of this type of scheme is that it can be organized so as to include the poorest members of the community. However, it must be recognized that, as these schemes usually operate in rural areas and focus on those outside the formal employment sector, they may represent a mechanism whereby 'the poor simply cross-subsidize the health care costs of other poor members of the population' (Bennett *et al.* 1998).

Thus, although community-based insurance schemes are an appealing alternative to out-of-pocket payments, ultimately health care financing mechanisms that promote cross-subsidies (both from the healthy to the ill and from high-income to low-income groups) in the overall health system are required. Greater health financing contributions by wealthier and healthier households will ensure that the burden of at least some of the direct costs of illness is removed from households with vulnerable livelihoods, which are also the households most likely to experience ill health. This could occur through risk-equalization and cross-subsidy mechanisms between individual community-based schemes that cover those in the non-formal sector and health insurance schemes covering formal sector workers, possibly as part of a mandatory insurance system as is being introduced in Ghana (Government of Ghana 2003). However, particularly in low- and middle-income countries, tax funding will remain a key financial protection strategy in relation to ensuring access to health services when needed, without suffering catastrophic consequences for the poorest. While government resources are extremely limited, there is scope for increasing the allocations to the health sector, particularly in the context of debt relief and recent debt cancellation initiatives. For example, the Heads of State of the Organisation of African Unity (now the African Union) committed themselves in April 2001 to devoting at least 15 per cent of government budgets to the health sector (OAU 2001). Most African countries remain far below this target. As budgetary allocations increase, attention should be paid to ensure that the poorest benefit most from these additional resources.

The evidence from the literature highlights that direct costs related to payments for health services and medicines are only one component of the economic consequences for households. Other direct costs, such as transportation and food supplementation costs, combined with indirect costs may be of even greater consequence. In this context, financial protection mechanisms not specific to the health sector also require policy consideration. The important role of old-age pensions for improving a household's ability to manage illness costs and to contribute to improved health status has been highlighted in some studies (Case 2001). Community-based strategies such as local solidarity or savings clubs and micro-credit schemes can be of considerable value in enabling households to cope with the full range of economic consequences of ill health. However, these strategies are no substitute for tax-funded social security systems, but merely complementary mechanisms that have the benefit of promoting local social solidarity.

Conclusion

The literature highlights the substantial direct and indirect costs incurred by a household when one of its members falls ill. These costs are sometimes of such a magnitude that the household could be impoverished. The characterization of economic costs of illness and the subsequent portrayal of different ways of struggling or coping with these costs have made it possible to single out some key criteria that define households' access to successful coping strategies and conditions for sustainability, which means the preservation of livelihoods over time. There is, however, a need for more cross-sectoral research that considers the economic consequences of ill health from a broader perspective by including other livelihood risks, such as those of an agricultural economy, and environmental effects on economic and social security. Only the full picture will allow the development and implementation of an adequate and comprehensive set of policy measures to prevent households from experiencing catastrophic shocks.

In terms of appropriate policy responses, the lessons drawn from households' observed responses to the economic costs of illness indicate that community-based schemes fulfil the set of criteria that characterize successful coping. It is evident from the literature that community-based insurance schemes are preferable to out-of-pocket payments as a health care financing mechanism, given the financial protection they offer households. However, health care financing mechanisms that improve cross-subsidies throughout the health system, such as risk-equalization between individual insurance schemes and increased tax funding for health services, must be prioritized. It is only when fragmentation between existing health care financing mechanisms is reduced, and local contributions are seen as merely complementary to a core of equitably allocated tax funding for health services, that health services can be accessed in a way that does not lead to catastrophic consequences for households.

Acknowledgements

The authors are grateful to Jane Chuma and to Vimbayi Mutyambizi for their assistance in locating many of the studies reviewed in this chapter. The authors are also grateful to the editors of this book for their valuable comments which assisted in refining earlier drafts. This chapter is based on, and is a further development of, research carried out as part of an Affordability Ladder Programme (ALPS) on equity and health sector reforms in developing and developed countries, funded by the Rockefeller Foundation. The researchers are independent of the funders.

6 Coping with the costs of illness :

Vulnerability and resilience among poor households in urban Sri Lanka

Steven Russell

Introduction: conceptualizing illness and household poverty

This chapter examines the ways poor households in urban Sri Lanka cope with illness costs and the consequences of these costs and responses for household livelihoods and poverty. These empirical findings are intended to illustrate the factors, particularly household assets and health services, mediating the links between illness and impoverishment at the micro-level, discussed in Chapter 5. This chapter specifically highlights the factors contributing to household resilience or vulnerability to illness shocks.

Figure 6.1 presents the conceptual framework used to guide the research in Sri Lanka. It is based on studies that have investigated household illness costs and coping strategies and their economic consequences (Russell 1996; Sauerborn *et al.* 1996a; Russell 2001), and is set within a broader sustainable liveli- hoods framework (Carney 1998; Scoones 1998).

At the household level, the presence and perception of illness (box 1) leads to decisions about whether to seek treatment and from which source (box 2). At this point, depending on the policy context and people's access to services, indi- viduals may have access to health policy resources outside the household (box 6). Illness may cause direct and indirect costs (box 3) to the household. Direct costs refer to expenditure incurred in seeking treatment, including non-medical expenses for transport or special foods. Indirect costs refer to the loss of house- hold productive labour time and income for patients and caregivers. Health care spending and income losses may threaten household members' minimum con- sumption levels and trigger coping strategies (box 4) that mobilize household assets (box 5) or cut consumption levels.

Household vulnerability or resilience to illness costs is defined here as the capacity to cope with illness costs without long-term damage to household assets and impoverishment. First, it is linked to severity of illness (box 1), with higher costs and less sustainable coping strategies likely as severity increases (McIntyre and Thiede 2003). Common acute illnesses such as coughs and colds usually pose least threat to household budgets and assets, whilst chronic ill- nesses such as diabetes and tuberculosis impose higher direct costs over time and may also prevent people from working over extended periods. Long-term

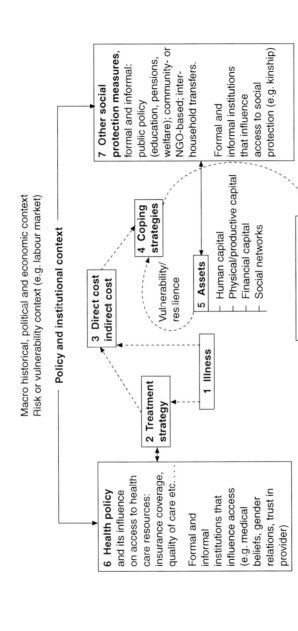

Macro historical, political and economic context
Risk or vulnerability context (e.g. labour market)

— **Policy and institutional context** —

7 Other social protection measures, formal and informal: public policy (education, pensions, welfare); community- or NGO-based; inter-household transfers.

Formal and informal institutions that influence access to social protection (e.g. kinship)

4 Coping strategies

3 Direct cost indirect cost

Vulnerability/res lience

5 Assets
— Human capital
— Physical/productive capital
— Financial capital
— Social networks

1 Illness

2 Treatment strategy

8 Livelihood outcomes

6 Health policy and its influence on access to health care resources: insurance coverage, quality of care etc....

Formal and informal institutions that influence access (e.g. medical beliefs, gender relations, trust in provider)

Figure 6.1 Conceptual framework for analysing the economic burden of illness for households.

terminal illnesses such as human immunodeficiency virus (HIV)/acquired immunodeficiency syndrome (AIDS) are likely to cause sustained production and income losses, high treatment costs, and asset strategies that lead to impoverishment.

Second, capacity to cope is influenced by household asset portfolios and their management (box 5). The main asset categories used in the analysis are described in Figure 6.1 and include less tangible assets such as 'social capital', narrowly used in this chapter to refer to social networks on which claims can be made to obtain resources that enhance capacity to pay. Networks include relatives and friends, work colleagues and employers, influential contacts, and also access to local financial institutions such as revolving savings groups (known locally as *seetu*) and credit societies.

Third, policy-related resources can add to people's asset portfolios (boxes 6 and 7). Health care services have already been identified as an important resource for households when illness strikes. Other public policy measures that contribute to household asset portfolios and resilience (box 7), broadly labelled as social protection (Moser 2001), include other essential public services, but more specifically social security, pensions, and welfare grants for vulnerable groups. Other sources of social protection derive from formal and less formal civil society organizations such as community- and non-governmental organization (NGO)-based savings and credit societies and inter-household transfers via social networks. The framework's inclusion of policy and institutional contexts that enhance resilience encourages the analysis of entry points for health and social protection interventions.

Illness costs and coping strategies have implications for asset portfolios and impoverishment, here termed 'livelihood outcomes' (box 8). These can be measured in terms of changes to asset portfolios, working days lost, income and consumption levels, debt, and vulnerability to future shocks (Scoones 1998).

The remainder of the chapter uses this framework to analyse the processes at household and community level that influence and moderate the links between ill health and impoverishment. Although it is recognized that these processes are nested within wider macro-historical, political, and economic contexts, these are not discussed further in the chapter. The next two sections briefly describe the research setting and design and provide a profile of treatment and household illness cost patterns across the study sites, using cross-sectional household survey data. The chapter goes on to examine the case study households' illness costs and coping strategies over eight months, distinguishing between groups of households with different levels of income-poverty and vulnerability to illness costs. Livelihood outcomes are briefly examined before conclusions are drawn on some of the complex processes that mediated links between illness and poverty at household level and the factors that might inform health and wider social protection policy debates.

Research setting and design

Data on illness and its livelihood impact were collected between 1998–9 in two low-income areas of Colombo, the capital of Sri Lanka. The research objectives were to measure the household costs of illness (direct and indirect) and assess the coping strategies and their consequences for the household economy. From these findings the research aimed to identify factors that made households resilient or vulnerable to illness costs. A household was defined as a group of individuals who share the same residence or room and consumption of meals. The household was the preferred unit of analysis for assessing the costs and consequences of illness because decisions about treatment and coping are based on negotiations within the household (but not necessarily from an equal bargaining position), illness costs are incurred by caregivers as well as the sick, and costs fall on the household budget (Berman *et al.* 1994; Sauerborn *et al.* 1995).

The two urban study sites were characterized by poor and overcrowded housing, poor drainage and sanitation, drug abuse problems, and low incomes from unskilled daily manual labour or service jobs. Labour markets in the wider urban system were often a source of covariant risk (risk affecting groups of households and communities) for livelihoods in the two communities because a labourer's daily wage was low and work was not always available. Inability to work due to sickness or other factors meant a breadwinner did not bring home a wage that day and the household had to obtain food through other means, such as credit from local shops. This risk or vulnerability context is relevant to understanding the impact of illness on household poverty.

The research design involved two main phases spanning an 18-month period. First, a household survey covering 423 households (out of 2,100 in both communities), or 2,197 individuals, produced a profile of household income (expenditure) and assets, illness episodes, treatment actions, illness costs, and coping strategies. The survey recorded information about three categories of illness, chosen because of the different costs and coping strategies they were likely to cause: acute illness (except hospital admission); chronic illness, categorized as such if the respondent reported it as 'chronic illness' (*nidangata rogiya*) or named it as a known chronic condition (such as diabetes, high blood pressure) or if it had persisted for over one month; and hospital inpatient treatment.

A two-week recall period was used for reported acute illness and associated treatment and costs, but for chronic illness a one-month recall period was used in order to capture any regular monthly visits to health care providers. For hospital inpatient treatment, a one-year recall period was used to maximize serious illness events recorded by the survey tool. For analysis, all illness cost data were converted to a cost per month figure. Days off work due to illness for the sick person and caregiver(s) were converted to a lost income figure using an average daily wage of Rs.150 ($2.30) calculated from the survey data. Only lost days of productive or paid work were included in the indirect cost calculations.

Despite the importance of lost unpaid activity days (e.g. childcare), only lost days of paid work were included in the indirect cost calculations because valuing unpaid activities is fraught with difficulties and less immediately relevant to productive or income losses that could threaten livelihood sustainability. Thus if a husband took a day off work to care for his sick wife who did unpaid work at home, the husband's wage loss was recorded but the woman's loss of unpaid activity days was not quantified. If a friend looked after the children, no indirect cost for the household was recorded. Clearly there are costs to such strategies, e.g. the woman may face an obligation to return the favour, but instead of placing a monetary value on any obligation, the strategy of making claims on friends was documented and its consequences explored through the case study work and qualitative methods.

For the second phase of research, the survey data were used to select purposefully 16 case study households for in-depth longitudinal study over eight months. The research objectives required a longitudinal case study design to enable intensive study of processes contributing to household vulnerability or resilience. Each case study household was visited every two weeks to record information relevant to the study objectives, using structured interview formats for more quantitative variables (expenditure, treatment, illness costs, borrowing), semi-structured or more open interviews to generate complementary qualitative data, and observation.

To select the households, survey data on income distribution were used to categorize households into income quartile groups, which were adjusted for household size and composition by calculating a per capita income figure, with children under ten years allocated a value less than one (<1 year = 0.35; 1–3 years = 0.5; 4–9 years = 0.75) because of their lower resource demands. The case study households were chosen to represent the four per capita income quartile groups, different degrees of vulnerability based on a simple assessment of asset portfolios, and different levels of 'illness' in the household based on reported illness and its costs (Table 6.1). Households in the lowest two quartiles earned less than $1.00 per capita per day (less than $30.00 per capita per month), and even in the upper quartile, most households earned only $40.00–$50.00 per capita per month or between $1.00 and $2.00 per capita per day. Despite their relatively high cash income in these poor areas, many families classified as 'better-off' were, therefore, only marginally above the World Bank's internationally recognized poverty line of $1.00 per day.

A local basic-needs poverty line was also constructed based on residents' perspectives and comprised a commodity bundle of food for three meals per day, fuel, soap, bus fares, clothing, electricity and water bills, and a small amount for social events. The poverty line excluded health and education expenses, so it could be used to estimate disposable household income available to pay for health care after basic needs had been met (e.g. in Figures 6.3 and 6.5). The local poverty line was $21.00 (Rs.1,354) per capita per month or $0.70 per capita per day, a harsher poverty line than the internationally recognized poverty line. Among the 16 case study households, seven in the poorest quartile fell below this line and struggled to meet basic food and fuel needs on a daily basis, and any additional costs, such as those incurred for health care, inevitably triggered coping strategies.

Table 6.1 Location of case study households in the community income profile[a]

| | Income quartile | | | |
	1 LPL	2	3 WBPL	4
Household per capita income: $/month[b] (Rs./month)	$0–21 (0–1,352)	$21–29 (1,353–1,880)	$29–40 (1,881–2,609)	$40+ (2,610+)
Households with illness	Nimal Jayasinghe Valli	Nishanthi Sumithra	Raja Rani	Dilani
Households without illness	Kumudu Selvaraja Amali Geetha		Pushpa Mayori	Mary Renuka

Notes
a Case study households have been given pseudonyms for confidentiality.
b At the time of research US$1.00 = Sri Lankan Rupees (Rs.) 65.00.
LPL = Local Poverty Line estimated by the author, US$21.00 per capita per month (Rs.1,354 per month).
WBPL = World Bank International Poverty Line, US$30.00 per capita per month.

As case study data are not statistically representative, aiming to strengthen understanding of complex processes rather than achieve statistical generalization, sample size was of less concern than the quality of data and depth of understanding generated (Mitchell 1983; Yin 1994; Seeley *et al.* 1995). The case studies were, nevertheless, chosen to be 'typical' of different household types in the two communities so that their processes and experiences might be analytically generalized to other households with similar characteristics in the same communities.

Treatment patterns and illness costs: an overview

The survey data showed that for serious illnesses requiring hospital admission, the vast majority of people in the two communities, from all income groups, used one of the large public hospitals in the city. Patients with chronic illness (e.g. diabetes) who sought regular outpatient treatment, particularly those among the two poorest-income quartile groups, used public providers more frequently than private providers, although patients from the relatively 'better-off' income group used private providers more often than they used public providers. In contrast, for acute illnesses requiring outpatient treatment, the use of health care providers outside the home was more equally split between public and private sectors, with the private sector slightly more dominant (Russell 2005). Even in the poorest-income quartile group, a considerable proportion of patients (26–66 per cent using a 95 per cent confidence interval) used private doctors and pharmacies when they sought treatment outside the home. The majority of patients from 'better-off' households (quartiles 3 and 4, still only earning between $1.00 and $2.00 per capita per day) used private providers more often than public providers when they sought treatment outside the home.

The household survey data found that 323 households (out of 423) experienced illness, and median total health care spending was $2.10 (Rs.138) per household per month, or equivalent to just under an average day's wage. The median indirect cost per month was zero because, among households that experienced illness, the majority (71 per cent or 228/323) did not lose income (see below).

The mean direct cost ($7.50 per household per month) and indirect cost of illness ($5.10) were higher than median costs because a minority of households experienced high costs that pulled the mean above the median. This disparity between mean and median costs indicates the need to analyse the distribution of illness costs across households. Here the distribution of illness cost *burdens* is analysed, illness cost having been defined as a proportion of household income. A 10 per cent cost burden in developing countries is commonly used as a threshold beyond which costs are assumed to be damaging (or 'catastrophic') for the household economy, likely to cause asset depletion, debt, and cuts to food consumption below minimum needs (Prescott 1999; Ranson 2002).

The majority of households incurred low illness cost burdens under 10 per cent of monthly income (Figure 6.2): 45 per cent (143/323 households) experienced a direct cost burden of 1 per cent or less and 77 per cent (250/323) a burden of 5 per cent or less. Indirect cost burdens were also low for the majority.

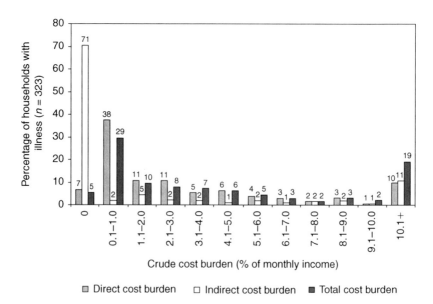

Figure 6.2 Distribution of illness cost burdens across households (*n* = 323).

Many illnesses did not cause income loss because children of school age disproportionately suffered from acute illnesses, a large proportion of acute illnesses
experienced by economically active adults were not serious enough to affect
work, and many people experiencing chronic illness and hospital admission
were elderly or economically inactive. With respect to total illness cost burdens,
65 per cent (211/323) experienced a burden of 5 per cent or less and 81 per cent
(261/323) a burden of less than 10 per cent.

However, a significant minority (19 per cent or 62/323 households) experienced burdens above 10 per cent (Figure 6.2). Notably, it was the poorest group
of households that were disproportionately affected by high burdens, with nearly
a quarter (24 per cent) experiencing a burden over 10 per cent, compared with
nearly a fifth (19 per cent) overall, partly explained by the very low incomes of
some of the poorest households, which meant even a small illness cost caused a
high burden.

Low direct cost burdens for the majority derived from the protection
offered by free and relatively good quality public health care services in the
capital. In particular, these services protected the majority against the high
costs associated with regular treatment of chronic illness and inpatient care.
Average direct cost burdens were higher for outpatient treatment of acute illnesses because a larger proportion of patients used private providers to avoid
long waiting times and cursory consultations at public facilities. Patients were
willing to pay for a longer consultation, greater patient focus, and the
opportunity to develop closer relationships with a private 'family' general
practitioner (GP).

Public health care services could not protect households from all illness costs.
Across income groups, patients preferred to use a private doctor for many types
of moderate illness due to public sector inter-personal quality weaknesses. There
were also non-medical expenses for transport, and, perhaps most significantly, a
minority of households coping with more serious illnesses suffered losses of
income. Household members therefore had to rely on other assets to manage
these costs.

Illness costs and coping among case study households

Coping with the costs of illness: why money matters

Most case study household incomes fluctuated from month to month because
work was not always available or members fell ill. Figure 6.3 presents average
household incomes remaining after basic needs had been met. It shows that half
(eight) of the households did not earn enough income to meet basic needs and
had no surplus cash for health care expenses:

> There are many very poor households who can't even eat . . . Around here
> there are many people who just live for that day.
>
> (Nishanthi, income quartile 2, less vulnerable)

The other eight households earned above basic needs due to higher wages and less frequent income losses (members worked in the formal government or private sectors, more workers in the household). However, higher income did not guarantee its availability to all household members or for health care, as illustrated by the case of Renuka at the end of this section, whose husband used their income to fund his heroin addiction.

Broad categories of vulnerability to economic shocks caused by illness have been added to Figure 6.3. A household's position on the vulnerable–resilient spectrum, when research began, was based on a simple audit of its tangible assets: levels of education, the number of workers and job security; physical or productive capital including house construction and connection to water and electricity services; and financial capital such as savings, jewellery, and levels of debt. Three of the four households in the highly vulnerable category were in a precarious situation because of previous serious illness that had depleted assets and earning capacity. Yet some of the lowest income households (Amali, Nimal, and Geetha) were not in the most vulnerable category because of stronger assets and capacity to cope with shocks.

Figure 6.4 summarizes the households' average direct and indirect cost burdens per month over eight months. Average cost burdens conceal higher burdens in one or two months. For example, Geetha's average monthly direct cost burden of 31 per cent reflects very high burdens concentrated in months 6–8

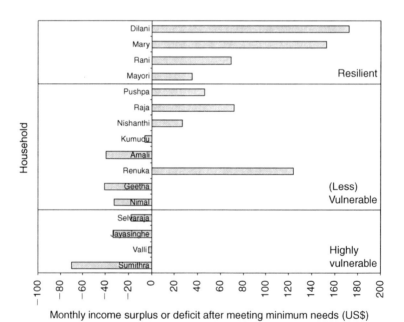

Figure 6.3 Average household income surplus or deficit after meeting minimum needs (per month).

(141, 47, and 47 per cent, respectively) when she had a hysterectomy operation and was diagnosed as diabetic. These concentrated or 'lumpy' costs were harder to manage, but she was helped by the free inpatient treatment received at a public tertiary hospital. The high direct costs actually stemmed from 'hidden' non-medical costs for visitors' transport and food.

Households below the local poverty line

To differing degrees, these eight households experienced frequent financial difficulties and struggled on a daily basis, e.g. eating only two meals per day or going without fish or meat:

> Illness is something we are all scared of here. How can we live without working? If my husband is ill, we have to get money from somewhere for food and for the medicine, we have to borrow.
>   (Selvaraja, poorest-income quartile, most vulnerable)

Income losses caused by illness and other factors were experienced most frequently by Valli and Amali; their income was often reduced to below the basic-needs poverty line, illustrated by the case of Valli in Figure 6.5. For Valli's household, the indirect costs of illness (caused by her arthritis) were more damaging than direct costs (Figure 6.4). For example, in month 2 (see Figure 6.5) she lost 18 days' work ($25.00/Rs.1,600) due to illness and in the same month faced high treatment costs ($7.80/Rs.507 or 10.1 per cent of income). Other income losses were caused by her husband's inability to find work each day, which was partly linked to his drinking problem. As this household had no savings or jewellery left to pawn, Valli borrowed money from her employer and her husband went to a moneylender to cope with these cost burdens. The income peak in month 6 was because they rented out a room in their house and took a deposit from the tenant, demonstrating the importance of housing as an asset in this urban context. Amali's household also suffered frequent income deficits, but they could mobilize resources to smooth consumption (adequate food and health care) without depleting assets because of their strong social networks (as discussed further below).

Low-income households spent a high proportion (70–90 per cent) of their monthly income on food, an indicator of severe budget constraint. Even a common illness such as flu or fever that prevented the breadwinner from working or required money for treatment would trigger coping strategies. Between 25 and 50 per cent of households in the two communities lived with these budget constraints and affordability problems (Table 6.2), so the protection provided by free health care services was an important resource for these households, illustrated by the case of Selvaraja in Case Study Box 6.1 and Table 6.2.

Spending decisions within the household, governed by gender and other relations, also influenced the resources available to meet illness costs for

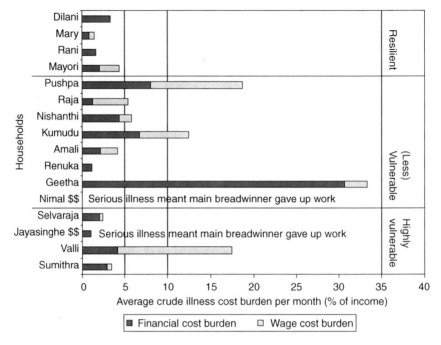

Figure 6.4 Average illness cost burden per month over eight months.

Note
$$ Nimal and Jayasinghe were the main breadwinners in their households but had been forced to stop work due to serious illness before research started. Ongoing indirect cost burdens were therefore hard to calculate. Nimal experienced a serious illness (leg injury) during the research but the high direct cost burden (over 100 per cent) is not represented here because their almost negligible income made the burden a little meaningless, and all direct costs were paid by extended family members.

different family members. The social norm was for male heads of households to delegate or exert control over spending decisions, so the money available for the family's minimum needs and health care was often dependent on the husband's priorities, including narcotics. Among the poorest households, male spending on alcohol, cigarettes, and other narcotics was common and had serious consequences for other members' capacity to pay for health care. Even five cigarettes per day cost $0.40 (Rs.30), a considerable proportion (15–20 per cent) of an average daily wage ($2.30–$3.00/Rs.150–Rs.200):

> People don't manage things well here ... Drugs are a big problem ... Some husbands spend their money on *kassipu* (illicit alcohol) ... Go and look. You can see the ones that improve, they are the ones that don't drink, or the ones that sell the drugs!
>
> (Key informant from study sites, female)

Nandawathi's husband is drinking and he spends her small earnings from the rice packets she sells ... But that is not all. Her son takes heroin and she

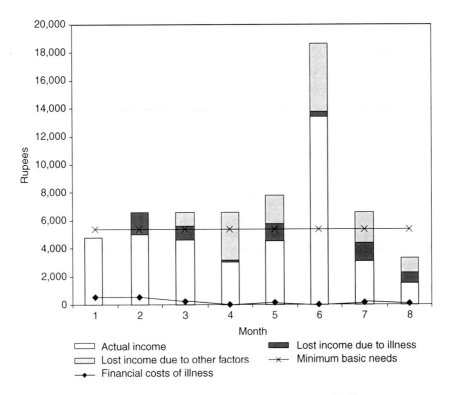

Figure 6.5 Illness, income fluctuations and basic needs: the case of Valli.

has to give him Rs.50 a day. They can only eat, nothing else. If there is a marriage or other social event, she does not go . . .

(Dilani, upper income quartile, resilient)

Households above the local poverty line

Those in the resilient subcategory rarely experienced financial stress that led to coping. In most months they had money remaining available to meet health care expenses for common acute and chronic illnesses and usually visited private doctors. The vulnerable subgroup spent a lower proportion (50–60 per cent) of their income on food than households below the local poverty line and could meet the costs of treatment for common acute and chronic illnesses (see the example of Pushpa in Case Study Box 6.1 and Table 6.2). However, in months when workers lost earnings or when illness coincided with other essential expenses such as education, coping strategies were necessary. Illness costs should not be seen in isolation from other expenses and their effects on ability to pay (Table 6.2).

Pushpa's household illustrated the vulnerability of some of the households

---

Box 6.1 Budget constraints and coping with illness costs: the cases of Selvaraja and Pushpa

For the poorest households, even the costs of common illnesses were beyond daily budgets. In month 5, Selvaraja's husband lost one day's work due to rain and one day because of shoulder pains (which often recurred). On these two days the household had to purchase food on credit from the local shop. Lost income from those two days, $6.00 (Rs.400), meant the cost of daily necessities that month was beyond income (107 per cent of income – see Table 6.2) and had to be financed through credit, cutting consumption of meat and milk powder (for their young daughter), and delaying payments on bills and debts.

For vulnerable households below the poverty line, protection against high direct illness costs was important. In the same month, the three children in the household suffered illness concurrently (fever with vomiting) and Selvaraja took them to a public hospital OP department, a visit which incurred a direct cost burden of only 0.5 per cent of monthly household income ($0.50/Rs.30). The remaining Rs.320 ($5.00) spent on health care that month (Table 6.2) was due to private sector use by Selvaraja's husband (for quick treatment to avoid wage losses) and by her mother (for a tooth extraction - there was a long waiting list at the public hospital). These private visits imposed a direct cost burden of 5.4 per cent of monthly household income, resulting in the household having to borrow from an ex-employer (Rs.500) and delay repaying debt to the local shop, paying the electricity bill, or redeeming a ring that Selvaraja had pawned in an earlier month to pay for health care.

In contrast, households above the basic needs poverty line had money available to meet the costs of common illnesses when workers could work. However, combined expenses were often beyond the scope of monthly income, illustrated by the case of Pushpa in Table 6.2. Pushpa's high direct illness cost burden (10 per cent of household income) that month was financed with available income, and even the combined cost burdens of health care, education, clothes and debt repayments were within the scope of that month's budget because earnings were relatively high that month. However, *seetu* payments pushed spending beyond the monthly budget. That month Pushpa's household purchased through credit from the local shop, pawned jewellery ($13.00/Rs.850) and borrowed $9.00 (Rs.600) from a friend (no interest charged).

Table 6.2 Income and spending patterns for households below and above the local poverty line: two examples

Household spending on:	Selvaraja (month 5) (below local poverty line)		Pushpa (month 2) (above local poverty line)	
	Rs.	% of monthly income	Rs.	% of monthly income
Daily necessities				
Food	5,345	91	4,220	51
Fuel	280	5	280	3
Transport	260	4	132	2
Cleaning/hygiene	240	4	232	3
Mosquito coils	96	2	126	1
Narcotics	90	1	508	6
Sub-total	**6,311**	**107**	**5,498**	**66**
Non-daily or unexpected needs				
Rent/mortgage				
Health care	***350***	***6***	***856***	***10***
Education	200	3	590	7
Electricity	66	1		
Water				
Clothes			440	5
Social				
Household goods			160	2
Debt repayment			600	7
Sub-total	**616**	**10**	**2,646**	**31**
Other ('less essential') items				
Savings or *seetu*			2,570	31
Other				
Sub-total	**0**	**0**	**2,570**	**31**
Total spending	**6,927**	**117**	**10,714**	**128**
Total income	5,900		8,300	

above the poverty line. Her household experienced high illness cost burdens (Figure 6.4). Both she and her husband lost work days each month due to adult and child illnesses: her husband had asthma and an episode of serious tooth decay; Pushpa had migraines and also had to care for her sick daughter (coughs and colds) and son (mumps) on occasions. Their high average direct cost burden (Figure 6.4) was explained by frequent use of their private 'family' doctor. In one month, both Pushpa and her husband had extended time off work due to illness, incurring an indirect cost burden of 39 per cent ($54.00/Rs.3,500) and a direct cost burden of 20 per cent. Puspha had to pawn her wedding ring to purchase basic food needs and pay for treatment, but burdens over 10 per cent were not 'catastrophic' because of the household's assets and capacity to cope (see below).

The implications of male spending on narcotics were felt less acutely in this group than in poorer households. Although Dilani's husband spent more that 10 per cent of household income on alcohol in all months, they still had enough money to save and pay for health care after meeting basic needs. However, Renuka's household illustrates how male spending undermined capacity to pay for health care. The husband's vegetable business earned a relatively high income ($7.70/Rs.500 per day), but the husband spent about 50 per cent on heroin and other narcotics, leaving barely enough income for Renuka and their four sons' food needs. To finance health care or education expenses, Renuka had to rely on friends, borrow from moneylenders, or cut other consumption. Although an extreme case, such cases are not unusual in these parts of Colombo.

Coping with the costs of illness: household and community-based assets

Coping strategies can be defined as actions that aim to manage the costs of an event or process, such as illness, that threatens the welfare of one or more members of the household. In this chapter, our concern is for the implications of illness-related coping strategies for the household economy or livelihood outcomes (box 8 in Figure 6.1). This includes consideration of whether strategies are 'successful' or 'sustainable' in terms of preserving assets and sustaining production, or whether strategies damage asset portfolios, reduce income and consumption, and threaten the sustainability of the household economy and its existence as a social unit. Ultimately, coping strategies seek to sustain the economic viability of the household (Sauerborn *et al.* 1996a).

Household asset portfolios and the social and financial resources available to people in the wider community (boxes 5 and 7 in Figure 6.1) influenced capacity to cope with illness costs. People's social networks were, in particular, an important source of non-financial and financial support (a gift or loan) at times of illness or other shocks. Community- or NGO-based financial institutions were also available (but not necessarily accessible) to poor households. Traditional rotating savings groups (*seetu*) were an important means of raising a lump sum of money. In their simplest form, these consisted of a group of about 10 individuals (usually known to each other and usually women) who contributed each month to a pool managed by a *seetu* organizer, and each month it was a woman's turn to take the lump sum. NGO and government initiatives had also established women's saving and credit societies, based on the *seetu* tradition, and these offered relatively small loans ($1.50–$15.00/Rs.100–Rs.1,000) for micro-enterprise development or essential needs. The main motivation to join a credit society was the low interest rate of 1 per cent per month compared with

Table 6.3 Strategies used to cope with illness costs

Common sequences and levels of risk	Strategy	
	Mobilize additional resources	*Adjust spending*
Frequently used and convenient strategies of low cost or risk to livelihood	Credit from local shop or seller for essential food and fuel items	Delay payments for electricity and water bills
	Seek/accept financial gifts from close family, relatives or an employer	
	Use financial assets: savings or *seetu* lump sum	
	Borrow small sum at no or low interest from friends and family, work colleagues, NGO credit society	Delay repayment of loans
	Borrow small sum at high interest from moneylender	
	Rent out room, taking a year's rent as deposit	Delay redemption of pawned jewellery
	Pawn jewellery	Cut spending on social events
	Diversify income: spouse or oldest child seek work	Cut spending on school items (books) or extra tuition
	Borrow large sum at no or low interest from relatives or employer	Cut spending on expensive food items like meat, fish, powdered milk for children, fruits
Higher cost strategies	Borrow large sum at high interest from moneylender	Cut other food consumption, from three to one or two main meals per day
	Sell any productive assets	

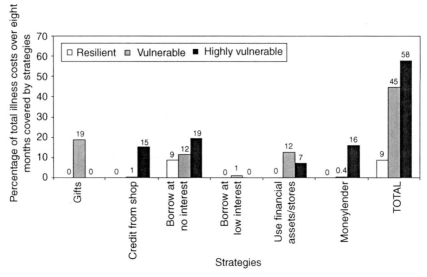

Figure 6.6 Strategies used by households of different vulnerability.

the 15–20 per cent charged by moneylenders. Pawnbrokers and moneylenders were, however, frequently used to obtain larger sums of credit. There was a notable absence of public social protection policy (box 7 in Figure 6.1) provided by the state to informal sector workers, e.g. pensions or unemployment benefit.

The findings so far presented have already identified a range of strategies that were used to manage illness costs. Table 6.3 summarizes these strategies, presenting them in an order that represents a common sequence moving from lower to higher risk for the household economy. Of particular importance for coping with illness costs were a household's social networks, financial capital (savings and jewellery that could be pawned) and access to financial institutions offering credit. Households of different levels of vulnerability had different asset portfolios at their disposal and so adopted strategies of different costs to livelihoods. Figure 6.6 summarizes the main strategies used by each vulnerability group (based on assets as defined above) to mobilize resources to cope with illness costs, and these are reviewed below.

Strategies used by highly vulnerable households

These households had weak asset portfolios, often due to earlier asset depletion, and were highly vulnerable to financial shocks. Their assets included:

- human capital: members had less formal education and they relied on one (or sometimes two) worker(s) with low wages and insecure work;
- physical or productive capital: a small wooden or poorly maintained cement block house with no electricity or water connection;

- financial capital: no savings and household members did not participate in *seetu* or credit societies; all jewellery had been pawned and lost, in some cases due to a previous illness (Jayasinghe and Valli), or the household was down to its last items (Selvaraja);
- social capital (networks): weak social networks characterized by a small number of contacts with limited financial resources to offer help. Family networks could be extensive but for various reasons the support available was limited, due to impoverishment or family feuds that had weakened ties. There were only a few close friends whom household members could rely on for support, and these contacts could not offer much financial help.

Women in the poorest-income households found it very difficult to save money and were often unwilling to join or were excluded from *seetu* groups because of their inability to make regular payments. Well-established members of *seetu* networks argued that they were reluctant to admit poorest-income women, particularly those with husbands who drank, because they posed a financial risk to other *seetu* members. Although NGO-based credit societies attempted to extend financial institutions to the poorest women by making saving regimes lower (a few rupees per day) and more flexible, women from the poorest households again appeared to be reluctant to join or were excluded from them.

Due to their low incomes on average, this group had to cover a high proportion of total illness costs through asset and borrowing strategies (58 per cent) (Figure 6.6), and their strategies reflected weaker asset portfolios. Compared with the less vulnerable group, their weaker social networks meant they could not rely on financial support through gifts. Instead, they relied more heavily on borrowing, mainly from shops or from employers (wage advances or gifts in some cases) at no interest, although 16 per cent of loans were from higher-cost moneylenders. The case of Selvaraja (Case Study Box 6.1) illustrates some of the strategies used by this group, including pawning jewellery and cuts in food consumption.

Strategies used by less vulnerable households

To differing degrees, these households had stronger asset portfolios than the most vulnerable group and hence stronger coping capacity. Adults were, in general, better educated (Nimal, Geetha, Amali, and Pushpa) or the household had more workers (Raja, Pushpa, and Nishanthi). Some (Nishanthi, Amali, Kumudu, Raja, and Pushpa) had more financial capital, with women participating in one or more *seetu* groups or credit societies (although Nimal's wife, Geetha, and Renuka were not involved due to their impoverishment). Some had savings (Geetha) or jewellery available to pawn (Geetha, Amali, Kumudu, Raja, and Pushpa), but others no longer had such resources due to a previous illness (Nimal – see Case Study Box 6.2 below – and Nishanthi).

This group could not cover a considerable proportion (45 per cent) of their illness costs through usual income sources and had to mobilize asset and borrowing strategies (Figure 6.6). However, what particularly distinguished this group of households from the more vulnerable group were their stronger social networks, characterized by more family and friendship contacts with resources to offer. Nimal, Amali, Pushpa and Nishanthi had strong family networks and the flow of help was often one way, with no expectation or obligation to repay (generalized as opposed to balanced reciprocity – see Sahlins 1972). Compared with the highly vulnerable group, they relied more heavily on gifts from family and less on borrowing. Fourteen per cent of illness costs were covered by borrowing (compared with 50 per cent in the previous group), predominantly from family and friends, with no interest and flexible repayment schedules.

Strategies used by resilient households

These households had the strongest asset portfolios, including more workers and higher salaries. Their relatively strong financial assets and social networks were linked to their ability to invest more heavily in them, through saving, gifts, lending, quick repayment of debts, and participation in *seetu*. Their higher disposable incomes allowed investment strategies and lubricated the wheels of trust and reciprocity. They faced few or no financial stresses over the eight months and had to cover only a small proportion (9 per cent) of total illness costs through borrowing strategies of low cost or risk (Figure 6.6). If households in this group did need to raise extra money, it was usually to invest (in housing, business, a productive asset, and education) and not to pay for health care or sustain consumption.

Illness and its consequences for livelihood change

Livelihood change over the study period was evaluated by analysing changes to livelihood outcomes using quantitative and qualitative data. Changes to six dimensions of livelihood were assessed: the number of workers and job and income security; income levels; physical capital; financial capital; debt levels; and consumption. Households were then placed into three broad categories of livelihood change over eight months: struggling (impoverishment); coping (stability); investing (improvement). A household was judged to be struggling if there was a decline in four or more of the six livelihood variables, to be coping if there was no change to four or more variables, and to be investing or improving if four or more variables improved. There was, not surprisingly, a strong link between vulnerability and livelihood change category. Referring back to Figures 6.3 and 6.4, all the highly vulnerable households struggled and became more impoverished; most of the middle group (less vulnerable) were coping, although to different degrees, and a few improved; and all the resilient households improved.

Did illness cost burdens play a role in these trends? Figure 6.4 suggests there was not a clear link between cost burden and livelihood change. Some of the middle group ('less vulnerable') incurred high average burdens of 5–10 per cent or even over 10 per cent per month, but managed to cope. In contrast, highly vulnerable households with lower burdens struggled and fell further into poverty. The lack of a clear link between cost burden and livelihood change was because illness was only one factor influencing livelihood trajectories. Previous events and processes had placed households on longer-term trajectories of struggling, coping or improving, and path dependency continued to influence livelihood change over the brief research period. Illness cost burdens, unless high and persistent, were unlikely to make a major difference to these paths except to exacerbate existing vulnerability and decline. Yet for some households, assets and health services played an important role in mitigating the impact of illness on poverty.

Highly vulnerable households: struggling and impoverishment

These households experienced a decline in four or more out of six dimensions of livelihood. These included the loss of an income earner or growing insecurity of work and the pawning of last items of jewellery. But perhaps the most telling dimensions of impoverishment were a spiral of debt, often from earlier debts that were carried through to the research period, and lasting cuts to food consumption or education.

Three of these four households had been on a path of decline triggered by illness before the research started. Due to cancer, Jayasinghe had been forced to give up work. Despite excellent treatment, free at the point of delivery, at the specialist cancer hospital, the loss of the main breadwinner had had serious social and economic consequences for the household.

Sumithra's household had experienced a series of accidents that had undermined assets and caused high levels of debt. Their youngest son had suffered a serious leg fracture in a road accident a few years earlier, and after doctors at the public hospital said they could not fix the bone, they took him to a private Ayurvedic specialist. The prolonged treatment entailed high direct costs (both medical and non-medical), and they had to sell saris, pawn jewellery, and take out a large loan. Then, in 1997, Sumithra's husband suffered life-threatening burns and was in a public hospital for three months, incurring high indirect costs and non-medical direct costs (transport). They tried to manage these costs by withdrawing two sons from school to work and by additional borrowing. When research started, the household's assets were depleted and they were heavily in debt.

Arthritis had caused Valli to give up her relatively well-paid job working as a cleaner at an international NGO office. Her household had also borrowed heavily (with interest) to finance two legal cases, one pertaining to her son's possession of heroin and the other pertaining to her husband selling illicit alcohol. Valli's husband had to promise their small plot of land as a security for repayment of the loans, effectively mortgaging the house, and they had pawned all their jewellery. When research started they were already on a path of impoverishment, arthritis was still affecting Valli's ability to work, and her husband was drinking.

What role did illness costs, health services, and assets play in continuing impoverishment over the eight-month period? Three of the households incurred low average burdens per month (Figure 6.4), but these were either (a) concentrated over one or two months and forced risky borrowing strategies because the households lacked assets, or (b) were lower but more frequent cost burdens that constituted a persistent attack on budgets and assets, illustrated by the case of Selvaraja (Case Study Box 6.1, Table 6.2). A direct cost burden of 6 per cent forced strategies that resulted in debt, failure to repay credit from the shop which later ended their credit facility, failure to redeem Selvaraja's ring that was subsequently lost, and long-term cuts to food consumption. In the same month, however, the protection provided by public health care services was also demonstrated: despite a gradual slide into deeper poverty, the health system mitigated that decline.

(Less) vulnerable households: coping or gradually improving

These households experienced little change to at least four dimensions of livelihood outcome. In general, levels of debt had not increased due to strong social networks, and if people had borrowed, it was from low-cost and flexible sources such as family, friends, and local credit societies. Household members sustained basic expenditure and consumption levels.

Historically, these households were on steady livelihood paths characterized by income poverty and vulnerability but fewer shocks, including no history of serious illness events (Pushpa, Raja, and Kumudu). Gradual improvements were evident in the cases of Kumudu and Puspha, and this continued during the research period despite their high illness costs (Figure 6.4) because of capacity to cope. Other households (Nimal, Geetha, Renuka, Amali, and Nishanthi) were coping to differing degrees. Nimal's household was difficult to categorize. It had suffered earlier a dramatic decline due to serious illness (Case Study Box 6.2) and so could have been located in the struggling group. However, when research started they were coping (at a lower level) and not suffering further impoverishment, thanks to strong networks of family support and free health services that protected the household against high direct illness costs.

What role did illness costs and resources play in livelihood stability over eight months? This group experienced higher cost burdens than the highly vulnerable group (Figure 6.4), partly because of their more frequent use of private providers, with four of the eight households experiencing high cost burdens concentrated in a few months (Nimal, Geetha, Kumudu, and Pushpa). However, none of these burdens, over 100 per cent in some months for Geetha and Nimal, were damaging to livelihood outcomes because of a combination of strong assets and public protection against high hospital inpatient costs.

Overall, a combination of factors explained this group's coping. Private providers were often used for outpatient treatment of acute and, to a lesser extent, chronic illness, but they had the income and assets to manage the direct

---

Box 6.2 Impoverishment associated with illness: the case of Nimal

As a direct result of a serious illness, Nimal's household experienced a decline into poverty from a position of relative wealth. Before a road accident in 1994, Nimal was earning a good salary as the manager of a rice mill and owned two three-wheeler taxis that he hired out to drivers. He described the accident as '*the worst experience of my life and the beginning of our financial problems and difficult life we face today*'. He was admitted to hospital for one month where they took many x-rays. Although his broken bones began to heal, he became very sick, and at the end of the year doctors diagnosed a disease of the bone marrow called 'aplastic anaemia' (blood cell deficiency caused by failure of bone marrow).

Since 1994, Nimal (aged about 50 at the time of the study) has been unable to work and needs to raise a substantial sum of money to privately finance a bone marrow transplant (not provided in Sri Lanka). At the time research started, he and his wife, Sita, lived in a small wooden house having undertaken a sequence of asset strategies that had left them impoverished and vulnerable (their daughter was married and living nearby). They had sold their brick house and moved to a small wooden house, sold productive assets (two three-wheelers), used all their savings including those from when Nimal had worked in the Middle East, and pawned all Sita's jewellery worth $307 (Rs.20,000) and friends' jewellery.

Despite this decline in assets and income, Nimal and Sita could obtain adequate food and other basic needs due to their strong social networks. They relied on gifts of food and money from Nimal's daughter and from his wife's younger sister whose husband was running a successful business. Friends gave blood to the hospital blood bank so that Nimal could obtain his regular transfusions free of charge (patients have to pay for blood if it is not replaced). Free check-ups and blood counts at the general hospital also protected Nimal, Sita and those who helped them from any direct medical costs associated with those regular visits.

---

cost burdens. In addition, the public sector was available to protect patients against the direct costs of more serious illness, and this group had assets with which to manage indirect costs. Free public treatment enabled households to access care without adopting risky asset strategies and made households more resilient to other shocks.

Resilient households: investing and improving

This group experienced improvement in four or more dimensions of livelihood: usually an increased level and diversity of income due to an older child starting work, investment in physical assets such as housing or electrical goods, and investment in savings and jewellery. Nearly all borrowing was for investment purposes.

Historically, these households were on steady trajectories of investment and improvement, despite starting from socio-economic backgrounds similar to the other households. Notably, no breadwinners had been affected by serious illness in the past. Also underlying their more successful paths were better education and higher-paid and more reliable jobs, possibly obtained through stronger social networks, or higher incomes that were partly due to sound investments in business. Strong social networks had also allowed them access to resources for investment or for support when the need arose.

The group experienced relatively low cost burdens (Figure 6.4). Members of these households used private providers more often than public providers for outpatient treatment of acute and chronic illness but relied on the safety net of the public sector for inpatient care. Free public inpatient treatment protected assets, and by protecting assets or keeping debts low, made households more resilient to other shocks. The safety net of low-cost inpatient hospital care also allowed households to release surplus income to saving and investment purposes and so enabled livelihood investment strategies, for example in housing and small businesses.

Conclusion

This chapter has introduced an adapted livelihoods framework that can be used in investigating the links between illness and household poverty. The framework supports the interdisciplinary approach to such investigation, which can capture the diverse resources (economic, social, and policy-based) and institutions (kinship obligations and traditional savings groups) people mobilize to cope with shocks (Berman *et al.* 1994; Wallman and Baker 1996). The chapter has also touched on social relations (e.g. gender) that influence access to resources and institutions. A research design that combined survey and case study tools generated complementary data, and the case study work allowed analysis of some of the complex processes linking illness and impoverishment, some of which are illustrated in Case Study Boxes 6.1 and 6.2.

The framework presented at the start of this chapter (Figure 6.1) proposed three broad factors that influence capacity to cope with illness costs: severity and duration of illness, household asset portfolios, and, linked to these, their access to policy- and community-based resources. The findings from Sri Lanka provide a case study of the complexity of these factors and add empirical and analytical detail to the broad categories in Figure 6.1.

The survey and case study findings revealed that public health care services, free at the point of delivery in Colombo protected the majority of poor house-holds against high direct cost burdens, particularly the potentially high costs of hospital inpatient care and regular treatment of chronic illness. However, the data also identified the public sector's failure to protect a considerable minority of households (at least a fifth) from the costs of seeking acute care. Long waiting times, inter-personal quality weaknesses and the absence of a system of public 'family' GPs meant patients could not build close or trusting relationships with primary-level public sector doctors, which deterred them from using public care. Instead, patients were willing to pay to see a private family GP (Russell 2005). An important question for policy debate in Sri Lanka is, therefore, how to improve public service delivery arrangements at the primary level of care, such as a public GP or family doctor system so highly valued by patients.

Health care services were not designed to protect households against the indi-rect costs of illness, and there were no other public social protection measures for informal sector workers. This meant the link between illness and impoverish-ment was strongest and most observable when serious and long-term illnesses undermined breadwinners' capacity to work. In three of four cases, serious ill-nesses had started a path of impoverishment through asset and income depletion that was hard to change because of the household's limited earning potential and increased vulnerability to future shocks. These cases illustrate the vicious cycle of serious illness, asset depletion, and vulnerability to future shocks.

However, it was not just serious illness that caused asset strategies that con-tributed to impoverishment and vulnerability. For the poorest-income house-holds (which made up 25–50 per cent of households across the two communities), even a small treatment cost or a few days' lost wages imposed high cost burdens on small budgets barely adequate to meet basic needs. Low but frequent illness cost burdens, often suffered by households with a chroni-cally sick member or several young children, were a persistent shock to vulner-able households' income and assets, undermining attempts to save and invest or gradually pushing them into poverty. Public health services offered some protec-tion to mitigate these burdens, but households could not avoid non-medical direct costs and indirect costs.

The study also found that a relatively low direct illness cost burden could trigger coping strategies if it was combined with other essential but irregular expenses, e.g. on education, clothing, and funeral rites. Male spending on nar-cotics exacerbated this problem. Combined cost burdens highlighted the import-ance of a range of other public policy measures that added to household resources and reduced the impact of health care expenses on the overall house-hold budget, notably free education and urban housing projects. These findings point to the need for multipronged approaches to social protection for a range of shocks and expenses, including health and education policy, insurance against illness-related income losses, as well as drug awareness and rehabilitation pro-grammes.

Household assets and community-based resources also influenced vulnerabil-ity to illness costs. In addition to the more obvious assets (work and labour, physical and financial capital), less tangible assets such as organizational skills, shrewdness with money, and the strength of social networks were important factors influencing the links between illness and poverty. Other work has shown that a strong social network is a special asset within the household's asset portfolio because it can be used to gain access to other resources for livelihood development (Bebbington 1999) or support at times of illness (Wallman and Baker 1996):

> A relationship well-sustained is readily converted into the currencies of help and support – whether practical, financial or emotional.
>
> (Wallman and Baker 1996: 675)

The research found that the poorer-income households had weaker social networks and could access fewer financial resources, possibly because they did not have the money to engage in lending and borrowing activities or to join *seetu* groups. A weak network added considerably to vulnerability because it limited access to financial support or to institutions that could offer gifts or low-risk loans. Better-off households had built up stronger networks through their lending and borrowing activities, and were more likely to have access to network support or local financial institutions.

The weak asset portfolios of a large proportion of households in the two communities pointed to the need for an expansion of social protection through public and community-based initiatives. In Sri Lanka, public health and education services add to household entitlements and offer some protection. There were also examples of NGO-based financial institutions providing cheap pawning and credit facilities. However, little protection was available against the damaging income losses caused by serious or frequent illnesses. Such safety nets are commonly viewed to be beyond the capacity of the governments of developing countries or beyond the scope and responsibility of public health care policies. Yet there are examples of pensions and targeted social grants in countries such as South Africa that have increased household resilience and food security (Booysen 2004). Policy debates among government sectors and donor, NGOs, and community-based actors in Sri Lanka must explore the possibilities of establishing effective social protection measures that can mitigate household impoverishment caused by serious or frequent illness.

Part III

Restructuring health systems to reach the poor

7 Alternative approaches to extending health services to the poorest

Sara Bennett

Introduction

The evidence presented in previous chapters paints a depressing picture of the effectiveness of health systems in addressing the needs of the poor. People living in poverty are more vulnerable to disease and infection, yet have poorer geographical access to health care facilities. Even if the poor are able physically to access health services, the costs associated with care may be prohibitive, or may cause long-term damage to household budgets. While seeking care, the poor are likely to be treated with a lack of courtesy, or even with contempt – which may discourage them from future use of health care. Many health systems, although not all, perform worse in addressing the needs of the poor than addressing the needs of the more affluent. The reasons underlying this are multiple, including amongst others: less knowledge about health and health care issues among the poor; resource allocations that favour more affluent areas; lack of accountability of health workers, particularly to poorer clients; financing systems that create barriers to accessing care; and health services that fail to respond to the needs of the poor.

At the national level, failure to improve the performance of health systems vis-à-vis the needs of the poor is in part due to political reasons and the lack of voice and political power that the poor commonly have. This may have been compounded by international commitments that do not prioritize the needs of the poor: for example, many global objectives, including the health Millennium Development Goals, do not distinguish between the poor and the non-poor. It is typically much easier to extend coverage rates amongst more affluent subgroups of the population (and thus achieve aggregate targets) than to target the poor, and there may be a danger that in the push to achieve national and global health targets, the poor become further marginalized (Gwatkin 2002b).

There is, however, considerable current interest in and commitment to strategies that improve the position of the poor. Poverty Reduction Strategy Papers (PRSPs), which focus on strategies to alleviate poverty, have become the primary planning framework for countries seeking access to conditional loans through the Poverty Reduction Growth Facility, or debt relief under the Highly Indebted Poor Countries (HIPC) initiative. While PRSPs generally include a section addressing health, and this typically considers geographical and financial barriers to accessing services, the strategies proposed to address these problems typically do not appear to be well-focused on the needs of the poor (Laterveer *et al.* 2003; Dodd *et al.* 2004). Strategies proposed focus on high priority services (such as child health and maternal health) that are likely to benefit the poor disproportionately more than the rich, but they do not commonly analyse why efforts to expand these services have failed in the past, or which innovative strategies can be deployed to ensure greater benefits for the poor in the future.

Unfortunately, for policy makers seeking innovative strategies to reach the poor, there is very little consensus on which strategies work best and under what circumstances. As can be seen from previous chapters, the reasons why health systems fail to serve the needs of the poor are multiple and complex – and strategies to address them need to take into account this complexity. Furthermore, while there is substantial debate on which strategies are most likely to be effective in meeting the needs of the poor, there is only rather limited empirical evidence.

The final section of this book examines the question of, 'What changes can be implemented within the health sector in order to meet the needs of the poor better?'. This chapter provides a conceptual framework to help organize the different types of pro-poor approaches. It summarizes the debates regarding the strengths and weaknesses of different types of broad approaches, which are likely to be more or less effective, and the conditions under which such likelihood of effectiveness can be envisaged. The chapter also explores in some detail the effectiveness of three universal, supply-side approaches in addressing the needs of the poor.

Why health services do not address the needs of the poor

Chapter 4 describes the reasons why health services do not adequately address the needs of the poor. These are summarized here, as they provide the foundation for the typology of approaches for promoting more pro-poor health services.

Barriers to service utilization arise due to:

- *Lack of knowledge on the part of households*: poorer households suffer from a double burden in accessing knowledge relevant to health. First, lower levels of education may make it harder for them to access health information messages; second, health information campaigns may not reach the poor, due to their lack of access to mass media and health services (Ahmed *et al.* 2006). Accordingly, poor households may be less likely to make the decision to seek care in a timely fashion or take advantage of public health programmes.
- *Accessibility*: poor households, living in remote rural areas or in urban slums, are less likely to have geographical access to health services, as these have historically been located in urban and more affluent areas.
- *Affordability*: multiple financial barriers – both formal and informal – may

prevent poor households from seeking care. User fees, which are now relatively widespread in low-income countries for government-provided services as well as private services, may be a deterrent to seeking care, but so are travel costs and the opportunity cost (in terms of neglecting other work or duties) of seeking care.

- *Quality and responsiveness*: increasing evidence has demonstrated the fact that services, particularly publicly provided services, do not respond to the needs of poor households. Quality is often perceived to be poor, particularly when drugs are not available, and opening hours and the range of services offered may not match need. These problems are compounded by staff attitudes, which can be dismissive or downright unpleasant to poor people seeking care.

These barriers to service utilization are synergistic: the costs of accessing care for poor households are typically greater than those for non-poor households, due at least partly to the physical inaccessibility of services. Lack of knowledge about the benefits of seeking care may be compounded by staff attitudes to poor clients, with whom health staff may spend less time and make less effort to explain the cause of illness and treatment options.

While the problems listed here represent the direct barriers to seeking care that poor households face, these barriers are reinforced by imbalances in power between rich and poor and lack of voice for poor people (Narayan 2000). Given the pervasive and embedded nature of social institutions that disempower the poor, it is difficult to address the manifestation of these problems within the health sector without also seeking to address the fundamental issue of powerlessness.

A typology of approaches for making health services more pro-poor

Distinctions can be made between different approaches to making health services more pro-poor. One fundamental distinction is between so-called 'universal' approaches and 'targeted' approaches. A targeted intervention seeks to direct resources to specific subgroups of the population, so pro-poor targeting may identify relatively poorer communities, households or individuals and target benefits at these groups. In contrast, a universal approach does not seek to target particular population groups but is rather based on the notion that certain strategies that improve the overall functioning of the health system for everyone will benefit the poor too.

The arguments in favour of targeted approaches concentrate upon the fact that they constitute a better use of limited resources and that targeted approaches are more likely to avoid damaging the local economy (van de Walle 1998). The latter issue is particularly pertinent for commodities such as condoms or insecticide-treated nets, where there is likely to be a local market for these products. Widespread availability of highly subsidized products is likely to crowd out the private market, whereas targeted provision of subsidized products to particularly poor segments of the community is less likely to have this effect. The issue of crowding out markets is less problematic in certain contexts: for example, in rural areas of sub-Saharan Africa, where the local health care market is not developed for the majority of health care services, crowding out is not such an issue.

Targeted approaches are likely to have higher administrative costs than universal approaches: there is typically a cost to identifying individuals or households who should be targeted, although the nature of this cost depends significantly upon the type of targeting criteria used (see Chapter 8). Targeted approaches may also be subject to different types of failure. First, those who deserve to be targeted may not actually be captured, and second, the benefits associated with targeting could leak to those who are not eligible. Such failures may be particularly problematic in contexts where those administering the targeting programme are not held accountable and the targeting process is not highly transparent.

Universal approaches obviously avoid the costs of identifying the poor, who should be targeted to receive benefits, as well as the targeting errors noted above. The other important factor in their favour is that, as they also benefit the non-poor, it may be easier to secure and sustain political support for them. Some opponents have argued that there is clear evidence that the universal approaches tried to date, such as the promotion of primary health care, have frequently been captured by the non-poor (Gwatkin 2001), and the evidence presented in earlier chapters seems to support this. However, as discussed above, the capture of benefits of universal programmes by the non-poor occurs because of the broader political context, and it would seem likely therefore that, over the medium term, targeted programmes may also be subject to such political capture.

Table 7.1 groups different strategies to address barriers to health care for the poor, according to whether they are universal or targeted in nature. While on paper the distinction between targeted and universal strategies sounds clear, in practice this distinction can be fuzzy. Many of the universal strategies identified in Table 7.1 could be implemented in a somewhat targeted manner. For example, essential packages could be designed in such a way that they guarantee a basic minimum of services which would benefit primarily the remote, rural poor who currently have access to very limited care. Moreover, universal and targeted strategies may be highly complementary. For example, a policy of providing universal access for all to a basic package of services might be best implemented through the provision of contracts to non-governmental organizations (NGOs) to provide services to the rural poor in remote areas. Even if governments chose to promote universal strategies for improving access to health services, it may be necessary to complement those with targeted interventions that aim to empower the poor and give them greater voice, in order to sustain and expand their rights within the health system.

Another key distinction, while on the subject of alternative approaches to reaching the poor, is between demand-side interventions and supply-side

Table 7.1 Classification of possible strategies to address barriers for the poor

Barrier addressed	Demand side		Supply side	
	Targeted	Universal	Targeted	Universal
Lack of knowledge	Social marketing; Conditional cash transfers	Behaviour change communication		
Lack of access			Contracting for services for the poor; Geographical resource targeting	Essential package; Strengthening private sector; Extending service infrastructure closer to communities
Affordability	Vouchers; Conditional cash transfers	Community-based health insurance	User fee exemptions	Social health insurance; Increased tax financing
Poor service responsiveness	Vouchers	Decentralization; Participatory decision making (e.g. hospital boards)	Performance-related contracts (specific to poor)	Essential package; Decentralization; Performance-related contracts (general)

interventions. Demand-side interventions are targeted at individuals, households and communities who are the recipients of health services. Demand-side interventions may be of two primary sorts (Standing 2004): they may focus primarily upon changing the knowledge and behaviour of households (thus addressing the first of the barriers to service utilization noted above) or they may focus upon harnessing consumer or user power in an effort to make both policy makers and service providers more accountable and more responsive to the communities whom they serve. This may be achieved through market-based competitive mechanisms (sometimes referred to as 'making the money follow the patient'), or through non-market-based mechanisms such as promoting consumer voice (e.g. through community participation on hospital boards). The *World Development Report 2004* discusses both of these options to improve service delivery and argues that, for some services, where outputs are difficult to specify and the market is not contestable (i.e. it is difficult for new providers to enter the market), increasing consumer voice within the public sector is the most appropriate strategy to improve responsiveness. However, for services which are more suited to market-based delivery (such as the provision of health-related commodities like condoms or vector control measures), promoting market-based competition is more likely to be effective.

While behaviour-change communication strategies have been widely used in the past, the notion of promoting accountability of policy makers and providers to communities has recently been spotlighted (particularly through the *World Development Report 2004*), perhaps partly as a consequence of increasing evidence from the broader development literature about how good governance, accountability and the role of civil society can positively affect development paths (Burnside and Dollar 2004). Interest in accountability may also reflect increasing recognition amongst policy makers of just how unresponsive service providers (especially those of the government) may be, particularly to poor clients (Narayan 2000). Multiple recent reforms, as diverse as decentralization, use of vouchers for health services, establishment of hospital boards and community-based health insurance schemes have an element within them that focuses upon strengthening user roles and promoting accountability (Brinkerhoff 2003).

Supply-side interventions directly target providers in order to address problems of accessibility, affordability and responsiveness, which inhibit poorer people from seeking care. So, for example, supply-side interventions may include promoting a basic package of essential primary health care services or giving providers performance-based contracts that present incentives to get services to the poor.

Both supply- and demand-side strategies may be targeted or universal, as illustrated in Table 7.1.

Clearly, for any decision-maker concerned with improving health services for the poor, it is important to understand the characteristics of the poor, what makes people poor, and their experience of poverty. The ease with which the poor can be identified through objective and reproducible measures is likely to guide the choice between targeted and universal strategies. If targeting is to be used, then the criteria to use for targeting (geographic, gender, means assessment) must be decided. Recent literature, however, stresses the relational nature of poverty; poverty can exclude people from social relationships, thus further exacerbating both their vulnerability and their sense of exclusion. The way in which health services are structured and operated can exacerbate or ameliorate this sense of exclusion (Tibandebage and Mackintosh 2005), and policy makers should also pay attention to this issue.

Decision-makers need to understand the nature of the barriers which currently prevent the poor from making appropriate use of health services. For some barriers, such as lack of knowledge, demand-side interventions are likely to form the primary strategy. For other barriers, such as lack of access, supply-side barriers will offer greater promise. Both supply- and demand-side strategies need to be considered in order to address concerns about affordability or poor service responsiveness. It is common, however, for the poor to be affected by complex problems that require multiple complementary strategies to resolve. For example, the poor may frequently seek care from low quality informal private providers because they find formal government services too inaccessible and expensive. Measures to address this issue may include improving the quality of care in the private sector, but enhancing the affordability and access of government services is also likely to be critical, particularly for those services which the private sector fails to provide or provides poorly.

Chapter 8 focuses upon improving the performance of health systems vis-à-vis the poor through targeted approaches. Chapter 9 then considers alternative approaches to promoting the affordability of health services for the poor. Chapter 10 looks at the emerging demand-side strategies which seek to promote greater accountability and responsiveness within health systems, particularly to poor clients. The following section of this chapter focuses, therefore, upon three universal approaches that have on occasion been advocated as means to extend health services for the poor; these are: (i) strengthening the private sector provision of services, (ii) introducing essential health packages and (iii) decentralization. These three universal approaches complement the approaches discussed in the other chapters (as indicated in Table 7.1) and represent alternative means to promote the accessibility and responsiveness of services for the poor.

Evidence on the effectiveness of three universal approaches to reach the poor

Private provision of services

Interest in the private health sector as a potential means to improve the access of the poor to health services springs from two sources. First, it has been proposed in the past (World Bank 1989) that promoting private sector providers for the more affluent segments of a society may free up government resources, which can then be better targeted at the poor. This argument is essentially an argument about improving the targeting of government resources and therefore is not dealt with further in this chapter.

Second, during the past 20 years, substantial evidence has been amassed demonstrating that, even for very poor households, the private sector, broadly defined, constitutes a widely used source of care. For example, a review of Demographic and Health Surveys from 38 countries demonstrated extremely high use of private sector providers even amongst the poor; for children in the poorest-income quintile, 34–96 per cent of children seeking treatment for diarrhoea received treatment in the private sector, while proportions of children seeking care for acute respiratory tract infection varied from 37 to 99 per cent (Gwatkin *et al.* 2000). Moreover, private providers, particularly unqualified, informal sector ones, may be much more physically accessible to the poor population than formal sector providers. For example, in rural Tanzania, a study found that there was a health facility for every 5,222 people, a retailer selling antimalarials for every 931 people and a retailer selling drugs of any kind for every 260 people (Goodman *et al.* 2004).

Private providers may be preferred by the poor because of a perceived greater degree of confidentiality and privacy, greater attention paid by such providers to being courteous and respectful and because such providers may offer more convenient services (in terms of waiting times and opening hours) (Palmer *et al.* 2003; Russell 2005). However, the clinical quality of care provided by private providers is extremely mixed and, frequently, rather poor (see Box 7.1). Such poor quality care may be due to lack of knowledge on the part of providers, who may have limited and outdated training, but is also due to financial incentives, which may, for example, lead private providers to refer unnecessarily or provide drugs which are not useful to the patient, as this increases their revenues. Sometimes the very responsiveness of private providers may compromise the clinical quality of care. For example, a study of malaria patients in India documented the fact that private providers working in low-income areas were particularly likely to skip blood smear tests for febrile patients and provide ineffective, one-day treatments, citing patients' inability to pay as the reason for doing so (Kamat 2001). Furthermore, although the nature of services offered by private providers varies from country to country, in some contexts private providers offer only limited services of public health importance (such as immunization, antenatal care, tuberculosis (TB) care, etc.).

If it were possible to enhance the quality of care and the range of services provided by private providers (while ensuring that prices do not increase dramatically), then this might significantly increase the access of poor people to quality health services and accordingly promote their health status.

There are several different mechanisms through which government could

---

Box 7.1 Quality of care issues in the private sector

- Unnecessary use of antibiotics for treatment of diarrhoeal diseases and non-complicated acute respiratory infections (Egypt, Pakistan)

- Insufficient use of oral rehydration salts for treatment of dehydration (Bangladesh, Nigeria, Pakistan, Sri Lanka and Yemen)

- Under-dosing of antimalarials (Vietnam)

- Inconsistent and non-standardized prescribing of antiretrovirals (Zimbabwe, Senegal)

- Important shortcomings in diagnosis and case-management of TB patients by private practitioners including reliance on radiological diagnosis alone, inappropriate treatment regimens, failure to educate patients and poor case holding (India, Pakistan)

Sources: Brugha (2003), Bustreo *et al.* (2003).

seek to promote improved quality of care, or greater coverage of priority services, by private health care providers (Bennett *et al.* 2005). Some of these mechanisms, such as contracting for services, the use of vouchers and social marketing, typically target specific subgroups of society for coverage by private sector services, and these are dealt with in Chapter 9. There are, however, a range of mechanisms that do not target specific population groups. These include: (i) training private health care providers, (ii) franchising arrangements, (iii) regulation of service providers, (iv) accreditation of service providers and (v) programmes that provide additional inputs (such as equipment or pre-packaged drugs) to private providers.

Programmes aimed at *training private health care providers* represent some of the earliest forays into the field of improving the quality and range of services offered by private providers. Such programmes have variously attempted to work with private allopathic providers (e.g. Chakraborty *et al.* 2000), private traditional providers (Hamid Salim *et al.* 2006) and private drug sellers (Kafle *et al.* 1992). Evaluations of such programmes suggest that although there were some successes, frequently a key obstacle remained in the shape of the financial incentives faced by private providers. Financial incentives for private providers (such as the widespread use of fee-for-service payment) often do not support improved quality of care and may even create incentives for poor quality (Chakraborty and Frick 2002).

Given the findings of earlier studies, more recent efforts have targeted both knowledge and incentives. For example, studies in Vietnam and Thailand have used a combination of education, regulation and peer review to address poor dispensing practices among private drug sellers (Chuc *et al.* 2002; Chalker *et al.* 2005). These studies concluded that multifaceted interventions can have significant beneficial impacts upon dispensing practices in the private sector, but these effects depend upon the context and the way in which the interventions are implemented.

Franchising models attempt not only to ensure the quality of the service provided, but also to brand the service, so that individual private providers who become franchisees may benefit from mass marketing conducted by the franchiser. The franchisee may also benefit from the possibility of the bulk supply of goods at reduced cost. There is therefore an incentive for the franchisee to remain a franchisee (and accordingly to maintain quality standards) and an incentive for the franchiser to ensure quality of franchisees (so that public trust in the franchise is not diluted). Of course, the extent to which these incentives can actually be brought into play depends considerably on the extent of asymmetric information between franchiser and franchisee, and accordingly the cost of monitoring quality (Ruster *et al.* 2003).

Besides the basic question of whether franchises are effective in securing the goals that they seek, there is also the concern of whether this mechanism serves the needs of the poor. There appear to be no studies which explicitly look at the impact of franchising upon access of the poor to health services, but analyses suggest that a key factor in the success of franchising is for potential clients to be willing to pay for services provided (Montagu 2002). Franchise arrangements typically do not include special arrangements for the poor and may price poorer consumers out of the market.

Regulation encompasses a variety of specific mechanisms designed to maintain minimum quality of care standards in both public and private health care sectors. The three principle types of quality-related regulation encompass:

• setting standards for the physical infrastructure of facilities, through licensing of private health care providers (typically done by the Ministry of Health);
• setting minimum standards for the qualification of health staff (through professional licensing typically conducted by professional associations);
• investigating and punishing medical malpractice and medical negligence through legal channels such as consumer protection law.

Given evidence regarding the very poor quality of care provided by certain private health providers, that may even jeopardize the health of patients, regulation to protect consumers seems essential. Nonetheless, it is difficult to design regulation in such a way that it protects the most vulnerable, namely the poor. For example, if the standards for physical infrastructure are set too high, then this may close down those private providers who serve the poor, even if they offer adequate clinical quality. Similarly, while medical malpractice legislation and consumer protection is important, the evidence suggests that in order to win such cases the plaintiff typically has to have the authority and education to stand up to the medical profession, to get medical records from providers, and to prosecute in a court of law (Mills *et al.* 2001). Few poor people may feel equipped to take on the medical profession in this way.

As discussed above, very targeted regulatory mechanisms, in conjunction with other interventions such as education, have been proven, in small-scale interventions, to have positive effects (Chalker *et al.* 2005), but improving quality of care in the private sector through broad regulatory measures appears difficult.

Accreditation seeks to promote quality standards in the private sector by accrediting health care providers who meet certain standards and by making lists of accredited providers publicly available so that potential users can employ such information in their decision-making process. Accreditation appears to be most effective in contexts where there is a large institutional purchaser, which limits its purchasing to accredited providers and thus offers very clear financial incentives to providers to be accredited. Without such a consolidated purchaser, accreditation may have little impact. Thus, as a strategy for improving quality of private sector health care for the poor, formal accreditation appears to have considerable limitations. Substantial consolidated purchasers are relatively rare in low-income contexts, and if they do exist, they are likely to serve a relatively affluent population who may be using private providers different to those used by the poor. Accreditation may also increase the cost of care; the poor may therefore have to resort to facilities outside the accredited network, which may be providing a very substandard quality of care.

Qualitative research among the poor in Tanzania has indicated that there are active information exchange networks among health care users and that private facilities can rapidly acquire poor reputations for providing substandard care (Tibandebage and Mackintosh 2005). Further research is needed to establish what sort of public policy mechanisms could be used to make these information networks more effective, through a kind of informal accreditation.

A further possible approach to strengthening private sector provision is *supporting the provision of resources to private providers*. For those private providers serving the poor, the poverty of the client base may indeed create financial obstacles that prevent private providers from having appropriate resources (e.g. diagnostic equipment) at their disposal. However, frequently, the quality of care issues which arise with respect to the private sector are not simply about lack of resources, but also about establishing appropriate incentive structures. Establishing mechanisms to offer loans to private providers is unlikely to address these incentive issues. Certain innovative resourcing strategies do attempt to address the incentive issues; for example, one approach has been to prepackage drugs for common conditions in order to prevent drug sellers from selling partial courses of treatment to poor clients who cannot afford the whole course of treatment (Mills *et al.* 2002). However, even such strategies can be subverted, through, for example, breaking the packet open.

So, in conclusion, while the intensive use of private providers by the poor is well documented, as are the clinical quality of care problems associated with private sector provision, there are currently few clearly effective strategies to improve quality of care in the private sector for poor populations. Certain measures to ensure quality of care (such as regulation) are clearly essential, but governments need to pay special attention to the concerns of the poor as they implement such measures. Other mechanisms, such as franchising, appear to hold promise but are as yet rather unproven, at least on a large scale. Typically, it seems that multifaceted interventions are necessary in order to achieve results.

Essential health packages and primary care

Government primary care services are typically much more pro-poor than other types of government services (see Chapter 4), although the rich may still benefit from them more than the poor. Expanding primary care services may therefore be seen as one way to improve the access of the poor to services. This strategy, backed up by the Alma Ata Declaration of 1978, was widely pursued throughout the developing world and had many notable successes. For example, during the 1970s Costa Rica expanded primary health care services throughout the country through its Rural Health Program and its Community Health Program (which worked in rural and urban areas, respectively). These programmes have been argued to be the major drivers of large improvements in health outcomes during the 1970s (Jaramillo *et al.* 1984). An evaluation in Niger of the impact of access to primary health care services on child mortality suggested that children living in villages near health dispensaries were 32 per cent less likely to die than children without access to primary health care services (Magnani *et al.* 1996).

However, in many countries there seems to be a 'glass ceiling' in terms of what percentage of government funding can be devoted to primary care. Frequently, pressure from an articulate, urban middle class means that it is extremely difficult for governments to allocate resources away from more expensive tertiary facilities to primary care services. There are some counter examples, such as Zambia, where for a period during the 1990s quite significant resource shifts were made towards primary care services (Lake *et al.* 2000), but examples such as these often exploited unique political windows of opportunity, and over time pressure builds up to reverse these achievements.

Frequently, allocation of government resources among different services, and different levels of service, is made in a very implicit and somewhat opaque manner. The *World Development Report 1993* proposed that countries use burden of disease data and cost-effectiveness criterion to identify a package of basic services that could be offered through primary health care facilities throughout the country (World Bank 1993a). This notion of establishing an 'essential package' is pro-poor in the obvious sense that it tries to promote the funding of cost-effective (largely primary health care) services for all, thus implying a reallocation of resources away from less cost-effective and less accessible tertiary facilities, which typically serve the more affluent. However, approaches used by the World Bank to identify elements of the essential package downplay the role of communities in prioritizing health interventions. Literature from the industrialized world, in contrast, emphasizes the importance of engaging communities in more explicit discussions around prioritization and resource setting (Ham 1997); this is particularly important so that the values of community members can be reflected in the prioritization.

Many countries have espoused an essential service package policy, and several have put this policy into practice, but there is remarkably little evidence about its effectiveness and, in particular, whether it improves access to services for poor people. One study from Bangladesh is instructive (Ensor *et al.* 2002). The essential service package designed for Bangladesh was very much focused upon diseases of the poor, but a detailed analysis of expenditure patterns subsequent to the implementation of the package found that other barriers still prevented access by poor groups. For example, informal fees acted as a financial barrier to utilization, and while behaviour-change communication formed part of the essential package of services, this programme was insufficient to create adequate demand for services. Furthermore, budgeting and financial structures had changed little so it was not clear that resources intended for the essential package were actually being used for the intended services; staff continued to moonlight in their private practices and it seems likely that resources also leaked into the private sector.

The definition and implementation of an essential package of services was also a core element of the Tanzania Essential Health Interventions Project

(TEHIP) (de Savigny *et al.* 2004). Unlike the Bangladesh experience, TEHIP worked at the district level and focused upon two districts alone. Furthermore, the tools on disease burden and cost-effectiveness were combined with other district-level decision-making tools and operational research, with modest increases in health budgets, rehabilitation of health facilities and district-level capacity building and with improvement of quality of care through the introduction of the Integrated Management of Childhood Illness (IMCI) package. This combination of interventions appears to have had quite impressive impacts: health spending in the intervention districts was brought much more closely in line with disease burden, substantial increases in service utilization were observed and child mortality rates in the two study districts declined by over 40 per cent in the five years after the introduction of the planning tools. As the study implementers note:

> In a country where the majority of people are poor, a minimum package of essential interventions addressing the diseases that account for the largest segments of the burden of disease will by definition benefit the poor. It is the poor who suffer the most from these diseases (such as malaria), so it is the poor who have the most to gain.
>
> (De Savigny *et al.* 2004).

One of the difficulties in considering the lessons from the TEHIP experience is that it is not entirely clear which of the several interventions implemented had the greatest impact on improving health services for poor people and how the different interventions complemented each other.

Decentralization

Decentralization entails the transfer of authority to lower levels of government. This may be lower levels of the Ministry of Health, such as district health management teams, or local government bodies. Decentralization has been one of the most widely implemented reforms in developing countries during the past 15 years, but it is also a widely heterogeneous reform, taking very different forms in different country contexts. It has the potential to have far-reaching implications for the poor – their access to health decision-making, and the financial accessibility and quality of services provided to them.

Decentralization has frequently been driven by forces outside the health sector – particularly by political forces for greater local autonomy and/or the redistribution of power (Hutchinson and LaFond 2004). However, within the health sector, the primary rationales for decentralization are typically said to be:

- *increasing responsiveness and accountability* – by putting decision-making functions closer to communities, it should be possible to make decision-makers more accountable to such communities and more responsive to their needs;

- *improving efficiency* – by giving local decision-makers control over resources (such as finances and human resources), they can use their intimate knowledge of local conditions to decide how best to deploy those resources. For example, decentralization may enable local decision-makers to move health staff to clinics in particularly underserved communities, or reshape budgets so as to reflect particular local priorities.

In addition to these primary rationales, decentralization also entails a reshaping of the accountability relationship between the centre and local decision-making units. This sometimes (although not always) encompasses a move away from a direct hierarchical relationship, towards a relationship where decentralized units are responsible via implicit or explicit contracts for certain priority outcomes. Such a shift towards performance-based agreements can make it possible to create stronger incentives for the provision of efficient and high quality health care services to the poor. Finally, decentralization creates an opportunity to reshape how central government resources are distributed among decentralized units. Reform of such resource allocation mechanisms can lead to the explicit financial targeting of poor or vulnerable communities and is discussed in Chapter 8.

At the country level, decentralization is occasionally presented as a reform to promote equity of access to care (Blas and Limbambala 2001a) or to reduce inequality in the distribution of publicly financed health care (World Bank 2004). But even if decentralization does not have as its core focus a concern for extending services to the poor, the primary rationales (responsiveness and efficiency) imply that the poor would benefit from a decentralized health system. In practice, evidence from the health sector on the impact of decentralization upon the poor, or access to services for the poor, is both limited and mixed. One study of the impact of decentralization in Bolivia suggested a strong correlation between spending patterns and social need under the decentralized system (Faguet 2001). In Zambia, decentralization was associated with an increase in the share of resources allocated to basic care at health centres compared with district offices and hospitals (Bossert *et al.* 2003a). In contrast, in Uganda, decentralization led to a considerable drop in spending on priority services compared with less essential services and management spending (Hutchinson 1999). In India, similar concerns arose as panchayats (local government authorities) were found to spend less on health than state governments had done prior to decentralization; furthermore, decentralization appeared to exacerbate inequities between rich and poor panchayats (Varatharajan *et al.* 2004).

Studies outside the health sector have similarly mixed conclusions regarding the impact of decentralization upon the poor. An Organization for Economic Cooperation and Development (OECD) review of 21 country experiences with decentralization determined that only three (in Bolivia, the Philippines and West Bengal) could be said to have had positive impacts upon the poor and classified a further four as 'somewhat positive' (Jütting *et al.* 2004). The impacts on the poor in the remaining 14 case studies were determined to be negative or somewhat negative. Similarly, a detailed case study-based analysis of the impact of decentralization upon different aspects of poverty in five sub-Saharan African countries indicates extremely limited success (Crook 2003). There are success stories, nonetheless, such as that of the Brazilian state of Ceara, where strong local leadership and local autonomy led to considerably improved social services, including health care (Tendler 1997). However, in this case, success was not due to decentralization alone, but rather to a potent combination of factors, including charismatic local leadership and strategic political action that enabled the local government to secure improvements in health services for the poor.

So what explains the mixed and somewhat discouraging picture regarding the effectiveness of decentralization in improving services for the poor? It has been recently argued that a critical factor relates to the central government's motivation for and commitment to decentralization and poverty reduction (Crook 2003; Jütting *et al.* 2004). In contexts where the central government is strongly committed to poverty reduction, decentralization and imposing stronger lines of accountability to local users can challenge local conservative elites and lead to highly positive results. But in many contexts, particularly in the poorest countries and those with the most limited degree of accountability to start with, decentralization often serves more as a means to 'consolidate an alliance with local elites based on availability of patronage opportunities' (Crook 2003). Under such circumstances, decentralization appears more likely to have negative than positive effects upon the poor.

One study supporting this thesis and specific to the health sector was that undertaken in Ceara, Brazil, which modelled health sector performance based upon: (i) indicators of formal organization including decentralization, (ii) indicators of informal management style and (iii) indicators of political culture (Atkinson and Haran 2004). It concluded that decentralization alone is insufficient to lead to improved health system performance, whereas political culture substantially influences performance directly and mediates the impact of decentralization upon performance. Other relevant evidence specific to the health sector centres around the nature of social participation in local government or other local power structures (such as hospital boards). There is evidence from several studies to suggest that participation may be restricted to certain elite groups; for example, in Zambia members of community health boards opposed to the government were removed and replaced with ruling party representatives (Blas and Limbambala 2001b). Such elites may also capture the 'spoils' of decentralization; for example, in Uganda some health unit management committees were accused of misappropriating user fee revenues to pay themselves 'sitting allowances' (Hutchinson 1999).

Conclusions

This chapter discussed alternative types of approaches to address barriers to health care for the poor. While the terms 'universal' and 'targeted' are convenient labels to identify alternative types of strategy, in practice the distinction may not always be clear, and successful interventions often combine the two approaches. Universal approaches to strengthening services for the poor are often complex and involve multiple, complementary elements. There is no single 'magic bullet' that can rapidly transform the accessibility, quality and responsiveness of health services and public health interventions for the poor. Instead, successful strategies are likely to combine a number of interventions, including, strengthening of district-level planning and management capacity, the institutionalization of an effective system of regulation and quality assurance for both public and private providers as well as enhancing lines of accountability and governance.

For all three of the universal approaches examined here, there is limited evidence on impact and even more limited data that distinguishes between impact on the poor and the non-poor. Much remains to be learnt about how best to scale up access for the poor through universal approaches. For example, while it appears imperative to improve the quality of care offered by many private and informal health care providers, who constitute an important source of care for the poor, effective mechanisms for doing this have not been fully developed or proven on a large scale. There have been small-scale successes, for example with respect to promoting the quality of drug dispensing by private pharmacies and drug vendors, but none of these initiatives have achieved nationwide coverage for a full range of drugs. With respect to essential health care packages, it seems that defining and implementing an essential package alone is unlikely to be sufficient to improve services for the poor, and this strategy needs to be supplemented by a broader range of interventions that enhance demand, strengthen the planning and management of services and thus improve access and quality of care. Finally, decentralization can be effective at improving services for the poor, but only if it is designed in a way that challenges local power elites and gives the poor a seat at the table. This is most likely to happen when strong, pro-poor central governments are in place.

Given the uncertainty about the effects of many universal approaches to improving access for the poor, and the conditions under which such approaches work, it is particularly important that these strategies are monitored and evaluated. Information collected from evaluations, and routine sources, should attempt to understand impacts in terms of different socio-economic groups, so that adjustments can be made to policy and the global knowledge base can be strengthened.

The discussion in this chapter has focused around how universal strategies might directly advantage the poor in terms of improving their access to health care. However, such strategies may also bear broader, indirect and less-easy-to-measure benefits for the poor through promoting a greater sense of social solidarity. For example, the US health care system addresses the needs of the poor largely through targeted approaches such as Medicaid. By and large, this is viewed to be an ineffective approach, but the health system both reflects the individualistic values of the society and reinforces them. Surveys of US citizens suggest that while they are supportive of greater equity in access to services, they oppose reforms which would limit provider choice or increase their own costs (Berk *et al.* 2006). This conundrum has presented a major obstacle to health care reform in the US. Similar lessons come from South Korea, which also has a very targeted and fragmented system of health financing. Despite a strongly pro-poor administration, reforms to expand health insurance coverage for the poor failed. This has been explained by societal values that emphasize individual responsibility and commercialism, and this is a society where poor people have very limited voice (Shin 2006). Again, the historical organization of the health system both reflected and reinforced these values. In Bangladesh, programmes aimed at benefiting the ultra-poor, developed by BRAC (a large NGO in Bangladesh focusing on poverty alleviation), added a component designed to capture support from village elites for the ultra-poor programme (Hossain and Matin 2004). Programme managers had realized that without support from elites to reinforce the externally supported programme and offer the ultra-poor greater protection within their village, the programme was likely to fail. The authors of the BRAC report, quoting Blair (2003), note the need for 'the poor to ally tactically and as necessary with the non-poor and elites on agendas with potentially wide benefits'. This was particularly thought to be the case as it was almost impossible 'to cobble together a constituency large and powerful enough to realise the pro-poor agenda on any exclusive basis' (Hossain and Matin 2004). The reality of political power, and especially of the politics around pro-poor reform, suggests that universal strategies to reach the poor and, at the same time, to promote social solidarity, are an important part of any policy to redress inequities.

8 Targeting services towards the poor

A review of targeting mechanisms and their effectiveness

Kara Hanson, Eve Worrall and Virginia Wiseman

Introduction

As the existence of socio-economic differentials in health and health service utilization becomes more widely recognized, policy makers at the national and international levels have become more concerned with how best to redress these inequalities. A key strategic choice is whether to target increased resources directly towards the poor or to provide the same benefits to all, irrespective of their income; and if targeting is to occur, how best to do it. In this chapter we use the definition of targeting given by Mooij: the identification and selection of certain groups, households or individuals and the distribution of benefits to them (Mooij 1999). We review the alternative approaches to targeting that have been used in health and other sectors, and draw together the existing evidence about their effectiveness.

In selecting examples of targeting, we have been challenged by the need to define the boundary between approaches that attempt to target resources towards the poor versus those which attempt more generally to improve equity. We feel the answer lies in drawing a distinction between 'principles of equity' and 'operationalizing equity'. Targeting essentially involves positive discrimination by treating different groups of individuals differently. This is consistent with the principle of vertical equity that is defined as the unequal, but fair, treatment of unequals (Mooney 1996). In recent times there has been increasing acknowledgement that vertical equity can, and should, be considered in any formulation of equity (Mooney and Jan 1997). However, in acknowledging vertical equity, an additional layer of value judgements is necessarily brought into the analysis. These are perhaps more difficult to address than in the case of horizontal equity (the equal treatment of equals) because they require statements about the *extent* of any difference in how individuals or groups should be treated if vertical equity is to be achieved (Wiseman and Jan 2000). They also require statements about how these groups should be identified and the mechanisms and methods used to deliver resources to them. In this chapter, 'targeting' represents the means for putting into practice the principle of vertical equity.

Conceptual framework

The targeting definition introduced above emphasizes a number of key elements of targeting policies: how individuals or groups are selected, the nature of the benefits involved and the way such benefits are distributed. However, the literature on targeting uses a wide variety of terminologies and organizing principles for describing targeting approaches, largely because it emerges from a variety of fields including education, social policy and economics. In this chapter, we propose a unifying terminology and conceptual framework for describing the different elements and key choices involved in a targeted transfer programme (Worrall *et al.* 2003).

Why target? Targeted vs. universal programmes compared

At the heart of the targeting issue is the question of how best to raise the well-being of the poor by transferring resources to them. The debate is usually characterized as a choice between universal benefits vs. targeted benefits (see Chapter 7). Under universal programmes, all members of a given population are eligible to receive programme benefits, while targeted programmes restrict benefits to some sub-group of the population.

It is important to assess targeted approaches against their objectives. Too often these objectives are not clearly stated. There are a number of reasons why policy makers might choose a targeted approach to providing benefits. These can be broadly categorized as relating to equity, efficiency and sustainability.

Equity is commonly cited as an objective of targeting transfers. By focusing resources on those identified as being in greatest need, a targeted approach allows them to benefit disproportionately. Also, compared with a universal transfer, the per capita amount of resources transferred may be greater for a given budget if the resources are targeted to specific groups. Another dimension of equity is the level of social protection that some targeting programmes offer recipients. It has been noted that targeted resources may protect the vulnerable during periods of economic change (Alderman and Lindert 1998).

A second justification for targeting is *efficiency*. There are a number of issues involved here. First, with limited resources available for transfers, channelling them directly to those in greatest need or with greatest ability to benefit will ensure that these resources are most effectively used. This assumes that the cost of reaching all individuals is the same, but that certain groups will benefit more from each unit of subsidy. Second, targeting subsidies can reduce the overall cost of a programme, compared with universal benefits. A third dimension of efficiency relates to whether a transfer actually results in a change in individual behaviour. For example, if a subsidy to purchase a commodity, such as an insecticide-treated mosquito net (ITN), is provided to an individual who would otherwise have purchased the net at the full price, no change in behaviour is induced by the subsidy and it can be said to be inefficient. Targeting may be used to avoid this inefficiency by focussing on those who would not otherwise have been able to access the good in question. Efficiency can be further enhanced if resources are used to induce a desired action which has positive externalities.

A third argument in favour of targeting is *sustainability*. Sustainability has multiple dimensions in this context. First, fiscal sustainability will be influenced by the overall cost of the programme; to the extent that this cost can be reduced by focusing resources on those most in need, fiscal sustainability may be enhanced. A second issue is political sustainability, which relates to the continued political commitment and support for targeting. One risk of a targeted approach is what has become known as the 'paradox of targeting' (Besley and Kanbur 1993; Gelbach and Pritchett 1997; Conning and Kevane 2001). This refers to the fact that the more narrowly targeted a programme becomes, the less political support it may garner, eventually undermining its sustainability. Setting a broader target group may be necessary to 'buy off' potential opponents of a narrowly targeted scheme and avoid social division. A further dimension of sustainability relates to the potential for state programmes to crowd out the private sector, eliminating a potential future source of supply (Hanson *et al.* 2001). By narrowing the group of beneficiaries of public transfers, a targeted approach may help to reduce the impact of public action on the viability of an existing or potential private sector.

What is being targeted – defining the benefit

In health and social policy, a range of different types of resources has been targeted towards specific groups. These include products, services, vouchers and cash which are subsidized by a government or other public body. For instance, a programme in Kenya targeted free ITNs to pregnant women visiting public antenatal services (Guyatt *et al.* 2002). Many countries have policies to exempt patients from payment of user fees for health services on grounds of poverty (Gilson *et al.* 1995), which can be seen as a form of targeted subsidy. More recently there have been experiments to target the distribution of an entitlement to a good or service, in the form of a voucher which can be redeemed in full or in part payment. Social welfare programmes in a number of Latin American countries have developed programmes to distribute cash benefits to poor households in exchange for participation in priority social services such as education, health and nutrition (Mesoamerica Nutrition Program Targeting Study Group 2002). Finally, information or marketing messages, promoting specific commodities or behaviour change, can be targeted to specific groups through the choice of medium and location. Targeted marketing can channel information towards a specific high-risk group or can be used to reinforce the targeting of a product or service. For instance, the promotion of social marketing condoms (a product) can be targeted to lower income groups through information conveyed in media that are more likely to reach the poor, such as radio or community performances in rural areas.

Targeted resources vary in their degree of transferability, which will influence programme achievements. It is useful to distinguish reallocations between individuals (where a beneficiary can transfer the resource to a non-target person) and between goods/services (where a benefit can be exchanged for an unintended good).

Cash, products and vouchers can all be easily transferred between individuals, raising the possibility that a targeted benefit will 'leak' to a non-target individual. However, the nature of the benefit and the design of the distribution system may limit the degree to which such transfers occur. For example, a voucher programme in Nicaragua provided sex workers with vouchers for reproductive health services in nominated private clinics (Gorter *et al.* 1999). While it was possible for the initial recipient of the voucher to transfer it to somebody else, it is relatively unlikely that a non-sex-worker would want to receive and use the voucher. A national-level targeted voucher scheme for ITNs in Tanzania requires the woman's antenatal care card to be presented at the time of redemption, reducing opportunities for transfer. Other benefits such as exemptions from payment, or direct provision of services such as health services or training programmes, are least amenable to being transferred to other individuals.

Cash is highly transferable between people and across goods and services. A cash benefit intended to increase food consumption within the household, for example, may be used for other purposes. Depending on programme design and monitoring, it may be possible for vouchers to be redeemed against non-target goods and services, though the degree to which this happens in practice is unknown. Local market conditions may allow benefits in the form of products to be exchanged for other commodities; but payment exemptions and direct receipt of services cannot generally be transferred.

Who to target

Although the focus of this review is on programmes which target the poor, it is important to recognize that much of the experience with targeting in the health field derives from targeting of those who are at greatest health risk or with greatest capacity to benefit from an intervention (Culyer 1995). These groups may or may not overlap with the 'poor', depending on the degree of correlation of biological and economic vulnerability.

The size of the target group will have implications for resource requirements, though some of the gains from having a narrower group may be lost through the additional resources required to identify a smaller group of beneficiaries. There are also operational implications of choice of target group since methods to identify beneficiaries are needed. Where the intervention targets the poor, this raises the important issue of how best to identify them given the multi-dimensional and context-specific characteristics of poverty. Assessing the accuracy of targeting mechanisms also requires defining a 'gold standard' for identifying the population of interest. Most recent studies have used per capita consumption (with or without equivalence adjustment) as the gold standard measure of poverty. However, this narrow money-metric definition of poverty may fail to capture other forms of deprivation and capability (Sen 1985; Falkingham and Namazie 2002).

How to target: targeting methods and mechanisms

The literature contains a number of different classifications of targeting approaches (van de Walle 1998; Jaspars and Shoham 1999), none of which is entirely satisfactory as targeting is a complex process and there are always cases which fall into multiple categories. Different dimensions of targeting programmes include the degree to which they rely on administrative systems, community members or self-selection to identify beneficiaries: whether they involve individual assessments of economic status or rely on proxy indicators; and whether they attempt to identify individuals/groups or focus on categories of spending. Following Conning and Kevane (2001), we distinguish here between the targeting *method*, which refers to the way beneficiaries are identified, and the broader targeting *mechanism*, which refers to the broader delivery strategy which may include the choice of intermediary for identifying beneficiaries, the channels for delivery of the benefit and the overall organizational design.

Targeting methods

Three main methods for identifying beneficiaries can be distinguished: individual assessment; identification through categorical or geographical indicators; and self-selection.

Individual assessment: This involves identification of individuals who are eligible for a benefit on a case-by-case basis, usually through some kind of means test. Individual or household income can be assessed directly, though this is difficult, time consuming and subject to misreporting (Gilson *et al.* 1995). Alternatively, one or more proxy indicators of individual socio-economic status may be assessed, for example, ownership of land and other assets, sex of household head (with the presumption that female-headed households are poorer than male-headed ones). The multi-dimensional characteristics of poverty mean that it may be important to use multiple indicators which are able to capture different aspects of deprivation. For example, the social safety net programme that was implemented in Indonesia in the aftermath of the Asian economic crisis of the late 1990s used the following criteria to define eligibility: families who did not eat twice daily or did not bring their sick members to health centres, families whose head-of-household lost his/her job due to a mass dismissal and families with children who dropped out of school due to financial reasons. Eligible families were identified in each village by teams consisting of government and non-government workers and all those households defined as poor received a health card entitling them to free health services (Saadah *et al.* 2001; Suci 2006).

Categorical/geographical indicators: In contrast to individual assessment, this method involves identifying beneficiaries by an easily observable characteristic, such as demographic group (age, single mothers), ethnic group or even disease diagnosis (tuberculosis (TB) patients or human immunodeficiency virus (HIV)/acquired immunodeficiency syndrome (AIDS) patients). This also includes geographic targeting, in which all residents of a geographically defined area are eligible for the benefit. An important determinant of the effectiveness of a geographic targeting method is the degree of heterogeneity of the population in a given area, with greater heterogeneity associated with greater targeting errors (see below).

Self-selection: In this form of targeting, the benefit (e.g. a subsidy) is available to all, but is designed to be more attractive to the target population so that they self-select a product or into a programme, while non-members of the target group choose to remain outside. This approach is sometimes referred to as 'market segmentation', in which the available products or services are designed to appeal to different segments or sub-groups of the market, who choose according to their preferences, willingness and ability to pay and, in so doing, distribute themselves in a way that maximizes coverage (of the target group) and minimizes leakage. Social marketing projects often use this approach, supplying both higher-priced premium brand products, which appeal to the non-poor and free or very highly subsidized brands, which are available to everybody but more likely to be chosen by the poor (Thomas *et al.* 1998). In food relief programmes, subsidies may be provided for inferior products (such as yellow maize meal or dark, rough flour) that are disproportionately consumed by the poor and shunned by the rich (Alderman and Lindert 1998).

Differentiation on the basis of the quantity of a good supplied can also be used to encourage self-selection. For example, the small loans involved in micro-credit schemes offer a means of segmenting the market since only the poor are inclined to borrow such small amounts. Alternatively, self-selection may be achieved through the process by which the good or service is obtained, for example, requiring queuing or some form of stigmatization such as shopping in a ration shop (see Alderman and Lindert 1998). Attempts to attract the relatively better-off to higher-priced services have been made, for example providing a 'fast-track' for health services, in which the quality of care does not differ but the time spent in the queue does (Thomas *et al.* 1998). Marketing strategies can be used to reinforce market segmentation by influencing perceptions of the nature of the target group for each brand (e.g. affordability vs. quality) or by using advertising media that are more accessible to specific population groups.

This taxonomy of targeting methods is not mutually exclusive: targeting mechanisms can combine one or more of these approaches. For example, the PROGRESA programme in Mexico (now known as Opportunidades), providing cash benefits, combines geographic targeting with individual assessment within qualifying locations (Skoufias *et al.* 2001).

Targeting mechanisms

Targeting mechanisms refer to the broader delivery strategy. This can include the channels for delivery of the benefit and the choice of intermediary for identifying beneficiaries.

In terms of delivering the benefit, each of the methods for identifying beneficiaries can be used in a variety of different targeting mechanisms. Table 8.1

Table 8.1 Classification of targeting mechanisms by approach and method

Method	Mechanism	Examples
Individual assessment	User fee exemptions (on grounds of poverty)	Exemptions + equity fund in Cambodia
	Cash transfers	PROGRESA (Mexico)
Categorical/geographic	Resource allocation formula	South Africa, Zambia
	Contracting NGOs to provide primary health care in rural areas	Cambodia, Guatemala, Senegal, Madagascar
	User fee exemptions (using demographic categories)	Many countries
	Cash transfers	Nicaragua, Honduras
	Vouchers	ITNs to pregnant women in Tanzania, seeds for farmers affected by drought in East Africa, health services for sex workers in Nicaragua
Self-selection	Market segmentation: Programme decisions needed about what products to offer, how they will be differentiated (quality, price, quantity, outlet) and whether to reinforce through targeted marketing or information	Social marketing of condoms, contraceptives and ITNs

shows one classification of mechanisms and also gives examples of each. More specific details of these schemes and a review of the evidence of their effectiveness follow in the section 'Review of Evidence'.

A further dimension of targeting mechanisms is the intermediary responsible for actually identifying beneficiaries. These may be administrative authorities, health workers, community members or groups or, in the case of self-selection, the beneficiaries themselves. The choice of intermediary may influence the effectiveness of the targeting mechanism (coverage and leakage of benefits – see 'Criteria for evaluation' below), the cost of targeting and have other consequences such as the reinforcement or undermining of community cohesion (Conning and Kevane 2001).

There is a small but growing literature on the use of community-based intermediaries in targeting programmes. These studies have primarily figured in the complex emergencies literature where 'beneficiary selection is commonly carried out by its own community members' (Jaspars and Shoham 1999). This choice of intermediary has been a response to the inability of outsiders to effectively target on the basis of socio-economic criteria (Jaspars and Shoham 1999). Local representatives are commonly required to select households without livestock, with little available labour or female-headed households who are not receiving support from relatives. Targeting programmes may rely on community leaders or elders, local government or committees made up of representatives from the local community. They tend to be appointed by the community and their main responsibility is to identify vulnerable individuals and families to be targeted.

Using community members as intermediaries in targeting programmes has been advocated on the basis that superior information is often available to communities about their members' circumstances (Conning and Kevane 2001). Compared with external agents, community members may know more about each others' resources, needs and circumstances without having to gather any data beyond what they see in the course of daily transactions (Jaspars and Shoham 1999). Because community members are linked by multiple and complex relationships, there may be greater consequences from hiding or misusing information, possibly leading to less leakage and therefore more accurate targeting. Also, from the narrow perspective of the funding agencies, the costs may be lower because community members are often not paid for their time or expertise and the community, rather than the programme, meets expenses such as travel and communications costs. This raises concerns about the fairness of imposing these costs on the community. On the downside, communities may face internal political or power divisions that influence the allocation of resources in ways that may undermine equity. The objectives of communities may differ from those of an external agency. In this circumstance, it is important to recognize the potentially divergent goals of the different intermediaries.

Criteria for evaluation

The most common criteria used to evaluate targeted programmes are the degree to which the programme reaches its intended beneficiaries ('coverage') and the quantity of benefits that is captured by non-target groups ('leakage'). In this context, leakage refers to an error of targeting, rather than to its common use as a euphemism for losses due to stealing or corruption. These two concepts can be described in terms of the two-by-two table, Table 8.2, which relates the intended or targeted beneficiaries to the actual beneficiaries.

Table 8.2 Two-by-two classification of targeting outcomes

	Intended/targeted beneficiary	
	Yes	No
Actual beneficiary		
Yes	A	B
No	C	D

Notes
Coverage = $A/(A+C)$
Leakage = $B/(A+B)$

142   *K. Hanson* et al.

Under-coverage, which is the complement of coverage, and leakage are often described as 'targeting errors' (Cornia and Stewart 1993) and provide two criteria against which specific targeting approaches can be assessed, often in comparison with a universal approach. It is possible for a programme to experience both under-coverage and leakage simultaneously, with under-coverage arising from a failure to identify potential beneficiaries and address the barriers to uptake; and leakage arising from inaccurate identification of the target group, incentive effects and deliberate corruption. It is important to consider the appropriate timescale over which under-coverage should be measured, particularly when comparing across programmes. Longer-standing programmes might be expected to have achieved higher levels of coverage than more recently implemented ones.

While coverage and leakage are the primary outcomes considered in the targeting literature, other criteria are also important. These include the cost of targeting, its impact on the broader delivery system and political feasibility and sustainability. When considering targeting costs, a societal perspective should be taken to ensure that the full costs of contributions outside the administrative system, such as community involvement, are accounted for.

More recently, there has been interest in the effects of certain types of public intervention on the broader delivery system. One concern has been the degree to which the private sector is 'crowded out' by the public sector, with implications for efficiency and sustainability. It would be expected a priori that the more narrowly targeted the benefits, the lower the degree of crowding out; however, this has not been investigated empirically. The potential for crowding out by widely targeted benefits was shown in an evaluation of an ITN project, which found that sales of a more-subsidized net to all pregnant women and children under five years of age reduced the sales of a less-subsidized net (Hanson and Jones 2000).

Having set out these criteria, however, it is striking how little information is available to assess the effectiveness of targeting approaches. To the degree that the approaches described below were evaluated, most looked primarily at coverage of target groups and a few at the degree of leakage to non-target groups. Very few studies considered the costs of the targeting approach and hardly any the effects of the programme on broader public and private delivery systems.

Review of evidence

This section provides an overview of the way six different targeting mechanisms have been applied in the health sector (resource allocation formulae, contracting non-governmental organization (NGOs), user fee exemptions, cash transfers, vouchers and market segmentation strategies). These studies have been purposively selected on the basis that they are documented in the literature, they provide some insights into the strengths and weaknesses of the different mechanisms for targeting benefits to different groups and do so across a range of settings. Table 8.3 summarizes these different approaches in terms of the conceptual framework outlined above: who is targeted; what is the targeted benefit;

Table 8.3 Typology of targeting approaches with examples

Targeting mechanism, example[a]	What is targeted	Who is target group	Targeting method	Evaluation criteria
Resource allocation formulae (South Africa, Zambia)	Public health expenditure	Poor people; People with greater health need	Geographic	Equalization of (weighted) per capita expenditure
Provision of primary health care (PHC) in rural areas	PHC expenditure (usually primary care facilities)	Poor people	Broad (type of service); Geographic	Coverage; Leakage
Contracting NGOs to provide PHC in rural areas	Contracted health services	People living in rural areas	Geographic	Service utilization in lower socio-economic groups; Health expenditure in lower socio-economic groups
User fee exemptions	Exemptions from payment for services	Poor individuals; Demographic groups; People with specific conditions (e.g. tuberculosis)	Direct; Categorical	Coverage of target groups
Equity fund (Cambodia)	Exemptions from payment for services	Poor individuals	Direct	Coverage; Leakage; Cost per beneficiary; Cost per capita
Cash transfers	Cash	Poor people	Geographic; Geographic + direct	Coverage; Leakage
Vouchers for sex workers in Nicaragua	Sexual health services	Sex workers	Direct	Sexually transmitted infections treated
Vouchers for ITNs in Tanzania	Subsidy for ITNs	Pregnant women; Children <5	Characteristic	Coverage; Leakage
Social marketing of contraceptives	Public health commodities	People in lower socio-economic groups; Untargeted[b]	Self-selection	Coverage; Leakage (switching)
Social marketing of ITNs	Subsidized ITNs	Groups most vulnerable to malaria; Poor households	Self-selection; Characteristic	Coverage

Notes
a See text for references.
b Most projects do not directly target subsidies. The Malawi project targeted poor households by product differentiation and self-selection. The SMITN (Social Marketing of Insecticide Treated Nets) project in Tanzania initially marketed a more subsidized, differentiated product for sales to pregnant women and children <5 through health facilities.

what is the targeting method; and what evaluation criteria are used to assess impact.

Resource allocation formulae

Resource (re-)allocation mechanisms are usually adopted to address existing inequalities in the geographic distribution of health services, with socio-economic differences underlying these geographical patterns. In this case, the benefit being targeted is increased spending in specified geographic areas. Many such mechanisms trace their roots to the Resource Allocation Working Party (RAWP), which set out to redress inequalities in resource allocation in the UK National Health Service (RAWP 1976). According to the definition proposed in the Introduction, resource allocation formulae can amount to targeting where they set out to address a vertical equity objective, such as greater resources for those in greater health need. They therefore need to go beyond simply equalizing per capita allocations across geographic areas and include adjustments for socio-economic status (as a proxy for health need, assuming that health needs are greater for poorer individuals); and sometimes more directly for health indicators, such as standardized mortality ratios, age and sex distribution (Pearson 2002; Ensor *et al.* 2003; Goudge *et al.* 2003). A benefit of formula-based approaches is the transparency that may be brought to the process of resource allocation, though, in practice, this may be limited by keeping certain forms of funding outside the formula (e.g. conditional grants, top-slicing) and also political influence on allocation of actual expenditure compared with budgets.

While a number of low- and middle-income countries have considered proposals to adopt resource allocation formulae to increase the equity of health expenditure – such as Bangladesh (Ensor *et al.* 2003) and Balochistan province, Pakistan (Green *et al.* 2000) – few countries have fully implemented such approaches. Furthermore, not all resource allocation formulae have included measures of poverty or health need. This review located two examples where such policies were actually implemented: South Africa (Gilson *et al.* 1999) and Zambia (Lake *et al.* 2000). In Cambodia, a resource allocation formula was adopted which included only population and measures of cost and workload (Pearson 2002) and therefore did not address vertical equity. A study of the decentralization process in Chile and Colombia considered the degree to which decentralization policy provides opportunities to address geographic inequalities in health expenditure (Bossert *et al.* 2003b).

The main criterion against which such policies are assessed is their progress towards increasing need-adjusted per capita health expenditure. Of course, this criterion is unable to reflect the degree to which resources are actually consumed by the poor.

South Africa (source: Gilson *et al.* 1999): Two policy regimes in the post-apartheid period have attempted to address inequalities among provinces in per capita health expenditure.

An initial resource allocation formula took account of population size weighted by provincial per capita income in order to allocate proportionately greater resources to poorer provinces. In the second year, the formula was modified, replacing provincial per capita income with a measure of private health insurance coverage, as public resources were intended for those who did not have access to private sources.

From 1997/98 a fiscal federal regime has also used a population-based formula to allocate block grants ('global budgets') to the provinces, of which 85 per cent is to be spent on the social sector (education, health and social services). However, the provinces have greater discretion over how they allocate those funds. The formula used to allocate provincial global budgets includes population size but is also influenced by historical patterns of resource allocation and provincial contributions to tax revenue. This latter feature tends to reinforce existing patterns of economic privilege and, according to the definition of targeting adopted in this review, would be an inequitable vertical targeting approach.

In assessing the effects of the policy, greater progress appears to have been made in equalizing health expenditure per capita under the health sector resource allocation formula regime. In most provinces, expenditure per capita shifted towards the national average. This took place, however, in the context of an overall increase in resources available for health, which helped to soften the impact of the decreases in funds for the better-resourced provinces. The process of redistribution slowed under the fiscal federalism regime. Most of the richer provinces increased their relative share of expenditure and, in poorer provinces, progress was halted or even reversed. Lacking a mechanism at the national and provincial levels to promote equitable health spending, health allocations are subject to political influence at the provincial level.

Zambia (source: Lake *et al*. 2000): In 1994 a formula for allocating resources among districts was introduced in Zambia. The formula was initially based on population, with weights for population density (less densely populated areas were assumed to have higher costs) and the presence of referral facilities. In 1995, a more comprehensive formula was proposed, which included additional indicators of local costs (index of fuel prices), health need (prone to cholera/dysentery outbreaks) and deprivation (whether the district has a bank/service station).

The introduction of a formula-based approach in 1994 had a broadly positive effect on resource allocation, with inequities reduced in all but two provinces. It should be noted, however, that the formula excluded salaries and drugs and addressed only about 40 per cent of total district-level resources.

Contracting NGOs to provide health services in rural areas

Many countries are experimenting with contracting NGOs to provide health services in rural areas. NGOs are often favoured because of their greater capacity to serve marginalized populations. Contracting NGOs provides potential to target health services to the poor, where it is combined with specification of a service package which emphasizes primary health care. Contracting is being used within many current global initiatives (e.g. projects funded by the Global Fund to fight AIDS, TB and Malaria and by PEPFAR, the (US) President's Emergency Plan for AIDS Relief).

Cambodia has experimented with contracting of management and delivery of health services on a pilot basis, together with careful evaluation of the experience with a 'before-after with control group' research design (Bhushan *et al.* 2002). Two different contracting models at the district level were compared with a control group of directly managed government districts. In the 'contracted out' districts, contracted NGOs had full management control over the district, including employing staff. 'Contracted-in' districts involved NGOs in management support to public sector providers. Health facility and household surveys were conducted at baseline and 2.5 years after implementation.

The results of the final survey indicate that the contracted districts performed better than the control districts with respect to most of the health service coverage indicators. Additionally, both contracting models were associated with a substantially greater increase in curative visits by those in the poorest half of the population, with an increase of 1,096 per cent in the contracted out districts and 490 per cent in the contracted-in districts, compared with 82 per cent in the control districts. Higher use of preventive care by the poorest half of the population (as indicated by vitamin A distribution) was also noted among the contracted districts. Out-of-pocket payments by the poorest were significantly reduced in the contracted districts (with the exception of those contracted-in districts which did not introduce user fees, in which it was found that, because they could not pay adequate compensation to staff, under-the-table payments and private practice persisted). The improvements in equity arising in the contracting districts were attributed to a combination of improved service availability in more remote parts of the district, where the poor are more likely to live, decreased private expenditure on ineffective services and decreased travel costs.

A study of the process in one district with 'contracted-in' district management reveals some of the mechanisms through which these improvements were made (Soeters and Griffiths 2003). Following a period of individual health worker contracts which proved unwieldy, sub-contracts were agreed between the district management and individual facilities which decentralized authority to facility managers. Managers were able to choose the structure of incentive payments, control personnel management decisions and control the allocation of recurrent resources. Arrangements included incentives to traditional birth attendants to refer mothers to deliver at health facilities (leading to a 550 per cent increase in facility deliveries), probationary periods for staff and local recruitment of additional staff, where these were needed. This study also confirmed the importance of reduction in informal fee-charging resulting in the fall in out-of-pocket payments from a mean of $18 per capita annual expenditure before the reforms to $11 thereafter.

Guatemala has also contracted with NGOs with the specific aim of extending basic health services to remote, indigenous populations using a geographic targeting approach. The Programa de Extension de Cobertura de Servicios Basicos

(PECSB) (program to extend coverage of basic health services) began in the wake of the 1996 Peace Accords, with the first pilot agreements with NGOs in 1997 extended by 2002 to 160 agreements with 88 NGOs, covering 3 million people (La Forgia *et al.* 2005). NGOs are contracted to provide a basic service package including maternal and child care, illness management, emergency care and environmental services, and are paid on a capitation basis. There is little information available about the impact of PECSB. Some evidence indicates that the proportion of the population without access to health services (defined as >1 hour of travel from facility) fell dramatically over the period of implementation from 46 per cent in 1996 to 9 per cent in 1999, though there were a number of reforms under way at the same time. Immunization coverage rates are reported to have increased as has antenatal coverage (Nieves and La Forgia 2000; Gragnolati and Marini 2003).

User fee exemptions

Evidence of the effectiveness of systems to exempt certain groups from payment of user fees provides helpful insight into the effectiveness and feasibility of direct targeting, together with the interaction between targeting mechanisms and health system incentives. Exemptions may be targeted at individuals on the basis of poverty (direct targeting) or demographic group, disease status or profession (characteristic targeting). This literature has been comprehensively reviewed elsewhere (e.g. Gilson 1997). An important issue, however, is the conflict of interest faced by health workers where they carry the responsibility of deciding who to exempt from payment.

This conflict in health service objectives between equity and resource generation is addressed in experiments with an 'Equity Fund' in Cambodia (Hardeman *et al.* 2004). The approach recognized the problems of conflict of interest and lack of specialized skills and time to make individual exemption decisions. To address them, a NGO-administered Health Equity Fund was created that identifies the poor and pays user fees for hospital services on their behalf. An evaluation of the impact of the fund found a steady increase in the number of people benefiting from the fund, rising to about 30 per cent of all hospitalized patients. High levels of coverage of the poor and minimal leakage of the subsidy to non-target groups were achieved, with the fund supporting nearly all of those assessed as 'poor' or 'extremely poor' who came to the hospital and benefiting only one non-poor individual. A contributing factor to the success of the fund was the cessation of the practice of informal charges. The total cost of the fund was $1,084 per month, of which approximately 60 per cent went to direct financial assistance (fees, transport and other basic items) and 40 per cent for administration costs. The cost per beneficiary was $18.86 and per district resident just $0.06.

Cash transfers

Cash transfers have been targeted at the poor through large-scale social programmes in Honduras, Nicaragua and Mexico (Mesoamerica Nutrition Program
Targeting Study Group 2002). All three provide cash benefits to poor families in
exchange for participation in specified health, nutrition and education services.
The targeting criteria, benefits and service attendance requirements are summarized in Table 8.4. The Honduras and Nicaragua programmes use primarily geographic criteria, though, within selected census districts, households are
excluded if they own a vehicle or more than 14 hectares of farming land; these
criteria exclude only 2.5 per cent of the population in the selected districts. The
Mexico programme includes direct targeting within the identified localities,
using an index that includes household characteristics such as asset ownership.

A benefit incidence analysis of the effectiveness of the targeting procedures
was undertaken by comparing the results of the programme procedures with
national-level survey data on living conditions, which allowed deciles of per
capita expenditure to be constructed. The analysis allowed the share of benefits
captured by different expenditures to be calculated. All three programmes were
found to be relatively well targeted, with 22.1, 22 and 32.6 per cent of benefits
captured by the lowest decile in Honduras, Mexico and Nicaragua, respectively.
Cumulatively, nearly 90 per cent of benefits were captured by the poorest 50 per
cent of the population in Honduras and Nicaragua, with only 71 per cent captured by the poorest 50 per cent in Mexico. The poorer performance of the
Mexico programme was argued to be partly a result of the revision of household-level criteria in a later stage of the programme.

Vouchers

Vouchers provide an entitlement to a good or service, with the recipient generally free to choose among a number of different providers. The attraction of the
voucher approach is that it can create a degree of competition on the supply side,
with providers vying for customers on the basis of the quality or price of the
service they provide. Depending on the design of the system as a whole, there is
the potential for a voucher system to reinforce and strengthen a private sector
delivery system, thereby potentially contributing to sustainability.

Vouchers are better described as a targeting mechanism than a targeting
method, as a range of different approaches to identifying the beneficiaries and
distributing the vouchers themselves can be used. In the health field, the target
groups for voucher programmes have generally been those who are biologically
vulnerable rather than the poor. Two programmes for which evaluation results
are available are a programme delivering vouchers for reproductive health services for sex workers in Nicaragua and vouchers for ITNs for pregnant women
in Tanzania.

The Nicaraguan programme has been distributing vouchers to sex workers in
Managua since 1995, and allows these workers to receive a package of health

Table 8.4 Comparison of targeting approaches across three cash transfer programmes in Central America

Honduras	Mexico	Nicaragua
1 National survey data used to identify the 70 municipalities with the highest rates of stunting, and 40 of these randomly selected.	1 Fourteen states selected using multiple criteria, including the numbers of poor people.	1 Two departments selected on basis of poverty rates and accessibility of social services infrastructure.
2 All households with children under 3 years or pregnant women are eligible.	2 Locality-level marginality index calculated.	2 Municipalities selected which were involved in a planning intervention.
3 Transfer worth $4/month.	3 Household-level poverty index calculated within targeted localities.	3 Within municipalities, all census districts ranked on basis of marginality index, intervention implemented in randomly selected half of the poorest.
4 Recipients must keep up to date with prenatal checkups, growth monitoring and vaccinations.	4 Health and nutrition component transfer worth $13/month.	4 All households within selected census districts eligible for universal transfer except those owning a vehicle and larger landowners.
	5 Recipients must attend preventive health checkups; nutrition and health education sessions for pregnant women, children under 2, and malnourished children aged 2–5.	5 Transfer worth $19/month.
		6 Recipients must attend health education, attend child growth monitoring sessions, keep vaccinations up to date.

Source: Adapted from Mesoamerica Nutrition Program Targeting Study Group (2002).

services from designated providers. The agreements with the providers are renewed annually and provide opportunities for monitoring, training and, if services are inadequate, for replacement with alternative providers. Two thousand vouchers are distributed every six months to sex workers and, in later rounds, their partners or clients (Gorter *et al.* 1999; Sandiford *et al.* 2002).

From 1996 to 2000 the Kilombero-Treated Net (KINET) project in Tanzania distributed vouchers to pregnant women through maternal and child health (MCH) clinics, providing them with a discount of TSh.500 off the TSh.3,000, being the cost of a net, for purchase from designated social marketing retailers. An evaluation of the scheme found that, on the one hand, 97 per cent of all vouchers received by women were redeemed for a net but, on the other, only 12 per cent of pregnant women had used a voucher, indicating problems of information, knowledge and awareness among both women and MCH clinic staff (Mushi *et al.* 2003).

Voucher programmes require a mechanism for identifying eligible individuals and trying to maximize coverage and minimize leakage. In Nicaragua, sex workers were identified at 50–60 prostitution sites in and around Managua (Sandiford *et al.* 2002). In the Tanzanian programme, all pregnant women attending antenatal care services and children under five years of age were eligible (a characteristic targeting approach). This evidence reveals substantial problems of under-coverage with the Tanzanian project.

With a benefit in the form of a voucher, transferability across persons and across services is a potential risk. In the case of the sex worker programme, it was decided not to worry about transfers across individuals since the recipient was likely to be at as high, if not higher, risk of a sexually transmitted disease as the initial beneficiary. It was also unlikely in this programme that the provider-clinics would agree to provide some other kind of service in place of the designated sexual health package.

A recent study tracking vouchers in the KINET project from recipient through to redemption point reported only one case where the voucher had been transferred from one individual to another; though there were many cases where the original recipient of the voucher could not be located. The latter findings might be attributable to health workers making up names of recipients and selling or giving the vouchers to others outside the intended target group, or the women might have sold or given their vouchers to other people (Tami *et al.* 2004).

Market segmentation

As described above, market segmentation, using self-selection as a targeting method, relies on individual choices about what services and goods to consume and in what quantities. Often there is some manipulation of the service or commodity characteristics in order to increase its appeal to the target group and reduce its appeal to non-targeted individuals. This can also include influencing the locations where it is provided or sold and the media and messages used to promote it. The main criteria used to assess market segmentation as a mechanism are the degree of coverage and leakage, usually examined through the socio-economic characteristics of users of the targeted service, compared with alternatives.

Most of the evidence on market segmentation comes from the experience of targeting subsidized contraceptive commodities, especially when these are distributed and sold using a social marketing approach. In the health sector, social marketing involves the application of commercial marketing technologies to public health interventions and behaviours.

Evidence from Bangladesh, Honduras, Indonesia, Mexico, Nepal and Pakistan shows that users of subsidized contraceptive social marketing (CSM) sources came from lower socio-economic levels and not from the whole population of contraceptive users (Lande and Geller 1991). CSM users had lower family income (Nepal), lower ownership of key indicator goods (Mexico) and lower monthly expenditure (Indonesia). Stover and Bollinger (1989) found that more than 85 per cent of CSM users in the Dominican Republic, Barbados, Colombia and Jamaica came from lower socio-economic groups.

An important issue with self-selection is the degree to which new CSM users are switching from other sources of supply. To the extent that they are switching from full-priced commercial sources, this is seen as inefficient (subsidizing people to do what they were otherwise doing); if they are switching from more highly subsidized, free public sources, this may result in a net reduction in cost and therefore an efficiency increase. This assumes, however, that those who were previously willing to pay were not doing so at the expense of great sacrifice. Lande and Geller (1991) cite a review of eight programmes which found that new users are generally 30 per cent or more of the total and that the number of new users and switchers from other subsidized sources is generally higher than those from commercial sources. No evidence is available about the origins of switchers from other methods. In contrast, a study of oral contraceptive use in Honduras over the period 1984 to 1987 found that the introduction of the CSM programme was associated with only a very small change in oral contraceptive use over the period 1984–7 (Janowitz *et al.* 1992).

There may be geographic differences in market conditions that influence outcomes. Agha and Davies (1998) found that in large cities in Pakistan, users of the subsidized CSM brand were mostly switching from commercial products, while in smaller cities (where average incomes are lower) there were more new users (seven out of ten were switchers in large cities vs. two out of ten in small cities).

A recent study of the distribution of socially marketed condoms in Zambia examined the types of outlets stocking the social marketing brand (Agha and Kusanthan 2003). It concluded that the marketing strategy of focusing distribution on outlets in low-income neighbourhoods had a significant impact on improving condom availability among the urban poor. Demand-side evidence would be required to conduct a benefit incidence study which could look at the actual patterns of purchase.

An ITN project in Malawi has experimented with trying to 'segment' the ITN market through product differentiation of nets as a way to improve the targeting of a subsidy towards poorer rural households (PSI, http://www.psi.org/resources/pubs/itn.html, accessed 4 May 2004). Two products are sold through the project. One is a round blue net, sold to distributors at a mark-up above the direct product cost, through commercial outlets. This product has been found to be more popular among urban households sleeping on beds. The other product is a square green net, sold at a subsidy on the direct product cost, through rural public sector health facilities. No evaluation of this programme is yet available. A similar project in Tanzania targeted a more-subsidized, differentiated product towards pregnant women and children under five years of age through sales in MCH facilities (Hanson and Jones 2000).

Discussion

This chapter has reviewed the evidence regarding six different approaches to targeting resources towards the poor. A key finding from the review is the importance of programme design and implementation issues in explaining observed outcomes. For example, evaluation of the KINET voucher scheme in Tanzania found substantial under-coverage of key target groups, and attributed these in part to lack of knowledge about programme benefits and eligibility criteria (Mushi *et al.* 2003). The challenge of ensuring awareness among target populations is likely to arise across the whole range of targeting mechanisms. Successful programmes will need to identify these implementation issues and devote adequate resources (technical and financial) to overcoming them.

Unfortunately, most studies in the literature focus on measuring targeting outcomes (coverage, under-coverage and leakage) and few studies document the critical 'how and why' issues which both explain these outcomes and provide insights into how problems can be resolved through more careful design and implementation. Exceptions are the work on health financing reforms in South Africa and Zambia (Gilson *et al.* 1999; Lake *et al.* 2000). There is clearly a need for more research in this area. Nonetheless, a few general lessons emerge from existing work. These relate to the availability of information, the importance of incentive effects and the potential cost of targeting.

A critical issue is the availability of good information for programme design and evaluation. For resource allocation formulae, information is needed on population distribution and on indicators of deprivation (socio-economic or health-related). Also, information is needed about the distribution of other sources of funding so that the equity of the distribution of all resources can be looked at together, rather than focusing on the impact of individual sources. These other sources of funding will differ among contexts: in South Africa, it proved to be important to look at private insurance coverage; in Uganda, donor funding was an important source which needed to be considered in allocating the government budget.

Identifying individual beneficiaries raises a host of other informational requirements. The skill needed to conduct individual-level means testing was identified in the Equity Fund in Cambodia and social workers were used in place of health workers to do this. Measuring household income and expenditure is the 'gold standard' in some contexts for assessing household socio-economic status. However, rural livelihoods may be more complex in their seasonality, the importance of non-cash resources and the interlinking among households. In evaluating household socio-economic status, progress has been made recently in using 'asset indices' which combine indicators of housing material and house-hold asset ownership into a single measure (for more information see http://siteresources.worldbank.org/INTPAH/Resources/Publications/Quantitative-Techniques/health_eq_tn04.pdf, accessed 17 March 2005; Zeller *et al.* 2001).

A second issue is the importance of the incentive effects that targeting mechanisms may create to providers and users. For example, one reason why user fee exemption schemes have usually failed to protect the poor is that they are perceived to conflict with revenue generation to the health facility. This incentive may be magnified to the extent that health workers benefit directly from the user fee revenue (for example, through bonus payments), reducing their incentive to grant exemptions. The Equity Fund example from Cambodia is a promising approach to break the link between facility revenue and providing exemptions. In addition, strategic use of incentives can help to increase desired outcomes, as in the case of incentives to traditional birth attendants to refer mothers for institutional deliveries in Cambodia. On the user side, the design of targeting approaches needs to recognize the other financial and non-financial costs faced by users in taking up the targeted benefit. If the subsidy is only partial, cash constraints may still impede the poor from taking up the benefit. Other costs may be incurred in terms of time or travel costs, and there may be psychological costs such as stigma involved in taking up a targeted benefit. These barriers to uptake can be substantial. For example, in Tanzania, in their evaluation two years after the introduction of a discount voucher system for tar-geting treated bed nets, Mushi *et al.* (2003) reported that only 12 per cent of women used the vouchers.

A third issue is the potential cost of targeted approaches. In general, there is little evidence about the cost of targeting, yet the little information that is avail-able suggests that individual targeting can be costly (Devereux 1999). The costs of targeting in the PROGRESA programme in Mexico were estimated at 30 per cent of total programme cost, though this may have been particularly expensive because of the costs of household surveys needed to assess individual household eligibility within the targeted geographic areas. More generally, direct targeting costs are the costs of identifying eligible recipients and excluding others. This may require additional structures, for example, social workers to screen potential individual recipients and, even when this task is undertaken by existing staff, there is an opportunity cost to this time. These costs may be hidden if respons-ibility for identifying beneficiaries lies with unpaid community representatives. In this case, there are issues of fairness and, potentially, of sustainability common to all volunteer programmes. Self-selection incurs no direct targeting cost, but this needs to be set against the costs of product differentiation and branding, although these costs are largely fixed and should therefore decrease with programme size. The costs of targeting need to be compared with the alternative of universal benefits (see Chapter 7) to gain a full understanding of the relevant tradeoffs.

As noted above, most evaluations in this area have focused on the main targeting outcomes (coverage, under-coverage and leakage). They have neglected the other issues of concern to policy makers, such as cost and sustainability. The importance of implementation issues is only beginning to be recognized. Future research in this area needs to consider a broader range of outcomes, and more systematically compare the costs and consequences of alternative methods of directing resources towards those most in need.

9 Protecting the poor from the cost of services through health financing reform

Sara Bennett and Lucy Gilson

Introduction

Ill health often has devastating effects upon household economies, as illustrated in many of the previous chapters of this book. While loss of earnings and the indirect costs of seeking care may be considerable, direct payments for health services alone can throw households into poverty. The World Health Organization (WHO) estimates that 180 million people suffer financial catastrophe each year due to the costs of health care (WHO 2005b). This is particularly likely to occur for patients incurring hospitalization or for those suffering from long-term illness such as human immunodeficiency virus (HIV)/acquired immunodeficiency syndrome (AIDS). While the financial burden of paying for health services affects everyone, it is particularly significant for poor households. Hospital costs can easily throw vulnerable households into poverty, and even drug costs might cause other important expenditures, such as those on education, to be forgone. There is substantial evidence, as described in earlier chapters, that the costs of paying for health care deter many from seeking needed health services.

The system of health financing in a country encompasses how resources are raised for the health sector, how they are pooled or managed and how they are spent. In this chapter we focus in particular on the first two of these sub-functions: that is alternative approaches to raising and pooling revenue for the health sector and their implications for the poor. All sources of financing for health care, both external and domestic, are considered. As all developing countries rely on a mix of financing mechanisms, combining out-of-pocket payments with government tax revenues for example, in order to assess the overall equity impact it is critical to understand how the different financing mechanisms work together.

The chapter addresses strategies to improve both the fairness of health financing and the extent to which the health financing system offers financial protection, particularly for the poor. Understanding how fair or equitable a health financing system is requires asking who pays for and who benefits from services. Such analyses determine health systems to be more equitable if poorer people pay less and benefit at least as much from health services as richer people, if not more. Such analyses do not look only at out-of-pocket payments for care but all sources of revenue for health care. While a health financing system is said to be progressive simply because richer people pay a greater share of their income to finance health care than the poor, the overall effect may not be fair or equitable if this is also associated with much higher utilization rates among the rich. To judge fairness of a health financing system, both the sources of revenue and the use of services must be taken into account. The question of financial protection focuses instead upon the extent to which the health financing system protects the poor when they need to seek care, so that they do not suffer severe financial consequences from seeking care (or conversely do not seek care due to the financial consequences of doing so). While the chapter focuses on the issue of how to protect the poor in health reform, this is only one criterion against which a health financing reform should be assessed and governments contemplating reforms to protect the poor should also seriously consider the administrative efficiency and revenue-raising ability of the proposed system.

This chapter is particularly concerned with the challenges faced by low-income countries. With relatively low levels of formal sector activity in most developing countries, there is often a limited tax base on which to draw and there are many competing development priorities. In such contexts, government budgetary allocations to the health sector may be extremely low. The World Bank estimates that in low-income countries the average level of total health expenditure (government and private) is just $29 per capita per annum (World Bank data for 2002). In some, particularly post conflict countries, total expenditure is considerably lower than this: Burundi, Democratic Republic of Congo, Eritrea and Ethiopia have total health spending of less than $10 per capita. Such levels of expenditure are insufficient to provide services of adequate quality or to meet the needs of the whole population. Typically with such low levels of expenditures, the segments of the population whom it is easier to reach, and whom are also often more affluent, benefit more from government expenditures on health. Accordingly many governments have been interested in exploring measures that will increase the resources available to fund the health sector.

Health financing, perhaps more than any other element of health system development, has been strongly influenced by the international political environment. During the 1980s there was a move by some international agencies, particularly the World Bank, to increase the importance of user fees and social health insurance as a means of health financing (Akin *et al.* 1987). The user fee element of this policy was widely implemented, with many countries, particularly in sub-Saharan Africa, introducing or substantially increasing user fees. Social health insurance proved a much more complicated policy to pursue and few low-income countries moved in this direction, although social health insurance was sometimes adopted in middle-income countries, such as Thailand. A vibrant debate developed in the international literature on the consequences of the introduction of user fees (Gilson 1988; Kanji 1989). Overall a rather negative picture emerged, particularly in terms of consequences for the poor: user fees were widely shown to inhibit access to care for the poor. During the late 1980s and early 1990s, community-based health insurance (CBHI) schemes emerged as an alternative means to generate local revenue and improve the quality of care, while avoiding some of the most egregious problems of user fees. Initially, this strategy was supported by United Nations Children's Fund (UNICEF) as part of the Bamako Initiative; however, more recently it has acquired other advocates, including, notably, the Commission for Macroeconomics and Health (2001). While debates about the advantages and disadvantages of different health financing approaches have continued, some countries and many international agencies have now rejected user fees as a potential solution, at least at the primary care level.

While there has been much research, experimentation and documentation of efforts to reform mechanisms for raising domestic resources for health care (particularly user fees), perhaps the biggest development in health financing in low-income countries during the past five years has been the increase in external resources now flowing for health care. There is need for further consideration as to how new resources available from global health initiatives, debt relief processes for highly indebted countries and some emerging innovations in international financing can best be used to protect the poor.

The next section outlines alternative options for raising domestic resources and their implications for the poor. The section following it considers the same issue but with respect to external resources. We then move on to consider practical lessons for governments contemplating health financing reform and, in particular, how approaches to policy development and implementation can promote the rights and interests of the poor.

Generating domestic revenues

Health care systems, and particularly those in the developing world, depend on a mix of financing mechanisms; for example, user fees are generally implemented to complement resources raised through the tax system and CBHI is commonly initiated in settings where there are already substantial user fees. The degree to which a financing system as a whole is pro-poor, therefore, depends crucially on how the different financing mechanisms interact and compare (Kutzin 2001). For example, if a social health insurance scheme for those people employed in the formal sector co-exists with a tax-funded system for those outside of formal sector employment, then the equity effects depend largely on how well-funded the tax-based system is and whether it can deliver a similar package of benefits to the social health insurance system.

Box 9.1 describes the principal mechanisms for financing the health system. Amongst low-income countries as a whole, the primary source of health finance is typically private expenditure (see Table 9.1). In all but a few of the low-income countries, such private expenditure is made up almost entirely of out-of-pocket payments made directly to public and private providers. In terms of public spending, the bulk of such spending in low-income countries comes from general government tax revenues, with social security spending typically being

Box 9.1 Principal financing mechanisms

Tax-based financing: Health services are paid for out of general government revenue such as income tax, corporate tax, value added tax, import duties, etc. There may be special earmarked taxes (e.g. cigarette taxes – sometimes known as sin taxes) for health care.

Social insurance financing: Health services are paid for through contributions to a health fund. The most common basis for contribution is the payroll, with both employer and employee commonly paying a percentage of salary. The health fund is usually independent of government but works within a tight framework of regulations. Premiums are linked to the average cost of treatment for the group as a whole, not to the expected cost of care for the individual. Hence there are explicit cross-subsidies from the healthy to the less healthy. In general, membership of social health insurance schemes is mandatory, although for certain groups (such as the self-employed) it might be voluntary.

Private insurance: People pay premiums related to the expected cost of providing services to them. Thus people who are in high health risk groups pay more and those at low risk pay less. Cross-subsidy between people with different risks is limited. Membership is usually voluntary and the fund is generally owned by a private company, either for-profit or not-for-profit.

User fees: Patients pay directly, according to a set tariff, for the health care services they use. There is no insurance element or mutual support. This is the most common way of paying for care offered by private providers in developing countries, and is also used as a component of financing for public sector services.

Community-based health insurance: As for social health insurance, premiums are commonly set according to the risk faced by the average member of the community, i.e. there is no distinction in premiums between high and low risk groups. However, unlike social health insurance schemes, enrolment is generally voluntary and not linked to employment status. Funds are held by a private non-profit entity.

Table 9.1 Current patterns of health financing in low-income countries

	Public expenditure as % total health expenditure	Social security as % total government health spending	Out-of-pocket as % total private spending	Private prepaid schemes as % total private spending	Government expenditure on health as % of total government expenditure
Africa (35 countries)	45.6	3.1	83.4	3.2	8.9
South-East Asia (6)	43.8	1.1	83.4	0.2	5.9
Western Pacific (6)	55.3	9.2	77.9	3.8	9.0
Eastern Mediterranean (4)	37.8	24.5	91.6	N.A.	6.2

Source: WHO data (2003).

Note
N.A. = Not available.

very small. According to WHO statistics, of the low-income countries, only a very few (Mongolia, Pakistan, Senegal, Sudan and Vietnam) have social health insurance schemes that account for more than 15 per cent of government expenditure. While a number of CBHI schemes exist, it appears that their coverage is very limited.

What are the policy options for governments of low-income countries seeking to protect the poor through the health financing system? Those which are currently under the spotlight include:

- Repeal user fees;
- Expand tax-based financing;
- Expand the coverage of social health insurance and CBHI.

This section considers each of these policies in turn.

Repeal of user fees

As noted above, a large number of studies in the late 1980s and early 1990s concluded that user fees had negative effects upon the welfare of the poor (see McPake 1993; Gilson 1997). While there were a few isolated cases where user fees, combined with improvements in quality, had improved the position of the poor (Litvack and Bodart 1993), such cases were small-scale pilots rather than national reforms. User fee increases in the context of national reforms typically made relatively small contributions to revenue: in sub-Saharan Africa, income from user fees was typically less than 5 per cent of total government spending (Creese 1997) and appeared to contribute little to improving quality of care. While exemption mechanisms were sometimes proposed as a means through which to protect the poor while implementing or increasing user fees, studies of the application of exemption mechanisms have highlighted the difficulties of implementing fair exemptions policies (Russell and Gilson 1997; Newbrander *et al.* 2000; Gideon and Bitran 2002).

This accumulating evidence has led to a reversal of international policy advice on user fees: World Bank guidance on the design of Poverty Reduction Strategy Papers (PRSPs) now argues that governments should seek ways to reduce the role of user fees and out-of-pocket payments for health care (World Bank 2002). Some countries have repealed fees: South Africa removed user fees for children under six years and pregnant women in 1994 and extended this to all services at the primary care level in 1997. This had beneficial effects on the overall utilization of curative care services, although there were concerns that, due to lack of capacity at the primary care level, preventive services were squeezed (Wilkinson *et al.* 2001). In Uganda, user fees were abolished in all government health units in 2001, and this had a dramatic effect upon utilization rates, with an 84 per cent increase in outpatient attendances between 2001/2 and 2002/3 (Deininger and Mpuga 2005). Immunization rates and use of preventive services also increased, despite the fact that these had always been free of charge

(Burnham *et al.* 2004). Furthermore, there is evidence to suggest that the poor benefited disproportionately. Subsequent to the change, the utilization rate of government health centres of the poorest quartile was 0.99 visits per person per annum, compared with 0.77 of the wealthiest quartile. Unfortunately, data prior to the repeal of user fees is not disaggregated by income quartile, but overall rates were around 0.5 per person per annum (Deininger and Mpuga 2005). Similar patterns were observed in terms of hospital services. One study, however, suggested that there were costs associated with the repeal of user fees, in particular the loss of cost-sharing revenue negatively affected the sense of community governance of primary care facilities, as Health Unit Management Committees had become less active. There was also the potential for negative effects upon health worker motivation, stemming from the loss of bonuses which were previously paid from fee revenues (Burnham *et al.* 2004).

While repeal of user fees appears likely to increase financial accessibility, particularly for the poor, it needs to be complemented by other policies. As the evidence above indicates, utilization rates typically increase when fees are removed and, unless there are additional resources channelled to the health sector and adequate preparations made, the quality of health services may decline due to the twin impacts of increased utilization and diminished resources due to the loss of user fee revenues (Gilson and McIntyre 2005). As a stand-alone policy, therefore, the repeal of user fees is insufficient and must be complemented by other strategies such as those described below.

Even where there are no, or very limited, formal user fees for government health care services, patients will often need to pay a small bribe or informal payment in order to be able to access health services. This is particularly the case in many of the countries of the former Soviet Union and Eastern Europe where health worker salaries have suffered as a result of the transition (Lewis 2000), but the phenomenon occurs throughout the developing world. While there is some limited evidence that poorer segments of the population pay less in informal charges (Lewis 2000; O'Donnell *et al.* 2005), this is at least partially due to lower consumption and it is clear that informal charges act as a barrier to all population groups but particularly to the poor (Lewis 2000; Killingsworth 2002). While the nature and culture of informal charges vary substantially between countries, proposed approaches to controlling such fees typically include improving the funding of the health system from other sources and increasing transparency, particularly through making information on health service prices clear to users.

Expanding tax-based financing

Tax-based financing in mature economies tends to be progressive (i.e. households with higher incomes pay a higher proportion of their income in tax) and, as tax-based financing also removes fees at the point of contact with health care providers, tax financing also offers financial protection to the poor. Strategies to expand tax-based financing encompass: (i) increasing the tax base through economic growth; (ii) improving the efficiency of tax collection mechanisms; (iii) increasing the allocation in the government budget to health; and (iv) earmarking or hypothecating specific taxes (typically the so-called 'sin' taxes such as those on tobacco and alcohol) for health.

While government tax finance is generally progressive, there is widespread evidence that, in developing countries, affluent groups frequently capture more of the benefits, provided through government-financed public health care systems, than poorer ones (e.g. Castro-Leal *et al.* 2000; Sahn and Younger 2000). It is also typically the case that hospital care is less progressive than care at other types of facilities. However, recent findings from a regional study in Asia suggest some important nuances to this argument (O'Donnell *et al.* 2005). First, while public spending is not pro-poor, it is less pro-rich than other sources of health spending and therefore reduces inequality. Secondly, there are clear exceptions to the pro-rich bias in the distribution of government subsidies for health care. In the Equitap studies reported by O'Donnell *et al.* (2005), government subsidies in Hong Kong, Malaysia, Sri Lanka and Thailand were found to be pro-poor and this was largely explained by a more even distribution of hospital services. The authors of the study suggest that a policy emphasis on universal access to health services (including hospital services) is at the heart of the success in these countries. Relatively high levels of spending on health have been sustained not only by economic growth in the concerned countries, but also by political contexts that (for varying reasons) have strongly supported the expansion of access to services. These findings therefore suggest that expanding government tax-based financing for health care, including hospital services, may be an effective means to promote equity.

In terms of increasing the tax base in low-income countries, this is a policy measure which is largely outside the health sector. Particularly in fragile states, the scope for raising additional resources through tax revenues is likely to be very limited (High-Level Forum on the Health MDGs 2004). Increasing the proportion of government expenditure which goes to health may be a more feasible goal. The Abuja Declaration (approved by Ministers of the African Union) states that at least 15 per cent of government budget spending (after loan repayments) should be targeted to health. In practice, in low-income countries just 8.4 per cent (see Table 9.1) of the government budget goes to health. Although there are some low-income countries which allocate a considerably higher proportion of government spending to health than the average, none reach the 15 per cent target. While this figure of 15 per cent has little scientific basis, it is approximately what Organization for Economic Cooperation and Development (OECD) countries spend on health and in many instances would mean a doubling of government funding for health. Promoting stronger budgetary processes, greater capacity within Ministries of Health to present economic arguments for health sector investment and transparent decision making are all factors that would help achieve the set target.

Hypothecated taxes are simply taxes which have been earmarked for use for a particular purpose. There are several examples of using tax revenues from tobacco and alcohol to finance health services, but revenues from such taxes are typically limited and are used to finance a small part of health services (such as health promotion services). Other sorts of taxes (such as sales tax) could be hypothecated, and indeed the recent Ghana Health Insurance Act included an increment in sales tax, which was earmarked to support premium payment for the poor. Hypothecated taxes may help increase and stabilize funding for the health sector by protecting health expenditure from competition with other sectors. Hypothecation can also enhance transparency in terms of making it apparent to the population how much they are contributing to health care. However, there is also evidence that in an emergency hypothecation is frequently dropped, and health funds are raided for other more pressing purposes. Furthermore, Ministries of Finance typically dislike hypothecation, arguing that it reduces governments' flexibility to respond to emerging priorities (Savedoff 2004).

While tax-based financing holds promise in terms of developing equitable financing systems, in most developing countries steps must be taken to redress access inequity in the public health system and to enable the poorest to use health services, in order for this promise to be borne out in reality.

Expanding health insurance coverage

As Box 9.1 illustrates, there are three primary types of health insurance. In most low-income countries (with notable exceptions such as India where there is a large middle class), private health insurance is unlikely to be a viable option for financing the needs of anything but a small minority of the population.

Social health insurance typically works well in mature economies: it offers financial protection to all insured persons and should be at least neutral (with everyone contributing the same percentage of their income) if not progressive in its incidence. However, in low-income country contexts where relatively few people work in the formal sector, membership in a social health insurance scheme is likely to be limited, and there is a danger of such schemes being extremely inequitable. In particular, it is likely to be possible to enforce mandatory membership only amongst formal sector employees who may account for a small proportion of the total workforce. If coverage of the scheme is relatively limited, then scheme administration will not benefit from economies associated with a large scale of operations, and administrative costs are likely to be high.

Furthermore, formal sector workers often have some pre-existing health benefits and may be reluctant to lose these in order to participate in a social health insurance scheme: this has proved a problem in both Kenya and Thailand. If government starts to subsidize the social health insurance scheme in order to appease such powerful groups or to offer them special benefits, then this is likely to create inequity in the scheme.

Several low-income countries, including Ghana, Kenya and Tanzania, are at various stages of designing and implementing social health insurance schemes. In both Kenya and Tanzania, the road to implementation has been particularly rocky and paved with resistance by particular stakeholder groups (such as formal sector workers in Kenya, see Korte *et al.* 2004) and/or low enrolment (as in Tanzania, see Chee *et al.* 2002).

Several analysts have looked to CBHI as a means to pool risks and offer financial protection to people outside formal sector employment, as well as concentrating purchasing power. In some cases such schemes build upon traditional risk-sharing mechanisms. Despite the significant attention given to CBHI schemes, to date, their achievements in practice, with a few notable exceptions, have not lived up to expectations. For example, a systematic review of the evidence on CBHI concluded that:

> there is little convincing evidence that voluntary CBHI can be a viable option for sustainable financing of primary health care in low-income countries. These types of programmes have been found to mobilize insufficient amounts of resources ... there is evidence that CBHI provides financial protection by reducing out-of-pocket spending and by increasing access to health care, as seen by increased rates of utilization of care. The very low and diminishing population coverage rates, however, put the implications of this finding in doubt.
>
> (Ekman 2004)

Although it is frequently suggested that the very poor do not join CBHI schemes the evidence is somewhat mixed. For example a household survey in Rwanda found that although the majority of the scheme members were poor, the very poorest were less likely to join (Schneider *et al.* 2001b). A similar survey in Ghana suggested only a very weak impact of household income on enrolment (Sulzbach *et al.* 2006). In Gujarat state, India, the Self-Employed Women's Association (SEWA) scheme (see Chapter 12) included poor members of the community, and membership halved the percentage of households facing catastrophic levels of payments (payments which would bring households into poverty) (Ranson 2002). Like social health insurance, the degree to which CBHI schemes work in favour of the poor depends to a considerable degree on how they relate to the broader health financing system (Bennett 2004). In particular, as revenues in such schemes are pooled locally, there are dangers that without offsetting government subsidies, more affluent areas will be able to afford much better-funded schemes, whereas schemes in poorer areas will struggle to survive.

The most interesting current developments in health insurance for developing countries focus on efforts to extend health insurance coverage beyond formal sector employees. This may be achieved through: (i) targeting government funding to the poor through subsidized insurance premiums and (ii) linking social health insurance to existing CBHI schemes. Colombia, Ghana and Rwanda provide good examples of these trends.

In Colombia, prior to the 1993 health sector reforms, one out of six individuals in the first income quintile who fell ill did not seek care as they could not afford to pay (Escobar 2005). In addition, individuals from more affluent income quintiles crowded out the poor from public health facilities. Reforms introduced means-testing to target public subsidies and shifted from subsidizing health facilities to subsidizing insurance premiums for poor people. Services under the insurance scheme were contracted from both public and private providers. While universal coverage has not been achieved, there has been dramatic growth in coverage of individuals in the poorest income quintile, from 9 per cent coverage in 1992 to 49 per cent in 2003 and much more limited growth in the top income quintile (from 60 to 82 per cent over the same period). The increase in insurance coverage has translated into increased utilization. Evidence emerging from similar reforms implemented in Mexico in 2003 also suggests positive effects in terms of coverage of the poor and financial protection (Knaul *et al.* 2006).

In Ghana, the recently enacted National Health Insurance Act requires the establishment of district-level health insurance schemes managed by local government. Premiums from formal sector employees are paid directly into these schemes, while people outside the formal sector can join voluntarily. Subsidies for the indigent are also paid directly into the district funds (Sulzbach *et al.* 2006). It is too early in the implementation of the Ghanaian scheme to determine how successful it will be. Rwanda, however, has managed to roll out its 'prepayment' scheme to much of the population. Again, in Rwanda, these schemes, while locally owned and managed, fit within the broader health financing framework, and a percentage of revenues from the individual schemes are pooled at higher levels of the system to promote risk-pooling across a broader population. With government support, the growth of schemes in Rwanda has been rapid: expenditure by insurance schemes grew three-fold in real terms between 2000 and 2003. However, most of the growth in schemes was due to increased central government expenditures and population coverage was still relatively limited (Republic of Rwanda, Ministry of Health 2006). A recent grant from the Global Fund will allow for further expansion of the 'prepayment' schemes by providing 100 per cent subsidy of premiums for poor people and those living with HIV/AIDS and partial subsidy for other people outside formal sector employment.

While it is technically feasible for many of the mechanisms identified in Box 9.1 to be implemented in a way which promotes equity and improves the position of the poor, in practice this is not at all guaranteed. First, health financing systems typically depend upon multiple financing mechanisms and it is critical to assess how the different mechanisms work together and what their combined effect is upon equity. Secondly, the detailed design and implementation processes for health financing mechanisms frequently mean that they do not end up serving the needs of the poor. Understanding implementation processes and how they may be captured by non-poor groups is essential to any attempt to promote pro-poor health financing. This is a theme which is returned to later in the chapter.

External revenue sources

With many governments committed to achieving the Millennium Development Goals (MDGs), over the past five years there has been increased funding for the health sector from external revenue sources. It is estimated that development assistance for health from governments, multilateral and bilateral agencies rose from $6.7 billion per annum in the period 1997–9 to about $9.3 billion per annum in 2002 (Schieber *et al.* 2006). In the low-income countries of sub-Saharan Africa, donor funding accounts, on average, for about 20 per cent of total health expenditure. Much of the recent increase in donor funding has been focused on sub-Saharan African countries facing severe HIV/AIDS epidemics: in the period 2002–4 many of these countries saw 400–1,000 per cent increases in external aid flows to tackle HIV/AIDS (Lewis 2005). A considerable proportion of the growth in health financing has been channelled through new public/private partnerships, such as the Global Fund to Fight AIDS, TB and Malaria (the Global Fund) and the Global Alliance for Vaccines and Immunization (GAVI) and non-traditional sources such as the Bill and Melinda Gates Foundation and the Clinton Foundation.

Besides direct funding to the health sector from these new sources, additional domestic resources for health may become available to low-income countries through debt relief, notably through the programmes for Heavily Indebted Poor Countries (HIPC) and total debt write-off for HIPC eligible countries. Finally, although not yet fully implemented, there are a number of new global taxes or innovative methods being developed to increase the level of earmarked resources for developing country health sectors. Of particular note in this respect are the International Finance Facility (IFF) and the French-initiated airline tax. This section considers the extent to which the processes defined to use these external monies at the country level are likely to contribute to pro-poor strategies.

Global initiatives

The two primary global health initiatives which provide financial support to countries are the Global Fund and GAVI. The statement of purpose of the Global Fund declares that it aims to mitigate the impact of its three focal diseases [AIDS, tuberculosis (TB) and malaria] and thereby contribute to poverty reduction. GAVI does not have any defined poverty alleviation purpose or objective. While Global Fund guidance to countries states that applications by middle-income countries must focus on the poor or vulnerable, there is no specific guidance given to applicants to encourage a pro-poor focus. This is the same for GAVI.

Both GAVI and the Global Fund have created new coordination structures at the national level – the Interagency Coordinating Committee (ICC) for immunization and the Country Coordinating Mechanism (CCM) for the Global Fund which requires representation of affected communities on the CCM. In principle, these new mechanisms create opportunities for giving poor people greater voice in the way in which resources are spent. However, evaluations of the operations of CCMs have often highlighted the fact that these committees tend not to be representative and that the selection of individuals to serve on such committees often lacks transparency and due process (Doupe and Flavell 2003).

Recently there has been much discussion about how global initiatives may increase transaction costs and distort local priorities (McKinsey and Company 2005). Such concerns arise for a number of reasons:

- Countries which are recipients of grants from the global health initiatives and indeed the Initiatives themselves are under substantial pressure to meet targets and demonstrate rapid results. This may well inhibit approaches which aim to meet the needs of the poorest and hardest to reach or which include consultation with the poor or other vulnerable groups as part of their planning processes (Stillman and Bennett 2005).
- Pressure to achieve results rapidly also leads to the bypassing of existing systems, so, for example, sometimes parallel systems are set up to deliver drugs or track utilization data. By not building on existing systems, the sustainability of the approaches used is questionable.
- There are substantial concerns about the sustainability of external sources of finance, which also raises concerns for the poor: if future funding is not secure, government may not be willing to invest in new facilities needed to improve access for remote, rural populations.

Debt relief

In contrast with the global health initiatives, resources freed up by debt relief are clearly specified to be targeted at poor and vulnerable groups. Debt relief holds the potential for increasing government tax financing of health services (as discussed above). The programming of additional funding associated with debt relief is governed by processes agreed by the World Bank, International Monetary Fund (IMF) and G7 countries, which include the development of PRSPs. According to World Bank guidelines, the development of such strategies should include consultation with representatives of poor and vulnerable groups. There has been much debate in the broader development literature about the extent to which PRSPs and the resources associated with them really do benefit the poor (Cheru 2006). However, perhaps the bigger issue concerns the magnitude of likely fiscal impacts from debt relief. First, countries must qualify for debt relief through establishing a good track record in the implementation of programmes supported by the World Bank and the IMF. Once this track record is established, countries reach a 'decision point', at which a potential debt relief package is agreed on. However, the debt relief package only becomes effective after a further period of good performance (known as the completion point). To date, just 29 countries have reached the decision point, meaning that many highly indebted countries are not yet benefiting (IMF 2006). Second, even in countries which are benefiting, the amounts of debt relief may be small. For example, in Ethiopia, debt relief under the HIPC Initiative in 2002–3 amounted to just $62 million (0.9 per cent of gross domestic product (GDP) and considerably less than external commitments to fight HIV/AIDS) (IMF and IDA 2004 cited in McIntyre *et al.* 2005).

A review that looked explicitly at how PRSPs addressed health and the extent to which they targeted the poor concluded that, while it was quite common for PRSPs to employ geographical criteria to target the poor (for example, focusing on deprived regions or districts), it was much less common for PRSPs to use targeting criteria that explicitly identified the poorest households. Of 21 PRSPs reviewed, only eight moved beyond broad geographical criteria in order to target resources in the health sector at the poorest and, interestingly, in four of these cases the purpose was to reduce financial barriers for the poor in seeking care (Dodd *et al.* 2004).

Innovative financing mechanisms

At the time of writing, the plans for new sources of funding to be raised under the IFF and the proposed airline tax are still taking shape. It is difficult therefore to assess the extent to which they will be pro-poor. It seems most likely that resources from these new forms of financing will flow through existing mechanisms such as GAVI and thus, unless special conditions are placed upon their use, they will be just as 'pro-poor' as the existing mechanisms are. They will also be likely to raise the same concerns regarding the creation of parallel structures in health systems and unpredictable financing.

Taken together, the new forms of international financing for health care in low-income countries raise complex management challenges for government. They frequently flow through extra-budgetary channels, making it difficult for governments to decide how to allocate budgetary resources in order to ensure an overall distribution of resources, which will be equitable and efficient. The extra-budgetary nature of such resources also challenges government's overall stewardship role in the health sector. External resources also appear highly volatile, with large changes from year to year which further exacerbates planning problems for government. Finally, the duration of future aid flows is also uncertain. Some of the external sources of funding are meant to be relatively short term in nature, while some depend on performance-based funding, which means that countries could lose or face severely diminished support from these sources if targets are not met and, while there is high-level commitment to increasing aid in order to achieve the MDGs, international political commitment to particular aid mechanisms is not a given. In the face of this uncertainty, some low-income country governments have questioned whether it makes sense to implement expensive (and sometimes irreversible) adjustments to health programmes based upon the anticipated influx of new external resources. For example, policy makers in Malawi were very concerned about the adoption of artemisin-based combination therapy for malaria, as recommended by the

Global Fund as part of the Global Fund grant to Malawi, given the much higher cost of this treatment than monotherapy (Mtonya *et al.* 2005).

While there is current interest in developing some kind of global pooled funding for health that could enhance predictability and sustainability of aid flows to a particular country, the feasibility of developing such a mechanism remains to be seen.

Reforming financing systems in practice

Shaping values through health financing reform

In planning the implementation of health care financing reform, it is critical to allow for the fact that health financing mechanisms act as important signals of value within any health system. Changing the existing configuration of financing mechanisms can, therefore, signal new values – with consequences for how patients experience health care. Such implications need to be considered in managing the policy implementation process.

The role of financing mechanisms in this regard is perhaps most clear in relation to user fees. In the 1980s, the introduction of user fees was often proposed to signal a value change from the position that a person's ability to pay should not influence who gets access to care to the position that paying for care leads people to value services – and so reduces unnecessary use of care, promotes appropriate use of referral services and encourages greater health worker accountability to patients (e.g. Akin *et al.* 1987). The removal of fees may represent the reverse value change, as in South Africa in the 1990s and Uganda in the 2000s. In order for policy implementation to proceed smoothly, such value changes have to be accepted by influential actors, including those responsible for implementation, who are typically front-line health workers. The mixed views of South African health workers about this value change was, therefore, one reason why the removal of fees encountered unexpected implementation problems, including a worsening of provider–patient relationships (Walker and Gilson 2004).

Importantly, the values implied in the new financing mechanism have a strong potential to influence patient experience of care. Where fees are introduced or increased, patients may be faced with two new barriers to access. The increased cost of access is the most obvious barrier, but this cost may itself create the expectation , amongst the poorest groups, of exclusion from the health system and so add to their experience of poverty (Tibandebage and Mackintosh 2005). Given the wider and common experiences of poor provider attitudes towards patients, inability to pay often also seems to become a cause of anger and resentment in provider–patient relationships, leading to further humiliation for poor patients trying to access care (Walker and Gilson 2004; Tibandebage and Mackintosh 2005). Not surprisingly, therefore, investigation of influences over patient trust of health care providers worldwide generally highlights the influence of payment mechanisms over such trust. User fee systems are a common cause of patient suspicion of provider behaviour, whilst systems free at the point of care may be seen more favourably in this regard (Gilson 2005a; Russell 2005).

The political nature of health care financing reform is, therefore, partly a function of the fact that such reforms are commonly founded in changing values. Financing reforms directly affect the performance of any health system in terms of the basic goals of equity and efficiency. They are both ideological in nature and have direct consequences on how population groups experience the health system. Insurance reforms may, for example, have the specific goal of enabling greater cross-subsidy within the health system between rich and poor, so as to reduce the influence of ability to pay over health care access. Or such reforms, depending upon how they are designed, may seek to allow patient choice of provider and permit access to greater levels of care for those who can afford to pay. Finally, community prepayment schemes may, at least partly, seek to encourage local communities to take responsibility for, and exercise account-ability over, their local health services.

Managing the implementation of financing reform is, therefore, not just a technical task but, ultimately, a task of political management. A central element of such management will be how to market and sell the value change represen-ted in new financing mechanisms and strategies to generate adequate political support to sustain implementation.

Managing the policy process

Health financing reform is, therefore, an innately political task and likely to be highly politically contested – particularly if the reforms aim to advantage the poor at the expense of more affluent stakeholder groups which are frequently better organized. For example, in the Dominican Republic, the physicians' association and private clinics were judged to be highly opposed to a package of health reform measures that included stronger regulation and expansion of social security coverage to those previously uninsured, whereas non-governmental organizations (NGOs) and community groups, who would be likely to support measures to improve access for the poor, were largely non-mobilized (Glassman *et al.* 1999). Similarly, in Mexico, health worker trade unions and existing bene-ficiaries of social security schemes were viewed to be strong and mobilized opponents to health financing reforms aiming to achieve universal coverage (Barraza-Lorens *et al.* 2002). Groups which are highly mobilized against reforms may either sink the reform process before it has started or seek modifi-cations in the substance of the reforms in order to secure their own interests. For example, in Korea, physician opposition to pharmaceutical reform, which would adversely affect physician income, led to increases in medical fees in order to compensate physicians for income loss (Kwon 2003).

In order to secure the successful adoption of contested health financing pol-icies, policy champions are likely to need to engage in a conscious strategy to manage the political process (Thomas and Gilson 2004). Strategies may include, for example, mobilizing groups which stand to benefit from reforms, creating strategic alliances with actors who are not close to the reform process but are powerful and are supportive of it and effectively communicating the nature of the reform. Evidence suggests that too often health financing proposals appear technically impenetrable (Gilson *et al.* 2003) and this means that, even if they are well designed, they may be unable to garner sufficient support for their implementation. Arguments for and against financing reforms need to be communicated in simple and accessible terms, in order for the ideas to gain currency and support amongst a broader set of actors, including, for example, civil society groups.

Managing the implementation process

How health financing reforms are developed, planned and implemented significantly affects their impact upon the poor. If health financing reforms are not well conceived and well planned, then it is likely that implementers – whether they are health staff or local governments or a national health insurance council – will have to adapt the design as part of the implementation process. It is at this point that many reforms are distorted in such a way that they do not achieve their original goals. For example, while the repeal of user fees in both Uganda and South Africa appeared successful overall, failure to anticipate the resource needs for the substantial increase in utilization of services and for payment of compensation to health workers for loss of income from fee revenues could have led to the downfall of the policy. Similarly, while there were theoretical arguments to support the original introduction of user fees in the late 1980s, in practice, the failure to develop effective exemption mechanisms and the fact that increased revenues did not lead to increased service quality undermined any arguments that may have existed for user fees being 'pro-poor'.

Health workers are key stakeholders in the reform process as they generally have responsibility for implementing reforms and as they often work in distant health facilities where it is difficult to monitor their behaviour closely. The extent to which health workers understand and buy into health financing reforms is therefore likely to significantly influence the effectiveness of reform implementation. For example, the availability of clear guidelines regarding exemptions and effective communication of such guidelines to health workers were found to be important factors determining the successful implementation of exemptions (Gideon and Bitran 2002). In a study of nurses' experience of the repeal of user fees in South Africa, Walker and Gilson (2004) highlight how health workers' own experience of a policy change influenced their response to it. In the South African context, nurses felt excluded from the policy-making process and believed that they faced harder working conditions as a consequence of the reform. This led them to blame patients for the situation in which they found themselves. Ensuring appropriate consultation with health workers from the early stages of health financing reform design through to implementation appears critical. As argued elsewhere by Gilson (2005b), 'instead of imposing change and expecting implementation, health system leaders must always pay attention to the importance of consultation, communication and engagement among the network of actors responsible for implementation.'

Frequently, policy reform is undertaken during a political window of opportunity, or as part of an election promise (Gilson *et al.* 2003). While legislation or reform documents may be developed relatively quickly, it often takes a lot longer to work out the details of the reform process. While the Health Insurance Act in Ghana had been passed in August 2003, the decree that provided details of how the health insurance schemes would be established was not produced until 18 months later. In Kenya, proposals to establish a national health insurance scheme were produced in May 2004, and it was said that the scheme would be implemented in July 2004 – but this proved wildly optimistic, and the scheme is still not implemented (McIntyre *et al.* 2005). During the preparatory period, governments need to manage expectations carefully so that the battle for people's hearts and minds is not lost before it has even started.

Careful thought should also be given to the phasing of health financing reforms and to the consideration of how this affects the poor. For health insurance in particular, new institutional capacities may need to be developed and reforms may need to be phased in due to lack of capacity. For example, it is common that national health insurance schemes are designed in such a way that those in formal sector employment, who are often amongst the better off, get covered first and poorer groups only gain coverage at a later date. The design of the Ghanaian scheme tried to avoid this by offering subsidies to districts from the start so that the indigent could receive immediate coverage. Where there are doubts about the specifics of the design of a health financing reform or how it might affect the poor, implementing and evaluating a pilot can be effective: this was done with the prepayment scheme in Rwanda. Early evaluation identified and fixed flaws in the organizational structure and also demonstrated that the schemes had improved equity in service use (Saunders 2004).

Finally, monitoring and evaluation is critical in order to determine the actual effects of implementation upon the poor and it is also critical to track processes of implementation and allow learning through doing. Monitoring systems need to be timely, providing 'live data' so that, if necessary, corrective action can be taken.

Conclusions

Low-income countries face complex challenges in terms of developing health financing systems that both facilitate access for the poor and protect them from financial catastrophe. In many low-income countries and especially those facing significant HIV/AIDS epidemics, external resources are perhaps the most important new source of funding for health. Determining how best to manage the influx of external resources is a pressing challenge for health policy makers, particularly in terms of promoting the predictability of external revenues and ensuring that they are applied in a manner which matches national priorities. However, it would be dangerous to assume that the flow of such resources will be sustained over the long term. Low-income countries need to start planning now for how they might replace such external resources with domestic revenues. Increased flows of external resources may provide an opportunity for developing countries to explore alternative approaches to raising and managing domestic revenues. The use of Global Fund support in Rwanda to roll out the prepayment scheme and improve financial access for the poor and people living with HIV/AIDS is a good example of this.

The most obvious place to look for additional revenue for the health sector, that will not place an excessive burden on the poor, is government tax revenues. Few developing countries currently meet the Abuja target of 15 per cent of the government budget being allocated to health. Improved evidence on the effectiveness of health spending is needed to help convince Ministers of Finance to adjust allocations between sectors and greater societal discussion and consensus is needed regarding governments' investment priorities. Earmarking of tax revenues for health should also be explored further. It is important to realize that external resources currently flowing to the health sector are viewed by governments as just additional and not intended to facilitate a drop in government allocations to the health sector. The additionality of external funding requires close monitoring.

While there are interesting innovations in terms of extending social health insurance schemes to cover the informal sector, the effectiveness of such reforms in low-income country contexts has not yet been fully assessed. Such strategies typically place quite high demands upon local policy-making and implementation capacity and there is a danger that the development of such schemes in low capacity contexts may distract policy makers and health workers from more important tasks. In contrast, the evidence on the repeal of user fees seems more substantive: if supported by additional government or external funding to ensure sufficient resources to respond to increased demand, then the repeal of fees has beneficial effects for the poor. In all circumstances, it is important to think about the overall package of financing mechanisms in the country and how they will interact and not just analyse the effects of one particular financing mechanism.

Regardless of the design of health financing reforms, the process of reform management and implementation is often highly politically charged and yet critical to the success of the reform. Those responsible for designing and implementing financing reforms must understand the value changes that the reform embodies and will need to manage actively the political process of reform design and implementation. In terms of implementation, ensuring that those responsible for implementing the reform fully understand it and at least to some degree support it is likely to be critical to its success.

10 Building voice and agency of poor people in health

Public action within health systems

Rene Loewenson

Participation and governance as social dimensions of health

It is commonly stated that people are the centre of health systems and services (WHO 2000). Communities do indeed play many roles in health systems: as producers of health inputs and providers of goods and services for health; as consumers of health and health care inputs; as contributors to the financing of health systems; and as citizens in defining and guiding the implementation of the norms, standards and policies that shape health systems. Yet the level of inequality in health and access to health care globally indicates that many people in fact do not exercise these roles and are excluded from effective forms of participation in health systems (EQUINET/TARSC 1998). This signals the need for greater focus on how people as citizens are playing the role of defining, guiding and monitoring the policies that shape health systems.

This chapter explores the voice of communities, or their participation, involvement and profile, in health systems. It further explores the agency of people, or the extent to which they can effectively represent and collectively act on their interests, take action on the structures and factors that affect their health and influence the distribution of resources for health. The chapter outlines how these dimensions of health contribute to health outcomes. It outlines the mechanisms through which they can be structured within health systems. Finally, it briefly poses the challenges to be met in implementing such mechanisms and providing for community voice. It does so in the context of a world where decisions that influence health, such as what foods are produced and sold or how health services are financed, may be made in offices and boardrooms of global institutions and large foundations several thousand kilometres away from communities and therefore inaccessible to them.

Participation

'Community involvement in health' (CIH) or 'participation' has been recognized as a critical dimension of health systems for many decades. The 1976 World Health Organization (WHO) Alma Ata Declaration made participation a central feature of primary health care. The 1987 WHO Harare Declaration endorsed direct public involvement in health systems and the reorientation of political and health systems to support such participation. Participatory processes have been built across different functions of health systems, as shown in the examples in Table 10.1 (Loewenson 1999).

Despite a wealth of various forms of participation, the term 'participation'

Table 10.1 Examples of community involvement in improving the functioning of health systems

Health system function	Example of community participation
Health promotion	Community food production schemes and village food plots support supplementary feeding programmes for children linked to early childhood education and care schemes at community level. Such schemes improve child nutrition even in poor communities, and complement and sustain state and non-government interventions (Chopra 2004).
Prevention and care of illness	HIV-positive persons as 'champions' have been effective in reducing barriers to use of Voluntary Counselling and Testing as an entry point to AIDS interventions, including treatment and care (various sources cited in Loewenson 2004).
	A community-based participatory intervention significantly reduced neonatal (newborn) and maternal mortality in rural Makwanpur district, Nepal. Between 2001 and 2003, neonatal mortality in the intervention group was 26.2/1,000 live births and 36.9/1,000 in the control clusters. The maternal mortality rate was 69/100,000 live births in the intervention clusters compared with 341/100,000 in the controls. Women in the intervention group were more likely to have antenatal care, institutional delivery, trained birth attendance and hygienic care (Manandhar *et al.* 2004).
Policy and priority setting	The Tanzania Essential Health Interventions Project has worked with state services to integrate evidence and preferences from communities within district health planning and in selecting priority interventions, with positive impacts in reducing disease burdens (Reid and Kasale 2000).
Mobilization of resources for health	Communities in Zimbabwe played a role in mobilizing the resource inputs for malaria spraying and in organizing and sustaining spraying programmes in co-operation with the Ministry of Health (Oxfam Canada *et al.* 1999)
Monitoring health policies and interventions	Civil society organizations raised social debate and pressure in promoting the Framework Convention on Tobacco Control and act as a watchdog of implementation of tobacco control measures at local level (INFACT 1999).

continues to be used inappropriately and often ambiguously in health systems. The same term is used to represent very different patterns in the distribution of control in decision-making and over resources between communities and health services. It also describes a large range of partnerships, with different degrees of sharing of values, goals, agendas, capacities and resources (see Figure 10.1) (Loewenson 1999). As Figure 10.1 indicates, 'participation' may be used to represent passive receipt of information, having some voice in being consulted or advising on health systems and greater amplification of voice such that citizens have more direct influence over policy and spending decisions and have recognized roles in health interventions.

Studies suggest that there is a potential positive impact of participation on the performance of health systems and in health outcomes and that greater degrees of cooperation between communities and health services do enhance these outcomes. In a review of over 60 case studies of community–health service relationships, Goetz and Gaventa (2001) found that the potential for and

Degree High	Community participation	Example
	Has control	Organization asks community to identify the problem and make all key decisions on goals and means. Willing to help community at each step to accomplish goals.
	Has delegated power	Organization identifies and presents a problem to the community, defines the limits and asks community to make a series of decisions which can be embodied in a plan which it will accept.
	Plans jointly	Organization presents tentative plan subject to change and open to change from those affected. Expect to change plan at least slightly and perhaps more susequently.
	Advises	Organization presents a plan and invites questions. Prepared to modify plan only if absolutely necessary.
	Is consulted	Organization tries to promote a plan. Seeks to develop support to facilitate acceptance or give sufficient sanction to plan so that administrative compliance can be expected.
	Receives information	Organization makes a plan and announces it. Community is convened for informational purposes. Compliance is expected.
Low	None	Community told nothing

Figure 10.1 Levels and forms of community participation (source: Loewenson 1999).

responsiveness of services to citizen voice depended on the nature of the service provided and the features of communities. In relation to services, community voice was less evident where services were more technologically complex, provided less as a shared public good than an individual intervention and where the service–community interface was not prolonged (Goetz and Gaventa 2001).

Work carried out by the Training and Research Support Centre (TARSC) and the Community Working Group on Health (CWGH) in Zimbabwe in 2003 sought, for example, to understand better the relationship between health centre committees (HCCs), as a mechanism for participation in health and specific health system outcomes. HCCs have roles in identifying priority community needs and actions, planning the resource inputs to meet these needs and making organized demands on health services and health budgets for these needs and actions. The presence of a HCC was either for historical reasons (it was created some time ago and had continued) or was due to efforts by communities, the CWGH or the health services to revive these structures. Areas without HCCs had all these elements (community leaders, health service personnel and CWGH activities) but without HCCs being present. A case-control study was used, with four case sites with HCCs and control sites of clinics without HCCs in the same districts, with sufficient distance between catchment areas to avoid spillover of results (Loewenson *et al.* 2004). Findings from a cross-sectional community survey of 1,006 respondents and health information system analysis showed that HCCs at clinics were associated with significantly higher levels of knowledge and uptake of services for antenatal care and tuberculosis treatment, use of oral rehydration solution for diarrhoea and improved environmental health outcomes in communities (Chi square $p < 0.05$) (see, e.g., Table 10.2). Communities in areas with HCCs had a better knowledge of the roles of health personnel and the

Table 10.2 Primary health care indicators, Health Centre Committee Survey 2003

	With HCC		Without HCC	
	No.	*% total*	*No.*	*% total*
Children <5 yrs with diarrhoea in the past two weeks	57	11.2	68	13.8
Diarrhoea treated with oral rehydration salts	47	82.5	51	75.0
% pregnancies attended antenatal care	69	82.1	72	37.1
Environmental health technician visited in the past month	190	37.1	95	19.2
Average number of immunization outreach campaigns in the year (2002)	11.3		0.5	
Know what the district nursing officer does	54	10.5	23	4.6

Source: Loewenson *et al.* (2004).

organization of their health services. There was some evidence, in terms of drug availability and staffing, of improved health resources at clinics with HCCs. HCCs with good co-operative relationships with health authorities performed better than those that were less well accepted by these authorities. Key informant and communities interviews indicated that the HCCs provided an important mechanism for enhancing communication flow between communities and health services and for promoting health action within communities, particularly where health personnel themselves had a strong orientation towards primary health care (Loewenson et al. 2004).

In a similar assessment, CHESSORE in Zambia found that HCCs improved health system performance and enhanced resource flow to low-income rural communities between 1994 and 1998 through a range of mechanisms. They improved information flow on activities for malaria prevention in the community, established channels of communication between communities and health services and made input to local public health programmes. Key informant interviewees cited a number of benefits achieved through the HCCs, including imparting knowledge through health education, creation of new health posts through their influence on construction and sitting of posts and improving community preparedness for disease outbreaks. These improvements were reported to have led to reductions in prevalence rates for malaria and sexually transmitted infections (Ngulube et al. 2004).

However, these two studies also reported a number of factors constraining the representativeness, performance and power of HCCs, including weak participation from the poorest groups, limited access to resources, information and training, resistance from health professionals who perceive them as interfering in primarily technical decisions and weak formal authority (Loewenson et al. 2004; Ngulube et al. 2004). The same problems have been found to affect participatory mechanisms (e.g. committees, boards) in a range of studies (Gilson et al. 1994b; Bennett et al. 1995; Kahssay and Baum 1996; Mubyazi and Hutton 2003; Rifkin 2003; Macwan'gi and Ngwengwe 2004). Programmes that aim to build participation thus need to explicitly recognize and deal with such barriers and do so in a sustainable and consistent manner if they are to build more meaningful forms of participation, particularly for poor communities (Rifkin 2003) (see, e.g., Box 10.1).

Governance, values and power

The concrete mechanisms and forms of participation are located within the wider framework of relationships and interactions between the state and society and the wider context of how power is exercised.

Public action, often but not exclusively by governments, can reduce inequalities in the social and economic conditions that affect health. Such action influences the distribution of assets or the various forms of public provisioning that impact on the lives of poor people and include land redistribution, health care provision for the poor, subsidized food provision, livelihood support and pro-

---

Box 10.1 The WAMMA programme Tanzania

The WAMMA programme operates in the Dodoma region of Tanzania covering 438 villages and 1.5 million people. It is a co-operation between the government of Tanzania and a UK-based NGO called WaterAid that has been operating in the same district for over a decade. The NGO spent some time building its relations and working with the state, to form joint teams for the programme. Flexibility and mutual compromise was noted as important in building this relationship and in introducing a participatory approach. WaterAid resisted pressure from its donors to speed the pace of results at a possible cost to building strong working relations and methods. The programme in Dodoma took the national water policy and developed guidelines appropriate for district and village level implementation, including the establishment of water committees and rules for management of village water funds.

The work begins with participatory mapping in which map building, focus group discussions and other participatory methods (PRA) are used to identify preferences and design the local scheme. Villagers are directly involved in digging trenches and construction of distribution points, and set tariffs for the village water fund (lower than prior payments to water vendors). However, they formally contract the state for other inputs. The village water fund, which is managed by the villagers, is used to upgrade and maintain the system. The community also runs a hygiene education programme. The programme significantly improved community access to safe water supplies, in a manner that locates sustainability within community structures. It demanded changes at state, NGO and village level, in terms of approaches used, management of conflicts of interest, mutual respect. This has in turn demanded patience and flexibility.

Source: Jarman and Johnson (1997).

---

gressive taxation. Examples of such action are found in China, Sri Lanka, Cuba, and Kerala state in India (Dreze and Sen 1989).

Sen (1990) proposes that such public action should be seen in a broad perspective to include not only what is done *for* the public by the state, but also what is done *by* the public for itself by demanding state action and through making governments accountable. Such action is argued to promote the political incentive for governments to be responsive, caring and prompt. The public is both beneficiary and primary instrument.

These relationships between citizen and state are changing, as are the values that inform them. For example, Europe in the early 1900s and Africa in the early post-independence period shared features of state-driven welfare systems organized around principles of solidarity, universality and equity, with outreach from state services used to build trust and legitimacy. The relationship between state and citizens was centred around political systems and parties that backed public sector and welfare-driven redistribution policies to achieve health gains (Navarro *et al.* 2006).

From the late 1990s onwards, liberalization policies transformed these relationships, particularly in low-income developing countries where they were applied as 'structural adjustment programmes'. Flexible labour markets and public sector reforms undermined the tax base, income and employment security that underpinned the welfare state. Privatization and commercialization of state-owned enterprises undermined the quality and outreach of state services. This was associated with increased out-of-pocket financing (e.g. user fees), reduced risk pooling and cross-subsidization needed for equitable finance of services and increased poverty and exclusion from services (EQUINET/TARSC 1998, 2000; Breman and Shelton 2001; Bond and Dor 2003b). According to the Commission on Macroeconomics and Health, 'the majority of studies in Africa, whether theoretical or empirical, are negative towards structural adjustment and its effects on health outcomes' (Breman and Shelton 2001).

Global trade policies further limited the authority and policy flexibility of the state. The weakened public sector was not able to implement the redistributive role of the health sector critical for equity, de-legitimizing the state and demoralizing communities (Bond and Dor 2003b; Mackintosh and Koivusalo 2004). Post-independent governments in Africa had, for example, significantly widened coverage of and access to primary health care and district health services primarily through the expansion of public sector services, particularly to underserved, low-income rural communities (EQUINET/TARSC 1998; EQUINET Steering Committee 2000). While many of these improvements were implemented in a manner where decision-making was centralized and weakly transparent to communities, trends towards commercialization of health services through fee charges and privatization of essential health-related services like water supplies changed the status of communities – from citizens with public rights and responsibilities into consumers with market power, or lack of it. This weakened the ability of poor communities to demand and access such services (Van Rensburg and Fourie 1994; MSP 2004).

Within this scenario, non-state organizations and associations of people within civil society became more prominent and more diverse, raising demands for accountability, participation and compliance with human rights. One indicator of this is the growth in numbers of civil society organizations. Chuengsatiansup (2001) reports, for example, that non-profit organizations in Africa increased from 1,506 in 1985 to more than 20,000 in 1994. Similar massive rates of growth were recorded also in East and West Europe and in the United States. States were challenged to take on new roles of facilitating and coordinating the roles of these actors and of ensuring legitimacy of and operation around national policies and values.

While this may appear to have opened up the space for people's participation in health systems, there is also evidence that it has been the more powerful medical interest groups or the wealthier urban elites who have been able to exact concessions under these reforms, sometimes at the cost of the poorer, less organized rural health workers as well as the urban and rural poor (Van Rensburg and Fourie 1994; Bennett *et al.* 1995). Tudor Hart's inverse care law posits that the availability of good medical care tends to vary inversely with the need for it in the population served (Hart 1971). The distribution of benefits from new technologies and services generally follow this law. New medical technology is often first available through the private sector and so preferentially distributed in favour of wealthier groups (Victora *et al.* 2001). The stronger voice of these groups may also crowd out less effectively voiced demand by poorer sections for the health inputs they need.

This has raised new debates on how to strengthen the voice of poor communities in health. While the primary focus for communities is at national level, marginalized communities now also need to gain voice in systems where decisions affecting health and livelihoods are made beyond the national level in global institutions and exchanges and within the boardrooms of foundations and multinational companies. What forms of state–citizen interaction and what vehicles of state authority can speak with, rather than only speaking for, such communities and in so doing strengthen the accountability and authority of states? What forms and rules of fair process are needed to give voice and weight to the health claims of poor communities within this environment (Storey 1989; Lafond 1991; Kalumba 1997)?

Organizing power: institutions and processes for people's voice in health

Historically, public health planning has tended to be a top-down process, based on expert identification of priorities and the strategies to address them. This is intensified by curative medical systems that are hierarchical, mystified and paternalistic to clients, that have been built on traditions of clinical autonomy in decision-making and that are poorly prepared to take on other interests in decision-making. Communities on their side often lack the 'language', information, cohesion, organizational structures and capacities for effectively engaging in these competing spheres of authority and can become powerless and distrustful in the process. The competing claims for health resources have sharpened the demand for forms of 'public action' that overcome such historical barriers, particularly if the Tudor Hart inverse care law is to be addressed. Such action may raise the visibility, recognition and inclusion of community voice and roles in health systems.

This section focuses on two aspects of such public action:

- How do people, and particularly marginalized communities, strengthen their social organization to claim health entitlements and demand state and private sector action? What forms of action can communities take themselves?

- How does public action ensure responsiveness and accountability of states, and private and donor funded services? How is public action reinforced by policy and institutional change?

Social organization to claim health entitlements

Communities organize through a range of voluntary associations that draw from neighbourhood, work, social and other connections to satisfy shared necessities or interests and to relate collectively to the state. Civil society is the sphere where interest groups and individuals come together, formulate and articulate their interests and negotiate conflict. It is a bridge between individual citizen interests and the state.

Social networks, faith-based organizations, trade unions and other community organizations have provided an important means for poor households to respond to a range of health challenges. As noted in the section 'Governance, values and power' in this chapter, while these organizations have been a long-standing feature of health systems, there has been a growth in diversity and number of civil society organizations, both in terms of those that network community groups and those that deliver services.

The acquired immunodeficiency syndrome (AIDS) epidemic has, for example, brought new recognition to these forms of community organization, given their many roles in the response to AIDS. These include promoting societal debate over gender violence, negotiating the employment rights of workers with human immunodeficiency virus (HIV), organizing the sharing of responsibilities in communities for caring, providing employment to families of the deceased, carrying out collective production and group gardens for households affected by AIDS and providing counselling and social support (Williams and Ray 1995; Blinkhoff et al. 1999; UNESCO/UNAIDS 2000; SAfAIDS 2000–2003).

These social networks have also enabled people to organize collectively over their health claims. Community-based organizations draw information and social attitudes from communities and bring these to the attention of authorities. These organizations use participatory appraisal methods that involve community members to identify poor households and their needs. These methods have been found to be more valid, more transparent and more acceptable to communities in identifying beneficiaries of programmes than administrative measures used by bureaucracies (Simanovitz 1998; Gwatkin 2000b). Hence, for example, the Tanzania Essential Health Interventions Project has strengthened the use of evidence on disease burdens and cost-effectiveness of available interventions in health planning. Within this framework, participatory methods have been used to draw evidence on community priorities and ratings of disease burdens and to prioritize health interventions to bring into this system (Reid and Kasale 2000; Mbuyita et al. 2004). Public opinion has also been brought into health planning through opinion surveys, anonymous postal surveys, focus groups and citizens' juries. Despite the range of initiatives, the systematic integration of community preferences with health planning is an area where there is scope for new innovation and methodology.

There is also concern for how the poorest social groups, who are often least organized, obtain a voice and representation in these processes. As noted in the earlier discussion on HCCs, obtaining a sustained representation from the poorest groups is difficult, particularly where their organizations have limited resources. One option has been to link more strongly with weaker groups in civil society (see Box 10.2).

Building accountability and responsiveness of health systems

In addition to the HCCs discussed earlier, there are a number of formal mechanisms available to the public within health systems to build accountability and responsiveness of health services. Such accountability mechanisms may apply to the way systems raise and use their funds (financing), to how services deliver on promised outputs and goals (performance) and to the overall manner in which

---

Box 10.2 The Community Working Group on Health (CWGH) in Zimbabwe

The CWGH is a network of national and local level membership-based civil society organizations, including private and public formal sector workers, small-scale farmers, informal sector workers, youth, residents, women, churches, human rights, disabled persons, people with AIDS, traditional/rural environmentalists and consumers. It was started when trade unions, residents, consumers and church-based organizations, responding to a strike by health workers in 1997, carried out a survey of constituent organizations' membership views on health and the health sector. This survey was backed by technical papers on the major views raised. Members gathered around shared health priorities and strategies to pursue these priorities, to add weight to their negotiations over health policy and to health actions.

The CWGH as a network has been stronger in raising their health sector strategies with health professional associations, parliamentarians and state authorities than their individual members. The network has pooled institutional resources and encouraged co-operation to take issues forward at district level meetings with health care providers, to provide health education to its members, to promote dialogue at local level on promotion, prevention and management of health problems, and to strengthen informed participation in local health planning.

Source: Loewenson (1999).

---

systems build trust, integrate citizen interests and respond to social priorities (political and democratic) (Brinkerhoff 2003). District and national health boards, hospital boards, national coordinating committees, and councils and other bodies involve services, authorities and communities to provide mechanisms for dialogue and consultation over health services. New mechanisms have emerged in recent years, like the Country Coordinating Mechanisms, at national level that involve civil society organizations and that review and monitor the plans for resources from the Global Fund for AIDS, TB and Malaria.

Like the HCCs discussed earlier, such mechanisms have been reported to suffer from ambiguity between their powers and responsibilities. The powers and roles allotted to hospital boards and their degree of autonomy from the ministry of health were found in one review, for example, to be an important factor in their success (Bennett *et al.* 1995). Boards that had little influence over capital investment and financial and personnel policy also had limited impact on efficiency or service provision. The role of an enabling legal framework and adequate resources to support these forms of public action has been noted across studies as necessary, even if not sufficient (Bennett *et al.* 1995; Loewenson *et al.* 2004) (see Box 10.3).

Brinkerhoff (2003) summarizes both the complexity and the situation-specific context for the strategies within health systems for building accountability. These strategies include regulation, oversight, monitoring, public reporting (particularly for financial issues), ensuring clear and short feedback chains between management and service providers and providing incentives for responsive performance. Decentralization policies, introduced under health reforms in the 1990s, were argued to strengthen such mechanisms and improve accountability and quality of services by bringing authority closer to the people (Mogedal and Hodne Steen 1995; MoHCW/SDU 1997).

In practice, the extent to which the policy intentions of decentralization delivered on promises of services being more responsive and transparent to communities depended in part on how far the services themselves were given greater powers at district and local levels, on the adequacy and control over resources and on the extent of investment in local structures to take on new roles. The policies were introduced in some places with poor communication to communities and local health workers and thus poor understanding of their content or implications (Community Working Group on Health 1997). Improved information flow and dialogue between providers and communities has been found to be critical to accountability mechanisms and a potential gain in decentralization (George 2003; Hutchinson and LaFond 2004). Poor communication thus undermines this gain and raises the potential for conflict over authority (George 2003).

The policies reflected dilemmas facing both central and local authorities. Where the appointment of hospital boards was done by central government, studies reported little accountability to the public. Where few responsibilities were delegated in practice, particularly over revenue raising and retention, financial controls and staffing, boards had weak ability to make significant impacts on

Box 10.3 Participation in urban planning and management in Bolivia

In Bolivia, the Law of Popular Participation (LPP) (1994) provides a legal framework for participation of local institutions inside municipal boundaries:

- In planning, to draw up participatory plans to determine how new resources made available by the LPP should be spent by municipal governments;
- In management, to oversee management of projects in participatory plans;
- In auditing, to ensure stipulations of the LPP are respected and that funds are disbursed and accounts transparent.

The LPP makes available a range of new resources:
- 100 per cent increase in central government grants to cover new responsibilities;
- Direct funding from international funding agencies;
- Counterpart donor-government funds such as the social investment fund and the campesino development fund.

No more than 10 per cent of these funds is to be spent on running costs and 90 per cent is for implementation of projects.

The LPP recognizes various forms of local councils or committees (OTBs) that are made up of local groups, have jurisdiction over a territory, and are responsible for co-managing LPP resources and auditing how muncipalities manage assets and incomes. Municipal strengthening units have assisted in training and facilitation of local plan development. Participatory methods (PRA) are used, mixed with stakeholder analysis, working with local NGOs. Vigilance committees link councils to OTBs as a watchdog of local government activities, and have the right also to report directly to the Finance Ministry, who must investigate their complaint.

The LPP is reported to have made a real shift in authority, transferring revenue and authority from central to local level, providing concrete legally backed measures for participation, introducing new participatory planning methods, and involving NGOs in capacity and technical support.

Source: Blackburn and Holland (1998).

hospital performance (Bennett *et al.* 1995). Where boards were free of central control, studies found them to have become more self-interested, placing interests of local politicians above those of consumers (Mills 1997). In some places, weak links with the central ministry of health weakened public health surveillance and planning based on population indicators and led to greater bureaucratic inputs to decision-making, with a negative impact on services that have public-good characteristics like immunization and with little evidence of enhanced community participation or inter-sectoral coordination (Lauglo and Molutsi 1995; Khaleghian 2003). In others, local level planning linked with centrally imposed budgets left little room for local discretion (Gilson *et al.* 1994b).

Across many countries, local planning was found to be weak where inadequate specific measures were put in place to enhance accountability and weak capacities built for participation, even where budget devolution took place (Gilson *et al.* 1994b; Gaventa and Robinson 1998). Beyond ensuring specific measures for enhancing participation and accountability, it would thus appear from the studies cited above that decentralization policies have extremely mixed outcomes when implemented under conditions of poorly defined legal frameworks and with inadequate resources, including staffing and planning capacities (Hutchinson and LaFond 2004). Under-resourced health workers in such situations may perceive public demands for accountability and greater control as a burden rather than an asset and thus resist or be non-responsive to such demands.

Securing voice in the context of local poverty and global policy

Experiences of community voice and agency have been primarily located within public sector health services within countries, i.e. at national level. Yet, as described earlier, national health policy is increasingly influenced by policies and institutions at global level and within the private sector. The commercialization of health services and the liberalization of trade through global (World Trade Organization, WTO) and bilateral trade agreements have imposed limits on the ability of governments to regulate the private and public sectors. Multinational corporate interests have become more powerful in many areas that impact on public health, including health services (Hong 2000; EQUINET Steering Committee 2004). How do low-income communities (and countries) build voice within this context?

Within civil society there has been a growing level of concerted action and networking to engage global and private sector policy influence in health. The earliest expression of this in health was in the baby milk controversy. Civil society intervention was reported to be fuelled by public health practitioners moving into the public domain the issue occasioned by Nestlé's legal suit against professional/civic lobbies and by referral of the issue to the United Nations. Civil society organizations like International Baby-Food Action Network (IBFAN), Oxfam and War on Want played a role in negotiating and drafting the code on breast-milk substitutes, informing the public on the code, supporting government regulatory action and monitoring and publicizing violations of the code (Chapman 1999; IBFAN n.d.).

The most recent expression has been in the negotiation of the WHO Framework Convention for Tobacco Control (Yach and Bettcher 2000). Civil society organizations campaigned in favour of Thailand's resistance to US efforts to use the WTO to force access by US cigarette multinationals to Thai markets. Civil society strengthened public lobbies in support of the South African government in its conflict with industry over its tobacco regulation policies (Dale 2001; Van Wallbeek 2001). Civil society intervention at local, national and global level has also complemented state efforts in Africa, Asia and Latin America to secure for states the authority to obtain essential drugs under the WTO Trade-Related Aspects of Intellectual Property Rights (TRIPS) agreement at Doha, to resist challenges from pharmaceutical companies, to challenge excessive mark-ups of drug prices and to push for global action to make antiretroviral treatment available. National civil society organizations have formed pressure and watchdog groups to promote and ensure implementation of these public health policies (Chapman 1998; HAI 2001; Oxfam 2001a, 2001b).

There is debate on whether such global campaigns strengthen the voice of poor communities. The 'voice' in these processes has largely come from larger, better-resourced, internet-linked organizations in the North, with greater access to funding and power, with less input from those in the South that are organized at community level. Within a rapidly changing situation, this is an issue for further investigation, particularly focusing on the extent to which these influences shape the understanding of the roots of the social crises that lead to global campaigns and the responses to them (Paul 1996; Deacon 1999; Deacon *et al.* 2000; Ottaway 2001).

Conclusions

The previous section highlights some of the new challenges facing work on bringing community voice and agency into health systems. These challenges also raise new questions for such work, which have yet to be adequately answered. For example, global information flow has grown, including that on values and policy frameworks in health. There are new global conventions, such as the Framework Convention on Tobacco Control, new financing arrangements, such as the Global Fund for AIDS, TB and Malaria, new systems for public accountability, such as the UN Millennium Development goals and new and wider social movements, such as the People's Health Assembly and the World Social Forum (Koh 2000; Sheehan 2000). Do these global trends counterbalance and confront the social marginalization of poor communities and the disruption to civil society and state relations brought about by widening inequality and poverty? Do they enhance the voice and agency of communities in low-income countries and low-income households in communities?

The chapter outlines the benefits to health and health services from involving users and communities in the planning and running of services. It presents evidence to show that such benefits cannot be assumed from the mere presence of participatory mechanisms like councils and boards. These need to be backed by clear legal frameworks, adequate resources and explicit investments, mechanisms and processes to support communication, sharing of information, inputs from communities and use of community inputs in health planning and management. The activities that reinforce participation cited in this chapter place demands on health workers, who may themselves need support to facilitate more productive interactions with clients and communities. As noted in the WAMMA and Bolivian case studies, building participation in health systems can take time and patience.

In the context of decades of public policy commitment to the enhanced voice of communities in health, the chapter discusses the various mechanisms for and experiences of participation and public action, and how these have been affected by wider political, economic and health policy. This discussion suggests factors that weaken public action and participation in health services, including resource constraints, information and capacity gaps, bureaucratic procedures, health worker attitudes and wider tensions over power and authority. The chapter highlights the more profound challenges that have grown under market-led reforms, particularly where these reforms have undermined the welfare systems and values of solidarity and equity that underpinned state–citizen relations.

The chapter outlines the responses to these challenges, in the form of growing public actions, social networking and civil society organizations and the measures used to make health services responsive and accountable to public interests. These measures have had mixed outcomes. At the same time, new challenges have arisen for the voice and agency of poor communities from the global and private sector influence on health policy.

The positive examples cited in this chapter, namely, civil society networking, community action, legal frameworks and public provisioning, signal that meaningful participation is underpinned by shared values of equity and solidarity. The positive and negative examples of community involvement provided in Zimbabwe, Bolivia and Tanzania suggest that, under decentralization and structural adjustment, community voice and action in health is also reinforced by health systems that provide specific resources, technical and service support to the primary health care interface between services and society.

Understanding the institutions and processes for achieving voice and agency cannot be divorced from the political, economic and social policies that shape people's lives and institutions. It is not 'participatory' to introduce policies that deprive people of access to basic services by using participatory methods or consultative workshops. While the process may give communities voice, the outcome undermines their effective use of that voice and their ability to act on their health problems. The harm to poor communities and the damage caused to civil society–state relations by policies that pose cost and other barriers to provision of and access to basic services, for example, outweigh the gains in social organization and consumer voice that has grown around these policies.

11 Improving equity in health through health financing reform:

A case study of the introduction of universal coverage in Thailand

Supasit Pannarunothai

Thailand D63 015 I18 I11

Introduction

Cross-country analysis suggests that health development and economic development are closely related (Karolinska Institute 2006). However, within a country, this relationship is not so clear-cut. Evidence suggests that the health of privileged groups improves greatly with economic development, while the health of poor households seems to be inelastic to economic development, so increasing the gap between the health status of the rich and the poor (World Bank 2004). Many countries have therefore sought to target economic policy to improve the working of market mechanisms, invest in human development, ensure strengthened institutions and empower people, especially the disadvantaged groups (World Bank 2005).

Barriers to access to health care are believed to be one of the key problems of poor households. Inaccessibility adversely affects both health status and household welfare more broadly. According to the rankings of the *World Health Report 2000*, Thailand performed much worse on the index of fair financing than on the indices of health outcomes and responsiveness (WHO 2000). In early 2001, concerns about the unaffordability of health care prompted the new government to introduce a universal coverage (UC) policy, in order to provide equal access to all citizens regardless of socio-economic status. A comprehensive benefit package is offered, with a user fee of only 30 baht ($0.70) payable per visit, except by the poor, the elderly and school children, who receive free care. The policy was rapidly implemented across the whole country and consolidated with the passage of the National Health Security Act in 2002.

This chapter addresses the origins of this policy and reviews the evidence on whether it has helped the poor. It examines the historical, economic and social context of the UC policy, and then draws upon a range of published and unpublished Thai studies that have sought to understand the implications of the UC policy for equity. No formal 'before and after' evaluations have been done, but time series data (from household surveys etc.) have been exploited to assess change in key indicators over time and several 'after' studies have compared households of different socio-economic status or with different health insurance coverage. The major part of the chapter is devoted to analysing the situation after implementation of the UC policy at household and provider levels with respect to access to care.

The Thai health system and household access to care is affected not just by domestic health and economic policy but also by globalization. International trade agreements have introduced international trade in health services. There is controversy on whether globalization will produce net benefits, given that privileged groups are likely to benefit and poor households may find their access to services decreased. The chapter therefore also speculates on the changes in the health system and impacts on accessibility to care among poorer households that may result from international trade agreements.

Historical, economic and social context

The base of the Thai economy has rapidly changed from agriculture to services and manufacturing according to the statistics of the National Economic and Social Development Board (NESDB), which established the first national economic and development plan in 1962. The share of agriculture decreased from 40 per cent of gross domestic product (GDP) in 1960 to 10 per cent in 2002, and manufacturing increased from 13 per cent to 37 per cent of GDP (MOPH 2001; NESDB 2004a). Economic growth has been impressive over these four decades despite the economic crisis in 1997. From 1987 to 1996, growth averaged about 10 per cent a year. The economic crisis brought a 60 per cent devaluation of the baht and negative growth for a few years. By 2001, economic growth was 2.1 per cent, it rose to 5.4 per cent in 2002 and back to 6.7 per cent in 2003 because of high investment and domestic consumption (NESDB 2004b).

Economic development and income distribution

Economic development in Thailand has been criticized for creating greater income disparity rather than narrowing the gap between the rich and the poor. Since the first national economic and social development plan in 1962, the Gini coefficient for income distribution increased from 0.414 in 1962 to a high point of 0.536 in 1992 and then fell slightly when the country faced economic crisis in 1997. The share of income of the poorest 20 per cent (quintile) was 7.9 per cent in 1962 and 4.2 per cent in 1999, while the share of the richest quintile was 49.8 per cent and 56.2 per cent in the same years. The proportion of the population under the poverty line was 57.0 per cent in 1962, 11.4 per cent in 1996 and slightly higher at 15.9 per cent in 1999 after the economic crisis. It decreased to 9.2 per cent in 2002 (NESDB 2004a).

One main reason for rising income disparity has been the lack of a national economic policy on income distribution in any of the national economic and social development plans. The plans stress high economic growth, but not more equal income distribution, although there were concerns as early as the drafting of the second national plan (1967–71) that 'the fruits of economic growth should be shared more equitably by people in the urban slums and rural areas' (Stifel

1981). This idea was put forward around the 1970s by Dr. Puey Ungphakorn (1981). An influential governor of the Bank of Thailand, as well as dean of the School of Economics and member of many committees on social and economic development, he proposed a complete social welfare framework. However, this equity orientation was criticized as communist by the military regime which seized power in 1976. This missed opportunity not only paved the way for the instability of the economy in 1997 (as unequal income distribution leads to unstable economic growth) but also led to social and health problems.

Social and health service inequities

The United Nations Development Programme (UNDP) human development index (HDI) can be used to rank countries on economic and social development. Thailand's HDI declined by 20 places over eight years, from 54th place in 1994 (UNDP 1994) to 74th in 2001 (UNDP 2003) compared with a decline by only ten places in GDP per capita (from 72nd to 82nd). Educational level of the active labour force advanced slowly: in 1998 about 70 per cent of the workforce had completed only primary school education and in 2003 the proportion was still as high as 63 per cent (NESDB 2004a).

Mental illness has become a big problem and has been related to unbalanced social development and economic crisis (NESDB 2004a). If family structure is used as an indicator for social cohesion, family life has deteriorated. The divorce rate increased from 22.5 per cent in 1997 to 29.2 per cent in 2002 (National Institute for Child and Family Development 2005). Prevalence of psychiatric diseases increased from 440 per 100,000 in 1997 to 828 per 100,000 in 2002. Depression cases also increased over this period, from 56 per 100,000 to 175 per 100,000 (NESDB 2004a).

The *World Health Report 2000* ranked Thailand 99th among member countries on life expectancy at birth, but 74th in terms of equality of child survival. The worst rank it secured was 128 for fairness of financial contribution to health systems. The highest rankings for Thailand were 33 for level of responsiveness of the health system and 50 for distribution of responsiveness of the health system (WHO 2000). Though this report created great controversy, it left a strong impression that Thailand had quite a responsive health system but that health outcomes were relatively poor and equity of health finance very poor.

In terms of inequitable distribution of health human resources, regional disparities have shown great improvement over the last two decades. The difference in ratios of health professionals per 10,000 population between the northeast (the poorest region) and Bangkok was 18-98 (depending on cadre) in 1979 and 6-10 in 2000 (recalculated from Kangwanpornsiri *et al.* 2003: 19). Better distribution was the result of building more public hospitals at provincial and district levels.

In some respects, Thailand has been more fortunate than other countries. With increased democracy, academics and the middle-class have been the driving force for three big areas of reform: political, bureaucratic and health (Poolcharoen *et al.* 2000). The people's constitution of 1997 laid down equity as an important principle for the society, including greater transparency in the bureaucracy as well as decentralization of power to local government. These circumstances are leading to the long-term development of sound social institutions including those of academia, the political sphere and civil society (Chuengsatiansup 2004; Phoolcharoen 2004).

Methodological challenges in monitoring health equity

To explore the effectiveness of health and economic policies in improving household welfare and health status, household-level data are the most informative. Some policies can be evaluated rapidly, such as access to health care, whilst many policies need a longer time frame, such as those to improve income distribution or health outcomes. Thailand has a long and valuable record of household surveys (health and welfare and socio-economic surveys, SESs).

However, household surveys are only one of a range of important sources of data. Table 11.1 illustrates the methodological tools that can generate data useful both for policy formulation and for monitoring policy effectiveness, especially among poor households.

The household health and welfare survey (HWS), which takes a sample of households in the general population, may not give sufficiently sensitive data disaggregated by socio-economic group. Cluster sampling techniques, taking a sample of poor and not so poor households in the same neighbourhoods, can be more helpful in exploring policy effectiveness (Kongsawatt and Pannarunothai 2005). Analytical methods to highlight inequities are also important. Recent studies have employed the concentration index to measure equity of health utilization as compared with health status (van Doorslaer *et al.* 1993). Standardization or regression techniques to remove the confounding effects of age and sex on illness and utilization can also be applied (Pannarunothai and Rehnberg 1998; Benjakul 2004).

Health facility data are valuable if their coverage is comprehensive. The value of administrative data can be strengthened by linking data from various sources, such as linking outpatient and inpatient data and dispensing data to explore the equity of access to drug therapy (Limwattananon *et al.* 2004).

Series of national health accounts studies improve understanding on levels and changes in health financing and expenditure (Myers *et al.* 1985; Tangcharoensathien *et al.* 1999a; International Health Policy Programme 2004). The share of out-of-pocket spending in total health expenditure is a good index for equitable financing. The share of total health expenditure in GDP reflects the macro-efficiency of the health system (OECD 2006).

Apart from quantitative studies, micro-level studies on the mechanisms patients use to cope with medical bills (Sujariyakul 2000) and qualitative studies on people's changing beliefs (Techowanich *et al.* 2005) can be informative in understanding the causes and consequences of reforms. Monitoring changes over time is also a crucial element in getting at the truth.

Table 11.1 Methodological tools for policy formulation and evaluation

Method	Target group	Purpose
Household survey (e.g. health and welfare survey, socio-economic survey)	General households, poor neighbourhoods	Study the impact of policy at household level, by random sampling to represent the big picture, or focusing on poor households. Data can be analysed to show equity changes.
Panel survey	General households	To be more confident about how policy affects the same households over time
Health facility data	Outpatient and inpatient services, dispensing data	Provide details on type of services used, comparing access to good quality services
National health accounts	The whole health system	To monitor levels and changes of financing sources and expenditure patterns at the national and programme levels
In-depth follow up studies	Certain groups of patients	To explore coping mechanisms of patients
Qualitative household studies	Random sampling of households or purposive sampling	To study beliefs

The situation before the UC policy

Incremental changes in the Thai health care system over 100 years had caused segmentation of target populations and inequity of access to health services. UC was proposed to provide access for all, but faced constraints inherited from the past.

Segmentation of the target population

The history of democracy in Thailand has led to more equal access to social and health services. During the absolute monarchy of King Rama V over 100 years ago, the first public western hospital was set up to provide access to all, especially the poor, after the King lost a very young son from an infectious disease. Expansion of health service coverage became the main approach to reach all, including the poor. Successive governments expanded the policy to build a public provincial hospital for every province (from 1940–60), a public community hospital for every district (from 1980–90) and a health centre for every sub-district (from 1990–2000). This supply-oriented model did not aim to provide financial protection when households seek care, since public facilities in Thailand charged user fees, though at a subsidized rate.

In terms of health insurance, the first scheme was the workmen's compensation scheme (WCS), introduced in 1973 to protect labourers from work-related injury and illness. At that time socialism had a bad name and it was not until 17 years later, in a period of greater democracy, that the Social Security Act could be passed by parliament. This Act provides comprehensive health (and social) protection to workers in the private sector. It shifted the focus of state intervention from service provision to financing, and this approach has proved to be much more effective in providing health security (Tangcharoensthien et al. 1999b; Mills et al. 2000) and in protecting against catastrophic health spending. The WCS still functions independently of the social security scheme (SSS) established later, even though their population groups are similar, covering about 10 per cent of the population.

The civil service has played a lead role in social development and modernization. Indeed, the civil servant medical benefit scheme (CSMBS) provides the most generous medical protection, covering all civil servants and their dependents (parents, spouse and children). This non-contributory tax-financed scheme has been heavily criticized (Tangcharoensathien et al. 2001; Mills et al. 2005) for escalating costs related to its retrospective reimbursement system based on fee-for-service (though costs are also increased by its relatively high share of elderly beneficiaries).

The rest of the population had implicit health coverage in the sense that they could always ask for free care at a public facility, but it was not until 1975 that the government set up an additional health budget to encourage public health facilities to exempt low-income households. They were excused user fees if they showed a low-income card which was issued every three years to individuals and households with income below the poverty line. The low-income card scheme (LICS) later expanded its coverage to other underprivileged groups such as the elderly, children younger than 12 years, the disabled as well as religious and community leaders. The scheme had the highest coverage – eventually more than 25 million people (40 per cent of the total population) – but with limited government subsidy (about 25 per cent of the total government health budget). The voluntary health card scheme (VHCS) emerged around 1983 to provide health coverage for those just above the poverty line, and reached its highest population coverage of 16 per cent after the economic crisis. Despite these various schemes, the uninsured population remained as high as one-third of the total population in 1999 (Pannarunothai *et al.* 2000).

Sources of finance and household contribution

When government policy was based on expanding coverage of health services to rural areas, the impact in terms of public health expenditure as a share of total health expenditure was minimal. Myers *et al.* (1985) first analysed health care financing in Thailand, finding that total health expenditure was 4.6 per cent of GDP, two-thirds was from household spending, and only 26.4 per cent of the total was contributed by the government and channelled through public facilities, with 3.8 per cent of the total channelled through the CSMBS. At that time, the contribution from the WCS was only 0.5 per cent of total health expenditure.

When Thailand introduced a contractual model of health financing with the SSS, it had little impact on the national health account (Tangcharoensathien *et al.* 1999a). By 1994 the SSS and WCS contributed only 3.0 per cent of total health expenditure, but the share of the CSMBS had increased from 3.8 per cent to 9.0 per cent. The government contribution had also increased to 36.7 per cent as the government expanded population coverage of the LICS. A subsequent financing study found that the share of household health expenditure in total health expenditure had decreased, suggesting that government health coverage policies (e.g. expanding the LICS and marketing the VHCS) were beginning to affect the national health account (Tangcharoensathien *et al.* 2004).

Subsequently, household out-of-pocket spending on health care decreased dramatically, from two-thirds of total health expenditure in 1984 to less than a third in 2001 (International Health Policy Programme 2004). Though this looks impressive, economic hardship resulting from medical care costs persisted within poorer households, as shown below.

Access to care before the UC policy

Measures of equity of health utilization using the concentration index (van Doorslaer *et al.* 1993) show that overall consumption of health care in 1996 in urban areas favoured the rich, but in rural areas, there was a slight bias towards the poor (Pannarunothai and Patmasiriwat 2001). The emphasis on expansion of health infrastructure in rural areas may explain these differences.

Payment for health services was more of a problem than health care utilization. Data from the national SES 1986–8 demonstrated that health financing was very inequitable, whether by the Kakwani index of progressivity (Pannarunothai and Patmasiriwat 2001) or by the fair financial contribution index (WHO 2000). It is widely accepted that a health system that relies on out-of-pocket payment (the most inequitable source of health finance) puts poor people at risk of reducing health care consumption as well as depleting household assets.

More sensitive evidence on the accessibility problems of the underprivileged came from provider studies and qualitative research. Gaining access to care may create loss of household welfare. A study on financially catastrophic illness in a southern province (Sujariyakul 2000) showed a high incidence of catastrophic illness (24 per cent of uninsured inpatients), defined as incurring bills which exceeded 15 per cent of annual household income. Most of these patients were poor, unskilled labourers with little education. Follow-up of these patients to study coping mechanisms found that about 3.2 per cent of these inpatients would find themselves in debt and 0.2 per cent had to remove their children from school.

The UC policy

As reviewed above in the section 'Economic development and income distribution', the most comprehensive or egalitarian approach to providing equal access to necessary health and social services was suggested in the 1970s. Despite the period of political dictatorship, the egalitarian concept stayed in the minds of many academics and social activists. Two decades later, in the 1997 Constitution, equity emerged as a guiding principle for academics and social activists. Their social movements successfully extended the egalitarian concept to a universal health coverage policy. In 2001, the new government won the first-ever parliamentary majority proposing many popular public policies, of which universal health coverage was one. A few months after coming to office, the government named UC '30 baht for all diseases', established a pilot in six provinces and fully implemented the programme within the first year (Pannarunothai *et al.* 2004). The main features of the 30 baht policy were:

- Protection to all Thais (except those covered by CSMBS and SSS);
- General tax as the main source of finance;
- Copayment of 30 baht per visit or admission;
- A comprehensive health package with the main exclusions being treatment for human immunodeficiency virus (HIV) and chronic renal failure.

Figure 11.1 illustrates the merging of the populations covered by the fragmented insurance schemes (LICS, VHCS) and the uninsured into the new UC scheme. The SSS/WCS and the CSMBS remained unaffected.

A key issue in the UC policy was the mechanism of payment between the purchasing organization and health care providers. The SSS experience of

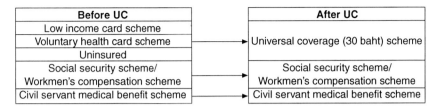

Figure 11.1 The merging of insurance schemes into a universal coverage scheme.

paying for all care through capitation suggested that the financing model for UC should combine capitation payment for outpatient services with case-based payment for inpatient care (based on diagnosis-related groups within a global budget) in order to avoid adverse selection problems at the tertiary level and reduce the risk of under-treatment (Health Systems Research Institute 2001).

The proposal was easy to recommend but difficult to implement. Restrictions on the additional funding made available to the UC scheme have meant that capitation payments and case-based payments have been lower than what was needed to cover fully the cost of care (Pannarunothai *et al.* 2004).

Effects of the UC policy

Various research activities were undertaken to evaluate the effectiveness of the UC policy. Their main findings are reviewed here.

Uptake of UC benefits by the insured

As early as six months after implementation, a household survey was undertaken in four pilot provinces to check for policy effectiveness (Pannarunothai *et al.* 2002). Of particular concern was the uptake rate (i.e. were people falling ill seeking care but paying out-of-pocket rather than using their UC benefit). Reasons for low uptake might include fear of substandard services or medicines provided by the scheme, especially given the cost-containment incentives. Data at the end of 2001 showed that the uptake rate for less expensive services such as outpatient care was lower than for hospitalization. The UC scheme performed better than the CSMBS but less well than the SSS for outpatient services (uptake rate of 60 per cent for UC, 47 per cent for CSMBS and 81 per cent for SSS). However, it was the worst for inpatient care (uptake rate of 72 per cent for UC, 82 per cent for CSMBS and 79 per cent for SSS) and for chronic care (uptake rate of 64 per cent for UC, 75 per cent for CSMBS and 68 per cent for SSS).

The poorest segment of the population (household income per capita below 2,500 baht per month) had much higher uptake at 74 per cent for outpatient care, 86 per cent for inpatient care and 79 per cent for chronic care. This at least signalled that the scheme was improving protection of the poorest.

These findings were supported by several other studies. A survey of eight provinces, also done around six months after implementation, found an uptake rate of 48 per cent for acute illness, 66 per cent for inpatient care and 66 per cent for chronic illness. The highest uptake rates were in rural areas and for the elderly (Chariyalertsak *et al.* 2004). The National Statistics Office (NSO) in a national household survey carried out two years after implementation found improved uptake for inpatients, but not for outpatients. For inpatients, uptake was 77 per cent for those paying the 30 baht copayment and 85 per cent for those exempted. Uptake rates were also higher in rural areas (Vasavid *et al.* 2004).

Effectiveness of financial protection

Household health expenditure for the poorest decile was 4.6 per cent in 2000, falling to 2.8 per cent in 2002, in contrast with the richest decile which spent 1.3 per cent of household income in 2000 and 1.7 per cent in 2002. In 2000, about 14.8 per cent of total households faced catastrophic spending but only 10.6 per cent did so in 2002; this fall has been attributed to the 2001 UC policy (Tangcharoensathien *et al.* 2004).

The 2001 four-province study, six months after implementation, analysed financial protection by insurance scheme. Out-of-pocket spending amongst households covered by the UC scheme was regressive, with the poorest quintile spending 7.5 per cent of household income and the richest quintile 1.2 per cent. A similar pattern was evident in the population of the CSMBS (the poorest quintile paid 3.4 per cent as against 0.6 per cent by the richest). In contrast, the SSS households had a progressive pattern (the poor paid about 1 per cent and the richest, 2.8 per cent) (Pannarunothai *et al.* 2002). A second wave of the four-province survey in 2003 showed an increase in service uptake within the UC scheme by all income brackets and a less regressive pattern of spending by the chronically ill (Pannarunothai *et al.* 2005).

To focus on the impact of the UC policy on poor households, a new study was performed covering the same four provinces but including Bangkok. The study purposively sampled poor families identified by hospital medico-social workers and took further samples of poor and less poor households in the same neighbourhood. The study revealed that relative to the rich, the poor were more likely to be uninsured, more likely to have an acute illness, more likely to use services and more likely to make use of UC benefits (Kongsawatt and Pannarunothai 2005). The higher uptake of benefits to some extent reduced the burden of out-of-pocket spending.

A household survey of the elderly in the poorest Thai province had very similar findings. Catastrophic spending related to health was very low among the elderly (experienced by only 3 per cent and 5 per cent of the elderly in urban and rural areas, respectively). How much of this was due to the UC policy was unclear, since the elderly were previously protected under the LICS. However, the uptake of UC benefits was much higher than under the previous scheme and so must have conferred a greater degree of financial protection (Srithamrongsawat 2004).

Implications of UC implementation for care seeking behaviour and quality of care

Although the great majority of the eligible population received a UC card, coverage was not 100 per cent. A household survey in an urban area in 2003 showed that 6 per cent of the urban population did not have any insurance card. Most of them were poor and very mobile and almost a half of them were denied their benefit for various administrative reasons (Suedee *et al.* 2004). There is evidence that many poor patients 'escaped' from hospital to avoid paying hospital bills even though they should have been covered by the UC scheme (Singkheaw *et al.* 2004). Hospitals were keen to charge patients more than 30 baht if they did not follow the referral line or were not able to show 'official documents' according to the rules and regulations for eligibility.

The quality of health care seeking demands more attention from researchers. The poor rely on self-prescribed treatment and services provided by non-professionals more than the rich (Tangcharoensathien *et al.* 2004; Kongsawatt and Pannarunothai 2005). These cheaper alternatives would not matter if outcomes did not differ; but a qualitative study of drug stores showed that the poor received lower quality of care than the rich in terms of drug information and drug safety (Panklang 2004). Moreover, the study of the elderly referred to above found that a greater proportion of care was provided by health centres and district hospitals in rural areas, in contrast to urban areas where there was greater use of higher-level hospitals (Srithamrongsawat 2004). While there is a strong case for preferring the use of lower levels of health care on the grounds of accessibility, there was also concern about quality of care, given that primary care staff was not specifically trained in meeting the needs of the elderly.

Disputes over differences in drug standards between the different health benefit schemes have been widespread. Capitation payment in the SSS has been associated with giving fewer medicines for chronic conditions as compared with the fee-for-service system of the CSMBS (Tangcharoensathien *et al.* 1999b; Mills *et al.* 2000). A retrospective cohort study of dispensing in public hospitals showed that UC patients had lower accessibility to more effective drugs than CSMBS patients. For example, the odds ratio of getting a statin drug to lower blood lipid levels was significantly lower for UC than CSMBS patients. The odds ratios were similar before and after the UC policy implementation, though overall rates of prescription appeared to have increased with the UC policy. This pattern was also observed for the prescription of inhaled corticosteroids, a high cost but effective drug for asthma (Limwattananon *et al.* 2004).

The extent of social solidarity

It is vital that a policy of UC be underpinned by a broad social consensus. In order to assess people's views, once they had had a chance to reflect on the relationships between policy, taxation and quality of services, representatives of the randomly sampled households in the four-province survey participated in one-day weekend meetings to discuss the philosophy, mechanisms, successes and weaknesses of the UC scheme compared with other schemes. People in poorer provinces were more egalitarian than in richer provinces, judging from their responses on targeting, source of finance and benefit package. The poor did not support a revision of the UC policy to target only the poorest segment of the population. They were willing to pay a little higher income tax to overcome the problem of inadequate financial support. The poor also did not agree with charging higher fees to raise more money or with reducing the benefit package to include catastrophic illness only. In contrast, the rich were willing to opt out of UC rather than pay higher income tax. They would like to reduce the size of the target group and trim down the benefit package in order to reduce the financial burden on the government. They supported increased user charges as a means of bringing income and expenditure into balance (Techowanich *et al.* 2005).

Impact of international trade law on poor households' access to care

With liberalization of international trade laws, Thailand has identified a comparative advantage in many areas such as tourism, medical and dental services (WHO/WTO 2002), traditional healing and health promotion (Janjaroen and Supakankunti 2002). However, there is likely to be a negative effect with the probability of 'crowding out' by foreign patients, who consume medical services and reduce the quantity available for the poor (WHO/WTO 2002).

Importing foreign patients or exporting Thai doctors and nurses abroad would worsen the imbalance of human resources in the Thai health system. Research on the impact of trade in health service on health manpower development has linked the success of the UC scheme with the success of trade liberalization. If both are successful, Thailand needs to scale up production of health personnel to respond flexibly to demand. If trade liberalization wins over the UC policy, private health care will flourish, draining personnel out of the public sector, leaving too small a workforce in public services to cater to the needs of the poor (Wibulpolprasert *et al.* 2002).

It has been modelled that if Thailand imports 100,000 foreign patients, this would draw a workforce of 200–400 doctors (plus other personnel) to the private sector. The corollary would be fewer doctors working for the public sector or for the UC system and a decline in quality would be anticipated. This would in turn encourage higher demand for health care in the private sector amongst the non-poor who can afford private health care. This additional demand would drain a total of 240–600 of doctors from the public sector (Pannarunothai and Suknark 2005).

Conclusions

Equity in health has many facets. Experiences in Thailand have shown that political and social development have played a significant role in developing a just health policy formulation. Economic development emphasized growth and trade and risked widening health inequalities. The policy of extending health care coverage was successful in improving equity of health care delivery as rural people had increased accessibility to health services, but did not achieve equity of health financing because the poor still paid regressive out-of-pocket user fees. The UC policy has increased financial access to care and provided protection from catastrophic health spending, especially amongst the poor. Since UC policy implementation is still in its first few years, the regressive pattern of health care financing has not been completely reversed. There is a risk that external factors such as international trade in health services could drain human resources to the internationally marketable services within the country or through export of human resources.

Lessons for Thailand

Thailand made extraordinary strides in its health policy on universal health coverage after the economic crisis. This was a political phenomenon supported by evidence from studies on health equity in Thailand. The egalitarian policy is widely supported by the poor and some academics while the ideology of the affluent groups is still libertarian. Thailand has to learn from these experiences to understand the philosophy required for balanced economic and social development and the capacities needed in health management to implement large-scale social programmes.

Providing equal access to health care for both rich and poor alike has not yet been fully accepted by Thai society, although the government won an even greater majority for its second term in office. To reach universal health coverage for all citizens is certainly more costly for the government budget than just targeting the poor. Many well-off people question why financial protection should be extended to the rich as they do not need it.

The quality of services delivered to the poor is still lower than that available to the rich. This problem needs to be addressed by improving the payment methods together with mechanisms to improve service provision quality. Health infrastructure at the primary care level, in particular, has to be improved in order to achieve equity of both health finance and health care delivery, because the poor are more likely than the rich to seek care from the primary level.

The community of health system research in Thailand should not be confined only to academic institutions. Civil society needs to be mobilized to take part in the reform processes. If both work together, they can monitor the changes of health and social systems to achieve the desired objectives.

Lessons for other countries

Developing countries have to realize that pushing economic policy towards an equity orientation is more difficult than encouraging growth-led economic policy. Technocrats alone are not sufficient to push in the right direction. Windows of opportunity may exist at points along the route of policy development, but the ultimate goal of policy change should be well understood by all involved.

To improve the well-being of poor households, Thai experience suggests that a good health financing policy is more effective than a good service provision approach. But there should be various monitoring systems to identify the positive and negative consequences of policies.

Thailand still retains a fragmented health insurance system and single fund management is not politically feasible at the moment (Mills *et al.* 2005). Fragmented health insurance schemes are very likely to be inequitable and not likely to work in the interests of the poor. Good databases are vital to compare how effective these schemes are in protecting against the costs of illness and in building good health.

Indeed, research more broadly played a significant role in supporting the arguments for UC, in helping design the policy and in monitoring its effectiveness. Although political momentum was vital, it was the researchers who supplied the information on which policy was developed.

Finally, Thai experience suggests that it is feasible to reform inequitable health financing and delivery systems if the right combination of conditions is in place: the economic crisis created a political situation which was open to reform, and fortunately there was both an evidence base to inform the decisions and some practical proposals. In this respect the Thai experience has similarities with Mexico (Frenk *et al.* 2003), where the health system has also managed to move from a system of fragmented and inequitable financing, to a more holistic and equitable system.

12 Promoting access, financial protection and empowerment for the poor:
Vimo SEWA in India

M. Kent Ranson, Tara Sinha and Mirai Chatterjee

Introduction

Vimo SEWA has been providing a voluntary integrated insurance, covering life, assets, and medical expenditure to informal sector workers in Gujarat, India, since 1992. 'Vimo' in the Gujarati language means 'insurance', and the insurance scheme is 'for the poor, and [administered/governed] by the poor'. Vimo SEWA was conceived with the primary goal of securing the financial assets of poor women against potentially catastrophic risks, including ill health, loss of life, and loss of home or working assets.

The objective of this chapter is to assess Vimo SEWA's impact on access to inpatient health care, financial protection, and empowerment. This scheme and others like it are often cited by health policy makers as mechanisms for: mobilizing health care resources, protecting the poor from the costs of health care, increasing access to health care among the poor, and improving the quality of health care. For example, *World Health Report 2000* noted that prepayment schemes represent the most effective way to protect people from the costs of health care and called for investigation into mechanisms to bring the poor into such schemes (WHO 2000). We hope that sharing of the Vimo SEWA experience will help others in designing and implementing insurance schemes for the poor.

We assess Vimo SEWA based on the extent to which it has:

1 made health care interventions more widely available/accessible for the poor;
2 ensured that the poor and near poor are adequately protected against health care costs; and
3 given the poor a voice in shaping health care services.

The data presented in this chapter come from a variety of quantitative and qualitative studies, as well as from Vimo SEWA's management information systems (MIS) and programme documents.

Vimo SEWA

Objectives of the scheme and its initiation

Self-Employed Women's Association (SEWA), the 'mother' organization with which Vimo SEWA is associated, is a trade union of poor women workers in the unorganized sector. The economic security of these workers is dependent on a variety of factors over which they have no control. Their income and employment are uncertain, reflecting fluctuations, among other things, in the local and national markets, in the needs and whims of their employers, in the adequacy of monsoon rains, and in the political situation. Adding further to this uncertainty are times of personal crisis that result from: sickness, disability or hospitalization, death of a family member; and loss of personal property due to fire, floods, riots, or earthquake.

Vimo SEWA was started in 1992 with the primary goal of providing self-employed women financial protection in times of crisis (Chatterjee and Vyas 1997). SEWA Bank's loan records (between its inception in 1974 and 1992) revealed that medical crises are one of the major costs borne by poor women and also a reason for non-repayment of loans.

Vimo SEWA was initiated at SEWA Bank with active support from a young woman officer of the United India Insurance Company (UIIC). For years, SEWA and SEWA Bank had intermittently met with representatives of the nationalized insurance companies. However, the insurers had not been prepared to offer 'non-life cover' (i.e. health and assets insurance) to a population that they felt would be unable to afford the premium and that had been perceived to be always in crises of one sort or another. But several factors contributed to the successful launch of the scheme in 1992. First, the UIIC officer understood the need for such insurance and was determined to see such a programme materialize. Second, the membership of SEWA Union had increased to 40,000 by 1992, which made it a potentially large business proposition for the insurance company. And third, SEWA Bank had grown to be a strong, financially viable institution of 30,000 depositors.

Health components of the scheme today

In order to join the scheme, adults must be between 18 and 55 years of age at the time of joining the scheme (although coverage extends up to the age of 70). Vimo SEWA offers three different policies. Table 12.1 shows the premium (including its breakdown) and the health insurance benefit under each of these policies. Adult women must first enrol themselves, and only then do they have the option of enrolling their spouse and/or children. Under the least expensive (and most popular) policy, those who pay the annual premium of Rs.85 (Rs.15.5 of which is earmarked for health insurance) are covered to a maximum of Rs.2,000 per year in case of hospitalization (at an exchange rate of US$1 = Rs.54). A woman, her husband, and children can all be insured for a total of

Table 12.1 Vimo SEWA policy premiums and benefits, calendar year 2004

	Policy I	Policy II	Policy III
Premiums for package inclusive of health, life and assets insurance:			
Female annual premium	85	200	400
Female fixed deposit	1,000	2,400	4,800
Male (spouse) annual premium	55	150	325
Male (spouse) fixed deposit	650	1,800	4,000
Amount (from above premiums) paid to formal insurance company for hospitalization	15.50		
insurance	38.05	67.08	
Hospital benefit, per annum	2,000	5,500	10,000
Share of members (%)	93	7	<1

Rs.240. The premium for children is the same regardless of the number of children; the total benefits available to the children are capped.

Women also have the option of becoming long-term members of Vimo SEWA by making a fixed deposit (Rs.1,000 for the first policy); interest on this is used to pay the annual premium and the deposit is returned to the woman when she turns 70. As an incentive for members to pay by fixed deposit, members who pay in this manner are provided with some additional benefits, including maternity benefit. The maternity benefit consists of Rs.300 paid in cash to the pregnant woman.

The children's health insurance is available only to couples (or single mothers) who have purchased insurance for themselves. A single policy is available. For a premium of Rs.100 per annum, all children in the household (aged older than three months and younger than 18 years), regardless of the number, are covered to Rs.2,000 per year in case of hospitalization.

The choice of health care provider is left to the discretion of the Vimo SEWA member. Members are eligible for reimbursement whether they use private for-profit, private not-for-profit or public facilities. After discharge from hospital, the Vimo SEWA member is required to submit the following documents within a 90-day period: a doctor's certificate stating the reason for hospitalization, the dates of admission and discharge, doctors' prescriptions, bills for medicines purchased, and reports of laboratory tests done during the hospital stay. After submission of these documents, the member is usually visited by a SEWA employee who verifies the authenticity of the claim. All documentation is reviewed by a consultant physician, and a final decision on the claim is then made by a claims committee made up of the members and the staff of SEWA. Finally, the Vimo SEWA member is notified of the committee's decision, and the member is paid by cheque when found eligible.

Exempted from coverage under Vimo SEWA are certain pre-existing diseases (e.g. chronic tuberculosis, certain cancers, diabetes, hypertension, haemorrhoids), normal deliveries, and disease caused by addiction. As is the case with other chronic illnesses, hospitalizations for complications of human immunodeficiency virus (HIV)/acquired immunodeficiency syndrome (AIDS) are covered *once only*, if the person is diagnosed with the illness after joining Vimo SEWA, or if the person has been a member of Vimo SEWA consecutively for a period greater than one year.

The scheme does not include coverage for the costs of outpatient care. Although members have expressed a demand for such coverage, it has been excluded for a variety of reasons. First and foremost, it is felt that covering outpatient care would be inefficient, as its cost is generally quite inexpensive, but the cost of processing claims (particularly if they were coming from a huge variety of outpatient providers across the north of Gujarat) would be quite expensive. Second, it would be difficult for Vimo SEWA to verify the authenticity of the claims for outpatient care and the need for such care. For inpatient care, the presence of illness can generally be verified by laboratory tests, e.g. X-ray results for those with fractures and biochemistry results for those with typhoid. But for outpatient care, patients receive services – some of them unnecessary, particularly intravenous injections and antibiotics – without any firm evidence of diagnosis of an illness. Finally, at the time of its initiation and during several years since then, Vimo SEWA has purchased its health insurance from one or more formal insurance companies, none of which has provided coverage for outpatient care.

SEWA, through Arogya SEWA (SEWA Health), directly provides limited preventive and curative services through health centres in and around Ahmedabad City, Gujarat, which are open to members of SEWA as well as non-members. In some cases, the health workers at these centres might refer women for higher levels of health care, and they may even accompany women to the nearest hospital. The centres do not function as an integrated referral network, however; they have no direct contact with hospitals and are not intended to prevent women from unnecessarily seeking hospitalization.

How the scheme has evolved

The design and management of Vimo SEWA's health insurance component have evolved considerably since 1992 (Figure 12.1). Initially, SEWA's health insurance was administered jointly by SEWA and the UIIC, one of four government-owned general insurance companies. SEWA negotiated with the UIIC to develop a special package to cover its members. In the beginning, coverage was for women only; included only allopathic, inpatient care; and did not include gynaecological illnesses. The maximum amount of reimbursement was Rs.1,000 per year. The collaboration with the insurance company proved to be a mixed experience. Difficulties arose in part due to the nature of the risks covered (more specifically, the exclusion from coverage of certain diseases common among Vimo SEWA members, including occupational and gynaecological illnesses) and also because these companies had very little experience in insuring the poor. Consequently, systems and procedures were slow and not suited to the reality of

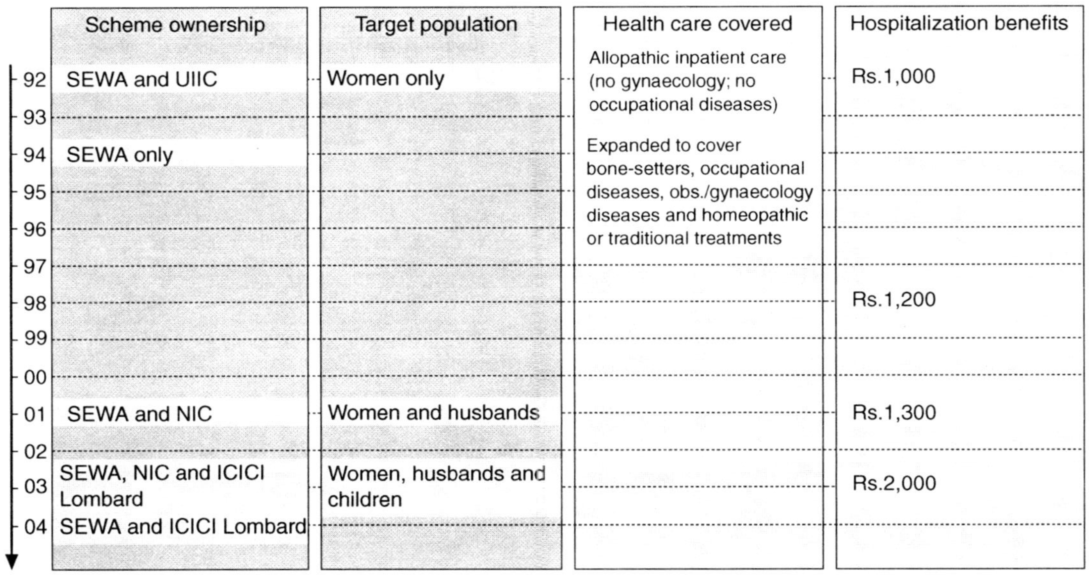

Year	Scheme ownership	Target population	Health care covered	Hospitalization benefits
92	SEWA and UIIC	Women only	Allopathic inpatient care (no gynaecology; no occupational diseases)	Rs.1,000
93				
94	SEWA only		Expanded to cover bone-setters, occupational diseases, obs./gynaecology diseases and homeopathic or traditional treatments	
95				
96				
97				
98				Rs.1,200
99				
00				
01	SEWA and NIC	Women and husbands		Rs.1,300
02				
03	SEWA, NIC and ICICI Lombard	Women, husbands and children		Rs.2,000
04	SEWA and ICICI Lombard			

Figure 12.1 Evolution of Vimo SEWA's health insurance component.

the situation of women workers. In 1994, Vimo SEWA assumed complete control of the medical insurance component of the fund.

In 1995, coverage was expanded to include treatment from traditional bone-setters, occupational diseases, obstetric and gynaecological problems, and, in exceptional cases, homeopathic or traditional medical care (still to a maximum of Rs.1,000 per year). In 1998, the maximum coverage was increased to Rs.1,200 per year. In 2001, Vimo SEWA began offering health insurance to men, implemented three different insurance policies, and increased coverage to Rs.1,300 (under the least expensive policy). Since 2001, Vimo SEWA has again started purchasing medical insurance from formal insurance companies (currently a private for-profit insurer, ICICI Lombard). However, Vimo SEWA remains fully responsible for the enrolment of members, approval, and process-ing of claims. The formal insurer simply receives premiums from Vimo SEWA once per annum and pays Vimo SEWA a lump sum on a monthly basis for all claims reimbursed. In 2003, Vimo SEWA increased the coverage of medical insurance to Rs.2,000 and also began offering voluntary health insurance for the children of insured members.

When Vimo SEWA was started in 1992, the primary thrust was on enrolling members in Ahmedabad city. This was because the members of the staff of Vimo and the SEWA Bank were located in Ahmedabad. As the insurance pro-gramme stabilized, it expanded to the rural members in 11 districts. Today, two-thirds of the members live in rural areas and one-third in Ahmedabad City. In calendar year 2004, Vimo SEWA had 104,794 members, comprising over 72,000 adult women and 32,500 adult men. One-third of the total membership (i.e. 33,029) in 2004 joined under the fixed-deposit scheme and two-thirds (71,765) under the annual premium scheme.

Table 12.2 compares the general rural Gujarati households with Vimo SEWA members, in the 16 sub-districts where Vimo SEWA has the most members, based on select indicators of socio-economic status. By most indicators, the Vimo SEWA members appear slightly 'poorer' than the general population – and significantly so for indicators of food security.

Protection against health care costs

Vimo SEWA is expected to protect its members from the costs of health care, by covering up to Rs.2,000 of the direct costs of inpatient care – i.e. bed, doctor, medicine, and laboratory fees. Protection against health care costs is measured in a variety of ways, including:

- the percentage of claimants who receive at least some reimbursement for their claim (i.e. their claim is 'accepted');
- among accepted claims, the mean and median percentage of self-reported 'total costs of hospitalization' that is actually reimbursed; and
- the extent to which reimbursement reduces the percentage of all claimants that experience 'catastrophic' health care expenditures, i.e. hospitalizations

Table 12.2 Comparison of rural Vimo SEWA members in 16 sub-districts with the general rural population by key socio-economic characteristics

SES characteristics	Vimo SEWA members		General population	
	Mean/Frequency	95% CI	Mean/Frequency	95% CI
Number of observations	n = 967		n = 780	
If wall brick or stone with plaster (%)	41.8	(36.2–47.6)	42.9	(34.7–51.5)
If gas for cooking (%)	5.7	(3.9–8.4)	8.0	(4.8–13.1)
If oil store ≥1 month, during last 12 months (%)	15.5	(11.5–20.5)	27.8	(21.0–35.9)
If millet store = 12 months (%)	8.9	(6.5–12.1)	17.7	(12.5–24.5)
If wheat store ≥1 month, during last 12 months (%)	34.2	(28.9–39.9)	55.0	(46.5–63.2)
If electrical connection, own or shared (%)	62.9	(55.9–69.5)	62.9	(53.2–71.7)
Number of rooms	1.8	(1.7–1.8)	1.9	(1.8–2.1)
Hh adults literate (%)	47.6	(45.0–50.1)	49.6	(43.5–55.7)
Hh adults attended college or univ. (%)	2.1	(1.2–2.9)	4.0	(2.5–5.6)
Number of refrigerators	0.04	(0.02–0.06)	0.08	(0.04–0.11)
Number of fans	0.81	(0.70–0.93)	0.90	(0.72–1.08)
Number of mattresses	0.56	(0.40–0.72)	1.03	(0.72–1.33)
Number of wrist watches	0.48	(0.40–0.57)	0.57	(0.47–0.67)

resulting in expenditure (net of reimbursement) exceeding 10 per cent of annual household income.

The degree of financial protection conferred by the scheme is known to be limited by certain aspects of scheme design and management, namely:

- The cap on reimbursement, currently set at Rs.2,000;
- The time lag between discharge from hospital and reimbursement – much of which is accounted for by delays by the insured members in submitting the claim to Vimo SEWA.

Another factor that limits the financial protection offered by the scheme – and may reflect problems on the demand side (e.g. failure to compile the necessary documents) and the supply side (e.g. failure to instil an adequate understanding of the scheme among members) – is the fact that some members do not submit an insurance claim, even if they have been hospitalized with an eligible illness.

Quantitative data suggest that the scheme does confer financial protection to poor people. In 2003, 13 per cent of claims were rejected. Of the 2,615 claims that were reimbursed, on average, 63 per cent of total expenditures (reported by the members) were reimbursed by Vimo SEWA. But Figure 12.2 (which includes only those members enrolled in Policy I) reveals that the financial protection provided to those who experience the most expensive hospitalizations is

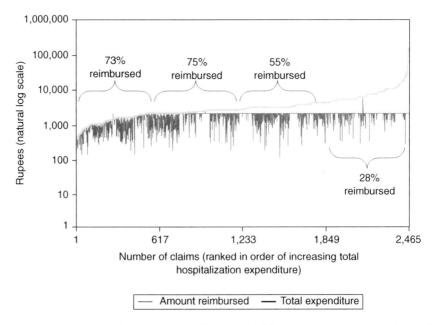

Figure 12.2 Total, self-reported, expenditure (ranked from least to most expensive) and total amount reimbursed, Vimo SEWA Policy I 'approved' claims, 2003 ($n = 2,465$)

limited. Among the least expensive quartile of hospitalizations (which ranged from Rs.190 to Rs.2,000), the mean level of reimbursement was 73 per cent, while among the most expensive quartile of hospitalizations (Rs.4,014 to Rs.151,003), the mean level of reimbursement was only 28 per cent.

An analysis of all claims submitted in the six years from 1 July 1994 through 30 June 2000 (Ranson 2002) revealed that claims were rejected in 11 per cent of cases. The mean rate of reimbursement for all reimbursed claims was 76.5 per cent (median 92.6 per cent). Reimbursement more than halved the percentage of catastrophic hospitalizations; for 35.6 per cent of claims, the total spent on hospitalization would have been otherwise catastrophic for the claimant, while expenditures by patients after reimbursement were catastrophic for 15.1 per cent.

Quantitative data suggest that certain elements of scheme design (aside from the Rs.2,000 cap) hinder the financial protection conferred by the scheme. For example, the relatively high rejection rates (ranging from 11 to 14 per cent of all claims annually) are accounted for in large part by claims rejected because of pre-existing or chronic illnesses. Among claims rejected between 1994 and 2000, the main reasons for rejection were: pre-existing disease (48 per cent), incomplete documentation (15 per cent), and fraudulent claim (10 per cent). A similar analysis for July 2001 through December 2002 found pre-existing disease or other excluded condition (56 per cent), incomplete documentation (5 per cent), 'invalid claim' (5 per cent), not actually admitted to hospital (13 per cent), and age older than 58 years (5 per cent). The fact that reimbursement occurs only after discharge from hospital and submission and approval of a claim also dilutes the financial protection. The average lag time between discharge from hospital and reimbursement improved considerably during the six years covered by the first analysis and was an average of 98 days by the last two years studied (1998–9 and 1999–2000). The 99 days between discharge and reimbursement could be broken down into 55 days from discharge to submission of the claim, 26 days from submission to the date of the panel's decision, and 18 days between the panel's decision and receipt of payment by the claimant.

Qualitative research has revealed that the cost of submitting a claim and the difficulties involved in compiling documents and certificates are among the factors that prevent members from submitting a claim or result in delays in claim submission.

The direct or indirect costs of compiling documents and submitting the claim to the local Vimo SEWA representative can be expensive:

> They (the members) are reluctant to come here (to the district office) because they cannot pay the transportation fare. So they cannot come here.
> (Woman Vimo *aagewan*, 28 years old, Surendranagar district)

> Interviewer: Did you submit a claim?
> Respondent: A visit to the Vimo office costs us twenty-five rupees.
> (Women Vimo SEWA member, 50 years old, Ahmedabad City)

Commonly the poor have limited literacy skills and also lack the confidence to negotiate with officials and formal systems. They therefore have greater difficulty in getting together all the required documents for submitting a claim. As one *aagewan* in Anand taluka explained:

> We ask the claimant for all bills for the hospitalization. If the doctor has not given these bills – many women are illiterate and don't ask for the certificates or bills at the time of discharge – then we ask them where they were admitted and we go along with them to collect the certificate and bills.
>
> (Woman Vimo *aagewan*, 33 years old, Anand district)

Access to health care interventions

Vimo SEWA, by reducing the financial barrier to seeking inpatient care (albeit retrospectively), may improve access to inpatient health care. This assumes that members, upon falling sick, weigh the potential costs of seeking health care against the benefits, and factor into this equation the possibility of being reimbursed under the Vimo SEWA scheme.

Figure 12.3 compares rates of claims submission to Vimo SEWA (2003) with self-reported rates of hospitalization in Gujarat from two recent representative surveys. In rural areas, the rate of claims on Vimo SEWA in 2003 was 26.6/1,000 members. This is very high in comparison with the rate of hospitalization estimated by the National Sample Survey Organization (NSSO) based on 1995–6 data (Mahal *et al.* 2000), which ranged from 13.3 hospitalizations/1,000 among rural women to 16.6/1,000 among rural men. But the rate of Vimo SEWA claims is low in comparison with the rate of hospitalization estimated by Sundar (1995) based on 1993 data, which ranged from 40.8/1,000 for rural men to 78.0/1,000 for rural women. The relationships are similar for the urban data, with the rate of Vimo SEWA claims high in comparison with NSSO estimates of hospitalization rate and low in comparison to Sundar's estimates. Thus, it is difficult to draw conclusions about the rate of Vimo SEWA claims relative to rates of hospitalization, given tremendous variability and uncertainty in estimates of the latter. The section below on 'Data and research needs' discusses the many complications involved in comparing claims rates with rates of hospitalization that derive from other sources.

There are recent indications that claims submissions may be increasing in Ahmedabad City. Claims rates in Ahmedabad (claims/1,000 members per year) more than tripled from 15.0 in 2000–1 to 46.7 in 2003. There was a one-time jump in the rate of rural claims between 2001–2 and 2003, but this is thought to have been due to lack of awareness about scheme membership among many 2001–2 rural members. It is quite difficult to determine whether the rising rate of claims in Ahmedabad is due to increased financial access (for many of those who truly need hospitalization) or due to a growing problem of adverse selection and/or moral hazard.

Two special studies have attempted to compare rates of claims among Vimo

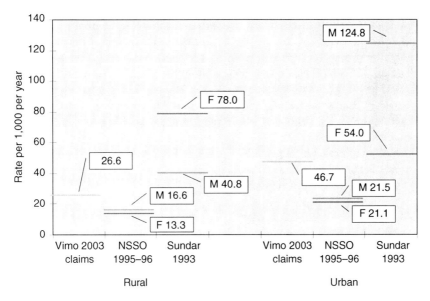

Figure 12.3 Rates of claims at Vimo SEWA (2003) compared with rates of hospitalization in Gujarat as assessed in two recent surveys, rural and urban (M = male;
F = female)

SEWA members and non-members. One study, conducted in 2000, compared
insured women, aged 18 to 58 years, in 242 Vimo SEWA households (in Anand
and Kheda Districts) with age-matched women in 381 non-insured households in
the same villages (Ranson 2004). This study found no significant association
between membership in Vimo SEWA and frequency of hospitalization, although
there was a trend towards higher rates of hospitalization among SEWA members.
Over the one-year period examined in the survey, Vimo SEWA members had
undergone 28 hospitalizations; but claims were submitted, and reimbursed, for
only five of the hospitalizations (18 per cent). The authors conclude (based on
qualitative interviews) that the failure to impact on utilization resulted from: lack
of awareness among members of the scheme or its benefits; the perception that
benefits of the scheme are low (relative to the total direct and indirect costs of hospitalization); and the high costs of submitting a claim to Vimo SEWA (e.g. transportation to the Vimo SEWA office and opportunity costs of missed work).

Another study was conducted in non-randomly selected areas of Ahmedabad
district (eight 'slum-dominated localities' and six neighbouring villages) in
1998–9 (Gumber and Kulkarni 2000; Gumber 2004). This study evaluated the
impact of Vimo SEWA on the utilization of ambulatory care, on choice of
private versus public facilities for inpatient care, and on out-of-pocket expenditure for inpatient care. It found that members of Vimo SEWA households were
significantly less likely (than the non-insured 'controls') to seek ambulatory
care. Out-of-pocket expenditures on hospitalization were not significantly

different among members of Vimo SEWA households in comparison with those of the non-insured. However, these findings are difficult to interpret given that: (1) it does not assess the impact of the scheme on utilization of inpatient care, although only inpatient care is covered by Vimo SEWA; (2) it appears to include all 357 households taken from a Vimo SEWA list as insured, although only half of these households stated that they had purchased insurance; and (3) the analysis seems to include all members of Vimo SEWA households as insured, although the insurance would only have covered select, adult women within these households.

Our discussions with Vimo SEWA staff, including *Aagewans* (local women insurance leaders), suggest that having insurance does increase the probability that members will seek inpatient care:

> Respondent: Suppose a woman is very poor, and she has become a Vimo member, and she knows that she will get reimbursed. Then somehow or other, even if it means selling something, she will get admitted. She will do her best to take advantage of the insurance ... If she has jewellery at home she will even sell it, but she will get admitted ... In Khambat there is a member, Jadaben, who is very poor, and she has only one son who does mason's work. He is young. This woman became very ill ... She sold her jewellery and used the money to get admitted to the hospital.
>
> (*Aagewan*, Anand district)

The scheme may also increase access to hospitalization by increasing, among its members, awareness about health, disease, and appropriate health care seeking. This heightened awareness might reduce the need for hospitalization by increasing demand for preventive health care or early, outpatient curative care:

> Respondent: Through our insurance scheme, women gain an awareness of their own health; that 'I must take care of myself then only I can take care of my house'. 'If I am not healthy then how will I take care of my house or my children or do my job?' So they themselves get aware about this.
>
> (ADMIN 3)

> Respondent: The purpose of this scheme is our members should know who are the quacks (the untrained and unlicensed doctors). And to whom they should go. And what is the fact. And what is the proper treatment. So this is one type of the health education also ... Suppose one member does not get the claim, or we say to her, okay, because of this problem (because she has taken health care from a quack) you are not getting the claim ... So, that will be one, this is also one type of the health education.
>
> (ADMIN 1)

On the other hand, our interviews suggest that even the insured face a variety of financial and non-financial barriers that may prevent them from seeking hospitalization. For the poorest, seeking care at an inpatient facility may simply not be an option, as they perceive such care to be unaffordable. One Vimo *aagewan* reported feeling helpless when called to see a young, insured woman living far from the nearest hospital:

> Respondent 1: The mother said, 'Bhartiben, you have sold my daughter insurance, and now she has a severe fever. We don't have a hospital here, so where do I take her?' I said, 'Either you get her admitted in Dhrangadhra or in Patdi.' She said, 'Sister, I don't have the money right now and look at the fever she is running.'
>
> (Woman Vimo *aagewan*, 28 years old, Surendranagar district)

Even when the insured have access to loans to pay for hospitalization, they may prefer to forego the hospitalization:

> Respondent: Many just stay at home because they do not have money to go to the doctor ... My husband does not go (to hospital). When there is no money, he says, 'What is the need to go?' ... (Even with insurance) the problem is, you have to borrow the money, go to the hospital and then return the money with interest.
>
> (Woman Vimo SEWA member, 32 years old, village in Gandhinagar district)

Some Vimo SEWA members live in remote villages, far from urban centres and hospital facilities. Transportation is expensive and sometimes unavailable. An *aagewan* in one of the focus group discussions felt that the cost of transportation, added to the cost of inpatient care, was enough to prevent poor insured women from going for hospitalization:

> Members living in the villages have to travel to the city in order to be admitted to hospital, and they find the cost of travel expensive. They feel that, 'The reimbursement from the insurance will only amount to what I spent on transportation, and nothing will be left with us.'
>
> (Woman Vimo *aagewan*, 28 years old, Surendranagar district)

Women's household responsibilities inhibit them from being hospitalized even when they need it:

> Sometimes if the woman has to cook, make tiffin (lunchbox), send her children for tuition, then she does not get admitted to hospital. She takes some pills and continues with her work.
>
> (Vimo SEWA *aagewan*, 37 years old, Anand district)

Empowerment for shaping health care services

Members play an active role in shaping the Vimo SEWA scheme. There is popular participation in managerial functions and scheme governance, such that scheme design and functioning reflects the wishes of Vimo SEWA members. And increasingly, the scheme is becoming a forum for communication between Vimo SEWA members and health care providers; Vimo SEWA is shaping itself as a strategic purchaser of health care services, so as to maximize the quality and cost-effectiveness of services available to its members.

Member participation in management and governance

SEWA believes in promoting member-based institutions where members are owners, managers and users. SEWA union and its allied organizations such as SEWA Bank, where Vimo SEWA was born, are governed by elected representatives of the members who are all self-employed women. The day-to-day operations of these organizations are carried out by teams composed of grassroots workers and professionals, under the guidelines provided by the elected representatives.

Community participation in Vimo SEWA governance occurs in two ways. First, the governing body is made up of representatives of the member community (including insurance members). Given the large membership of SEWA union (700,000 in January 2004) and in Vimo SEWA (over 100,000 in January 2004), members' interests are represented by elected representatives. Major decisions, such as premium and coverage amounts, and expansion of the scheme to new geographic areas, are taken in consultation with, and after approval by, the elected representatives. Second, members of the insurance programme actively express their feedback and their needs vis-à-vis the scheme to the workers who market and service the scheme. These inputs are incorporated into the design of the scheme to the extent possible.

When the scheme was introduced in 1992, the premium and coverage amounts were discussed in several fora with representatives of members to assess the usefulness and acceptability of the scheme. Only then was it launched. The modus operandi of collecting premiums and allocating the scheme's financial resources are also put to the elected representatives for approval.

A specific example of community participation is expanding the scheme to the members' families in response to their voiced need. Initially, the scheme was introduced only for the women members of SEWA union. When the women began to experience the benefits, they asked that the scheme be extended to their husbands, and health insurance for husbands of women members was introduced. Health insurance for children was also started in response to the needs voiced by members.

These changes in the scheme in response to the needs of some members did not mean that all members were forced to buy the expanded policy. Participation in the scheme is voluntary. A woman can choose whether she wants to buy insurance only for herself, or for both herself and her husband, or for the entire family. Consequently, members who need coverage for their families are able to get this benefit, leaving others to choose the extent of coverage they want for their families.

Community participation is facilitated due to community outreach by the programme and the doorstep approach of SEWA. To market the scheme to the community, Vimo SEWA conducts village-level meetings. These meetings are not only a means of enrolling new members, but also a forum for existing members to voice their grievances, which are addressed by the Vimo SEWA team at the earliest opportunity. Further, insurance is serviced by local-level workers (the *aagewans*) who visit members in their homes when they need to submit their claims. These regular visits by *aagewans* to the residences of members provide the opportunity for members to give feedback regarding the scheme.

Yet another mechanism for community participation in the scheme is the Claims Committee, which scrutinizes and approves claims that are submitted. The medical claim committee, which scrutinizes and decides on each health insurance claim submitted, is made up of SEWA *aagewans* representing different trades practised by SEWA members. This mechanism ensures community participation and transparency in the processing of decisions on the claims. It also reduces the information asymmetry that occurs when insurers and the insured belong to different socio-economic backgrounds.

Shaping health care services

Since its inception, Vimo SEWA has aimed to direct its members towards providers of high-quality health care. For example, members have been encouraged to use public health care services (generally acknowledged to provide better technical quality than the private for-profit sector), where available, and they have been provided with education about medical practices that are unnecessary or dangerous. For example, based on research among Vimo SEWA claimants in Anand/Kheda, it was found that more than 15 per cent of claims (from July 1994 to August 2000) were for hysterectomies and that the technical quality of care varied from potentially dangerous to excellent (Ranson and John 2001). So the staff and the members of SEWA were taught about the potential complications of unnecessary hysterectomy/oophorectomy, and there was a subsequent decrease in the rate of these procedures among members in these districts.

Vimo SEWA has helped to shape the health care services that are provided directly by Arogya SEWA (SEWA Health), another department within the SEWA family. Vimo SEWA provides the health programme with periodic (currently weekly) reports indicating disease incidence by geographical area, based on its medical claim data. These reports show the reasons for hospitalization in different areas. This information helps SEWA's health programme to provide preventive and curative services based on the health care needs of the area.

Increasingly, Vimo SEWA is shaping health care services provided by public, trust and private for-profit hospitals by purchasing health care from them on members' behalf. Under a recent pilot project, a maternity benefits package was purchased (at a price of Rs.200) from select public and trust hospitals, for pregnant, fixed-deposit members in Ahmedabad City. This intervention involved negotiating with hospitals to provide – at a low, fixed price – the antenatal package recommended by the World Health Organization. This was coupled with education of pregnant women, their husbands, and health care providers about optimizing maternal and child health and recognizing and dealing with problems during pregnancy and delivery. By actively purchasing maternity benefits for its members, Vimo SEWA caused a shift towards utilization of public and trust hospitals as against private for-profit hospitals, and those who chose to avail of these maternity benefits enjoyed significantly lower costs (inclusive of the costs of delivery). Furthermore, those who used the empanelled providers were far more likely to receive a check-up within 48 hours after delivery than were those who did not.

Vimo SEWA's responses to findings

This section focuses on changes that are being made or are likely to be made to Vimo SEWA in order to enhance financial protection, access to health care, and members' ability to shape health care services.

Changes aimed at increasing financial protection

Vimo SEWA has already begun to implement several interventions – launched in August 2004 – aimed at protecting its members from more expensive hospitalizations. On a pilot basis, in eight rural sub-districts (covering more than 10,000 women members and their insured spouses), Vimo SEWA is reimbursing its members cash in hand prior to their discharge from hospital. This intervention, termed 'prospective reimbursement', is enhancing financial protection in two ways. First, this benefit is available to the members only if they use select ('empanelled') hospitals, of which there are two in each district. These hospitals are (with only one exception) public and private not-for-profit facilities. They were selected because their services are much less costly than those of private for-profit facilities (historically, much more popular among Vimo SEWA's members, as they are perceived to provide faster and more courteous service) and also because they were deemed to provide more comprehensive and higher-quality services. Past evaluations have found that the cost of the same services at private not-for-profit and public hospitals is only a fraction of the cost of services at private for-profit facilities. Second, this intervention ensures that members have cash available at the time of discharge, in contrast to receiving reimbursement a month or more after their discharge.

A second intervention being piloted aims to increase the rate of submission of (appropriate) claims, particularly among Vimo SEWA's poorest members. This will be achieved primarily by improving the knowledge, capacity, and motivation of Vimo *aagewans* and by enhancing two-way communication between *aagewans* and members. The Vimo *aagewans* will receive training to ensure that they are (1) absolutely clear on scheme benefits and the process of claim submission and review and (2) sensitive to the problems that poorer members face in accessing scheme benefits (equity sensitivity). They will be motivated through 'supportive supervision' – supervision that incorporates self-assessment, peer-assessment, and community input (Marquez and Kean 2002) – and through timely reimbursement for their transportation expenses. Communication will be enhanced by ensuring that *aagewans* make regular (perhaps twice yearly) visits to each insured person, by providing households with a stamped/addressed postcard that can be mailed should they have a claim to submit and by providing households with a mirror (or wall-mounted decoration) that includes the name and telephone number for their local Vimo SEWA representative. It is hoped that these activities will make it easier for members to compile and submit a claim and ultimately will result in increased financial protection for members.

There has been a great deal of discussion around increasing the financial protection provided by the scheme by increasing the hospitalization coverage (under the least expensive policy) to Rs.5,000 or Rs.10,000. The cap has been maintained, however, at Rs.2,000, primarily because there have been concerns that such an increase would result in the submission of inappropriate (fraudulent) claims, particularly in Ahmedabad City, where there has already been a rise in claims over recent years. It has also been felt that the increase in premium that would be required would discourage the poorest from joining the scheme. So while the benefits paid out for natural death and loss of assets have recently been increased significantly (1.7 times and two times, respectively, between calendar years 2004 and 2005), hospitalization coverage has remained at Rs.2,000.

Changes aimed at increasing access to inpatient care

The 'prospective reimbursement' intervention, described above, is expected to improve access to inpatient care by removing some component of the financial barrier that might otherwise prevent people from seeking health care. Somewhat more difficult to address are the many non-financial barriers that prevent women – and those living in remote, rural areas – from accessing care, such as: the long distance between home and the hospital; the lack or expense of transportation; the inconvenience caused to the family when the woman is unavailable for childcare or for her other domestic responsibilities; and lack of knowledge about, or trust in, allopathic medical services.

Other departments at SEWA are helping to address these barriers. For example, Bal SEWA runs an extensive network of childcare centres – children can be left in the care of these centres while their mothers go to seek care, at least during working hours. Arogya SEWA teaches poor people about health and illness, thus facilitating early recognition of disease conditions, and teaches them when and where to seek help for illnesses.

But Vimo SEWA has been able to do little about barriers that relate to distance and transportation – perhaps the most important among all barriers for the rural poor. Increasing the number of inpatient hospitals or making ambulance facilities available in rural areas would simply not be feasible given the very wide geographic area over which Vimo SEWA's members are spread. There has been some discussion about providing claimants in towns and villages of the most rural sub-districts with a fixed transportation reimbursement (in the range of Rs.200–Rs.500). This has not been implemented, in part because it would not be part of the package purchased from the formal insurance companies, and thus would result in considerable administrative burden (e.g. a separate premium would have to be earmarked and it would have to be kept as a separate fund, administered by Vimo SEWA). Furthermore, it would mean treating members of Vimo SEWA differently depending on their place of residence, and while it might make the distribution of scheme benefits more equitable, it could cause discord between members and *aagewans* from different regions.

Changes aimed at enabling members to better shape health services

Working to further shape or improve the quality of health care services is likely to be a slow and difficult task for Vimo SEWA, particularly in rural areas. There are several reasons for this. First, outside Ahmedabad City, Vimo SEWA's member population is often sparsely spread over wide geographic areas; purchasing power is thus not sufficiently consolidated to influence provider behaviour. Hospital administrators have stated, for example, that they are unwilling to negotiate lower prices for Vimo SEWA members if they can only expect one or two hospitalizations per month from among the membership population. Second, it is very difficult to influence provider behaviour in a setting where there is minimal guidance (or support or reinforcement) from government or from any regulatory agency (such as the Indian Medical Association) as to appropriate treatment for common ailments. Finally, but much more easily remedied, Vimo SEWA does not currently have the public health and regulatory human resources that would be required for actively monitoring and reinforcing standard treatment protocols.

Discussion and conclusions

Summary of findings

Vimo SEWA has been providing comprehensive (life, assets, and hospitalization) insurance to its members since 1992. The scheme is in a constant state of evolution, with scheme administrators trying to fine-tune aspects of scheme design and management so as to better meet the perceived needs of the members. Available data suggest that the scheme does provide some element of financial protection, particularly for less expensive hospitalizations. The financial protection conferred by the schemes is limited by the cap of Rs.2,000 on hospitalization benefits, by the lag-time between discharge from hospital and reimbursement, and by the failure by some members who have been hospitalized to submit a claim. There is soft evidence to suggest that membership in Vimo SEWA is improving access to hospitalization among the urban membership. This does not appear to be the case among rural members, who may simply not be able to mobilize the necessary resources to seek hospitalization, or who face other barriers to seeking care, such as lack or high cost of transportation and childcare, work, and domestic responsibilities. It is a high priority of the scheme to respond to the needs of its members; as such, it has evolved mechanisms for regularly meeting with members and for incorporating their suggestions into the scheme. Increasingly, Vimo SEWA is acting to improve the quality of care accessed by its members through a combination of: educating members regarding available sources of high-quality health care, directly providing preventive and primary care, and purchasing health care from select, empanelled providers.

Data and research needs and challenges

There are several important problems with the data that we have used in assessing the financial protection provided by the Vimo SEWA scheme. First, when asked to provide information on the total cost of their hospitalization episode, members (and the *aagewans* responsible for collecting the information) have little incentive to provide information on costs exceeding the amount which can be reimbursed, i.e. costs beyond the 'cap'. It is remarkable, for example, that in 2003 (for the 2,995 claims, for which complete data are available), 13 per cent (352) of scheme 1 members reported total hospitalization expenditures of exactly Rs.2,000. This most likely represents underreporting of the total hospitalization expenditures and makes it look as if the scheme is providing greater financial protection than it really is.

Second, one can only assess the extent to which households are impacted by health care expenditures and protected by insurance mechanisms, by looking at how the household copes with the expenditures, e.g. borrowing from friends, family, moneylenders; selling off assets; and reducing expenditures on food, education, clothing, and health care for other family members. And ideally, such assessments should be longitudinal, i.e. covering the full time during which the household is likely to change its behaviour as a result of this financial shock. Quantitative researchers have attempted to assess such impacts by quantifying health care expenditures (Xu *et al.* 2003) and the impact of protective mechanisms (Pradhan and Prescott 2002; Ranson 2002) as a percentage of total household expenditures. Unfortunately, the data available on the socio-economic status of Vimo SEWA member households – total self-reported household income – is unreliable. As well, it would be useful and interesting to have qualitative data regarding how households deal with health care expenditures – along the lines of work done by Rosenzweig (1988), Sauerborn *et al.* (1996a), and Krishna *et al.* (2003) – and whether and how health insurance has influenced their response.

As already mentioned, quantifying any increase in rates of hospital utilization among members as against that among non-members has proved difficult. It is difficult to compare rates of hospitalization among members (using claims data that are kept as part of the ongoing MIS) with data for the general population (available from various health care utilization surveys). This is because (1) the MIS provides data only on hospitalization for which members actually submit a claim and (2) rates of hospitalization vary quite widely in Gujarat, across studies, and according to gender, age, place of residence (urban vs. rural, and from one rural area to another) and socio-economic status. Data are also difficult to collect from a single, cross-sectional study because (1) large study populations are required, as hospitalization is a relatively infrequent event, and (2) data on factors that may confound the relationship between insurance status and hospitalization, such as age, wealth/socio-economic status, and health status, are hard to measure reliably. But aside from performing a single, very large, cross-sectional study (or a smaller longitudinal study) of the non-insured and the insured populations at considerable expense, it is unclear how this lack of data can be addressed.

Discussion: implications of SEWA work for other countries and schemes

The lessons learnt from Vimo SEWA's experience have policy implications for community-based financing schemes in other settings and for governments and donors, more broadly.

First, the Vimo SEWA experience highlights just how tricky it is to use such schemes for targeting services to the poorest populations. On the one hand, the underlying ethos and objectives at Vimo SEWA are very much 'pro-poor', and this is reflected in the fact that the poorest, both in urban and rural areas, are proportionately represented amongst the membership. But the fact that urban members of Vimo SEWA have much higher claims rates than rural members illustrates how such schemes can potentially work against the interests of the poor, with cross-subsidies flowing from poor rural households to wealthier urban households. Thus, community-based financing schemes, governments, and donors need to pay heed to, and document, how well such schemes are actually working for the poor.

Second, there is only so much that a scheme can do to promote access for the poor. Coordinators of Vimo SEWA, through their research and years of experience, are aware of the many barriers that the poorest women and men face in accessing quality health care. But there are certain barriers (e.g. lack of transportation, limited access to telephones, poor quality roads, and distance to the closest *fully staffed* health care facility) that Vimo SEWA cannot tackle directly. So if governments wish to promote community-based health financing schemes, they have a responsibility to ensure that there are providers who are both physically accessible and offering adequate quality of care.

Third, Vimo SEWA provides a functioning and long-standing model of a 'private–public partnership (PPP)' where all sides have gained from the inter-action. Vimo SEWA interacts with the public sector in both its role as a provider of insurance (through the semi-autonomous Life Insurance Corporation and General Insurance Corporation) and its role as a provider of health care services. Over the years, Vimo SEWA has helped the public insurance companies in developing policies that are attractive to the poor and in delivering insurance services to the poor (thus helping the companies to meet their 'rural- and social-sector' mandates). In return, Vimo SEWA (and its members) has been able to draw on the experience, and technical skills, at the public companies, in devel-oping an actuarially sound insurance product and has also accessed a govern-ment subsidy (through the Life Insurance Corporation) that is only available to those who purchase insurance. Similarly, Vimo SEWA helps the public system for health care provision by encouraging its members to use public facilities because of their low cost and the technical skills of the public doctors and nurses. But at the same time, Vimo SEWA is trying to work with these providers to ensure that they are available to the poor and responsive to their needs.

Finally, the Vimo SEWA experience suggests that community-based financ-ing schemes form a good channel through which to provide subsidies to the poor, in the form of face-to-face education (e.g. about health, health care, insur-ance, or savings). Subsidies from government or donors should not be used to cover benefits under the scheme, as it would be difficult to prevent such benefits from being captured by less poor (urban) members. But such subsidies can very equitably be spent on the administrative costs of marketing, communication, and after-sales services. Such costs are predominantly spent in reaching households in poor and isolated areas. And while Vimo SEWA has not yet been able to do much in terms of improving access to health care among such households, the twice- or thrice-yearly visit from a representative of Vimo SEWA might be the only contact that they have with a formal financial institution and might be the only direct (face-to-face) message they receive about health or health care seeking.

Conclusions

Vimo SEWA, now in its twelfth year, has made many achievements. As a community-based insurer, it is relatively unique in terms of its large and varied membership, its geographic scope, and the responsiveness of its management to the needs of its target population. The scheme has proved itself to be viable; albeit with external support, it has weathered multiple natural and manmade dis-asters (floods, an earthquake, a typhoon, and riots) and has seen its membership gradually increase with time. But this case description also highlights some of the tensions that are faced by community-based insurers the world over: for example, the tension between a desire to protect members from the costs of even the most expensive hospitalizations and at the same time to set premiums suffi-ciently low as to make the scheme affordable to the poor; between a desire to deliver insurance to those who live in the remotest rural areas and the very high costs of marketing insurance and servicing claims, among such members; between a desire to increase access to hospitalization and a fear that a benefits package that is too attractive will be abused by members or health care providers; and between a desire to optimize the quality of health care accessed by members and the paucity of clinical guidelines and public health expertise to meaningfully impact on provider behaviour.

In a setting where a significant percentage of the population (roughly one-third) lives below the poverty line, where some live hours away from the closest functioning hospital, where the private health care sector is active but unmonitored and unregulated, and where the resources (financial and human) available to counter these problems are highly constrained, we must be realistic in our expectations. Vimo SEWA is by no means a solution to all of the problems of India's public health system. Yet there can be no question that it is a tremendous improvement on the alternative – a system where the poor and the illiterate fall into the hands of unregulated private practitioners of questionable service quality at high cost, with no hope of recovering the expenses they incur.

13 Conclusions

From evidence to action

Sara Bennett, Lucy Gilson and Anne Mills

Introduction

This book has covered three main themes: the links between health, economic development and poverty; evidence on the extent to which health systems serve the needs of the poor; and innovative measures to make health systems more pro-poor. While in the past, poverty was often defined in terms of lack of income, more recent concepts of poverty have emerged that emphasize the multidimensional nature of poverty, the fact that the poor are not a homogenous group and that people may move in and out of poverty for a variety of reasons (DFID 1999). It is recognized that poverty is a relative concept and that, in particular, social exclusion is an important facet of poverty. Various chapters of this book have highlighted differing dimensions of poverty. For example, Chapter 10 considers the role of social exclusion and the importance of the health system and deliberations around the health system as a means to combat social exclusion. Chapters 4–6 focus much more on the processes through which household interactions with the health system may contribute to their poverty.

The purpose of this final chapter is to examine the implications for action of the reviews and studies contained in the book. While some of the lessons derived are for developing country policy and decision-makers, others are relevant to civil society organizations, donors, multilateral organizations and the research community.

Five main issues and areas for action are identified, namely:

1 the need for political commitment and a stronger focus upon strategies to build political commitment;
2 recognition of the inter-linkages between health and other sectors and the imperative of inter-sectoral action;
3 the importance of an effective, well-functioning public health care system which is free at the point of use and has broad geographic coverage;
4 an increased focus on the specific details of policy design and process of implementation, as they may significantly affect the extent to which a policy or strategy serves the interests of the poor;

5   development of a stronger evidence base to guide innovative strategies within the health sector to make health systems better serve the needs of the poor.

Each of these five issues is discussed in turn.

Building and maintaining political commitment

'Political commitment' is commonly highlighted as a key factor determining the success of policy. Too often the term is left nebulous and it is not clear how political commitment can be built or how to overcome the problems associated with a lack of political commitment. In different contexts and for different policies, political commitment will mean different things. Sometimes political support may derive from a small group of politicians and this is sufficient to generate momentum for pro-poor reform. In other contexts, or for other reforms, it may be necessary to pull together a broader group of actors to generate sufficient political commitment. Political support, that is support from stakeholders with the power to influence policy development, appears to be particularly important in order to develop and implement policies that promote the interests of the poor.

As several chapters of this book have demonstrated, policies that benefit the poor are unlikely also to serve the interests of more powerful and affluent groups, who might therefore oppose the policy. For example, Pannarunothai (Chapter 11) highlights the difficulties of maintaining social consensus on, and political commitment to, the universal coverage reform in Thailand. In sub-Saharan Africa, reforms which have repealed user fees have sometimes failed to take into account the implications of this policy for health workers (in terms of increased workloads and potentially lower income) and this has the potential to undermine the reform (Bennett and Gilson, Chapter 9).

There is no simple 'magic bullet' to solve the problem of lack of political commitment to pro-poor reform, but there are a number of concrete steps that different stakeholders can take to help such reforms stand a better chance of success. First, it is important to acknowledge the political nature of the policy process and take account of it in developing and implementing reforms. This entails identifying the values that underlie reforms, considering which stakeholders may be supportive of such reforms and which are likely to remain opposed and using this knowledge to develop a strategy to sustain reforms (Bennett and Gilson, Chapter 9).

One common problem in mobilizing stakeholders who support the values embedded in pro-poor reforms is that such stakeholders may be dispersed and only weakly organized. Loewenson, in Chapter 10, points to the critical role that civil society organizations – such as women's groups and trade unions – can play in giving voice to poorer people and thus enabling them to influence decision-making. However, the nature of the political system will affect what space these groups are allowed, in order to engage in policy debates. It also typically takes time, investment and support for such groups to establish capacity to play effective roles in influencing policy development.

As discussed below, the impacts of a reform will frequently be strongly influenced by aspects of the design of the policy and by how the policy is implemented. Hence the coalition of support which is built for policy change needs to be maintained through policy refinement and implementation. In the case of contested reforms, such as the universal coverage policy in Thailand, policy champions may need to be active for several or more years, in order to ensure that the benefits achieved for the poor through the policy are not gradually eroded over time. The influence of policy implementation over the final effects of the policy also point to the critical importance of securing the support of 'frontline bureaucrats', such as health workers, responsible for policy implementation (Walker and Gilson 2004).

Inter-sectoral action

The Commission on Macroeconomics and Health provided substantive evidence of the strong links between health and economic development (Commission on Macroeconomics and Health 2001). In Chapter 2, Alsan *et al.* review this and more recent evidence that further demonstrates and explains the causal links from health to economic development. Such evidence is at least partly responsible for stimulating the increased international investment in global health that has occurred during the past six years. While there continues to be major international commitment to achieving the health Millennium Development Goals (MDGs) and continuing increased development assistance for this purpose, there is less clarity about the optimal balance of investment to achieve health gains. How should additional investment be balanced between strengthening health systems and services, increasing technological development for health care and investing in related sectors such as education and environment which may have direct impacts upon health? The question of comparative returns to different sectors in terms of reducing poverty and promoting growth lies outside the scope of this book, and there is relatively limited empirical evidence to answer this question.

While the final part of this book has focused on the question of how to achieve better health for the poor, most of the policies and mechanisms discussed concern health services or the broader health system. The increasing evidence regarding the links between strong health systems, equitable access to health and more equitable health outcomes (e.g. Anand and Barnighausen 2004) suggests that investments in health systems and services are important, but it is also clear that many effective interventions lie outside the health sector. Palmer in Chapter 4 demonstrated the importance of geographical access to health services. The increasing focus on rural infrastructure (particularly roads) at institutions such as the World Bank and the New Partnership for Africa's Development (NEPAD) appears to be an important element in overcoming this constraint and may also help to retain health staff in rural areas and ensure more timely delivery of drugs and supplies. Similarly, the chapters by Russell and Ranson highlighted the importance of risk-pooling arrangements, both in terms of formal insurance (as in Self-Employed Women's Association (SEWA), India) and informal arrangements (as in Sri Lanka) in terms of protecting the poor from the costs associated with ill health. The broader literature suggests there are a variety of mechanisms, such as the development of formal and informal insurance markets, financial markets and promotions of savings and food for work programmes, that can help poor people to cope with financial shocks stemming from ill health (Dercon 2004).

The 1978 Alma Ata Declaration (WHO 1978) stressed the importance of collaboration between the health sector and other sectors such as agriculture, education, housing and community development. However, during the past decade, with the notable exception of the human immunodeficiency virus (HIV)/acquired immunodeficiency syndrome (AIDS) sphere, an inter-sectoral approach has been lacking (People's Health Movement *et al.* 2005). A pro-poor lens reinforces the importance of coordination with other sectors and taking a holistic view of the experiences of the poor. It seems that there is, increasingly, a return to a broader, more all-encompassing vision of health and, in particular, the actions needed to promote the health of the poor. The work of the current Commission on the Social Determinants of Health underlines this (Doherty *et al.* 2006; Irwin *et al.* 2006).

If health is to be promoted through an inter-sectoral approach, then it is critical for health sector actors to engage fully in the development of Poverty Reduction Strategy Papers (PRSPs) and other tools for cross-sectoral planning that focus upon poverty alleviation. Too often it has been found that there is relatively limited participation by health sector actors in the development of PRSPs and presumably missed opportunities for promoting strategies that benefit the health of the poor (WEMOS 2006).

A strong public health care system

While on the one hand there is substantive evidence to suggest that public health care systems are often captured by the relatively affluent and subsidies are skewed towards the less poor, there is also increasing evidence indicating that, where such political capture is not strong, public health care systems are the most effective strategy to serve the interests of the poor (O'Donnell *et al.* 2005). The imperative to develop strong public health care systems has been highlighted by several other analysts and initiatives that have considered what policy changes are needed in order to improve health care for the poor (Freedman *et al.* 2005; People's Health Movement *et al.* 2005).

Clearly one of the biggest problems in terms of developing a broad and effective public health care system lies in ensuring that governance mechanisms are sufficiently strong to avoid both political capture of decision-making by the elites and capture of health sector resources by more affluent groups. Chapters 10 (Loewenson) and 4 (Palmer) respectively address these different types of capture (political and resource oriented). The foregoing discussion on political commitment is also relevant here.

For government-funded health care systems to benefit the poor, they need to have wide geographic coverage, provide good-quality services and be free at the point of use. There are of course substantial constraints that need to be addressed in order to create health care systems with these characteristics. Research has shown not only that households in poor communities have to travel longer distances to reach primary care facilities, but also that these facilities typically have fewer health care providers, drugs and medical equipment than primary care facilities in wealthier areas (Khan *et al.* 2006). The challenges to addressing these access barriers are considerable and, as noted, will require inter-sectoral action. It is well documented, and understandable, that trained health care staff are often unwilling to work in remote areas where their children may have poor access to schooling and their spouses to employment (WHO 2006). While multiple financial, educational and regulatory mechanisms have been used to encourage health staff to stay in rural areas, evidence about the relative effectiveness of these mechanisms is still emerging (Chopra *et al.* 2007). Similarly, improving the quality of health care for poor communities is a complex challenge which requires a multifaceted response. Improving supervision, training opportunities and work environment for health workers needs to be combined with measures that both enhance the responsiveness of providers to their poorer clients and create incentives for health workers to provide good-quality care (Agyepong 1999). Stronger logistical systems to ensure the availability of drugs and functional medical equipment are also needed.

Several chapters in this book have underlined the barriers to access that user fees constitute and their potentially impoverishing effects. These impacts are worse for the poor than for the non-poor. While during the late 1980s and the 1990s there was a push to introduce fees in government health care systems, the pendulum has since swung back, and some countries (notably South Africa, Uganda and Zambia) have repealed fees, particularly at the primary care level. The repeal of user fees requires careful planning, in order to avoid a situation in which health services, and particularly those serving remote or poorer populations, become under-resourced while facing increasing demand. Nonetheless, this policy shift appears to have had positive effects upon service utilization by the poor and, if planned properly, can strengthen this group's entitlement to public services.

The increasing emphasis upon developing a public health care system that provides free services to all also reflects growing understanding of the shortcomings of strategies that focus upon service delivery for one or two specific diseases. For funding bodies, global initiatives that focus on a handful of diseases or services (such as the Global Fund to Fight AIDS, TB and Malaria, GAVI, Stop TB, Roll Back Malaria and the Presidential Emergency Plan to Fight HIV/AIDS) have distinct advantages: it is easier to specify targets and assess the impact of development assistance. But, at the country level, there is a real danger that the combined effect of these initiatives undermines the public health care system, distorting local priorities, overwhelming country health system capacity and ultimately undermining the delivery of a package of primary care services that benefit the poor (Stillman and Bennett 2005). There is now increasing recognition of this danger, particularly in terms of the multiple demands made upon health workers and the dangers of denuding government services of staff. Analysts have called upon disease control programmes to ensure that their activities are integrated with general health care delivery, both in order to promote quality of care and to avoid undermining health systems (Unger *et al.* 2003). Some initiatives, such as the the GAVI Alliance, are now focusing on how they can contribute to resolving some of the broader health system issues, while still maintaining a focus on a particular package of diseases or services.

Finally, it should be stressed that the need for strong public health systems does not preclude the possibility of using specific forms of targeting in more rapidly expanding access to quality services for the poor. As Chapters 9 and 10 illustrated, targeted strategies and universal strategies are not mutually exclusive. Indeed, targeted strategies are likely to be complementary to universal approaches as they enable a speedier redirection of resources towards the poorest or the expansion of service coverage to marginalized groups who cannot immediately be brought within the health care system.

Maintaining a focus on policy design and policy implementation

A further lesson, that runs consistently through the chapters, is the need to focus not just on the major hurdle of getting policies approved as legislation or policy documents but also on the details of policy design and implementation. Governments work in different ways in different countries, but frequently policy legislation provides a broad enabling framework, within which the details of the reform must be worked out. It is often the details of the design features and the implementation processes that affect the success of the policy or strategy and its ability to reach the poor.

Unfortunately, detailed policy design can be a rather technical process and one tending to exclude non-specialist stakeholders. As a consequence, there is a real danger that pro-poor achievements in the overarching policy may be sapped by the accumulation of relatively minor design features. Even if the policy is so technical that a small specialist working group is needed to develop the design, it is important that this group consults regularly with a broader set of stakeholders. Finding ways to draw on the operational experience of those involved in implementation is particularly important in developing feasible policy designs. Engagement with the broader public and societal interest groups is also important in gauging potential support for, or opposition to, policy details and in developing strategies to sustain implementation.

Problems are also encountered during the implementation phase of a pro-poor policy or strategy. Exemption policies for user fees have been found rarely to operate as initially conceived: many poor people who were technically eligible for exemptions were not actually granted them (Russell and Gilson 1997). Reforms designed to create greater downward accountability of health services to beneficiary populations, particularly to the poor, have been distorted because more affluent groups gain control over the representative bodies (Brinkerhoff 2000). As noted, for many policies it is health workers who are the frontline bureaucrats responsible for policy implementation. Accordingly, it is particularly important to work with this group to ensure not only that they are aware of the rules and regulations of the reform but that they also understand its end objectives and the values underlying it. Ensuring that the nature of the policy is communicated in ways that are clear to potential beneficiaries is also always important in policy implementation.

However, given the difficulty of predicting and controlling for all implementation risks, it is essential to develop routine monitoring and evaluation processes which generate information to be fed back into policy implementation. Participatory evaluation and operational research, that involves a range of stakeholders (including beneficiaries) and is conducted in a timely manner, is also important. Such research should alert stakeholders to the fact that the strategy is not working as originally envisaged, and why that is, and so enable a change in direction. Communication with implementers and users, particularly poorer groups, therefore needs to occur at multiple stages, including consultation during the policy design phase, communication of the nature of reforms planned and consultation again with users about their experience of the reforms as part of the monitoring process (Gilson *et al.* 2003).

Strengthening evidence on implementing innovative strategies

While the final section of this book focused upon innovative strategies to extend health services to the poor and to better enable their access to care, for many strategies the evidence base is remarkably limited.

Innovative strategies are perhaps best developed and tested in terms of approaches to mitigate the financial consequences of seeking care. But even in terms of health financing, there are few systematic reviews of strategies and many remaining questions (Palmer *et al.* 2004). The evidence base is considerably weaker for strategies that deal with non-financial barriers to access. Although chapter authors derived general lessons about how to conceptualize and design strategies to target resources on the poor and promote their access to care, there is very limited clear evidence about which strategies are effective and under what conditions.

During recent years there have been some positive developments to improve knowledge in this field. For example, some policy interventions, such as the use of conditional cash transfers, have been subject to well-designed evaluations (e.g. Gertler 2000). Moreover, there have been increasing calls for the wider use of more rigorous impact evaluation methods (Center for Global Development 2006). But much still remains to be done in terms of developing a more robust evidence base to support decision-makers in addressing the needs of the poor. First, very few of those who are supporting major health sector initiatives to extend services to the poor include within them adequate funding for evaluation. The Commission on Macroeconomics and Health proposed that a minimum of 5 per cent of donor support to health sector projects be channelled to operational research (Commission on Macroeconomics and Health 2001), but it appears rare that this target is met. Second, even when rigorous evaluation methods are used, research methods do not always enable conclusions to be drawn about how a reform has affected the poor, in particular. Study designs need more commonly to disaggregate data across different subgroups of the population in order to understand how the poorest and most vulnerable are affected.

Third, much of the recent focus on evaluating policy has been around the use of randomized methods to assess the effectiveness of policy changes. While randomization is an ideal to be aspired to in some areas of public policy and to answer some types of questions, it is not always practical or feasible in a particular country context to use a randomized approach. Moreover, randomized studies, before and after impact evaluations with controls and interrupted time series studies are good at answering questions regarding effectiveness (does this intervention work in this particular context?), but there are also very pressing questions about *how* and *why* a policy change or strategy is effective, which such randomized impact evaluations can not always address. In the field of health systems, policies are often complex and multifaceted. For example, some policies, such as decentralization, take different forms in different countries and even within one country their form may change over time in response to political pressures. Other policies, such as establishing essential health packages, have often been only weakly or partially implemented. Understanding this complexity and the true nature of the policy reform is critical to be able to interpret findings regarding effects. Other types of study designs, such as case studies, particularly if conducted as part of a multi-country study, are better able to disentangle why a particular policy may be effective in certain contexts but not in others. This information is important for policy makers and other stakeholders if they are to apply global evidence to their own particular context. Understanding the mechanisms through which pro-poor policies work may also entail understanding the poor's own experiences of the policy: qualitative research employing in-depth interviews or participant observation may be effective in this respect.

Fourth, many of the evaluations which take place assess small-scale reforms: for example, the evidence on franchising or contracting for services typically comes from fairly small-scale experiments supported by external actors. It is thus difficult to predict how effective and sustainable such interventions may be if implemented more broadly. A further dimension to this question is the need for evidence on effective approaches to scaling up small programmes.

Systematic review methods, which have been widely used to synthesize evidence regarding clinical interventions, are increasingly being used to synthesize evidence on health systems and policy interventions (Effective Practice and Organization of Care Group 2006, http://www.epoc.uottawa.ca/). To date, such reviews have rarely focused on health system issues pertinent to developing countries, though there are initiatives to accelerate work in this field and develop review approaches more appropriate to the nature of low- and middle-income country health policy and systems research. Such reviews should both help map the existing knowledge base and also identify knowledge gaps and study designs that are best able to answer different types of health policy questions.

While research evidence will only ever be one among multiple influences upon policy making, better and more accessible evidence might at least encourage policy makers and civil society representatives to seek and use evidence in their decision-making. In some industrialized countries there are interesting initiatives to promote the use of evidence in policy (Nutley 2003), but few, if any, developing countries have similar strategies, although some such initiatives are now beginning to emerge (Van Kammen *et al*. 2006). If real progress is to be made in terms of strengthening health services for the poor, not only is greater political commitment and more strategic building of political support required, but also stronger information about which strategies may be effective, under what conditions and how they can be implemented.

Conclusions

The links between health, economic development and poverty are well documented, and recent research has reinforced the message that health is critical to economic development and has underscored the fact that poverty is a critical contributor to ill health as well as an impediment to people's ability to access quality health care services.

There seems to be greater commitment than ever before to improving the health of the poor in the developing world. This is reflected in the UN MDGs, but also in the increased resources now being channelled to global health, both from foundations such as the Gates Foundation and from industrialized country governments. Nonetheless, developing and implementing policies and strategies which are better able to meet the needs of the poor can seem like a frustratingly mammoth task. There are few simple and discrete interventions that are proven to be successful. A successful policy will typically have multiple interrelated components that have been tailored to match the local context. So, for example, a targeting strategy will need to be tailored to local market conditions and will require an effective communications strategy in order for it to work well. Even for those interventions or policies where there is robust evidence regarding their effectiveness and the conditions under which they are effective, problems may arise during implementation. Above all, developing and maintaining political commitment to the reforms can be a complex and challenging task.

Ultimately, it is not surprising that reforming health systems so that they better meet the needs of the poor is a long and difficult process, with no magic bullets. The close links between a country's broader economic development and the health of its people point to the many complex ways in which health, the health system and the broader economic and political environment are linked. While it may be possible, as countries such as Costa Rica, Cuba and Sri Lanka

234 of S. Bennett et al.

have demonstrated, to achieve health status beyond that predicted by their stage of economic development, this is clearly contingent upon a number of strongly political factors. Stakeholders within the health sector need both to understand the technical advantages and disadvantages of different policies to improve the health of the poor and to appreciate the political challenges in implementing these.

Bibliography

Abel-Smith, B. and Rawal, P. (1992) 'Can the poor afford "free" health services? A study of Tanzania', *Health Policy and Planning*, 7: 329–41.

Ableidinger, J., Case, A. and Paxson, C. (2002) 'Orphans in Africa', NBER Working Paper 9213, Cambridge, MA: National Bureau of Economic Research.

Acemoglu, D. and Johnson, S. (2006) 'Disease and development: the effect of life expectancy on economic growth', NBER Working Paper 12269. Online. Available at: www.nber.org/papers/w12269. Last accessed 25 April 2007.

Acemoglu, D., Johnson, S. and Robinson, J. (2003) 'Disease and development in historical perspective', *Journal of the European Economic Association*, 1: 397–405.

Acharya, L. and Cleland, J. (2000) 'Maternal and child health services in rural Nepal: does access or quality matter more?', *Health Policy and Planning*, 15: 223–9.

Agha, S. and Davies, J. (1998) 'Contraceptive social marketing in Pakistan: assessing the impact of the 1991 condom price increases on sales and consumption', PSI Research Division Working Paper No. 14, Washington, DC: Population Services International.

Agha, S. and Kusanthan, T. (2003) 'Equity in access to condoms in urban Zambia', *Health Policy and Planning*, 18: 299–305.

Agyepong, I.A. (1999) 'Reforming health service delivery at district level in Ghana: the perspective of a district medical officer', *Health Policy and Planning*, 14: 59–69.

Ahmed, S., Adams, A., Chowdhury, M. and Bhuiya, A. (2003) 'Changing health care seeking behaviour in Matlab, Bangladesh: do development interventions matter?', *Health Policy and Planning*, 18: 306–15.

Ahmed, S.M., Petzold, M., Kbair, Z.N. and Tomson, G. (2006) 'Targeted intervention for the ultra poor in rural Bangladesh: Does it make any difference in their health seeking behaviour?', *Social Science and Medicine*, 63: 2899–911.

Akin, J., Birsdall, N. and de Ferranti, D. (1987) 'Financing health services in developing countries: an agenda for reform', a World Bank Policy Study, Washington, DC: World Bank.

Alderman, H. and Lindert, K. (1998) 'The potential and limitations of self-targeted food subsidies', *World Bank Research Observer*, 13: 213–29.

Alliance for Health Policy and Systems Research (2004) *Strengthening health systems: the role and promise of health systems research*, Geneva: Alliance for Health Policy and Systems Research.

Alsan, M., Bloom, D.E. and Canning, D. (2004) 'The effect of population health on foreign direct investment', NBER Working Paper 10596, Cambridge, MA: National Bureau of Economic Research.

Anand, S. and Barnighausen, T. (2004) 'Human resources and health outcomes: cross-country econometric study', *The Lancet*, 364: 1603–9.

Andersen, H. (2004) '"Villagers": differential treatment in a Ghanaian hospital', *Social Science and Medicine*, 59: 2003–12.

Anwar, A., Killewo, J., Chowdhury, M. and Dasgupta, S. (2004) 'Bangladesh: inequalities in utilization of maternal health care services – evidence from Matlab', HNP Discussion Paper, Reaching the Poor Program Paper No. 2, Washington, DC: World Bank.

Arora, S. (2001) 'Health, human productivity and long-term growth', *Journal of Economic History*, 61: 699–749.

Asenso-Okyere, W.K. and Dzator, J.A. (1997) 'Household cost of seeking malaria care: a retrospective study of two districts in Ghana', *Social Science and Medicine*, 45: 659–67.

Asian Development Bank (1997) *Emerging Asia, Changes and Challenges*, Manila: Asian Development Bank.

Atkinson, S. and Haran, D. (2004) 'Back to Basics: does decentralization improve health system performance? Evidence from Ceara in north-east Brazil', *Bulletin of the World Health Organization*, 82: 822–7.

Atkinson, A. and Haran, D. (2005) 'Individual and district scale determinants of users' satisfaction with primary health care in developing countries', *Social Science and Medicine*, 60: 501–13.

Attanayake, N., Fox-Rushby, J. and Mills, A. (2000) 'Household costs of "malaria" morbidity: a study in Matale district, Sri Lanka', *Tropical Medicine and International Health*, 5: 595–606.

Audibert, M. (1986) 'Agricultural non-wage production and health status: a case study in a tropical environment', *Journal of Development Economics*, 24: 275–91.

Ayé, M., Champagne, F. and Contandriopoulos, A.-P. (2002) 'Economic role of solidarity and social capital in accessing modern health care services in the Ivory Coast', *Social Science and Medicine*, 55: 1929–46.

Babu, B.V., Nayak, A.N., Dhal, A.S., Acharya, A.S., Jangid, P.K. and Mallick, G. (2002) 'The economic loss due to treatment costs and work loss to individuals with chronic lymphatic filariasis in rural communities of Orissa, India', *Acta Tropica*, 82: 31–8.

Baker, J. and van der Gaag, J. (1993) 'Equity in health care and health care financing: evidence from five developing countries', in E.V. Doorslaer, A. Wagstaff and F. Rutten (eds) *Equity in the finance and delivery of health care: an international perspective*, New York: Oxford University Press.

Balabanova, D. and McKee, M. (2002) 'Understanding informal payments for health care: the example of Bulgaria', *Health Policy*, 62: 243–73.

Baltussen, R., Ye, Y., Haddad, S. and Sauerborn, R.S. (2002) 'Perceived quality of care of primary health care services in Burkina Faso', *Health Policy and Planning*, 17: 42–8.

Barraza-Lorens, M., Bertozzi, S., Gonzalez-Pier, E. and Gutierrez, J.P. (2002) 'Addressing inequity in health and health care in Mexico', *Health Affairs*, 21: 47–56.

Barro, R. (1996) 'Health and economic growth', mimeo, Harvard University.

Barro, R. (1997) '*Determinants of economic growth: a cross-country empirical study*' (Lionel Robbins Lectures), Cambridge, MA: MIT Press.

Barro, R. and Sala-i-Martin, X. (1995) *Economic growth*, New York: McGraw-Hill.

Bebbington, A. (1999) 'Capitals and capabilities: a framework for analysing peasant viability, rural livelihoods and poverty', *World Development*, 27: 2021–44.

Becker, G.S., Philipson, T.J. and Soares, R.R. (2005) 'The quantity of life and the evolution of world inequality', *American Economic Review*, 95: 277–91.

Behrman, J.R. and Deolalikar, A.B. (1988) 'Health and nutrition', in H. Chenery and

T.N. Srinivasan (eds) *Handbook of development economics*, Amsterdam: Elsevier Science Publishers B.V.

Benjakul, S. (2004) 'Equity of health care utilization by the elderly population in Thailand during the periods of the economic bubble and after the economic crisis: policy options', unpublished PhD thesis (medical and health social sciences), Faculty of Graduate Studies, Bangkok, Thailand, Mahidol University.

Bennett, S. (2004) 'The role of community-based health insurance within the health care financing system: a framework for analysis', *Health Policy and Planning*, 19: 147–58.

Bennett, S., Russell, S. and Mills, A. (1995) 'Institutional and economic perspectives on government capacity to assume new roles in the health sector: a review of experience', The Role of Government in Adjusting Economies Working Paper 4, Birmingham: International Development Department, University of Birmingham.

Bennett, S., Creese, A. and Monasch, R. (1998) 'Health insurance schemes for people outside formal sector employment', ARA Paper No. 16, Geneva: Division of Analysis, Research and Assessment, World Health Organization.

Bennett, S., Hanson, K., Kadama, P. and Montagu, D. (2005) 'Working with the non-state sector to achieve public health goals', Making Health Systems Work: Working Paper No. 2, Geneva: World Health Organization. Online. Available at: www.who.int/management/Making%20HSWork%202.pdf. Last accessed 25 April 2007.

Berk, M.L., Gaylin, D.S. and Schur, C.L. (2006) 'Exploring the public's views on the health care system: a national survey on the issues and options', *Health Affairs*, 25: 596–606.

Berman, P., Kendall, C. and Bhattacharyya, K. (1994) 'The household production of health: integrating social science perspectives on micro-level health determinants', *Social Science and Medicine*, 38: 205–15.

Besley, T. and Kanbur, R. (1993) 'Principles of targeting', in M. Lipton and J. van der Gaag (eds) *Including the poor*, Washington, DC: The World Bank.

Bhargava, A., Jamison, D., Lau, L. and Murray, C. (2001) 'Modeling the effects of health on economic growth', *Journal of Health Economics*, 20: 423–40.

Bhushan, I., Keller, S. and Schwartz, B. (2002) 'Achieving the twin objectives of efficiency and equity: contracting health services in Cambodia', ERD Policy Brief No. 6, Manila: Asian Development Bank.

Biggs, T. and Shah, M. (1997) 'The impact of the AIDS epidemic on African firms', RPED Discussion Paper No. 72, Washington, DC: The World Bank.

Bill and Melinda Gates Foundation (2006) '2005 Annual Report', Seattle, WA: Bill and Melinda Gates Foundation.

Bils, M. and Klenow, P.J. (2000) 'Does schooling cause growth?', *American Economic Review*, 90: 1160–83.

Blackburn, J. and Holland, J. (eds) (1998) *Who changes? Institutionalising participation in development*, London: Intermediate Technology Publications.

Blair, H. (2003) *Civil Society, dispute resolution and local governance in Bangladesh: ideas for pro-poor programme support*, report prepared for the Department of International Development, Dhaka: UK High Commission.

Blas, E. and Limbambala, M.E. (2001a) 'User-payment, decentralization and health service utilization in Zambia', *Health Policy and Planning*, 16: 29–43.

Blas, E. and Limbambala, M.E. (2001b) 'The challenge of hospitals in health sector reform: the case of Zambia', *Health Policy and Planning*, 16 (Suppl. 2): 29–43.

Bleakley, H. (2003) 'Disease and development, evidence from the American South', *Journal of the European Economic Association*, 1: 376–86.

Bleakley, H. (2006) 'Disease and development: comments on Acemolgu and Johnson', remarks delivered at the NBER Summer Institute on Economic Fluctuations and Growth, 16 July. Online. Available at: http://home.uchicago.edu/~bleakley/Bleakley _Comments_Acemoglu_Johnson.pdf. Last accessed 25 April 2007.

Blinkhoff, P., Bukanga, E., Syamalevwe, B. and Williams, G. (1999) *Under the Mupundu Tree: volunteers in home care for people with HIV/AIDS and TB in Zambia's Copperbelt*, Strategies for Hope Series, No. 14, London: ActionAid.

Bloom, D.E. (2005) 'Education and public health: mutual challenges worldwide: Guest Editor's overview', *Comparative Education Review*, 49: 437–51.

Bloom, D.E. (2006) 'Education, health, and development', in J.E. Cohen, D.E. Bloom and M. Malin (eds) *Universal basic and secondary education: what, why, and how*, Cambridge, MA: MIT Press.

Bloom, D.E. and Canning, D. (2001) 'Demographic change and economic growth: the role of cumulative causality', in N. Birdsall, A.C. Kelley and S. Sinding (eds) *Population does matter: demography, growth, and poverty in the developing world*, New York: Oxford University Press.

Bloom, D.E. and Canning, D. (2003) 'The health and poverty of nations: from theory to practice', *Journal of Human Development*, 4: 47–71.

Bloom, D.E. and Canning, D. (forthcoming) 'The Preston Curve 30 years on: still sparking fires', *International Journal of Epidemiology*.

Bloom, D.E. and Mahal, A.S. (1997a) 'Does the AIDS epidemic threaten economic growth?', *Journal of Econometrics*, 77: 105–24.

Bloom, D.E. and Mahal, A. (1997b) 'AIDS, flu, and the Black Death: impacts on economic growth and well-being', in D. Bloom and P. Godwin (eds) *The economics of HIV and AIDS: the case of South and South East Asia*, New Delhi, India: Oxford University Press.

Bloom, D.E. and Williamson, J.G. (1998) 'Demographic transitions and economic miracles in emerging Asia', *World Bank Economic Review*, 12: 419–55.

Bloom, D.E., Canning, D. and Malaney, P. (2000) 'Demographic change and economic growth in Asia', *Population and Development Review*, 26 (Suppl.): 257–90.

Bloom, D.E., Canning, D. and Graham, B. (2003) 'Longevity and life-cycle savings', *Scandinavian Journal of Economics*, 105: 319–38.

Bloom, D.E., Canning, D. and Sevilla, J. (2004a) 'The effect of health on economic growth: a production function approach', *World Development*, 32 (1): 1–13.

Bloom, D.E., Canning, D. and Jamison, D. (2004b) 'Health, wealth and welfare', *Finance and Development*, 41: 10–15.

Bloom, D.E., Canning, D., Graham, B. and Sevilla, J. (2006) 'Improving health: a key to halving global poverty by 2015', in M.R. Agosín, D.E. Bloom, G. Chapelier and J. Saigal (eds) *Solving the riddle of globalization and development*, London: Routledge.

Bloom, D.E., Canning, D., Mansfield, R. and Moore, M. (forthcoming) 'Demographic change, savings, and international capital flows: theory and evidence', *Journal of Monetary Economics*.

Bobonis, G.J., Miguel, E. and Puri-Sharma, C. (forthcoming) 'Anemia and school participation', *Journal of Human Resources*.

Bond, P. and Dor, G. (2003b) 'Neoliberalism and poverty reduction strategies in Africa', EQUINET Discussion Paper 3, Online. Available at: www.equinetafrica.org.

Booysen, F. (2004) 'Social grants as safety net for HIV/AIDS-affected households in South Africa', *Journal of Social Aspects of HIV/AIDS Research Alliance*, 1: 45–56.

Bossert, T., Chitah, B. and Bowser, D. (2003a) 'Decentralization in Zambia: resource allocation and district performance', *Health Policy and Planning*, 18: 357–69.

Bossert, T.J., Larrañaga, O., Giedion, U., Arbelaez, J.J. and Bowser, D.M. (2003b) 'Decentralization and equity of resource allocation: evidence from Colombia and Chile', *Bulletin of the World Health Organization*, 81: 95–100.

Bossyns, P. and van Lerberghe, W. (2004) 'The weakest link: competence and prestige as constraints to referral by isolated nurses in rural Niger', *Human Resources for Health*, 2: 1.

Bourgignon, F. (1999) 'Absolute poverty, relative deprivation and social exclusion', Villa Borsig Workshop series 1999, Inclusion, Justice and Poverty Reduction. Online. Available at: www.gdsnet.org/classes/BourgignonRelativeDeprivation.pdf. Last accessed 25 April 2007.

Breman, A. and Shelton, C. (2001) 'Structural adjustment and health: a literature review of the debate, its role players and presented empirical evidence', Commission on Macroeconomics and Health Working Paper Series, No. WG6:6, Geneva: World Health Organization.

Brinkerhoff, D.W. (2000) 'Democratic governance and sectoral policy reform: tracing linkages and exploring synergies', *World Development*, 28: 601–15.

Brinkerhoff, D. (2003) 'Accountability and health systems: overview, framework and strategies', Technical Report No. 018, Bethesda, MD: Partners for Health Reform*plus* Project, Abt Associates Inc.

British Broadcasting Corporation (BBC) (2002) 'Aids ravages ranks of teachers', 8 May.

Brockerhoff, M. and Hewett, P. (2000) 'Inequality of child mortality among ethnic groups in sub-Saharan Africa' *Bulletin of the World health Organization*, 78: 30–41.

Brugha, R. (2003) 'Antiretroviral treatment in developing countries: the peril of neglecting private providers', *British Medical Journal*, 326: 1382–4.

Bulatao, R. and Ross, J. (2002) 'Rating maternal and neonatal health services in developing countries', *Bulletin of the World Health Organization*, 80: 721–7.

Burnham, G.M., Pariyo, G., Galiwanog, E. and Wabwire-Mangen, F. (2004) 'Discontinuation of cost sharing in Uganda', *Bulletin of the World Health Organization*, 82: 187–95.

Burnside, C. and Dollar, D. (2004) 'Aid, policies and growth: revisiting the evidence', Policy Research Working Paper 3251, Washington, DC: World Bank.

Buse, K. and Walt, G. (2000) 'Global public–private partnerships: Part II', *Bulletin of the World Health Organization*, 78: 699–710.

Bustreo, F., Harding, A. and Axelsson, H. (2003) 'Can developing countries achieve adequate improvements in child health outcomes without engaging the private sector?', *Bulletin of the World Health Organization*, 81: 886–94.

Cao, X.Y., Jiang, X.M., Dou, Z.H., Rakeman, M.A., Zhang, M.L. *et al.* (1994) 'Timing and vulnerability of the brain to iodine deficiency in endemic cretinism', *New England Journal of Medicine*, 331: 1739–41.

Carney, D. (ed.) (1998) *Sustainable rural livelihoods: what contribution can we make?*, London: Department for International Development.

Case, A. (2001) 'Does money protect health status? Evidence from South African pensions', NBER Working Paper 8495, Cambridge, MA: National Bureau of Economic Research.

Castro-Leal, F., Dayton, J., Demery, L. and Mehra, K. (2000) 'Public social spending in Africa: do the poor benefit?', *Bulletin of the World Health Organization*, 78: 66–74.

Center for Global Development (2006) 'Call for an international initiative to foster independent impact evaluation of social sector programs and policies'. Online. Available at: www.cgdev.org/section/initiatives/_active/evalgap/calltoaction. Last accessed 25 April 2007.

Center for the Study of Human Rights (2001) *25+ Human Rights Documents*, New York: Columbia University Press.

Chakraborty, S. (2004) 'Endogenous lifetime and economic growth', *Journal of Economic Theory*, 116: 119–37.

Chakraborty, S. and Frick, K. (2002) 'Factors influencing private health providers' technical quality of care for acute respiratory infections among under-five children in rural West Bengal, India', *Social Science and Medicine*, 55: 1579–87.

Chakraborty, S., D'Souza, S.A. and Northrup, R. (2000) 'Improving private practitioner care of sick children: testing new approaches in rural Bihar', *Health Policy and Planning*, 15: 400–7.

Chale, S., Swai, A., Mujinja, P. and McLarty, D. (1992) 'Must diabetes be a fatal disease in Africa?', *British Medical Journal*, 304: 1215–17.

Chalker, J., Ratanawijitrasin, S., Chuc, N.T., Petzold, M. and Tomson, G. (2005) 'Effectiveness of a multi-component intervention on dispensing practices at private pharmacies in Vietnam and Thailand – a randomized controlled trial', *Social Science and Medicine*, 60: 131–41.

Chambers, R. (1989) 'Editorial introduction: vulnerability, coping and policy', *IDS Bulletin*, 20: 1–7.

Chapman, J. (1999) 'The response of civil society to the globalisation of the marketing of breast milk substitutes, Ghana', *Journal of the Society for International Development*, 42: 103–7.

Chatterjee, M. and Vyas, J. (1997) *Organizing insurance for women workers: the SEWA experience*, Ahmedabad, India: Self-Employed Women's Association.

Chee, G., Smith, K. and Kapinga, A. (2002) 'Assessment of the community health fund in Hanang District, Tanzania', Bethesda, MD: Partners for Health Reform*plus*, Abt Associates Inc.

Cheru, F. (2006) 'Building and supporting PRSPs in Africa: what has worked well so far? What needs changing?', *Third World Quarterly*, 27: 355–76.

Chopra, M. (2004) 'Food security, rural development and health equity in Southern Africa', EQUINET Discussion Paper 22. Online. Available at: www.equinetafrica.org.

Chopra, M., Munro, S. and Vist, G. (2007) *Evidence from systematic reviews to inform policy-making about optimizing the supply, improving the distribution, increasing the efficiency and enhancing the performance of health workers*, Geneva: Alliance for Health Policy and Systems Research, World Health Organization.

Chowdhury, M.E., Ronsmans, C., Killewo, J., Anwar, I., Gausia, K. *et al.* (2006) 'Equity in use of home-based or facility-based skilled obstetric care in rural Bangladesh: an observational study', *The Lancet*, 367: 327–32.

Chuc, N.T., Larsson, M., Do, N.T., Diwan, V.K., Tomson, G.B. and Falkenberg, T. (2002) 'Improving private pharmacy practice: a multi-intervention experiment in Hanoi, Vietnam', *Journal of Clinical Epidemiology*, 55: 1148–55.

Chuengsatiansup, K. (2001) 'Civil society and health: broadening the alliance for health development', mimeo, paper prepared for the Ministry of Public Health, Thailand.

Chuengsatiansup, K. (2004) '*Deliberating health agenda: civil society and health systems reform in Thailand*', Nonthaburi: Health Systems Research Institute.

Claeson, M., Griffin, T., Johnston, M., McLachlan, A., Soucat, A. *et al.* (2001) 'Health, nutrition and population', in World Bank, *Poverty Reduction Strategy Papers' Sourcebook*, Washington, DC: The World Bank.

Collins, K.J., Brotherhood, R.J., Davies, C.T., Dore, C., Imms, F. *et al.* (1976) 'Physiological performance and work capacity of Sudanese cane cutters with Schistosoma mansoni infection', *American Journal of Tropical Medicine and Hygiene*, 25: 410–21.

Commission on Macroeconomics and Health (2001) *Macroeconomics and health: investing in health for economic development*, Geneva: World Health Organization.

Committee on International Science, Engineering, and Technology Policy (CISET) (2006) *Global microbial threats in the 1990s*. Online. Available at: http://clinton1.nara.gov/White_House/EOP/OSTP/CISET/html/iintro.html (accessed 14 September 2006).

Community Working Group on Health (1997) 'Health in Zimbabwe: community perceptions and views', Research Report, November 1997, supported by OXFAM and TARSC, Harare: Community Working Group on Health.

Conning, J. and Kevane, M. (2001) 'Community based targeting mechanisms for social safety nets', Social Protection Discussion Paper No. 0102, Washington, DC: The World Bank.

Corbett, J. (1988) 'Famine and household coping strategies', *World Development*, 16: 1099–112.

Cornia, G.A. and Stewart, F. (1993) 'Two errors of targeting', *Journal of International Development*, 5: 459–96.

Cornwall, A., Lucas, H. and Pasteur, K. (2000) 'Accountability through participation: developing workable partnership models in the health sector', *IDS Bulletin*, 31(1).

Crook, R. (2003) 'Decentralization and poverty reduction in Africa: the politics of local-central relations', *Public Administration and Development*, 23 (1): 77–88.

Cropper, M.L., Haile, M., Lampietti, J.A., Poulos, C. and Whittington, D. (1999) *The value of preventing malaria in Tembien, Ethiopia*, Washington, DC: The World Bank.

Creese, A. (1997) 'User fees: they don't reduce costs, and they increase inequity', *British Medical Journal*, 315: 202–3.

Culyer, A.J. (1995) 'Need: the idea won't do – but we still need it', *Social Science and Medicine*, 40: 727–30.

Cutler, D.M., Deaton, A.S. and Lleras-Muney, A. (2006) 'The determinants of mortality', *Journal of Economic Perspectives*, 20: 71–96.

Dale, S. (2001) 'How Thailand took on the transnational tobacco titans', *IDRC Reports*, 20 April 2001.

Deacon, B. (1999) 'Towards a socially responsible globalisation', GASPP Occasional Paper No. 1, Helsinki: STAKES.

Deacon, B., Disney, J., Stubbs, P., Wedel, J. and Wood, A. (2000) 'Civil society, NGOs and global governance', GASPP Occasional Paper No. 7, Helsinki: STAKES.

Deininger, K. and Mpuga, P. (2005) 'Economic and welfare impact of the abolition of health user fees: evidence from Uganda', *Journal of African Economies*, 14: 55–91.

de la Croix, D. and Licandro, O. (1999) 'Life expectancy and endogenous growth', *Economic Letters*, 65: 255–63.

Demery, L. (2000) *Benefit incidence: a practitioner's guide*, Washington, DC: World Bank.

Dercon, S. (2004) *Insurance against poverty*, Oxford: Oxford University Press.

De Savigny, D., Kasale, H., Mbuya, C. and Reid, G. (2004) *Fixing health systems*, Ottawa, Ontario: International Development Research Centre and the Ministry of Health, Tanzania.

Devereux, S. (1999) 'Targeting transfers: innovative solutions to familiar problems', *IDS Bulletin*, 30: 61–74.

de Waal, A. (1989) 'Is famine relief irrelevant to rural people?', *IDS Bulletin*, 20: 63–7.

DFID (1999) *Key sheets for sustainable livelihoods: overview*, London: UK Department for International Development and Overseas Development Institute. Online. Available at: www.keysheets.org/overview.pdf. Last accessed 25 April 2007.

Dodd, R., Hinshelwood, E. and Harvey, C. (2004) *Poverty reduction strategy papers: their significance for health. Second synthesis report*, WHO/HDP/PRSP/04.1, Geneva: World Health Organization.

Doherty, J., Gilson, L. and EQUINET (2006) 'Proposed areas of investigation for the KN: an initial scoping of the literature', Discussion Document No. 1, Health Systems Knowledge Network (KN), WHO Commission on Social Determinants of Health. Online. Available at: www.who.int/social_determinants/resources/health_systems.pdf (accessed 1 September 2006).

Donaldson, C., Gerard, K., Jan, S., Mitton, C. and Wiseman, V. (2004) *Economics of health care financing: the visible hand*, Basingstoke: Palgrave Macmillan.

Doupe, A. and Flavell, S. (2003) 'A multi-country study of the involvement of people living with HIV/AIDS (PLWHA) in the Country Coordinating Mechanisms (CCM)', Amsterdam: Global Network of People living with HIV/AIDS (GNP+).

Dreze, J. and Sen, A. (1989) *Hunger and public action*, Oxford: Clarendon Press.

Easterlin, R. (1999) 'How beneficent is the market? A look at the modern history of mortality', *European Review of Economic History*, 3: 257–94.

Easterly, W. (1999) 'Life during growth', *Journal of Economic Growth*, 4: 239–76.

Economist, The (2001) 'The worst way to lose talent', *The Economist*, 8 February.

Ekman, B. (2004) 'Community-based health insurance in low-income countries: a systematic review of the evidence', *Health Policy and Planning*, 19: 249–70.

Elwan, A. (1999) 'Poverty and disability: a survey of the literature', Social Protection Discussion Paper No. 9932, Washington, DC: World Bank.

Ensor, T., Dave-Sen, P., Ali, H., Hossain, A., Begum, S.A. and Moral, H. (2002) 'Do essential service packages benefit the poor? Preliminary evidence from Bangladesh', *Health Policy and Planning*, 17: 247–56.

Ensor, T., Hossain, A., Dave Sen, P., Ali, L., Begum, S.A. and Moral, H. (2003) 'Geographic resource allocation in Bangladesh', in A.S. Yazbeck and D.H. Peters (eds) *Health policy research in South Asia: building capacity for reform*, Washington, DC: The World Bank.

EQUINET Steering Committee (2000) 'Turning values into practice: equity in health in Southern Africa', EQUINET Policy Series No.7, Harare: EQUINET.

EQUINET Steering Committee (2004) 'Reclaiming the state: advancing people's health, challenging injustice: equity in health in southern Africa', EQUINET Policy Series No. 18, Harare: EQUINET.

EQUINET/TARSC (1998) 'Bibliography and overview: equity in health in the Southern African Development Community (SADC) Region', EQUINET Policy Series Policy No. 2, Harare: EQUINET.

EQUINET/TARSC (2000) 'Report of the TARSC/EQUINET regional meeting on public participation in health, in co-operation with IDRC (Canada) and WHO (AFRO/HSSD)', EQUINET Policy Series No. 5, Harare: EQUINET.

Escobar, M. (2005) 'Health sector reform in Colombia', *Development Outreach*, May 2005. Online. Available at: www1.worldbank.org/devoutreach/may05/article.asp?id=295. Last accessed 25 April 2007.

Ettling, M. and Shepard, D. (1991) 'Economic cost of malaria in Rwanda', *Tropical Medicine and Parasitology*, 42: 214–18.

Ettling, M., McFarland, D.A., Schultz, L.J. and Chitsulo, L. (1994) 'Economic impact of malaria in Malawian households', *Tropical Medicine and Parasitology*, 45: 74–9.

Faguet, J.-P. (2001) 'Does decentralization increase responsiveness to local needs? Evidence from Bolivia.' *World Bank Police Research Working Paper*: World Bank 2516

Falkingham, J. (2004) 'Poverty, out-of-pocket payments and access to health care: evidence from Tajikistan', *Social Science and Medicine*, 58: 247–58.

Falkingham, J. and Namazie, C. (2002) 'Measuring health and poverty: a review of approaches to identifying the poor', London: DFID Health Systems Resource Centre.

Feachem, R.G. and Sabot, O.J. (2006) 'An examination of the Global Fund at 5 years', *The Lancet*, 368: 537–40.

Fenwick, A. and Figenschou, B.H. (1972) 'The effect of Schistosoma mansoni infection of the productivity of cane cutters on a sugar estate in Tanzania', *Bulletin of the World Health Organization*, 47: 567–72.

Filmer, D. and Pritchett, L. (2001) 'Estimating wealth effects without expenditure data – or tears: an application to educational enrolments in states of India', *Demography*, 38: 115–32.

Finlay, J. (2006) 'The role of health in economic development', mimeo, Harvard University Program on the Global Demography of Aging.

Fogel, R.W. (1990) 'The conquest of high mortality and hunger in Europe and America: timing and mechanisms', NBER Working Paper No. 16, Cambridge, MA: National Bureau of Economic Research.

Fogel, R.W. (1994) 'Economic growth, population theory and physiology: the bearing of long term processes on the making of economic policy', *American Economic Review*, 84: 369–95.

Foster, R. (1967) 'Schistosomiasis on an irrigated estate in East Africa: effects of asymptomatic infection on health and industrial efficiency', *Journal of Tropical Medicine and Hygiene*, 70: 185–95.

Foster, A. (1994) 'Poverty and illness in low-income rural areas', *American Economic Review*, 84: 216–20.

Fox, M., Rosen, S., MacLeod, W., Wasunna, M., Bii, M. *et al.* (2004) 'The impact of HIV/AIDS on labour productivity in Kenya', *Tropical Medicine and International Health*, 9: 318–24.

Freedman, L., Waldman, R.J., de Pinho, H., Worth, M., Chowdhury, A.M.R. and Rosenfield, A. (2005) *Who's got the power? transforming health systems for women and children*, New York: UN Millennium Project Task Force on Child Health and Maternal Health.

Frenk, J., Sepulveda, J., Gomez-Dantes, O. and Knaul, F. (2003) 'Evidence-based health policy: three generations of reforms in Mexico', *The Lancet*, 362: 1667–71.

Gakidou, E., Murray, C. and Frenk, J. (2000) 'Defining and measuring health inequality: an approach based on the distribution of health expectancy', *Bulletin of the World Health Organization*, 78: 66–74.

Gallup, J.L. and Sachs, J.D. (2001) 'The economic burden of malaria', *American Journal of Tropical Medicine and Hygiene*, 64 (1–2 Suppl.): 85–96.

Gaventa, J. and Robinson, M. (1998) 'Influence from below and space from above: non elite action and pro-poor policies', Mimeo, Brighton, UK: Institute of Development Studies.

Gelbach, J.B. and Pritchett, L.H. (1997) 'More for the poor is less for the poor: the politics of targeting', Policy Research Working Paper 1799, Washington, DC: The World Bank.

George, A. (2003) 'Accountability in health services: transforming relationships and contexts', Working Paper Vol. 1, No. 13, Boston, MA: Harvard Center for Population and Development Studies.

Gertler, P.J. (2000) 'Final report: the impact of PROGRESA on health', Washington, DC: IFPRI. Online. Available at: www.ifpri.org/themes/progresa/pdf/Gertler_health.pdf. Last accessed 25 April 2007.

Gertler, P. and Hammer, J. (1997) *Strategies for pricing publicly provided health services*, Washington, DC: World Bank.

Gideon, U. and Bitran, R. (2002) 'Waivers and exemptions for health services in developing countries', Washington, DC: The World Bank. Online. Available at: http://info.worldbank.org/etools/docs/library/80703/Dc%202002/courses/dc2002/readings/aldeman.pdf (accessed 26 May 2006).

Gill, C.J., Griffith, J.L., Jacobson, D., Skinner, S., Gorbach, S.L. and Wilson, I.B. (2002) 'Relationship of HIV viral loads, CD4 counts, and HAART use to health-related quality of life', *Journal of Acquired Immune Deficiency Syndrome*, 30: 485–92.

Gilson, L. (1988) 'Government health care charges: is equity being abandoned?' EPC Publication No. 15, London: London School of Hygiene and Tropical Medicine.

Gilson, L. (1997) 'The lessons of user fee experience in Africa', *Health Policy and Planning*, 12: 273–85.

Gilson, L. (2005a) 'Editorial: building trust and value in health systems in low and middle income countries', *Social Science and Medicine*, 61: 1381–4.

Gilson, L. (2005b) 'Applying policy analysis in tackling implementation gaps', Paper presented to Forum 9, Global Forum for Health Research, Mumbai, India, 12–16 September 2005. Online. Available at: www.equinetafrica.org/bibl/docs/GILmon092005.pdf. Last accessed 25 April 2007.

Gilson, L. and Mills, A. (1995) 'Health sector reforms in sub-Saharan Africa: lessons of the past 10 years', *Health Policy*, 32: 215–43.

Gilson, L. and McIntyre, D. (2005) 'Removing user fees for primary care in Africa: the need for careful action', *British Medical Journal*, 331: 762–5.

Gilson, L., Alilio, M. and Heggenhougen, K. (1994a) 'Community satisfaction with primary health care services: an evaluation undertaken in the Morogoro region of Tanzania', *Social Science and Medicine*, 39: 767–80.

Gilson, L., Kilima, P. and Tanner, M. (1994b) 'Local government decentralisation and the health sector in Tanzania', *Public Administration and Development*, 14: 451–77.

Gilson, L., Russell, S. and Buse, K. (1995) 'The political economy of user fees with targeting: developing equitable health financing policy', *Journal of International Development*, 7: 369–401.

Gilson, L., Doherty, J., McIntyre, D., Thomas, S., Briljal, V. and Bowa, C. (1999) *The dynamics of policy change: health care financing in South Africa, 1994–1999*, Major Applied Research Paper 1, Technical Paper 1, Bethesda, MD: Partnerships for Health Reform Project, Abt Associates Inc.

Gilson, L., Doherty, J., Lake, S., McIntyre, D., Mwikisa, C. and Thomas, S. (2003) 'The SAZA study: implementing health financing reform in South Africa and Zambia', *Health Policy and Planning*, 18: 31–46.

Gilson, L., Palmer, N. and Schneider, H. (2005) 'Trust and health workers performance: exploring a conceptual framework using South African evidence', *Social Science and Medicine*, 61: 1418–29.

Glassman, A., Reich, M.R., Laserson, K. and Rojas, F. (1999) 'Political analysis of health reform in the Dominican Republic', *Health Policy and Planning*, 14: 115–26.

Goetz, A.M. and Gaventa, J. (2001) 'Bringing citizen voice and client focus into service delivery', IDS Working Paper 138, Brighton, UK: Institute of Development Studies.

Goldman, N., Pebley, A.R. and Beckett, M. (2001) 'Diffusion of ideas about personal hygiene and contamination in poor countries: evidence from Guatemala', *Social Science and Medicine*, 52: 53–69.

Goodman, C., Kachur, P., Abdulla, S., Mwageni, E., Nyoni, J. *et al.* (2004) 'Retail supply of malaria-related drugs in rural Tanzania: risks and opportunities', *Tropical Medicine and International Health*, 9: 655–63.

Gorter, A., Sandiford, P., Segura, Z. and Villabella, C. (1999) 'Improved health care for sex workers: a voucher programme for female sex workers in Nicaragua', *Research for Sex Work* 2. Online. Available at: http://hcc.med.vu.nl/artikelen/gorter2.htm. Last accessed 25 April 2007.

Goudge, J., Khumalo, N. and Gilson, L. (2003) 'Policy options to improve the economic access of low-income households to state-provided health care', paper commissioned by the Affordability Ladder Programme, University of Liverpool. Johannesburg: Centre for Health Policy, University of the Witwatersrand.

Government of Ghana (2003) National Health Insurance Act (Act 650), Accra: Government of Ghana.

Gragnolati, M. and Marini, A. (2003) 'Health and poverty in Guatemala', World Bank Policy Research Working Paper No. 2966, Washington, DC: The World Bank.

Grantham-McGregor, S. and Ani, C. (2001) 'A review of studies on the effect of iron deficiency on cognitive development in children', *The Journal of Nutrition*, 131(2S-2): 649S–666S.

Green, A., Ali, B., Naeem, A. and Ross, D. (2000) 'Resource allocation and budgetary mechanisms for decentralized health systems: experiences from Balochistan, Pakistan', *Bulletin of the World Health Organization*, 78: 1024–33.

Gulliford, M., Figueroa-Munoz, J., Morgan, M., Hughes, D., Gibson, B. *et al.* (2002) 'What does access to health care mean?', *Journal of Health Services Research and Policy*, 7: 186–8.

Gumber, A. (2004) 'The potential role of community financing in India', in A. Preker and G. Carrin (eds) *Health financing for poor people: resource mobilization and risk sharing*, Washington, DC: The World Bank.

Gumber, A. and Kulkarni, V. (2000) 'Health insurance for informal sector: case study of Gujarat', *Economic and Political Weekly*, 35: 3607–13.

Guyatt, H.L., Gotink, M.H., Ochola, S.A. and Snow, R.W. (2002) 'Free bednets to pregnant women through antenatal clinics in Kenya: a cheap, simple and equitable approach to delivery', *Tropical Medicine and International Health*, 7: 409–20.

Gwatkin, D. (2000a) 'Health inequalities and the health of the poor: what do we know? What can we do?', *Bulletin of the World Health Organization*, 78: 3–18.

Gwatkin, D. (2000b) *The current state of knowledge about: targeting health programs to reach the poor*, Washington, DC: World Bank.

Gwatkin, D. (2002a) 'Reducing health inequalities in developing countries', in R. Detels, J. McEwen, R. Beaglehole and H. Tanaka (eds) *Oxford Textbook of public health*, Oxford: Oxford University Press.

Gwatkin, D. (2002b) *Who would gain the most from efforts to reach the millennium development goals for health? an inquiry into the possibility of progress that fails to reach the poor*, HNP Discussion Paper, Washington, DC: World Bank.

Gwatkin, D., Rutstein, S., Johnson, K., Suliman, E., Wagstaff, A. *et al.* (2005a) *Socio-economic differences in health, nutrition and population*, second edition, Washington, DC: The World Bank.

Gwatkin, D., Yazbeck, A. and Wagstaff A. (eds) (2005b) *Reaching the poor with health, nutrition and population services: what works, what doesn't, and why*, Washington, DC: World Bank.

Gwatkin, D.R. (2001) 'The need for equity-oriented health sector reforms', *International Journal of Epidemiology*, 30: 720–3.

Gwatkin, D.R., Rutstein, S., Johnson, K., Pande, R. and Wagstaff, A. (2000) *Socio-economic differences in health, nutrition, and population*, Washington, DC: Health, Nutrition and Population Department, World Bank.

Ha, N.T., Berman, P. and Larsen, U. (2002) 'Household utilisation and expenditures on private and public health services in Vietnam', *Health Policy and Planning*, 17: 61–70.

Haacker, M. (2004) 'HIV/AIDS: the impact on the social fabric and the economy', in M. Haacker (ed.) *The macroeconomics of HIV/AIDS*, Washington, DC: International Monetary Fund.

Haddad, S. and Fournier, P. (1995) 'Quality, cost and utilization of health services in developing countries: a longitudinal study in Zaire', *Social Science and Medicine*, 40: 743–53.

HAI (2001) 'Drug policy at the 54th World Health Assembly. WHO's growing partnership with the private sector: addressing public health needs or corporate priorities?', mimeo, Geneva: Health Action International.

Ham, C. (1997) 'Priority setting in health care: learning from international experience', *Health Policy*, 4: 49–66.

Hamid Salim, M.A., Uplekar, M., Daru, P., Aung, M., Declercq, E. and Lönnroth, K. (2006) 'Turning liabilities into resources: informal village doctors and tuberculosis control in Bangladesh', *Bulletin of the World Health Organization*, 84: 479–84.

Hamoudi, A. and Sachs, J. (1999) 'Economic consequences of health status: a review of the evidence', Working Paper No. 30, Cambridge, MA: Harvard Center for International Development.

Hansen, K., Woelk, G. and Jackson, H. (1998) 'The cost of home-based care for HIV/AIDS patients in Zimbabwe', *AIDS Care*, 10: 751–9.

Hanson, K. and Jones, C. (2000) *Social marketing of insecticide treated mosquito nets, Tanzania: end of project social and economic analysis*, London: Malaria Consortium, London School of Hygiene and Tropical Medicine.

Hanson, K., Kumaranayake, L. and Thomas, I. (2001) 'Ends versus means: the role of markets in expanding access to contraceptives', *Health Policy and Planning*, 16: 125–36.

Hanson, K., Ranson, M.K., Oliveira-Cruz, V. and Mills, A. (2003) 'Expanding access to health interventions: a framework for understanding the constraints to scaling-up', *Journal of International Development*, 15: 1–14.

Hardeman, W., Van Damme, W., Van Pelt, M., Por, I., Kimvan, H. and Meessen, B. (2004) 'Access to health care for all? User fees plus a health equity fund in Sotnikum, Cambodia', *Health Policy and Planning*, 19: 22–32.

Hartigan, P. (2001) 'The importance of gender in defining and improving quality of care: some conceptual issues', *Health and Policy Planning*, 16 (Suppl. 1): 7–12.

Hausmann-Muela, S., Ribera, J. and Nyamongo, I. (2003) 'Health seeking behaviour and the health system response', *DCPP* Working Paper No. 14, Disease Control Priorities Project, Washington, DC: World Bank.

Health Systems Research Institute (2001) *Proposal for Universal Health Coverage*, Nonthaburi: Health Systems Research Institute.

Heston, A., Summers, R. and Aten, B. (2006) 'Penn World Table Version 6.2', Philadelphia, PA: Center for International Comparisons of Production, Income and Prices at the University of Pennsylvania, September.

High-Level Forum on the Health MDGs (2004) 'Achieving the Health Millennium Development Goals in fragile states', High-Level Forum on Health MDGs, Abuja, December 2004.

Hill, Z., Kendall, C., Arthur, P., Kirkwood, B. and Adjei, E. (2003) 'Recognizing childhood illnesses and their traditional explanations: exploring options for care-seeking interventions in the context of the IMCI strategy in rural Ghana', *Tropical Medicine and International Health*, 8: 668–76.

Hjortsberg, C. and Mwikisa, C. (2002) 'Cost of access to health services in Zambia', *Health Policy and Planning*, 17: 71–7.

Hoddinott, J. (1999) *Targeting: principles and practice*, IFPRI Technical Guide No. 9, Washington, DC: IFPRI. Online. Available at: www.ifpri.org/themes/mp18/techguid/tg09.pdf (accessed 1/12/2006).

Hong, E. (2000) 'Globalisation and the impact on health: a third world view', paper prepared for the People's Health Assembly, Bangladesh, December 2000.

Horton, S. and Ross, J. (2003) 'The economics of iron deficiency', *Journal of Food Policy*, 28: 51–75.

Hossain, N. and Matin, I. (2004) Engaging elite support for the poorest? BRAC's experience with the Ultra Poor Programme, CFPR-TUP Working Paper No. 3, Dhaka: BRAC, Research and Evaluation Division, and Ottawa, Ontario: Aga Khan Foundation.

Hulme, D. and Shepherd, A. (2003) 'Conceptualizing chronic poverty', *World Development*, 31: 403–23.

Hutchinson, P. (1999) 'Decentralization of health services in Uganda: moving toward improved delivery of services', in P. Hutchinson, D. Habte and M. Mulusa (eds) *Health care in Uganda: selected issues*, Discussion Paper No. 404, Washington, DC: World Bank.

Hutchinson, P.L. and LaFond, A.K. (2004) *Monitoring and evaluation of decentralization reforms in developing country health sectors*, Bethesda, MD: Partners for Health Reform*plus* Project, Abt Associates Inc.

IBFAN (n.d.) 'The role of regulations in protecting infant health', International Baby Food Action Network. Online. Available at: www.ibfan.org/.

IMF (2006) 'Debt relief under the Heavily Indebted Poor Countries (HIPC) Initiative', International Monetary Fund Factsheet. Online. Available at: www.imf.org/external/np/exr/facts/hipc.htm (accessed 25 May 2006).

INFACT (1999) *Mobilising NGOs and the media behind the International Framework Convention on Tobacco Control*, WHO Framework Convention on Tobacco Control, Technical Briefing Series Paper 3, Geneva: World Health Organization. Document WHO/NCD/TFI/99.3.

International Health Policy Programme (2004) N*ational Health Accounts in Thailand 1994–2001*, Nonthaburi: Health Systems Research Institute.

Irwin, A., Valentine, N., Brown, C., Loewenson, R., Solar, O. *et al.* (2006) 'The commission on social determinants of health: tackling the social roots of health inequities', *PLoS Medicine*, 3: 0749–51.

Jaffar, S., Grant, A.D., Whitworth, J., Smith, P.G. and Whittle, H. (2004) 'The natural history of HIV-1 and HIV-2 infections in adults in Africa: a literature review', *Bulletin of the World Health Organization*, 82: 462–9.

Jamison, D.T., Mosley, W.H., Measham, A.R. and Bobadilla, J.L. (1993) *Disease control priorities in developing countries*, New York: Oxford University Press for The World Bank.

Jamison, D., Breman, J., Measham, A., Alleyne, G., Claeson, M. *et al.* (eds) (2006) *Disease control priorities in developing countries*, second edition, New York: The World Bank and Oxford University Press.

Janjaroen, W.S., Supakankunti, S. (2002) 'International trade in health services in the millennium: the case of Thailand', in N. Drager (ed.) *Trade in health services*, Washington, DC: Pan American Health Organization.

Janowitz, B., Suazo, M., Fried, D.B., Bratt, J.H. and Bailey, P.E. (1992) 'Impact of social marketing on contraceptive prevalence and cost in Honduras', *Studies in Family Planning*, 23: 110–17.

Jaramillo, J., Pineda, C. and Contreras, G. (1984) 'Primary health care in marginal urban areas: the Costa Rican model', *Bulletin of the Pan American Health Organisation*, 18: 107–14.

Jarman, J. and Johnson, C. (1997) *WAMMA: empowerment in practice*, London: WaterAid.

Jaspars, S. and Shoham, J. (1999) 'Targeting the vulnerable: a review of the necessity and feasibility of targeting vulnerable households', *Disasters*, 23: 359–72.

Jayawardene, R. (1993) 'Illness perception: social cost and coping-strategies of malaria cases', *Social Science and Medicine*, 37: 1169–76.

Jewkes, R., Abrahams, N. and Mvo, Z. (1998) 'Why do nurses abuse patients? Reflections from South African obstetric services', *Social Science and Medicine*, 47: 1781–95.

Jones, T. (1990) *The Panama Canal: a brief history*. Online. Available at: www.ilove languages.com/Tyler/nonfiction/pan2.html (accessed 23 September 2006).

Jütting, J., Kauffman, C., McDonnell, I., Osterrieder, H., Pinaud, N. and Wegner, L. (2004) 'Decentralisation and poverty in developing countries: exploring the impact', OECD Development Centre, Working Paper No. 236, Paris: OECD.

Kabir, M.A., Rahman, A., Salway, S. and Pryer, J. (2000) 'Sickness among the urban poor: a barrier to livelihood security', *Journal of International Development*, 12: 707–22.

Kafle, K.K., Gartoulla, R.P., Pradhan, Y.M., Shrestha, A.D., Karkee, S.B. and Quick, J.D. (1992) 'Drug retailer training: experiences from Nepal', *Social Science and Medicine*, 35: 1015–25.

Kahssay, H.M. and Baum, F. (eds) (1996) *The role of civil society in district health systems: hidden resources*, Geneva: World Health Organization. Document WHO/ARA/96.3.

Kalemli-Ozcan, S. (2002) 'Does mortality decline promote economic growth?', *Journal of Economic Growth*, 7: 411–39.

Kalemli-Ozcan, S., Ryder, H.E. and Weil, D.N. (2000) 'Mortality decline, human capital investment, and economic growth', *Journal of Development Economics*, 62: 1–23.

Kalumba, K. (1997) 'Towards an equity-oriented policy of decentralisation in health systems under conditions of turbulence: the case of Zambia', WHO Forum on Health Sector Reform, Discussion Paper No. 6, Geneva: World Health Organization.

Kamat, V. (2001) 'Private practitioners and their role in the resurgence of malaria in Mumbai (Bombay) and Navi Mumbai (New Bombay), India: serving the affected or aiding an epidemic', *Social Science and Medicine*, 52(6):885–909

Kangwanpornsiri, K., Saenchaipiangpen, A. and Waniswanathong, S. (2003) *Provincial Health Surveys Analysis*, Nonthaburi: Health Policy and Strategy Bureau, Ministry of Public Health.

Kanji, N. (1989) 'Charging for drugs in Africa: UNICEF's Bamako Initiative', *Health Policy and Planning*, 4: 110–20.

Karolinska Institute (2006) 'World health chart', Stockholm: Karolinska Institute. Online. Available at: www.whc.ki.se/index.php (accessed 30 June 2006).

Khaleghian, P. (2003) 'Decentralisation and public services: the case of immunisation', World Bank Policy Research Working Paper 2989, Washington, DC: World Bank.

Khan, M.M., Hotchkiss, D.R., Berruti, A.A. and Hutchinson, P.L. (2006) 'Geographic aspects of poverty and health in Tanzania: does living in a poor area matter?', *Health Policy and Planning*, 21: 110–22.

Killingsworth, J.R. (2002) 'Official, unofficial and informal fees for health care', World Health Organization, Draft Discussion Note #13, Third Health Sector Development Technical Advisory Group Meeting: Health Care Financing in the Western Pacific Region, 17–19 February 2002, Manila.

Killingsworth, J., Hossain, N., Hedrick-Wong, Y., Thomas, S., Rahman, A. and Begum, T. (1999) 'Unofficial fees in Bangladesh: price, equity and institutional issues', *Health Policy and Planning*, 14: 152–63.

Kim, A., Tandon, A., Hailu, A. *et al.* (1997) 'Health and labor productivity: the economic impact of onchocercal skin disease', World Bank Policy Research Working Paper 1836, Washington, DC: World Bank.

Kinney, E.D. (2001) 'The international human right to health: what does this mean for our nation and our world?', *Indiana Law Review*, 34: 1457–75.

Kivumbi, G. and Kintu, F. (2002) 'Exemptions and waivers from cost sharing: ineffective safety nets in decentralized districts in Uganda', *Health Policy and Planning*, 17 (Suppl. 1): 64–71.

Knaul, F.M., Arreola-Ornelas, H., Méndez-Carniado, O., Bryson-Cahn, C., Barofsky, J. *et al.* (2006) 'Evidence is good for your health system: policy reform to remedy catastrophic and impoverishing health spending in Mexico', *The Lancet*, 368: 1828–41.

Knowles, S. and Owen, P.D. (1997) 'Education and health in an effective-labour empirical growth model', *The Economic Record*, 73: 314–28.

Koh, H.H. (2000) 'Complementarity between international organizations on human rights/the rise of transnational networks as the "Third Globalisation" ', *Human Rights Law Journal*, 21: 307–10.

Kongsawatt, S. and Pannarunothai, S. (2005) 'Universal coverage policy and the access and utilisation of health care among the poor in Bangkok', *Journal of Health Science*, 14: 1008–21.

Koopmanschap, M. and Rutten, F. (1994) 'The impact of indirect costs on outcomes of health care programs', *Health Economics*, 3: 385–93.

Korte, R., Komm, B., James, C. and Nganda, B. (2004) 'National social health insurance: financial projections and future bilateral/multilateral cooperation', Joint WHO – GTZ Mission to Kenya, 21–26 June 2004. Online. Available at: www.who.int/ health_financing/countries/en/6th_who_gtz_mission.pdf. Last accessed 25 April 2007.

Krishna, A., Kapila, M., Porwal, M. and Singh, V. (2003) 'Falling into poverty in a high-grown state: escaping poverty and becoming poor in Gujarat villages', *Economic and Political Weekly*, 38: 5171–9.

Kutzin, J. (2001) 'A descriptive framework for country-level analysis of health care financing arrangements', *Health Policy*, 56: 171–204.

Kwon, S. (2003) 'Pharmaceutical reform and physician strikes in Korea: separation of drug prescribing and dispensing', *Social Science and Medicine*, 57: 529–38.

Kyomuhendo, G. (2003) 'Low use of rural maternity services in Uganda: impact of women's status, traditional beliefs and limited resources', *Reproductive Health Matters*, 11: 16–26.

LaFond, A. (1995) *Sustaining primary health care*, London: Earthscan Publications Ltd.

La Forgia, G.M., Mintz, P. and Cerezo, P. (2005) 'Is the perfect the enemy of the good? A case study on large-scale contracting for basic health services in rural Guatemala', in G.M. La Forgia (ed.) *Health system innovations in Central America*, World Bank Working Paper No. 57, Washington, DC: The World Bank.

Lake, S., Daura, M., Mabandhla, M., Masiye, F., Mulenga, S. *et al.* (2000) 'Analyzing the process of health financing reform in South Africa and Zambia: Zambia country report', Major Applied Research 1, Technical Paper No. 2, Bethesda, MD: Partnerships for Health Reform Project, Abt Associates Inc.

Lande, R.E. and Geller, J.S. (1991) 'Paying for family planning', *Population Reports*, Series J, No. 39, Baltimore, MD: Johns Hopkins University, Population Information Programme.

Laterveer, L., Niessen, L.W. and Yazbeck, A.S. (2003) 'Pro-poor health policies in poverty reduction strategies', *Health Policy and Planning*, 18: 138–45.

Lauglo, M. and Molutsi, P. (1995) 'Decentralisation and health systems performance: the Botswana case study', Gaborone, Botswana: DIS Centre for Partnership in Development and University of Botswana.

Lee, R. and Mason, D. (2006) 'What is the demographic dividend?', *Finance and Development*, 43: 16–17.

Lee, R., Mason, A. and Miller, T. (2000). 'Life cycle saving and the demographic transition: the case of Taiwan', *Population and Development Review*, 26 (Suppl.): 194–219.

Leighton, C. and Foster, R. (1993) 'Economic impacts of malaria in Kenya and Nigeria', Bethesda, MD: Abt Associates, Health Financing and Sustainability Project.

Leslie, J. and Jamison, D. (1990) 'Health and nutrition considerations in educational planning: the cost and effectiveness of school-based interventions', *Food and Nutrition Bulletin*, 12: 204–15.

Lewis, M. (2000) *Who is paying for health care in Eastern Europe and Central Asia?* Washington, DC: The World Bank.

Lewis, M. (2005) 'Addressing the challenge of HIV/AIDS: macroeconomics, fiscal and institutional issues', Working Paper No. 58, Washington, DC: Centre for Global Development.

Limwattananon, S., Limwattananon, C. and Pannarunothai, S. (2004) 'Cost and utilization of drugs prescribed for hospital-visited patients: impacts of universal health care coverage policy', Research report for the Health Systems Research Institute, Nonthaburi, Thailand.

Litvack, J. and Bodart, C. (1993) 'User fees plus quality equals improved access to health care: results of a field experiment in Cameroon', *Social Science and Medicine*, 37: 369–83.

Loewenson, R. (1999) 'Public participation in health: making people matter', IDS/TARSC Working Paper No. 84, Brighton, UK: Institute of Development Studies.

Loewenson, R. (2000) 'Putting your money where your mouth is: participation in mobilising and allocating health resources', paper presented to the TARSC/EQUINET Regional Meeting on Public Participation in Health, Harare, May 2000.

Loewenson, R. (2004) 'Community responses to HIV and AIDS: Strengthening social inclusion or carrying unfair burdens?', paper prepared for the UNRISD programme on Community Responses to HIV and AIDS, January 2004. Online. Available at: www.unrisd.org.

Loewenson, R., Rusike, I. and Zulu, M. (2004) 'Assessing the impact of health centre committees on health system performance and health resource allocation', EQUINET Discussion Paper 18, February 2004. Online. Available at: www.equinetafrica.org.

Lönnroth, K., Ming Thuong, L., Duy Lunh, P. and Diwan, V.K. (2001) 'Utilization of private and public health-care providers for tuberculosis symptoms in Ho Chi Minh City, Vietnam', *Health Policy and Planning*, 16: 47–54.

Lorentzen, P., McMillan, J. and Wacziarg, R. (2005) 'Death and development', NBER Working Paper 11620, Cambridge, MA: National Bureau of Economic Research. Online. Available at: www.nber.org/papers/w11620.

Lucas, H. and Nuwagaba, A. (1999) 'Household coping strategies in response to the introduction of user charges for social service: a case study on health in Uganda', *IDS Working Paper* 86, Brighton: Institute of Development Studies.

Mackintosh, M. and Koivusalo, M. (2004) 'Health systems and commercialization: in search of good sense', paper prepared for the UNRISD programme on Social Policy and Development, March 2004, Geneva. Online. Available at: www.unrisd.org.

Macwan'gi, N. and Ngwengwe, A. (2004) 'Effectiveness of district health boards in interceding for the community', The Institute of Economic and Social Research (INESCOR), University of Zambia, Equinet Discussion Paper 19, mimeo. Online. Available at: www.equinetafrica.org/bibl/docs/DIS19gov.pdf. Last accessed 25 April 2007.

Magnani, R.J., Rice, J.C., Mock, N.B., Abdoh, A.A., Mercer, D.M. and Tankari, K. (1996) 'The impact of primary health care services on under-five mortality in rural Niger', *International Journal of Epidemiology*, 25: 568–77.

Mahal, A. (2004) 'Economic implications of inertia on HIV/AIDS and benefits of action', *Economic and Political Weekly*, 39: 1049–63.

Mahal, A., Singh, J., Afridi, F., Lamba, V., Gumber, A. and Selvaraju, V. (2000) *Who benefits from public health spending in India?*, Washington, DC: The World Bank.

Makinen, M., Waters, H., Rauch, M., Almagambetova, N., Bitran, R. *et al.* (2000) 'Inequalities in health care use and expenditures: empirical data from eight developing countries and countries in transition', *Bulletin of the World Health Organization*, 78: 55–65.

Malthus, T.R. (1798) *An essay on the principle of population*, London: Pickering and Chatto, 1986.

Marks, S. and Mahal, A.S. (2006) 'Strategies for promoting children's rights and poverty reduction: economic and human rights perspectives', mimeo, Harvard School of Public Health.

Marquez, L. and Kean, L. (2002) 'Making supervision supportive and sustainable: new approaches to old problems', *MAQ Papers*, No. 4, Washington, DC: Maximizing Access and Quality (MAQ) Initiative, USAID.

Mbuyita, S., Makemba, A.M. and Mayombana, C. (2004) 'The voice of the community: development of a procedural framework to facilitate the incorporation of the preference and priorities of the people in district health planning, Tanzania', Mimeo, Ifakara, Tanzania.

McIntyre, D. and Gilson, L. (1998) 'Equity of health sector revenue generation and allocation: a South African case study', Washington, DC: Partnerships for Health Reform, Abt Associates.

McIntyre, D. and Thiede, M. (2003) 'A review of studies dealing with economic and social consequences of high medical expenditure with a special focus on the medical poverty trap', ALPS Systematic Literature Review 3, Cape Town: Health Economics Unit, University of Cape Town.

McIntyre, D., Gilson, L. and Mutyambizi, V. (2005) 'Promoting equitable health care financing in the African context: current challenges and future prospects', EQUINET Discussion Paper No. 27, Harare, Zimbabwe: Regional Network for Equity in Health in Southern Africa.

McKinsey and Company (2005) *Global health partnerships: assessing country consequences*, New York: McKinsey and Co.

McMichael, A.J., McKee, M., Shkolnikov, V. and Valkonen, T. (2004) 'Mortality trends and setbacks: global convergence or divergence?', *The Lancet*, 363: 1155–9.

McPake, B. (1993) 'User charges for health services in developing countries: a review of the economic literature', *Social Science and Medicine*, 36: 1397–405.

McPake, B., Hanson, K. and Mills, A. (1993) 'Community financing of health care in Africa: an evaluation of the Bamako initiative', *Social Science and Medicine*, 36: 1383–95.

Menken, J. and Rahman, O.R. (2001) 'Reproductive health', Chapter 3 in M. Merson, R. Black and A. Mills (eds) *International public health: diseases programs, systems and policies*, Gaithersburg, MD: Aspen Publishers.

Mesoamerica Nutrition Program Targeting Study Group (2002) 'Targeting performance of three large-scale, nutrition-oriented social programs in Central America and Mexico', *Food and Nutrition Bulletin*, 23: 162–74.

Miguel, E. and Kremer, M. (2004) 'Worms: identifying impacts on education and health in the presence of treatment externalities', *Econometrica*, 72: 159–217.

Mills, A. (1997) 'Reforming health sectors: fashions, passions and common sense', paper presented at the LSHTM conference on Reforming Health Sectors, London, UK, April 1998.

Mills, A.J. (2005) 'Public health classics: mass campaigns versus general health services; vertical versus horizontal approaches: what have we learnt in 40 years', *Bulletin of the World Health Organization*, 83: 315–6.

Mills, A., Bennett, S., Siriwanarangsan, P. and Tangcharoensathien, V. (2000) 'The response of providers to capitation payment: a case-study from Thailand', *Health Policy*, 51: 163–80.

Mills, A., Bennett, S. and Russell, S. (2001) *The challenge of health sector reform: what must governments do?*, Basingstoke: Macmillan.

Mills, A., Brugha, R., Hanson, K. and McPake, B. (2002) 'What can be done about the private health sector in low-income countries?', *Bulletin of the World Health Organization*, 80: 325–30.

Mills, A., Palmer, N., Gilson. L., McIntyre., D., Schneider, H. *et al.* (2004) 'The performance of different models of primary care provision in Southern Africa', *Social Science and Medicine*, 59: 931–43.

Mills, A., Tangchareonsathien, V. and Pannarunothai, S. (2005) 'Harmonization of health insurance schemes: a policy analysis', Report to the National Health Security Office, Nonthaburi, Thailand.

Mitchell, J.C. (1983) 'Case and situation analysis', *Sociological Review*, 31: 187–211.

Mkandawire, T. (2006) *Targeting and universalism in poverty reduction*, Geneva: UNRISD.

Mock, C., Gloyd, S., Adjei, S., Acheampong, F. and Gish, O. (2001) 'Economic costs of injury and resulting family coping strategies in Ghana', *Accident Analysis and Prevention*, 819: 1–10.

Modigliani, F. and Brumberg, R. (1954) 'Utility analysis and the consumption function: an interpretation of cross-section data', in K.K. Kurihara (ed.) *Post-Keynesian economics*, New Brunswick, NJ: Rutgers University Press.

Mogedal, S. and Hodne Steen, S. (1995) 'Health sector reform and organizational issues at the local level: lessons from selected African countries', *Journal of International Development*, 7: 349–7.

MoHCW/SDU (Ministry of Health, Strategic Development Unit Zimbabwe) (1997) 'Proposals for Health Sector Reform (Decentralisation) Roles and Relationships', Harare: Government Printers. November 1997.

Montagu, D. (2002) 'Franchising of health services in low-income countries', *Health Policy and Planning*, 17: 121–30.

Mooij, J. (1999) 'Real targeting: the case of food distribution in India', *Food Policy*, 24: 49–69.

Mooney, G. (1983) 'Equity in health care: confronting the confusion', *Effective Health Care*, 1: 179–85.

Mooney, G. (1996) 'And now for vertical equity? Some concerns arising from Aboriginal health in Australia', *Health Economics*, 5: 99–103.

Mooney, G. and Jan, S. (1997) 'Vertical equity: weighting outcomes? Or establishing procedures?', *Health Policy*, 39: 79–87.

Moser, C. (2001) 'Insecurity and social protection – has the World Bank got it right? *Journal of International Development*, 13: 361–8.

Mtonya, B., Mwapasa, V. and Kadzandira, J. (2005) 'System-wide effects of the Global Fund in Malawi: Baseline study report', Bethesda, MD: Partners for Health Reformplus, Abt Associates Inc.

Mubyazi, G. and Hutton, G. (2003) 'Understanding mechanisms for integrating community priorities in health planning, resource allocation and service delivery: results of a literature review', EQUINET Discussion Paper 13, October 2003. Online. Available at: www.equinetafrica.org.

Mumtaz, Z. and Salway, S. (2005) '"I never go anywhere": extricating the links between women's mobility and uptake of reproductive health services in Pakistan', *Social Science and Medicine*, 60: 1751–65.

Municipal Services Project (MSP) (2004) *Services for all* (MSP Newsletter), No. 4, February 2004, p. 8. Online. Available at: www.queensu.ca/msp/.

Munthali, S.M. (1998) 'Socio-economic impact of HIV/AIDS on Malawi: focus group discussions on community impacts and coping strategies', Report submitted to NACP Malawi, OATUU Health Safety and Environment Programme.

Murray, C. and Lopez, A. (1996) *The global burden of disease*, Cambridge, MA: Harvard University Press.

Musau, S.N. (1999) Community-based health insurance: experiences and lessons learned from East and Southern Africa, Technical Report No. 34, Bethesda, MD: Partnerships for Health Reform Project, Abt Associates Inc.

Mushi, A.K., Armstrong Schellenberg, J.R.M., Mponda, H. and Lengeler, C. (2003) 'Targeted subsidy for malaria control with treated nets using a discount voucher system in southern Tanzania', *Health Policy and Planning*, 18: 163–71.

Mutangadura, G., Mukurazita, D. and Jackson, H. (1999) *A review of household and community responses to the HIV/AIDS epidemic in the rural areas of sub-Saharan Africa*, UNAIDS Best Practice Collection, Geneva: UNAIDS.

Myers, C.N., Mongkolsmai, D. and Causino, N. (1985) *Financing health services and medical care in Thailand*, Bangkok: US Agency for International Development.

Nahar, S. and Costello, A. (1998) 'The hidden cost of "free" maternity care in Dhaka, Bangladesh', *Health Policy and Planning*, 13: 417–22.

Najera, J.A., Bernhard, H.L. and Hammer, J. (1993) 'Malaria', in D.T. Jamison, W.H. Mosley, A.R. Measham and J.L. Bobadilla (eds) *Disease control priorities in developing countries*, Oxford: Oxford University Press for the World Bank.

Narayan, D. (2000) *Voices of the poor: can anyone hear us?*, Oxford: Oxford University Press.

National Institute for Child and Family Development, Mahidol University (2005) 'Research results'. Online. Available at: www.cf.mahidol.ac.th (accessed 2 May 2005).

Navarro, V. (1999) 'Health and equity in the world in the ear of "Globalisation"', *International Journal of Health Services*, 29: 215–16.

Navarro, V. (2004) 'The world situation and the WHO', *The Lancet*, 363: 1321–3.

NESDB (2004a) *Thailand national income 2002 by system of national accounts*, Bangkok: National Economic and Social Development Board.

NESDB (2004b) 'GDP Quarter 4/46', Press release 8 March 2004, Bangkok: National Economic and Social Development Board.

Newbrander, W., Collins, D. and Gilson, L. (2000) *Ensuring equal access to health services: user fee systems and the poor*, Boston, MA: Management Sciences for Health.

Ngulube, T.J., Mdhluli, L., Gondwe, K. and Njobvu, C.A. (2004) 'Governance, participatory mechanisms and structures in Zambia's health system: an assessment of the impact of Health Centre Committees (HCCs) on equity in health and health care', EQUINET Discussion Paper 21, December 2004. Online. Available at: www.equinetafrica.org.

Nieves, I. and La Forgia, G.M. (2000) 'Large scale government contracting of NGOs to extend basic health services to poor populations in Guatemala', The Challenge of Health Reform: Reaching the Poor, Europe and the Americas Forum on Health Sector Reform, San Jose, Costa Rica, May 2000, Washington, DC: The World Bank.

Njau, J., Goodman, C., Kachur, S.P., Palmer, N., Khatib, R. *et al.* (2006) 'Fever treatment and household wealth: the challenge posed for rolling out combination therapy for malaria', *Tropical Medicine and International Health*, 11: 299–313.

Nordhaus, W. (2003) 'The health of nations: the contribution of improved health to living standards', in K.H. Murphy and R.H. Topel (eds) *Measuring the gains from medical research: an economic approach*, Chicago, IL: University of Chicago Press.

Nur, E.T. (1993) 'The impact of malaria on labour use and efficiency in the Sudan', *Social Science and Medicine*, 37: 1115–9.

Nutley, S. (2003) 'Bridging the policy/research divide: reflections and lessons from the UK', Keynote paper presented at 'Facing the future: engaging stakeholders and citizens in developing public policy', National Institute of Governance Conference, Canberra, Australia, 23–4 April 2003. Online. Available at: www.st-andrews.ac.uk/~cppm/Bridging%20Research%20Policy%20Divide.pdf#search=%22Nutley%20bridging%20the%20policy%2Fresearch%20divide%22 (accessed 27 August 2006).

OAU (2001) *Abuja Declaration on HIV/AIDS, tuberculosis and other related infectious diseases*, Addis Ababa: Organisation of African Unity.

O'Donnell, O., van Doorslaer, E., Rannan-Eliya, R., Somanathan, A., Adhikari, S.R. *et al.* (2005) 'Who benefits from public spending on health care in Asia', EQUITAP Project Working Paper #3, May 2005, EQUITAP. Online. Available at: www.equitap.org/publications/wps.htm.

OECD (2006) 'OECD health data 2006', Paris: Organisation for Economic Cooperation

OECD (2006) 'OECD health data 2006', Paris: Organisation for Economic Cooperation and Development. Online. Available at: www.oecd.org/dataoecd/60/28/ 35529791.xls (accessed 30 June 2006).

O'Keefe, E.A. and Wood, R. (1996) 'The impact of human immunodeficiency virus (HIV) infection on quality of life in a multiracial South African population', *Quality of Life Research*, 5: 275–80.

Onwujekwe, O. (2005) 'Inequities in healthcare seeking in the treatment of communicable endemic diseases in Southeast Nigeria', *Social Science and Medicine*, 61: 455–63.

Onwujekwe, O., Chima, R. and Okonkwo, P. (2000) 'Economic burden of malaria illness on households versus that of all other illness episodes: a study in five malaria holoendemic Nigerian communities', *Health Policy*, 54: 143–59.

Ottaway, M. (2001) 'Corporatism goes global: international organizations, non-governmental organization networks and transnational business', *Global Governance*, 7: 265–92.

Oxfam (2001a) 'Cutting the cost of global health', Oxfam GB Parliamentary Briefing No. 16, February 2001. Oxford: Oxfam.

Oxfam (2001b) 'South Africa vs the Drug giants', Oxfam GB Policy Papers, February 2001. Oxford: Oxfam.

Oxfam (Canada), ORAP/ZPT/ Dabane/MOTSRUD (1999) Personal Communication on Nutrition and Health Programme, Bulawayo.

Palmer, N., Mills, A., Wadee, H., Gilson, L. and Schneider, H. (2003) 'A new face for private providers in developing countries: what implications for public health?', *Bulletin of the World Health Organization*, 81: 292–7.

Palmer, N., Mueller, D., Gilson, L., Mills, A. and Haines, A. (2004) 'Health financing to promote access in low income settings – how much do we know?', *The Lancet*, 364: 1365–70.

Panklang, N. (2004) 'Equity in health: a case study of self-medication in Chiang Mai Province', unpublished Masters Thesis, Faculty of Social Science and Humanities, Mahidol University, Bangkok, Thailand.

Pannarunothai, S. and Mills, A. (1997) 'The poor pay more: health-related inequality in Thailand', *Social Science and Medicine*, 44: 1781–90.

Pannarunothai, S. and Patmasiriwat, D. (2001) *Macro-economic indices for measuring equity in health finance and delivery 1986–1998*, Nonthaburi: Health Systems Research Institute.

Pannarunothai, S. and Rehnberg, C. (1998) 'Equity of health care delivery in Thailand', A research report to the Swedish–Thai Collaboration in Health System Development, Nonthaburi: Health Systems Research Institute.

Pannarunothai, S. and Suknark, K. (2005) 'How free trade in health services affects Thai population and Thai physicians?', *The Thai Medical Council Bulletin*, 34: 155–75.

Pannarunothai, S., Srithamrongsawat, S., Kongpan, M. and Thumvanna, P. (2000) 'Financing reforms for the health card scheme in Thailand', *Health Policy and Planning*, 15: 303–11.

Pannarunothai, S., Patmasiriwat, D., Kongsawatt, S., Srithamrongsawat, S., Suttayakom, W. and Rodsawaeng, P. (2002) 'Sustainable universal health coverage: household met need', Research report to Japan International Cooperation Agency and Health Systems Research Institute, Nonthaburi, Thailand.

Pannarunothai, S., Patmasiriwat, D. and Srithamrongsawat, S. (2004) 'Universal health coverage in Thailand: ideas for reform and policy struggling', *Health Policy*, 68: 17–30.

Pannarunothai, S., Patmasiriwat, D. and Kongsawatt, S. (2005) 'How far the universal health coverage policy has reached households in Thailand? The second wave of household survey', *The Journal of Public Services*, 12: 29–47.

Parker, M. (1992) 'Re-assessing disability: the impact of schistosomal infection on daily activities among women in Gezira Province, Sudan', *Social Science and Medicine*, 35: 877–90.

Partnerships for Health Reform (2000) 'Brazil contracts NGOs to fight HIV/AIDS', *PHR Report*, June 2000, pp. 1–2.

Paul, J.A. (1996) 'NGOs, civil society and global policy making', paper for the Global Policy Forum, USA, June 1996.

Pauly, M.V. (1997) *Health benefits at work: an economic and political analysis of employment-based health insurance*, Ann Arbor, MI: University of Michigan Press.

Pauly, M.V., Nicholson, S., Xu, J., Polsky, D., Danzon, P.M. *et al.* (2002) 'A general model of the impact of absenteeism on employers and employees', *Health Economics*, 11: 221–31.

Pearson, M. (2002) 'Allocating public resources for health: developing pro-poor approaches', London: DFID Health Systems Resource Centre.

People's Health Movement, Medact and GEGA (2005) *Global Health Watch 2006–6: an alternative world health report*, London: Zed Press.

Périn, I. and Attaran, A. (2003) 'Trading ideology for dialogue: an opportunity to fix international aid for health?', *The Lancet*, 361: 1216–19.

Phoolcharoen, W. (2004) *Quantum leap: the reform of Thailand's health system*, Bangkok: Health Systems Research Institute.

Poolcharoen, W., Chunharas, S., Wibulpholprasert, S., Chuengsatiansup, K. and Sri-ratanabun, J. (2000) *Towards the national health system reform*, Nonthaburi: Health Systems Research Institute.

PHR*plus* (2004) *Health care utilisation, expenditures and insurance: household survey findings from Suez Governorate, Egypt*, Bethesda, MD: The Partners for Health Reform*plus* Project, Abt Associates Inc.

Picard, J. and Mills, A. (1992) 'The effect of malaria on work time: analysis of data from two Nepali districts', *Journal of Tropical Medicine and Hygiene*, 95: 382–9.

Pradhan, M. and Prescott, N. (2002) 'Social risk management options for medical care in Indonesia', *Health Economics*, 11: 431–46.

Prata, N., Montagu, D. and Jefferys, E. (2005) 'Private sector, human resources and health franchising in Africa', *Bulletin of the World Health Organization*, 83: 274–9.

Prescott, N. (1999) 'Coping with catastrophic health shocks', paper presented at the Conference on Social Protection and Poverty, Washington, DC: Inter-American Development Bank.

Preston, S. (1975) 'The changing relation between mortality and level of economic development', *Population Studies*, 29: 231–48.

Pritchett, L. and Summers, L. (1996) 'Wealthier is healthier', *The Journal of Human Resources*, 31: 841–68.

Psacharopoulos, G. and Patrinos, H.A. (2004) 'Returns to investment in education: a further update', *Education Economics*, 12: 111–34.

Ramu, K., Ramaiah, K.D., Guyatt, H. and Evans, D. (1996) 'Impact of lymphatic filariasis on the productivity of male weavers in a south Indian village', *Transactions of the Royal Society of Tropical Medicine and Hygiene*, 90: 669–70.

Ranson, M.K. (2002) 'Reduction of catastrophic health care expenditures by a community-based health insurance scheme in Gujarat, India: current experiences and challenges', *Bulletin of the World Health Organization*, 80: 613–21.

Ranson, M.K. (2004) 'The SEWA medical insurance fund in India', in A. Preker and G. Carrin (eds) *Health financing for poor people: resource mobilization and risk sharing*, Washington, DC: The World Bank.

Ranson, M.K. and John, K.R. (2001) 'Quality of hysterectomy care in rural Gujarat: the role of community-based health insurance', *Health Policy and Planning*, 16: 395–403.

Republic of Rwanda, Ministry of Health (2006) *Rwanda National Health Accounts 2003*. Online. Available at: www.who.int/nha/country/Rwanda_NHA_Report_2003.pdf.

Reid, G. and Kasale, H. (2000) 'Tanzania essential health interventions project', paper presented to the TARSC/EQUINET Regional Meeting on Public Participation in Health, Harare, May 2000.

Ribero, R. and Nunez, J. (2000) 'Adult morbidity, height and earnings in Columbia', in W.D. Savedoff and T.P. Schultz (eds) *Wealth from health*, Washington, DC: Inter-American Development Bank.

Rifkin, S. (2003) 'A framework linking community empowerment and health equity: it is a matter of CHOICE', *Journal of Health Population and Nutrition*, 21: 168–80.

Robertson, K.R., Robertson, W.T., Ford, S., Watson, D., Fiscus, S. *et al.* (2004) 'Highly active antiretroviral therapy improves neurocognitive functioning', *Journal of Acquired Immune Deficiency Syndrome*, 36: 562–6.

Rosen, S. and Simon, J.L. (2003) 'Shifting the burden: the private sector's response to the AIDS epidemic in Africa', *Bulletin of the World Health Organization*, 81: 131–7.

Rosen, S., Vincent, J.R., MacLeod, W., Fox, M., Thea, D.M. and Simon, J.L. (2004) 'The cost of HIV/AIDS to businesses in southern Africa', *AIDS*, 18: 317–24.

Rosenzweig, M.R. (1988) 'Risk, implicit contracts and the family in rural areas of low-income countries', *The Economic Journal*, December: 1148–70.

Ruebush, T., Kern, M., Campbell, C. and Oloo, A. (1995) 'Self-treatment of malaria in a rural area of Western Kenya', *Bulletin of the World Health Organization*, 73: 229–36.

Rugalema, G. (1998) 'It is not only the loss of labour: HIV/AIDS, loss of household assets and household livelihood in Bukoba District, Tanzania', paper presented at the East and Southern Africa Regional Conference on Responding to HIV/AIDS: Development Needs of African Smallholder Agriculture, Harare, 8–12 June 1998.

Rugalema, G. (2000) 'Coping or struggling? A journey into the impact of HIV/AIDS in southern Africa', *Review of African Political Economy*, 86: 537–45.

Ruger, J., Jamison, D.T. and Bloom, D.E. (2005) 'Health and the economy', in M. Merson, R. Black and A. Mills (eds) *International public health: diseases, programs, systems and policies*, second edition, Boston, MA: Jones and Bartlett Publishers.

Russell, S. (1996) 'Ability to pay for health care: concepts and evidence', *Health Policy and Planning*, 11: 219–37.

Russell, S. (2001) 'Can households afford to be ill? The role of the health system, material resources and social networks in Sri Lanka', PhD Thesis, Department of Public Health and Policy, London School of Hygiene and Tropical Medicine, University of London.

Russell, S. (2004) 'The economic burden of illness for households in developing countries: a review of studies focusing on Malaria, Tuberculosis, and Human Immunodeficiency Virus/Aquired Immunodeficiency Syndrome', *American Journal of Tropical Medicine and Hygiene*, 71 (Suppl. 2): 147–55.

Russell, S. (2005) 'Treatment seeking behaviour in urban Sri Lanka: trusting the state, trusting private providers', *Social Science and Medicine*, 61: 1396–407.

Russell, S. and Gilson, L. (1997) 'User fee policies to promote health service access for the poor: a wolf in sheep's clothing', *International Journal of Health Services*, 27: 359–79.

Ruster, J., Yamamoto, C. and Rogo, K. (2003) *Franchising in health*, Washington, DC: World Bank.

Rutenberg, N. and Watkins, S. (1997) 'The buzz outside the clinics: conversations and contraception in Nyanza,' *Studies in Family Planning*, 28: 290–307.

Saadah, F., Pradhan, M. and Sparrow, R. (2001) 'The effectiveness of the Health Card as an instrument to ensure access to medical care for the poor during the crisis', Washington, DC: The World Bank.

SAfAIDS (2000–2003) Series of booklets for policymakers on Men and HIV for Zimbabwe, Zambia, Lesotho, Swaziland, in partnership with PANOS and UNAIDS, Harare: SAfAIDS.

Sahlins, M. (1972) *Stone Age economics*, Chicago: Aldine-Atherton.

Sahn, D.E. and Younger, S.D. (2000) 'Expenditure incidence in Africa: microeconomic evidence', *Fiscal Studies*, 21: 329–47.

Sandiford, P., Gorter, A. and Salvetto, M. (2002) 'Vouchers for health: using voucher schemes for output-based aid', Public Policy for the Private Sector Note No. 243, Washington, DC: The World Bank, Private Sector and Infrastructure Network.

Sauerborn, R., Shepard, D.S., Ettling, M.B., Brinkmann, U., Nougtara, A. and Diesfeld, H.J. (1991) 'Estimating the direct and indirect economic costs of malaria in a rural district of Burkina Faso [see comments]', *Tropical Medicine and Parasitology*, 42: 219–23.

Sauerborn, R., Ibrango, I., Nougtara, A. and Diesfeld, H.J. (1995), 'The economic costs of illness for rural households in Burkina Faso', *Tropical Medicine and Parasitology*, 46: 54–60.

Sauerborn, R., Adams, A. and Hien, M. (1996a) 'Household strategies to cope with the economic costs of illness', *Social Science and Medicine*, 43: 291–301.

Sauerborn, R., Nougtara, A., Hien, M. and Diesfeld, H.J. (1996b) 'Seasonal variations of household costs of illness in Burkina Faso', *Social Science and Medicine*, 43: 281–90.

Saunders, M. (2004) 'The role of pilots: community based health insurance in Rwanda', in PHR*plus* (ed.) *The role of pilot programs: approaches to health system strengthening*, Bethesda, MD: Partners for Health Reform*plus*, Abt Associates Inc.

Savedoff, W. (2004) 'Tax-based financing of health systems: options and experiences', Discussion Paper No. 4, EIP/FER/DP.04.4, Geneva: World Health Organization.

Sawyer, D. (1993) 'Economic and social consequences of malaria in new colonization projects in Brazil', *Social Science and Medicine*, 37: 1131–6.

Schellenberg, J.A., Victora, C.G., Mushi, A., de Savigny, D., Schellenberg, D. *et al.* (2003) 'Inequities among the very poor: health care for children in rural southern Tanzania', *The Lancet*, 361: 561–6.

Schieber, G., Baeza, C., Kress, D. and Maier, M. (2006) 'Financing health systems in the 21st Century', in D.T. Jamison, J.G. Breman, A.R. Measham, G. Alleyne, M. Claeson *et al.* (eds) *Disease control priorities in developing countries (2nd edition)*, New York: Oxford University Press.

Schneider, P., Schott, W., Bhawalkar, M., Nandakumar, D.K. and Diop, F. (2001a) *Paying for HIV/AIDS services – Lessons from National Health Accounts and community-based health insurance in Rwanda, 1998–1999*, UNAIDS Best Practice Collection, Geneva: UNAIDS.

Schneider, P., Diop, F. and Leighton, C. (2001b) 'Pilot testing prepayment for health services in Rwanda: results and recommendations for policy directions and implementation', Bethesda, MD: Partners for Health Reform*plus*, Abt Associates Inc.

Schuler, S. Bates, L. and Islam K. (2002) 'Paying for reproductive health services in

Bangladesh: intersections between cost, quality and culture', *Health Policy and Planning*, 17: 273–80.

Schultz, P. (1999) 'Productive benefits of improving health: evidence from low-income countries', mimeo, Yale University.

Schultz, T.P. and Tansel, A. (1997) 'Wage and labour supply effects of illness in Côte d'Ivoire and Ghana: instrumental variable estimates for days disabled', *Journal of Development Economics*, 53: 251–86.

Scoones, I. (1998) 'Sustainable rural livelihoods: a framework for analysis', *IDS Working Paper* 72, Brighton: Institute of Development Studies.

Seeley, J., Kajura, E. and Mulder, D. (1995) 'Methods used to study household coping strategies in rural South West Uganda', *Health Policy and Planning*, 10: 79–88.

Sen, A. (1981) *Poverty and famines*, Oxford: Clarendon Press.

Sen, A. (1985) *Commodities and capabilities*, Amsterdam: North Holland.

Sen, A. (1990) 'Public action to remedy hunger', TANCO Memorial Lecture, London, 2 August 1990. Online. Available at: www.thp.org/reports/sen/sen890.htm. Last accessed 25 April 2007.

Sen, A. (1999) *Development as freedom*, New York: Alfred A. Knopf.

Sepehri, A., Chernomas, R. and Akram-Lodhi, H. (2005) 'Penalizing patients and rewarding providers: user charges and health care utilization in Vietnam', *Health Policy and Planning*, 20: 90–9.

Shastry, G.K. and Weil, D.N. (2002) 'How much of cross-country income variation is explained by health?', *Journal of the European Economic Association*, 1: 387–96.

Sheehan, M. (2000) 'The role of NGOs in building security in south Eastern Europe', *Central European Issues*, 5: 44–9.

Shin, Y. (2006) 'Policy context of the poor progress of the pro-poor policy: a case study on the Medical-Aid policy during Kim Dae-Jung's Government (1998–2002) in the Republic of Korea', *Health Policy*, 78: 209–23.

Simanovitz, A. (1998) 'Effective strategies for reaching the poor', *Grameen Dialogue*, 34: 1–5.

Singkheaw, P., Thissayakorn, W. and Kaukul, W. (2004) 'Reasons for patient escape from Buddhachinaraj Hospital in first trimester in 2004', unpublished research, Buddhachinaraj Medical College, Faculty of Medicine, Naresuan University, Thailand.

Skoufias, E., Davis, B. and de la Vega, S. (2001) 'Targeting the poor in Mexico: an evaluation of the selection of households into PROGRESA', *World Development*, 29: 1769–84.

Soeters, R. and Griffiths, F. (2003) 'Improving government health services through contract management: a case from Cambodia', *Health Policy and Planning*, 18: 74–83.

Sommer, A. and West, Jr, K.P. (1996) *Vitamin A deficiency: health, survival and nutrition*, New York: Oxford University Press.

Soriano, E., Dror, D.M., Alampay, E. and Bayugo, Y. (2002) 'Attitudes toward solidarity, risk, and insurance in rural Philippines', Chapter 19 in D.M. Dror and A.S. Preker (eds) *Social reinsurance: a new approach to sustainable community health financing*, Washington, DC: The World Bank and ILO.

Srithamrongsawat, S. (2004) 'Financial protection and enabling access to care for Thai elderly: the role of public assistance', unpublished PhD thesis, Department of Public Health and Policy, London School of Hygiene and Tropical Medicine, University of London.

Standing, H. (2004) 'Understanding the "demand side" in service delivery: definitions, frameworks and tools from the health sector', Issues Paper, London: DFID Health Systems Resource Centre.

Stanecki, K. (2004) *The AIDS pandemic in the 21st century*, Washington, DC: U.S. Census Bureau.

Stifel, L.D. (1981) 'Recollections of Dr Puey', in Komol Keemthong Foundation. *Collected articles by and about Puey Ungphakorn, a Siamese for all seasons*, Bangkok: Suksit Siam.

Stillman, K. and Bennett, S. (2005) 'Systemwide effects of the global fund: interim findings from three country studies', Bethesda, MD: Partners for Health Reform*plus*, Abt Associates.

Storey, P. (1989) 'Health care in South Africa: the rights and responsibilities of the community', *Medicine and Law*, 7: 649–55.

Stover, J. and Bollinger, L. (1989) 'Are contraceptive social marketing programs reaching their target markets?', SOMARC Occasional Paper, Washington, DC: The Futures Group.

Strauss, J. and Thomas, D. (1994) 'Health and labour productivity: sorting out the relationships', in G.H. Peters and D.D. Hedley (eds) *Agricultural competitiveness: market forces and policy choices: proceedings of the Twenty-Second International Conference of Agricultural Economists held at Harare, Zimbabwe*, Harare, Zimbabwe: Ashgate.

Suarez-Berenguela, R. (2002) 'Policy tools for achieving more equitable financing of and access to health care services in Latin America and the Caribbean', *Revista Panamericana de Salud Pública*, 11: 418–24.

Suci, E. (2006) 'Child access to health services during the economic crisis: an Indonesian experience of the safety net program', *Social Science and Medicine*, 60: 2912–25.

Suedee, T., Yimcharoen, W., Tapho, W., Buadung, L. and Jaitaingtam, S. (2004) 'Inaccessibility universal health coverage of the people in Amphur Muang, Nakhon Sawan Province', unpublished independent study for Master of Public Health, Naresuan University, Thailand.

Sujariyakul, A. (2000) 'Study on family ability to pay for hospital charges and financially catastrophic illness among inpatients in Songkhla province', unpublished PhD thesis, Prince of Songkla University, Thailand.

Sulzbach, S., Garshong, B. and Banahene, G. (2006) 'Evaluating effects of the National Health Insurance Act in Ghana: Baseline report', Bethesda, MD: Partners for Health Reform*plus*, Abt Associates Inc.

Sundar, R. (1995) *Household survey of health care utilisation and expenditure*, Working Paper No. 53, New Delhi, India: National Council of Applied Economic Research.

Sundari, T.K. (1992) 'The untold story: how the health care systems in developing countries contribute to maternal mortality', *International Journal of Health Services*, 22: 513–28.

Tami, A., Mbati, J., Nathan, R., Mponda, H., Lengeler, C. and Armstrong Schellenberg, J.R.M. (2004) 'Use and misuse of a discount voucher scheme as a subsidy for treated nets for malaria control in Southern Tanzania', unpublished manuscript.

Tangcharoensathien, V., Laixuthai, A., Vasavit, J., Tantigate, N.A., Prajuabmoh-Ruffolo, W. *et al.* (1999a) 'National health accounts development: lessons from Thailand', *Health Policy and Planning*, 14: 342–53.

Tangcharoensathien, V., Supachutikul, A. and Lertiendumrong, J. (1999b) 'The social security scheme in Thailand: what lessons can be drawn?', *Social Science and Medicine*, 48: 913–23.

Tangcharoensathien, V., Pitayarangsarit, S. and Srithamrongswat, S. (2001) 'Overview of health insurance systems', in P. Pramualratana and S. Wibulpolprasert (eds) *Health insurance systems in Thailand*, Bangkok: Desire Publishing, pp. 28–40.

Tangcharoensathien, V., Vasavid, C., Tisyaticom, K., Patcharanarumol, W. and Prakong-sai, P. (2004) *Financing of the universal health coverage system: present and future*, Nonthaburi: Health Systems Research Institute.

Techowanich, S., Buayaem, W., Tawornroongrote, S. and Pannarunothai, S. (2005) 'People's ideology towards universal health coverage', *Journal of Social Science*, 1: 177–95.

Tendler, J. (1997) *Good government in the Tropics*, Baltimore, MD: John Hopkins University Press.

Thiede, M., Palmer, N. and Mbatsha, S. (2005) 'South Africa: who goes to the public sector for HIV/AIDS voluntary counselling and testing?', in D. Gwatkin, A. Wagstaff and A. Yazbeck (eds) *Reaching the poor with health, nutrition and population services: what works, what doesn't and why*, Washington, DC: World Bank.

Thomas, S. and Gilson, L. (2004) 'Actor dynamics in financing reform: the contested process of health insurance policy development in South Africa, 1994–1999', *Health Policy and Planning*, 19: 279–91.

Thomas, S., Killingsworth, J.R. and Acharya, S. (1998) 'User fees, self-selection and the poor in Bangladesh', *Health Policy and Planning*, 13: 50–8.

Thomas, D., Frankenberg, E., Friedman, J., Habicht, J.-P., Hakimi, M. *et al.* (2005) 'Causal effect of health on market outcomes: experimental evidence'. Online. Available at: www.econ.duke.edu/~taroz/Iron_Indonesia05.pdf. Last accessed 25 April 2007.

Tibaijuka, A.K. (1997) 'AIDS and economic welfare in peasant agriculture: case studies from Kagabiro Village, Kagera Region, Tanzania', *World Development*, 25: 963–75.

Tibandebage, P. and Mackintosh, M. (2005) 'The market shaping of charges, trust and abuse: health care transactions in Tanzania', *Social Science and Medicine*, 61: 1385–95.

Topouzis, D. (1994) 'Uganda: the socio-economic impact of HIV/AIDS on rural families with an emphasis on youth', *Rome: Food and Agriculture Organisation* (TCP/UGA/2256). Online. Available at: www.fao.org/docrep/t2942e/t2942e00.htm (accessed 14 September 2006).

Topouzis, D. and Hemrich, G. (1994) 'The socio-economic impact of HIV and AIDS on rural families in Uganda: an emphasis on youth', HIV and Development Programme Study Paper No. 2, New York: UNDP. Online. Available at: www.undp.org/hiv/publications/study/english/sp2e.htm (accessed 25 November 2002).

Tudor Hart, J. (1971) 'The inverse care law', *The Lancet*, i: 405–12.

UNAIDS (2004) *Report on the global AIDS epidemic*, Geneva: UNAIDS.

UNAIDS (2006) *2006 Report on the global AIDS Epidemic*, Geneva: UNAIDS.

UNAIDS Reference Group on Estimates, Modelling and Projections (2002) 'Improved methods and assumptions for estimation of the HIV/AIDS epidemic and its impact: recommendations of the UNAIDS Reference Group on Estimates, Modelling and Projections', *AIDS*, 16: W1–14.

UNDP (1994) *Human development report 1994*, New York: Oxford University Press for the United Nations Development Programme, p. 94.

UNDP (2003) *Human development report 2003*, New York: Oxford University Press for the United Nations Development Programme, p. 238.

UNESCO/UNAIDS (2000) 'A cultural approach to HIV/AIDS prevention and care. Summary of country assessments and project design handbook', Mimeo, Paris: UNESCO, May 2000.

Unger, J.P., De Paepe, P. and Green, A. (2003) 'A code of best practice for disease control programmes to avoid damaging health care services in developing countries', *International Journal of Health Planning and Management*, 18 (Suppl. 1): S27–S39.

Ungphakorn, P. (1981) 'Looking back, looking ahead', in Komol Keemthong Foundation. *Collected articles by and about Puey Ungphakorn, a Siamese for all seasons*, Bangkok: Suksit Siam.

United Nations (2000) *4th report on the world nutrition situation: nutrition throughout the life cycle*. Online. Available at: www.unsystem.org/scn/Publications/4RWNS/4rwns.pdf (accessed 14 September 2006).

United Nations (2004) *5th report on the world nutrition situation: nutrition for improved development outcomes*. Online. Available at: www.unsystem.org/scn/Publications/AnnualMeeting/SCN31/SCN5Report.pdf (accessed 14 September 2006).

United Nations (2005) *World population prospects: the 2004 revision*, New York: United Nations.

UNDP (2003) *Human development report 2003: millennium development goals. A compact among nations to end human poverty*, New York: United Nations Development Programme.

UN Millennium Project (2005) *Who's got the power? Transforming health systems for women and children*, Report of the Task Force on Child Health and Maternal Health, London: Earthscan.

Valdivia, M. (2002) 'Public health infrastructure and equity in the utilization of outpatient health care services in Peru', *Health Policy and Planning*, 17 (Suppl. 1): 12–19.

van de Walle, D. (1998) 'Targeting revisited', *World Bank Research Observer*, 13: 231–48.

van de Walle, D. and Nead, K. (1995) *Public spending and the poor: theory and evidence*, Baltimore, MD: Johns Hopkins University Press for the World Bank.

van Doorslaer, E., Wagstaff, A. and Rutten, F. (1993) *Equity in the finance and delivery of health care*, Oxford: Oxford University Press.

Van Kammen, J., De Savigny, D. and Sewankambo, N. (2006) 'Using knowledge brokering to promote evidence-based policy-making: the need for support structures', *Bulletin of the World Health Organization*, 84: 608–12.

Van Rensburg, H.C. and Fourie, A. (1994) 'Inequalities in South African health care. Part II: Setting the record straight', *South African Medical Journal*, 84: 99–103.

Van Wallbeek, C. (2001) 'Effective development policies require political will: the example of tobacco control in South Africa', mimeo, IDRC Seminar, 13 June 2001, Cape Town, South Africa.

Vasavid, C., Tisyaticom, K., Patcharanarumol, W., Prakongsai, P. and Tangcharoensathien, V. (2004) *Financing of the universal health coverage system: present and future*, Nonthaburi: Health Systems Research Institute.

Victora, C.G., Barros, F.C. and Vaughan, J.P. (2001) 'The impact of child health interventions on inequalities: infant and child death in Brazil', in D. Leon and G. Walt (eds) *Poverty, inequality and health: an international perspective*, Oxford: Oxford University Press.

Varatharajan, D., Thankappan, R. and Jayapalan, S. (2004) 'Assessing the performance of primary health centres under decentralized government in Kerala, India', *Health Policy and Planning*, 19: 41–51.

Victora, C., Wagstaff, A., Schellenberg, J., Gwatkin, D., Claeson, M. and Habicht, J. (2003) 'Applying an equity lens to child health and mortality: more of the same is not enough', *The Lancet*, 362: 233–41.

Viscusi, W.K. and Aldy, J.E. (2003) 'The value of a statistical life: a critical review of market estimates from around the world', *The Journal of Risk and Uncertainty*, 27: 5–76.

Wagstaff, A. (2000) 'Socioeconomic inequalities in child mortality: comparison across nine developing countries', *Bulletin of the World Health Organization*, 78: 19–29.

Wagstaff, A. and van Doorslaer, E. (2003) 'Catastrophe and impoverishment in paying for health care: with applications to Vietnam 1993–1998', *Health Economics*, 12: 921–34.

Walker, L. and Gilson, L. (2004) ' "We are bitter but we are satisfied": nurses as street level bureaucrats in South Africa', *Social Science and Medicine*, 59: 1251–61.

Wallman, S. and Baker, M. (1996) 'Which resources pay for treatment? A model for estimating the informal economy of health', *Social Science and Medicine*, 42: 671–9.

Waters, H., Dougherty, L., Tegang, S.P., Tran, N., Wiysonge, C.S. *et al.* (2004) 'Coverage and costs of childhood immunizations in Cameroon', *Bulletin of the World Health Organization*, 82: 668–75.

Webber, D.J. (2002) 'Polices to stimulate growth: should we invest in health or education?', *Applied Economics*, 34: 1633–43.

WEMOS (2006) 'Why PRSPs matter for health'. Online. Available at: www.wemos.nl/en-GB/Content.aspx?type=Themas&id=1835 (accessed 1 September 2006).

Werker, E., Ahuja, A. and Wendell, B. (2006) 'Male circumcision and HIV/AIDS: the macroeconomic impact of a health crisis', HBS Working Paper No. 07–025, Boston, MA: Harvard Business School.

Whitehead, M., Dahlgren, G. and Evans, T. (2001) 'Equity and health sector reforms: can low-income countries escape the medical poverty trap?', *The Lancet*, 358: 833–6.

WHO (1978) 'Declaration of Alma-Ata: International Conference on Primary Health Care, Alma Ata, USSR, 6–12 September 1978'. Online. Available at: www.who.int/hpr/NPH/docs/declaration_almaata.pdf. Last accessed 25 April 2007.

WHO (1999) *World health report 1999: making a difference*, Geneva: World Health Organization.

WHO (2000) *The world health report 2000: health systems. Improving performance*, Geneva: World Health Organization.

WHO (2003) *World health report 2003: shaping the future*, Geneva: World Health Organization.

WHO (2004a) 'The Mexico Statement on Health Research', Geneva: World Health Organization. Online. Available at: www.who.int/rpc/summit/agenda/Mexico_Statement-English.pdf (accessed 20 October 2006).

WHO (2004b) 'Nutrition for health and development'. Online. Available at: www.who.int/nut/ (accessed 16 September 2006).

WHO (2004c) 'Making pregnancy safer', Fact sheet No. 276, Geneva: World Health Organization. Online. Available at: www.who.int/mediacentre/factsheets/fs276/en/.

WHO (2004d) *World health report 2004: changing history*, Geneva: World Health Organization.

WHO (2005a) *World health report 2005: make every mother and child count*, Geneva: World Health Organization.

WHO (2005b) 'Social health insurance: report by the secretariat', World Health Organization Executive Board 115th session, 2 December 2004, Provisional agenda item 4.5, EB115/8.

WHO (2006) *The world health report 2006: working together for health*, Geneva: World Health Organization.

WHO/WTO (2002) *World Health Organization and World Trade Organization, 2002: WTO agreements and public health. A joint study by the WHO and WTO Secretariat*, Geneva: World Health Organization.

Wibulpolprasert, S., Hempisut, P. and Pitayarangsarit, S. (2002) *Impact of liberalisation of trade on services on the human resource development in health*, Bangkok: USA Press.

Wilkes, A., Hao, Y., Bloom, G. and Xingyuan, G. (1997) 'Coping with the costs of severe illness in rural China', *IDS Working Paper* 58, Brighton: Institute of Development Studies.

Wilkinson, D., Gouws, E., Sach, M. and Karin, S.S.A. (2001) 'Effect of removing user fees on attendance for curative and preventive primary health care services in rural South Africa', *Bulletin of the World Health Organization*, 79: 665–71.

Williams, G. and Ray, S. (1995) 'AIDS in Africa: signs of hope from the workplace', in D. Fitzsimons, V. Hardy and D. Tolley (eds) *Economic and social impact of AIDS in Europe*, London: National AIDS Trust.

Wiseman, V. and Jan, S. (2000) 'Resource allocation within Australian Indigenous communities: a program for implementing vertical equity', *Health Care Analysis*, 8: 217–33.

Workneh, W., Fletcher, M. and Olwit, G. (1993) 'Onchocerciasis in field workers at Baya Farm, Teppi Coffee Plantation Project, southwestern Ethiopia: prevalence and impact on productivity', *Acta Tropica*, 54: 89–97.

World Bank (1989) *Financing health services in developing countries: an agenda for reform*, Washington, DC: World Bank.

World Bank (1993a) *World development report 1993: investing in health*, Washington, DC: The World Bank.

World Bank (1993b) *The East Asian miracle: economic growth and public policy*, New York: Oxford University Press.

World Bank (2002) *A sourcebook for poverty reduction strategies*, Washington, DC: The World Bank.

World Bank (2004) *World development report 2004: making services work for poor people*, Washington, DC: World Bank.

World Bank (2005) W*orld development report 2006: equity and development*, New York: Oxford University Press for the World Bank.

World Bank (2006) *World development indicators*, Washington, DC: The World Bank.

World Bank and World Health Organization (2002) *Dying for change*. Online. Available at: www1.worldbank.org/prem/poverty/voices/reports/dying/index.htm (accessed 14 September 2006).

Worrall, E., Wiseman, V. and Hanson, K. (2003) 'Targeting subsidies for insecticide-treated mosquito nets: a conceptual framework, experience from other sectors and lessons for ITNs', unpublished mimeo, Health Economics and Financing Programme, London School of Hygiene and Tropical Medicine.

Wyss, K., Kilima, P. and Lorenz, N. (2001) 'Costs of tuberculosis for households and health care providers in Dar es Salaam', *Tropical Medicine and International Health*, 6: 60–8.

Xu, K., Evans, D.B., Kawabata, K., Zeramdini, R., Klavus, J. and Murray, C.J. (2003) 'Household catastrophic health expenditure: a multicountry analysis', *The Lancet*, 362: 111–17.

Yach, D. and Bettcher, D. (2000) 'Globalisation of tobacco industry influence and new global responses', *Tobacco Control*, 9: 206–16.

Yin, R.K. (1994) *Case study research: design and methods*, London: Sage Publications.

Young, A. (2005) 'The gift of the dying: the tragedy of AIDS and the welfare of future African generations', *Quarterly Journal of Economics*, 120: 243–66.

Zeller, M., Sharma, M., Henery, C. and Lapenu, C. (2001) 'An operational tool for evaluating poverty outreach of development policies and projects', *IFPRI Discussion Paper*, No. 111, Washington, DC: International Food Policy Research Institute.

Index

private for-profit sector 208, 217; hospitals 218
private health care 200; providers 95–7, 110, 124, 132; services 75
private health insurance 158, 163; coverage 145, 152
private providers 87, 112, 122, 124; licensing of 126; responsiveness 123; use by the poor 127
private sector 69–70, 101–2, 123–4, 136, 181, 224; clinics 170; delivery system 148; doctors 72–3, 95, 97, 104, 113; facilities 16, 205, 213; influence 188; practices 128; quality of care 126; role of 64; services 11–13, 119, 127; workers 194
privatization 27, 180
productivity 21, 35, 43–6, 52; benefits 33; changes in 48, 49f; impact of health 41–2; reduction in 50t, 54; shortfall 52; time lost 75, 77, 79
programme design 135–7, 152
pro-poor approach 118–19, 222–3; central governments 132; funding 165, 168; health promotion 228; policies 232; reform 133, 226; strategies 166, 230
protection 55, 97, 99, 106, 110, 223; against costs of illness 102, 202, 208; from hospitalization costs 218; mechanisms 221; of the poor 17, 156, 160, 197, 203; social 9, 12–13, 92, 113–14, 135; sustainable 86–7; of the vulnerable 126
public health sector 151, 178, 181, 200, 223; care system 17, 225, 228, 230; cost of providing 66; facilities 72, 87, 165, 194–5, 205, 213; hospitals 191, 218; policy 92, 113–14, 186–8; provider 71, 95, 146; reforms 180; services 12, 75, 97, 111–12, 217; spending 68t, 157, 162; workforce 16

quality of care 13, 70–1, 97, 113, 117, 123–4, 127–9, 132, 160, 199, 203, 214, 221–4, 230; higher 75; poor 73–4, 126–7; technical 217
quality of service 69, 73, 119, 148, 161, 180, 184, 216, 220, 229; for the poor 201, 230; standards 126

reciprocity 86, 94
reference subjects 44–8, 49t, 50t, 52; HIV positive 53

referral 73, 146, 153, 169, 199, 206; facilities 145
reform 165, 172, 181, 191, 201; distortion of 171; health system 233; impacts of 227; multiple 122; national 160; politically contested 170, 173, 191; values underlying 226, 231
regulation 126, 132, 170, 184; agency 220
reimbursement 208, 211, 213; cap on 17, 205; from insurance 215; lag-time for 210, 221; prior to discharge 218; prospective 219; retrospective 194
research 2–4, 177, 196–7, 199–202, 211–13, 217, 221, 231–2; clinical 55; community 225; funders 18; opinion surveys 182; pilot schemes 172, 218
resources 8, 14, 113, 130, 167, 177, 220, 224; adequacy and control 176, 184–5, 188; allocation of 117, 128, 141, 146, 216; allocation formulae 14, 143t, 144–5, 152; available to health sector 39, 155–7, 168; captured 228; delivery 134; demands 94; diminished 161; effective use of 135; financial 114; generation 147; inadequate 186; increased 233; lack of 127; limited 107, 119, 178, 183; mobilization of 175t; needs unanticipated 171; non-cash 153; reallocation 136–7; redistribution 180, 230; social 76, 82, 85, 104; transferability 136, 150
responsiveness 17, 121–3, 129, 132, 182–4, 221, 223, of the health system 191; of providers 177, 229
revenue 155; cost-sharing 161; domestic 173; external sources 166; increased 171; limited 163; loss of 14; pooled 165; raising 153, 155–6
risk-equalization 87, 89
risk pooling 164–5, 180, 227
rotating savings groups 92, 104–5 see also seetu
rural areas 16, 195, 198, 220; health centres 152, 199; health workers 181; hospitalization claims 212; households 208; infrastructure 227; livelihoods 153; remote 215, 223, 229; sub-districts 218
Rwanda 164; costs ratio 78; prepayment scheme 165, 172–3

savings 34, 107, 111–12, 228; use of 83
seetu groups 114; organizer 105; participation 108; reluctance to join 107